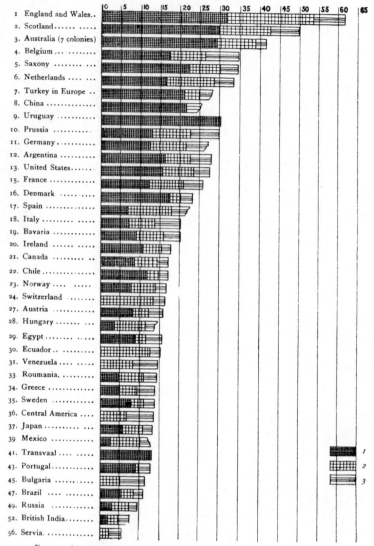

1. England and Wales..
2. Scotland........ ....
3. Australia (7 colonies)
4. Belgium ... .
5. Saxony ....
6. Netherlands ....
7. Turkey in Europe ..
8. China ....
9. Uruguay ....
10. Prussia ....
11. Germany..........
12. Argentina ....
13. United States......
15. France ....
16. Denmark ....
17. Spain ....
18. Italy ....
19. Bavaria ....
20. Ireland ....
21. Canada ....
22. Chile..............
23. Norway ....
24. Switzerland ....
27. Austria ....
28. Hungary ....
29. Egypt........ .....
30. Ecuador.. ....
31. Venezuela ....
33. Roumania. ....
34. Greece ....
35. Sweden ....
36. Central America ....
37. Japan ....
39. Mexico ....
41. Transvaal ....
43. Portugal............
45. Bulgaria ....
47. Brazil ....
49. Russia ....
52. British India........
56. Servia. ....

DIAGRAM (based on Table CXII, pp. 143-4) showing the percentage of population dwelling in cities at the latest censuses.

LEGEND.

1 Percentage of total population dwelling in cities of 100,000 +.
2   "   "   "   "   "   "   "   " 20,000 100,000.
3   "   "   "   "   "   "   "   " 10,000–20,000.

The entire length of the bars therefore represents the percentage of city dwellers in the total population of the countries named. Broken ends indicate lack of satisfactory statistics for exact measurements.

The Growth of Cities in the Nineteenth Century

A STUDY IN STATISTICS

By Adna Ferrin Weber

GREENWOOD PRESS, PUBLISHERS
NEW YORK

Originally published in 1899
for Columbia University by The Macmillan Company

Published in 1963 by the Cornell University Press

First Greenwood Reprinting, 1969

Library of Congress Catalogue Card Number 69-14142

PRINTED IN UNITED STATES OF AMERICA

"THE proportion between the rural and town population of a country is an important fact in its interior economy and condition. It determines, in a great degree, its capacity for manufactures, the extent of its commerce and the amount of its wealth. The growth of cities commonly marks the progress of intelligence and the arts, measures the sum of social enjoyment, and always implies excessive mental activity, which is sometimes healthy and useful, sometimes distempered and pernicious. If these congregations of men diminish some of the comforts of life, they augment others; if they are less favorable to health than the country, they also provide better defense against disease and better means of cure. From causes both political and moral, they are less favorable to the multiplication of the species. In the eyes of the moralist, cities afford a wider field both for virtue and vice; and they are more prone to innovation, whether for good or evil. The love of civil liberty is, perhaps, both stronger and more constant in the country than the town; and if it is guarded in the cities by a keener vigilance and a more far-sighted jealousy, yet law, order and security are also, in them, more exposed to danger, from the greater facility with which intrigue and ambition can there operate on ignorance and want. Whatever may be the good or evil tendencies of populous cities, they are the result to which all countries that are at once fertile, free and intelligent, inevitably tend."

—GEORGE TUCKER, *Progress of the United States in Population and Wealth in Fifty Years*, p. 127.

To

JACOB GOULD SCHURMAN

SCHOLAR, ADMINISTRATOR, STATESMAN

THIS ESSAY IS DEDICATED

WITH THE ESTEEM AND GRATITUDE

OF THE

AUTHOR

BIOGRAPHICAL NOTE

LEWIS MUMFORD is certainly correct in describing *The Growth of Cities in the Nineteenth Century* as a "classic pioneer work." It is the first really sound, comprehensive, and complete contribution to urban studies by an American. The only comparable studies at the time were French and German. Not only does Weber make a masterful synthesis of the vast but fragmentary work that preceded him, but he attempts to synthesize opinion on the urban questions he deals with. Furthermore, he brings to the field the dispassionate detachment of the social scientist seeking ways to study the city as an important social phenomenon. Mumford has also said of this book, "Important: All the more so because it has not tempted emulation." This is unfortunately true. Weber's outstanding qualities of scholarship and scientific method, building his own work on a solid foundation of knowledge of the work of others and attempting to find means of objectively investigating urban problems, have not characterized later American writers on the city. For any purposes except the most detailed scholarship, a review of the literature of urban studies can begin with Weber. It may be hoped this book will help to stimulate further studies that will be equally brilliant and thorough.

Adna Ferrin Weber was born on July 14, 1870, on a farm in Springville, Erie County, New York, and grew up in Salamanca, a village of 3,500 people then, about sixty miles south of Buffalo. He was one of seven children of Blanchard B. and Philena Ferrin Weber. At the age of twenty he entered Cornell University to commence studies toward the Bachelor of Philosophy degree. For all four of his undergraduate years Weber held one of the competitive McGraw Scholarships in Philosophy for mathematics. In his second and third years at Cornell, Weber supplemented his stipend by serving as the campus reporter for the *Ithaca Journal,* a post which brought him into close contact with professors and administrators throughout the University. His senior year was spent as private secretary to the newly elected president of the University, Jacob Gould Schurman, to whom he dedicated *The Growth of Cities.* He remained in this position the following year. While Schurman's secretary, Weber continued to write for the New York *Tribune* and the New York *Evening Post.* He also served in editorial capacities on the *Cornell Era* and the *Cornell Magazine.* In his senior year he was elected to the Sphinx Head senior society and Phi Beta Kappa.

Weber became well acquainted with many of the outstanding educators at Cornell through his undergraduate activities. Of particular importance were his contacts with Benjamin Ide Wheeler, Professor of Greek and Comparative Philology and later President of the University of California, and Charles Evans Hughes, Professor of Law and later Chief Justice of the United States. Weber subsequently served under Hughes when the latter was Governor of New York. However, the scholar who probably had most influence on the development of *The Growth of Cities* was Walter Francis Willcox, at that time a young Assistant Professor of Social Science and Statistics and Political Economy, now Professor of Economics and Statistics, Emeritus.

Upon completion of his Ph.B. in 1894, Weber enrolled in the Graduate School at Cornell and was appointed a Fellow in Political Economy and Finance, 1894–1895. It was during this time that he started work on *The Growth of Cities.* The following year he received a President White Fellowship in Political Science and took a year of study at the University of Berlin, where he continued his work on the volume. Returning to this country, Weber entered Columbia University as a University Fellow in Economics and Social Science. In 1898 he came back to Cornell for a year as Secretary of the Summer School and Assistant Registrar. He completed his work on the study that year and submitted it as his dissertation to Columbia. Columbia awarded the work the Grant Squires Prize, given every fifth year, and published a revised version in 1899.

Weber enjoyed the confidence of Theodore Roosevelt, who, as Governor of New York, appointed him Deputy Commissioner of Labor Statistics in 1899, a post he held until 1901. He married Mabel Norris on May 3, 1899. The couple had two sons. In 1901 Weber became Chief Statistician of the New York State Department of Labor and remained in this post until 1907. Most of his published work dates from this period. He was a special agent for the United States Bureau of the Census in 1902. Labor problems occupied Weber's attention increasingly, and most of his scholarly contributions were in this field. He was instrumental in introducing workmen's compensation in the United States and considers this one of his most important contributions. He was a founder and first secretary of the American Association for Labor Legislation, 1906–1907.

In 1907 Weber became Chief Statistician for the Public Service Commission of New York, First District (New York City), a position he retained until 1921 when he became the Chief of the Accounting Division of that agency. He edited the statistical volume of the Commission's annual report and was responsible for much of the Commission's activity in rate cases.

Weber is a Senior Fellow of the American Statistical Association and a member of the American Economic Association and the Academy of Political Science. From 1924 to 1932 he was a director of the Cities Census Committee, Inc.

In 1923 Weber lost his sight and was forced to retire. His activities have been limited since that time. He is now living on Long Island.

Barclay G. Jones

Cornell University, 1962

BIBLIOGRAPHY OF
ADNA FERRIN WEBER

"Professor Adolph Wagner, the Economist," *The Outlook*, 57 (October 9, 1897), 370–372.

"European Example for American Farmers," *North American Review*, 166 (February, 1898), 152–163.

"The Tramp and the Labor Colony in Germany," *The Chautauquan*, 26 (March, 1898), 605–610.

"Suburban Annexations," *North American Review*, 166 (May, 1898), 612–617.

The Growth of Cities in the Nineteenth Century: A Study in Statistics. (Studies in History, Economics and Public Law, edited by the Faculty of Political Science of Columbia University, vol. XI.) New York: The Macmillan Company for Columbia University, 1899.

Special Bulletins, edited by Adna Ferrin Weber. Albany, New York: Bureau of Labor Statistics (incorporated into Department of Labor in 1901), 1899–1907.

"The Compensation of Accidental Injuries to Workmen," in *17th Annual Report of the Bureau of Labor Statistics of the State of New York for the Year 1899,* Part II (transmitted to the Legislature February 5, 1900), pp. 555–1162.

"Tendencies in Trade Unionism," *International Monthly*, 2 (September, 1900), 252–278.

United States Bureau of the Census. *Population of New York by Counties and Minor Civil Divisions.* Bulletin Number 38 of the 12th Census of the United States. Washington: Government Printing Office, 1901.

"Growth of Cities in the United States: 1890–1900," *Municipal Affairs,* 5 (June, 1901), 367–375.

"The Workman's Position in the Light of Economic Progress"

(discussion), *Publications of the American Economic Association*, ser. III, **3** (1902), 228–229.

"Workmen's Compensation Acts of Foreign Countries," United States Bureau of Labor, *Bulletin*, **7** (May, 1902), 549–551.

"Employers' Liability and Accident Insurance," *Political Science Quarterly*, **17** (June, 1902), 256–283.

"Rapid Transit and the Housing Problem," *Municipal Affairs*, **6** (Fall, 1902), 409–417.

Rost gorodov v deviatnadtsatom stolietii. Trans. from English by A. N. Kotelnikova. St. Petersburg: Izd. E. D. Kuskovoi, 1903.

"The Report of the Victorian Industrial Commission," *Quarterly Journal of Economics,* **17** (August, 1903), 614–642.

Labor Legislation in New York. (Vol. II of monographs on social economics prepared under the direction of Hon. John McMackin; Exhibit at Louisiana Purchase Exposition.) Albany, N.Y.: New York State Department of Labor, 1904.

The Work of the Department of Labor of New York. With Leonard W. Hatch. (Vol. III of monographs on social economics prepared under the direction of Hon. John McMackin; Exhibit at Louisiana Purchase Exposition.) Albany, N.Y.: New York State Department of Labor, 1904.

The Growth of Industry in New York. (Vol. IV of monographs on social economics prepared under the direction of Hon. John McMackin; Exhibit at Louisiana Purchase Exposition.) Albany, N.Y.: New York State Department of Labor, 1904.

"The Significance of Recent City Growth: The Era of Small Industry Centers," *Annals of the American Academy of Political and Social Science,* **23** (March, 1904), 223–236.

"Wages Adjusted by Arbitration" (discussion), *Publications of the American Economic Association,* ser. III, **8** (1907), 38–42.

"The International Movement for Labor Legislation," *Charities and the Commons,* **17** (February 2, 1907), 833–838.

"Present Status of Statistical Work and How It Needs to Be Developed in the Service of the States," *Quarterly Publications of the American Statistical Association,* **14** (June, 1914), 97–102.

"Communication to the Regional Plan Committee," quoted and discussed on pp. 30–33 in *Population, Land Values and Government,* vol. II of *Regional Survey of New York and Its Environs,* prepared by Thomas Adams, Harold M. Lewis and Theodore T. McCrosky. New York: Regional Plan of New York and Its Environs, 1929.

Barclay G. Jones

PREFACE

THE present essay embraces the results of a statistical investigation of the growth of cities during the nineteenth century which was originally undertaken for a doctor's dissertation. In preparing the essay for a wider circle of readers than the specialists to whom the doctor's thesis primarily appeals, the author realized the difficulty of reconciling the aims of a scientific treatise, wherein sharply-defined technical terms and simple, abstract statements lend conciseness to style, with the requisites of a popular work; and in explaining technical terms and illustrating the propositions laid down or deductions drawn, he has had to expand the essay beyond his original intention. While its value may thereby have been somewhat impaired for the specialist, the subject itself is so important to present-day students that it will lend interest to almost any attempt to present the facts with clearness and impartiality.

The assistance rendered to the author by instructors, librarians and friends has been so generous that full acknowledgment cannot be given in this place. He is under especial obligation, however, to Dr. E. Blenck, director of the Royal Prussian Statistical Bureau in Berlin, through whose courtesy he was enabled to collect most of his statistical data in the unrivaled statistical library of the Bureau; to Professors Johannes Conrad, of the University of Halle, Max Sering, of the University of Berlin, and John B. Clark, of Columbia University, for helpful suggestions; and most of all to Professer Walter F. Wilcox, of Cornell University, for stimulating criticism and sound advice during almost the entire period of the preparation of the essay. Acknowledgments are also due to Professors Edwin R. A. Seligman and Richmond Mayo-Smith, of Columbia University, who read the proof. All responsibility for errors, however, rests upon the writer alone. While he has exercised due care in the copying and compilation of statistics, he does not hope for absolute accuracy, and begs the indulgence of his readers in their judgment of arithmetical errors.

ALBANY, *May* 15, 1899.

ABBREVIATIONS

Allg. St. Ar.—Allgemeines Statistisches Archiv.

Bleicher—Beiträge zur Statistik der Stadt Frankfurt am Main, Neue Folge, Erstes Heft: Statistische Beschreibung der Stadt und ihrer Bevölkerung, II. Theil: Die innere Gliederung der Bevölkerung. Bearbeitet von dem Vorsteher des Statistischen Amtes, Dr. H. Bleicher, 1895.

Conrad's Hdwbh.—Handwörterbuch der Staatswissenschaften, edited by Conrad. Elster, Lexis and Loening. First edition, 6 vols. + 2 sup. vols., Jena, 1890–97.

J. of St. Soc.—Journal of the Royal Statistical Society, London.

Levasseur—La Population Française, 3 vols.

St. Mon.—Statistische Monatschrift (pub. by Austrian Statistical Bureau).

11th Cen., Agr.—Eleventh Census of the United States (1890). Report on the Statistics of Agriculture.

11th Cen., Mfs.—Eleventh Census of the United States (1890). Report on Manufacturing Industries.

11th Cen., Pop.—Eleventh Census of the United States (1890). Report on Population.

11th Cen., Stat. of Cities—Eleventh Census of the United States (1890). Report on the Social Statistics of Cities (by Dr. J. S. Billings).

For the full titles of the works cited under the following abbreviations, the reader is referred to the bibliographical note at the end of the volume: (p. 476)

Harper.	Kuczynski.
Hassel, 1809.	Legoyt.
Hassel, 1822.	Supan.
Kolb.	Worcester.

CONTENTS

CHAPTER I

INTRODUCTION

CHAPTER II

THE HISTORY AND STATISTICS OF URBAN GROWTH

CHAPTER III

CAUSES OF THE CONCENTRATION OF POPULATION

CHAPTER IV

URBAN GROWTH AND INTERNAL MIGRATION

CHAPTER V

THE STRUCTURE OF CITY POPULATIONS

CHAPTER VI

The Natural Movement of Population in City and in Country

CHAPTER VII

THE PHYSICAL AND MORAL HEALTH OF CITY AND COUNTRY

CHAPTER VIII

GENERAL EFFECTS OF THE CONCENTRATION OF POPULATION

CHAPTER IX

TENDENCIES AND REMEDIES

MAP

CHAPTER I

INTRODUCTION

1790

Population of the United States	3,929,214
Population of cities of 10,000 and more	123,551
Proportion living in cities of 10,000 and more	3.14 per cent.

1891.

Population of the 7 colonies of Australia	3,809,895
Population of cities of 10,000 or more	1,264,283
Proportion living in cities of 10,000 or more	33.20 per cent.

THAT the most remarkable social phenomenon of the present century is the concentration of population in cities is a common observation, to which point is given by the foregoing comparison of two typical countries of different centuries. The Australia of to-day has the population of the America of 1790; it is peopled by men of the same race; it is liberal and progressive and practical; it is a virgin country with undeveloped resources; it is, to an equal extent, politically and socially independent of European influence. But Australia is of the nineteenth, rather that of the eighteenth century; and that is the vital fact which explains the striking difference in the distribution of population brought out by the introductory comparison. What is true of the Australia of 1891 is, in a greater or less degree, true of the other countries in the civilized world. The tendency towards concentration or agglomeration is all but universal in the Western world.

What are the forces that have produced such a shifting of population? Are they enduring? What is to be the ultimate result?

What are the economic, moral, political and social conse quences of the re-distribution of population? What is to be the attitude of the publicist, the statesman, the teacher toward the movement?

These are some of the questions to be answered, so far as may be, in the course of the present investigation. They are not questions capable of off-hand answers, for they are parts of a great problem. As Mackenzie says, " the growth of large cities constitutes perhaps the greatest of all the problems of modern civilization." [1] It is the problem of dwindling district schools, of city labor disputes, of the tenement house, of municipal transit, of agrarian reforms, of the " destitute" country village, of the "submerged tenth" and the physical wastes of civilization,—in short, it touches or underlies most of the practical questions of the day. " The social problem that confronts practical people is in a very great degree the problem of the city." [2] It is, therefore, of prime importance to ascertain the extent of the movement and its probable direction in the future; the forces that may be presumed to cause it; the more immediate as well as the ultimate consequences; and the possible remedies.

To a certain extent the distribution of the inhabitants of the earth is determined by man's physical environment.[3] Nature's mandate it is that explains why the arctic have fewer inhabitants than the temperate zones, why mountainous regions are not so densely settled as valleys. To study the distribution of population, geographers and statisticians calculate the density of population, the number of inhabitants to the square mile or acre, and then compare variations in density with variations in climate, soil, earth formation,

---

[1] *Introduction to Social Philosophy*, p. 101.

[2] Gilman, *Socialism and the American Spirit*, p. 30.

[3] Cf. Ratzel, *Anthropo-Geographie.*

political institutions, etc., in order to ascertain the causes that determine the distribution.

But the distribution of population is only partially explained by natural causes. With the same physical environment, the American people are differently distributed from the native Indians. The latter lived in tribes and congregated only in villages, because means of communication were too undeveloped and the population too small to permit the division of labor between city and country. Primitive peoples probably did not live in scattered dwellings, for man is a social being; at the present time, at least, the lowest races like the Australians and Terra del Fuegians dwell in small family groups. The group can never be very large as long as it derives its sustenance from the land it occupies. With the growth of transport facilities and the development of trade, the community may obtain its food-supply from outside sources in exchange for its own products. Then arises a differentiation of dwelling-centres and their functions, which increases *pari passu* with the development of methods of communication, and very noticeably affects the customs and modes of life of the inhabitants. That the townsman is different from the countrymen has long been recognized in politics, law and social science. The names "pagan" and "heathen" originally designated countrymen, while the adjective "urbane" and the nouns "citizen" and "politics" are derived from the Latin and Greek terms for city. In modern German "*kleinstädtisch*" is a term of reproach, while in nearly all languages there exists a strong antithesis between "citified" and countrified."

As our study proceeds, we shall discover fundamental differences in the structure of city and rural populations, which underlie and explain the ordinary manifestations of disagreement just noted. But the first step must be the determination of a method of measurement that can be used with some degree of refinement.   In other words, when does a dwelling centre cease to be rural and become urban?

One method of studying the spatial relations of men and communities to one another is by measuring the density of population; the more human beings to the square mile, the closer together must be their habitations. The limitations upon the use of this method are, however, very considerable. Given two districts of equal population and territorial extent, there will be equal density; but in one case, the population may be scattered in small communities, and in the other congregated in a few large centres.   In the latter case the average density will not be a true average; for example, to say that the average number of persons to the square kilometer in the province of Brandenburg, including the city of Berlin, is 112, is to give a ratio that is true neither of the rural part of the province (70) nor of Berlin itself (26,456). And when it is said that in California there are 7.78 persons to the square mile, in New Hampshire 41.81,[1] it does not follow that in California the people are scattered and in New Hampshire agglomerated.   On the contrary, 41 per cent. of the Californians dwell in towns of 10,000 or more inhabitants, and in New Hampshire only 25 per cent.[2]   Or compare Eng-

[1] Cf. Wilcox, " Density and Distribution of Population in the United States at the Eleventh Census," *Economic Studies* of Amer. Econ. Ass'n, ii, 395.

[2] Table CXV, *infra*. Objection may be made to the use of California in such comparisons, since its average density is not a true average.   But no such objection can be raised against Iowa, which, as Prof. Willcox says, (*op. cit.*, 418), " is perhaps the most evenly settled State in the Union as measured by the mean variation of the densities of population of its counties from the State average." Vermont and Mississippi also have small percentages of variation, yet how different the distribution of population !

TABLE I.

	Density.	Per cent. of population in cities of 10,000+.
Missouri	38.98	25.59
Vermont	36.39	7.93
Iowa	34.47	13.62
Mississippi	27.83	2.64
United States	17.99	27.59

land and Bengal. In density the two countries are as nearly equal as can be (Table CXIII), but in Bengal 4.8 per cent. of the population is urban, and in England 61.7 per cent. (Tables XCI and CXII).

The fact is, that in order to show the proximity of human habitations by density figures, the unit of territory must be too small for use in statistical studies. Only by means of maps and cartograms can the average density be made to portray the conditions of residence, considered with relation, not to the land, but to the people themselves. It is this fact, doubtless, that leads Professor Mayo-Smith in *Statistics and Sociology* to treat of density of population in the chapter on " Physical Environment; " of concentration of population in the chapter on " Social Environment." Density is far more dependent upon natural conditions than is agglomeration.

But it must be admitted that the study of agglomeration by means of percentages of the total population dwelling in centres of a specified size offers some difficulties that are escaped when the comparison is limited to density. What, for instance, is the real significance of the terms "urban population," " rural population? " Does urban population include the dwellers in villages and small towns as well as those in cities? What is the line of division between urban and rural districts?

In ancient times the distinction between urban and rural populations was easily drawn, because the term " urban " was suited only to the few large cities. There existed, indeed, smaller centres of population like our towns or villages, but these bore few or none of the characteristic marks of the city; they were closely identified with the scattered population, which was devoted to agriculture. The development of the arts and sciences, the prosecution of industry, and political activity—all the social forces going to make up civilization—were phenomena of the great capitals like Memphis, Thebes, Nineveh, Babylon. In classic antiquity, indeed, the identification of city and civilization becomes complete; the Greek republics were city states, and when Aristotle wishes to characterize man as a social or gregarious animal he says man is by nature a citizen of the city (πολίς). The essential identification of the city with all the higher interests of humanity by the Greeks and Romans is to be observed at the present day in the English word " city " and " civilization," both of which are derived from the Latin " *civis*." The tremendous influence of the classic city on the life of society has since been equaled by the mediæval city republics in Italy (Venice, Florence, Genoa) and Germany (the Hansa towns and free imperial cities). Society then entered upon a new phase of development, and it is only with the prodigious growth of the great centres of population and industry in the last half of the present century that the city has come once more to have something like the dominating influence that it exercised in antiquity.

The ancient city was a walled town and hence was easily distinguished from the surrounding rural districts. Similarly, in the middle ages the only places of collective residence were the enclosed towns which were absolutely cut off from the scattered population in the rest of the country. In such circumstances there could be but one distinction between city and country. This distinction, moreover, was recognized by the law, which by royal charter conferred certain privileges upon the towns as compared with the open country. The basis of the distinction was the pursuit of industry and commerce, *i. e.*, the cities were manufacturing or market places. Hence it was that the differentiation of population into town and country came to signify a contrast between manufacturing industry and commerce on the one hand, and agriculture on the other, and this distinction was the one made by scientific writers in Germany up to the most recent times.[1] In the eighteenth century the line between town and country was indeed a sharp one, and the opposition of their interests was clearly marked. The era of steam and machinery broke it down in England early in the present century, but on the Continent this influence has worked more slowly. An English writer in the middle of the century noted that the distinction was still sharp even in constitutional France and Belgium.[2] Town and country manifested a spirit of hostility toward each other rather than a desire for friendly intercourse; the cities maintained their walls, levied local taxes or duties (*octroi*) on goods brought in, and carried out a searching examination of every peasant's cart that was driven through the city's gate. The towns, with their special privileges, lived an isolated life and exerted little influence on the country population. Thus the movements following the February Revolution (1848) were confined to a few town populations like Hamburg, Berlin, Munich, Dresden, Frankfort. The cities were the " oases of civilization; " "the people outside were in the same condition as they had been for ages."[3]

But in the last half-century all the agencies of modern civilization have worked together to abolish this rural isolation; the cities have torn down their fortifications, which separated them from the open country; while the railways, the newspaper press, freedom of migration and settlement,

---

[1] Cf. Süssmilch, *Die göttliche Ordnung*, Berlin, 1740; Wappäus, *Allgemeine Bevölkerungsstatistik*, Leipzig, 1861, vol. ii, who says that " it is rather the nature of the occupation and not the mere place of dwelling " that explains the difference in the vital statistics of city and country.

[2] Laing's *Observations on the State of the European People*, 1848–9, p. 273.

[3] It is worthy of note that this mediæval separation of town and country still exists in Sweden and Norway, where all places of collective residence are still called " cities," though some of them have fewer than 500 inhabitants. Wagner-Supan, *Bevölkerung der Erde*, ix, 50–51.

etc., cause the spread of the ideas originating in the cities and lift the people of the rural districts out of their state of mental stagnation. Industry is also carried on outside of the cities,[1] so that the mediæval distinction between town and country has lost its meaning in the advanced countries. In Hungary, which is a relatively backward country, there were in 1890 thirteen legal "cities" having less than 3,000 inhabitants each, while 38 other places that had more than 10,000 inhabitants each had not attained the dignity of "cities." The old distinction between town and country is still preserved in the Prussian statistics, and in the census of 1895, 192 places of from 5,000 to 50,000 or more inhabitants with an aggregate population of 1,800,000 were included in the legal rural population.[2]

In the light of such facts, the absurdity of holding to the mediæval classification of dwelling-centres long since became patent to statisticians, and they have been seeking some other method. That there is a difference in the conditions of life of a city-dweller and a farmer is very evident, but on what basis are we going to separate the two? Hitherto each governmental statistical bureau has framed its own definition. The Russian government in one of its official documents,[3] affirms that "in Russia the urban population forms 12.8 per cent. of the total, as compared with 29 per cent. in the United States." But the fact is not there noted that, in the Russian estimate, towns of 2,000+ are rated as urban, while in the United States only places of at least 8,000 are called urban. On the 2,000 basis the comparison would be 37.7 and 12.8 per cent., on the 8,000 basis 29.2 and about 9 per cent.

[1] See especially the English censuses, and Lommatzsch, *Die Bewegung des Bevölkerungsstandes im Königreich Sachsen*, 14, ff., and Losch, *Die Entwicklung der Bevölkerung Würtembergs von 1871–1890*, in *Württ. Jahrbuch für Stat. und Landeskunde*, 1894.

[2] See *infra*, ch. ii, sec. 4.

[3] *The Industries of Russia* (published for the Chicago Exposition), iii, 42.

One of the modern methods of distinguishing between dwelling-places is to divide the population into agglomerated and scattered. The agglomerated population includes all persons living in houses immediately contiguous to one another or separated only by parks, streets, etc., while the remainder of the population, generally speaking, is agricultural. But with the increasing density of population, agglomeration must naturally increase, and it becomes increasingly difficult to determine the distance which must separate houses in order to count their inhabitants in the "scattered" population. Italy and France have classified their populations as agglomerated and scattered, with these results:

FRANCE.[1]		ITALY.[2]	
1872	60.7	1871	74.3
1876	60.4	1881	72.7
1881	60.1		
1886	61.0		
1891	60.5		

England expressed somewhat the same idea by giving the average distance between houses at various censuses, but has latterly abandoned the method. The mere fact of agglomeration, however, is probably less significant than some of the European statisticians would have us believe, and it seems to attract less attention in the census bureau than it formerly did; nor is it very important. One may well doubt if there exists any considerable difference between the rural population of France, parts of Germany and some other European countries, on the one hand, and the rural population of America on the other, that can be traced to the fact that in the one case peasants live in hamlets, and in the other case on their own farms; yet, in the former case, the per-

[1] *Résultats statistiques du dénombrement de 1891*, p. 61.

[2] Rauchberg, Art. *Bevölkerungswesen*, in Conrad's *Handwbh.*, ii, 431.

centage of agglomerated population would be much larger than that of the latter.

It is thus evident that agglomeration alone does not furnish a true means of distinguishing urban population from rural population according to the meaning attached to those terms in common parlance. An urban population must indeed be agglomerated; but it must also exceed a certain number of inhabitants or it will remain practically rural in character. A German *Dorf* or village containing, say, 300 peasants, is just as properly called rural as an American township containing 300 farmers living perhaps half a mile apart. Thus it is that modern statisticians have agreed upon a numerical boundary line between city and country. Many objections to this conclusion can of course be raised. It is rightly said to ignore the individuality of communities. Here is a suburban village in close contact with a manufacturing city and possessing most of the characteristics of city life; if its population does not reach the arbitrarily chosen number selected as the qualification for entrance to the urban group, it must be put in the rural class along with the veriest farming community. Here again is the townsman with a country residence; he is in the country but not of it. Nevertheless he must be counted in the rural population. The young manufacturing place, a harbor, a thousand-year-old village, a residence town, all places of the same size must be thrown into one class if we follow numerical distinctions. Then again, as population becomes more dense one naturally expects to find the average size of the town or village increasing; the town of 5,000 now plays the role in the formation of social judgments formerly taken by the village of 1,000. Hence the geographical statistician Supan favors a sliding line of division, varying in different countries with the density of population. In his *Ortsstatistik* he has included all places with over 1,000 inhabitants in thinly settled countries like Australia, all over 2,000 in countries with a somewhat denser population (United States, Russia, Peru, Greece and the Balkan countries), and in thickly populated countries like most of the older European states only such places as have 5,000 or more inhabitants.[1] These objections to the numerical line between city and country, however, do not outweigh its advantages.[2] For statistical purposes no other distinction is so available; hence this distinction has been sanctioned both in theory and in practice.

But no such agreement has been reached as regards the determination of the numerical boundary. It is not altogether easy to define the distinguishing characteristics of a city, but in a general way the student will observe that, when a community attains a certain size, new needs and purposes manifest themselves. The close association of a large body of people alters even the material conditions of life. The artesian well and cistern must give way to a common water supply brought from distant springs; a sewerage system must be introduced, likewise street lighting, and rapid transit between the home and the workshop. The liberty of the individual to do his own sweet pleasure must be curtailed for the common benefit; the streets may not be used as depositories of materials for new buildings; noises must be abated, such as music practice with open

---

[1] *Petermann's Mitteilungen, Ergänzungsheft*, No. 107: *Die Bevölkerung der Erde*, ix, Wagner und Supan.

[2] Some statisticians still identify rural and agricultural populations. The *Statesman's Year Book* (1897, p. 678), for example, takes such a position in the following: "In Northern Italy the population is scattered over the country, and there are few centres. In Southern Italy, and in the islands, the country people live in the towns, coming and going to cultivate their own plots of land; consequently there are many populous centres where, if numbers alone were considered, the population would be regarded as urban, though it is in truth almost exclusively rural."

windows during the sleeping hours; nuisances are prohibited, and the like.   In response to the new wants of the
community, the framework of the local government undergoes alteration, the law itself recognizing the difference between urban and rural populations.   Not only are new wants
to be satisfied, but they must be satisfied by new methods.
In the country village, where every citizen knows every
other citizen, the town meeting, or primary assembly in its
pure form, is the ideal governing body, but with every increase in the size of the town, representation must be given
fuller play.   Officials are multiplied by the score and hundred, and must be appointed rather than elected, since the
voters are unable to inform themselves concerning the merits
of so many candidates.

In the United States, then, the law usually provides for
three forms of local government: (1) for the township, the
primary civil division, (2) for the village, the smallest
agglomeration, whose charter of incorporation is granted by
the administration in accordance with general laws, (3) the
city, whose charter of incorporation is usually a special act
of legislation.   But as regards the requirements for these
grades there is no uniformity of practice.   In some of the
Western States almost any town may aspire to the dignity
of city.   Thus North Dakota contained four places which in
1890 severally had a larger population than 2,000 and all
were "cities," namely, Bismarck, 2,186; Fargo, 5,664;
Grand Forks, 4,979; Jamestown, 2,296.[1]   Kansas has no
villages or towns; every place sufficiently large to be incorporated is dubbed "a city."   Kingman county has
three "cities": Norwich with a population in 1890 of 301;
Spivey 205, and Kingman 2,390.[2]   The climax of absur-

---

[1] *Compendium of the 11th Census*, vol. i, population by minor civil divisions.
Pembina " city " with its three wards had a population of 670.

[2] *Op. cit.*, i, 167.

dity is reached in the case of the "city" of Mullinville, Kiowa county, with 79 inhabitants! It is greatly to be regretted that the word "city" is thus degraded, for it is thus coming to lose its peculiar significance. In the East, however, the meaning has been preserved and no one calls a place a "city" unless it possesses claims to the superior influence that accompanies a large population. In Massachusetts, all communities and areas are under the town (township) government until they attain a population of 12,000, when they are incorporated as cities; that is to say, the town meeting is then replaced with a representative legislature and executive. In New York, there is no rigid limit, but in practice a population of about 10,000 is required for incorporation as a city. There are now six cities in New York that had a population of 8,000–10,000 in 1892. But taking the United States as a whole, it must be admitted that the legal city is much less populous than the statistical unit (8,000), for there are 1,628 incorporated cities in the United States, and only 448 towns exceeding 8,000 population.[1]

In England, the municipality corresponding to our city is the borough; the term "city," when used at all, referring by tradition to a borough that happens to be the residence of a bishop. But for the exercise of the important and numerous functions connected with sanitation the country is divided into urban and rural sanitary districts. When the local government board finds an unusually high death-rate prevailing in a country district, it may by order create an urban sanitary district, which is endowed with greater powers in regard to the preservation of health. And it is the urban sanitary districts that contain the urban population of England. There are few districts with a smaller population than

---

[1] Gannett, *The Building of a Nation*, 32.

3,000, but a large number under 10,000 and even under 5,000.[1]

In France, all communes are governed in accordance with the provisions of one municipal code, excepting only the cities of Paris and Lyons. The law thus makes no distinction between urban and rural populations.

In Germany and Austria-Hungary, as already observed, the law regarding municipal corporations has not developed in recent years and largely preserves mediæval distinctions, with the result of producing anomalies.

The conclusion is forced upon us that the legal definition of urban population lacks uniformity. The law-givers do indeed recognize a vital distinction between urban and rural populations, but they do not help us to draw the line. What, now, is the opinion of statistical scientists on the question?

The disagreement is not so great here as in the preceding cases, for of late years the numerical boundary (2,000) chosen by France in 1846 has made its way through most of Continental Europe, and its adoption in 1887 by the International Institute of Statistics[2] makes it reasonably certain that it will be the generally accepted line of division for many years to come. If we hold in mind the distinction commonly made in America between city and town, we shall see that the difference in the meaning attached to the word "urban" by European and American statisticians rests simply on this fact: that in America the "town"[3] is regarded as rural and in Europe as urban. The question of

---

[1] See further ch. ii, sec. 2, Introduction.

[2] See *Bulletin de l'Institut International de Statistique* (1887), ii, 366.

[3] In American usage generally, the town is something between village and city, a kind of inferior or incomplete city. The thing which the town lacks, as compared with the complete city, is . . . . municipal government." Fiske, *Civil Government in the United States*, p. 103. But Fiske says the town is urban rather than rural.

classification is always more or less of an empty one, but in determining the position of a town it may be well to note that the authority of one of the most eminent statisticians of this century is practically on the American side. Gustav Rümelin in discussing the *Landstadt*, which, like the American town, occupies a middle position between the country and the great city, says that as a rule it has more of the characteristics of the *Dorf* (hamlet or village) than of the *Grossstadt* (large city).[1]

And on consideration one must incline to the view that the peculiar marks of a city as described in a foregoing paragraph do not pertain to the village or town. The American legal practice of making broad the distinction between village and city, rather than that between village and rural district, is the sound one. In England, too, the limit 10,000 is important; boroughs containing not less than 10,000 inhabitants may themselves regulate matters of local concern which in other cases are attended to by the county council.[2] While, then, a population of 10,000 will in the comparative tables be accepted as the minimum limit of an urban agglomeration, in studying the several countries it will be convenient to follow the official definition. Germany, in particular, does not recognize the line of 10,000, but divides the dwelling-centres into these four groups:[3]

Landstädte	2,000-5,000	inhabitants
Kleinstädte	5,000-20,000	"
Mittelstädte	20,000-100,000	"
Grossstädte	more than 100,000	"

[1] *Stadt und Land*, in *Reden und Aufsätze*, i, 352 : "Die kleine Landstadt liegt in der Regel von der Grossstadt noch viel weiter als vom Dorf . . . . Die kleinen Städte sind die Vermittlungskanäle für den Wechselverkehr von Stadt und Land," etc. As will appear later on, the age distribution in the town differs considerably from that of the city; this fact, almost entirely a resu't of emigration or immigration, is of vast importance in determining the social character of a community.

[2] Goodnow, *Comparative Administrative Law*, i, 244.

[3] For the basis of these distinctions, see *Statistik des Deutschen Reichs, Neue Folge*, Bd. 32, p. 29.*

In order to avail ourselves of the best statistics it will therefore be necessary at times to regard as urban population all the inhabitants of places of 2,000 or more.

As the foregoing table indicates, Germany divides the urban population into classes. The practice is a common one among official statisticians, but they seldom agree on the lines of division. In most cases 10,000 appears as one limit; France and Austria add 50,000, etc. But in nearly every instance, a separate class is made of cities that exceed 100,000 souls in population. Such cities are rightly called great cities (*Grossstädte, les grandes villes*). They differ from smaller cities in that their influence extends not merely beyond their county, but beyond the commonwealth or province, becoming national or even international. Hence the *grande ville* has become recognized not only in the official statistics, and in the writings of *savants*, but also in the legislation of many modern states. The Institut International de Statistique made it the only sub-class in the urban portion of the population.[1]

The discussion on classification of population according to the size of dwelling-place may be summarized in the following manner:

Rural Population.	{ Scattered. { Agglomerated. { 1. Hamlets and villages (less than 2,000 pop.). { 2. Towns (from 2,000 to 10,000 pop.).
Urban Population.	{ 3. Cities (more than 10,000 pop.). { a. Great cities (more than 100,000 pop.).

One point still calls for notice regarding the comparability of urban statistics, namely, the area that constitutes the urban unit. In American usage, outside of New England, it is the incorporated village or city within the township;[2]

[1] *Bulletin*, ii, 366.

[2] " Township," is the common American name of the primary political division. But there are numerous variations, *e. g.*, " parish " in Louisiana, " precinct " in

but in New England, where there are no other incorporated communities than the city, the township is the statistical unit. Obviously, this variation in practice destroys the comparability of urban statistics, since a township is large enough to contain several villages and a large number of scattered dwellings besides. The census returns should designate communities within the township.

The percentage of error in such cases will of course vary directly with the extent of territory and inversely with the number of inhabitants. Given a large township, there still may not be a single community or dwelling-centre of 2,000 population, although the entire township may contain 10,000 people. This is indeed an extreme case, though it can doubtless be paralleled in the statistics of Spain, where the dwelling centres are never separately returned. In Italy, where both the agglomerated population, or inhabitants of communities, and the total communal or township population are returned, important differences are found. Brescia township contained, in 1881, 60,630 inhabitants; Brescia,

---

Texas, "district" in Virginia, etc. In New England the term "town" is unfortunately substituted for township. Historically, this latter usage is incorrect, as well as confusing. In primitive Anglo-Saxon times, "township" (tunscip) was, without much doubt, regularly used to designate the municipality in its entirety (*i. e.*, the whole area within the hedge or walls); and "town" (tun) meant the settled portion (Cf. W. F. Allen, "Town, Township and Tithing" in *Essays and Monographs*). In the course of time, however, the term "town" usurped the name "township," being applied to the whole area : and in this significance was brought to America by the Pilgrims. Consequently, in New England, the word means the entire municipality, while the settled portion is variously designated as the "village," the "middle of the town," etc. The use of the word "town" for "township," is, moreover, productive of confusion, because "town" is also frequently used to designate a dwelling-centre of a size intermediate between the village and the city. On the other hand, the English use it constantly in the place of the word "city;" with them London is always a "town." But the American practice is far more logical and convenient and conforms more closely with historic usage; for "city" has always signified a town of high rank and dignity, as appears in the classic phrase, "free and imperial city."

the community, 43,354. Chiari township, 10,414; Chiari, the town, 6,000.[1] The average area of the Italian township is 35.3 square kilometers, as compared with 54 for the Spanish township. In Servia, where the township is also large (38.2 sq. km.), the population in townships of more than 2,000 inhabitants constituted, in 1890, 36.5 per cent. of the population; but the population in cities, towns and villages of 2,000+, only 13.25 per cent. In Germany where the *Gemeinde* (township) is very small,[2] the respective figures in 1890 were 47 and 42.5 per cent. France has a method of her own; holding to the commune or township as the unit, she counts as urban communes only such as possess an agglomerated population exceeding 2,000. Theoretically, this is indefensible because it adds villages and isolated farmers to the urban population; but it is better than the German or New England method of counting as urban those townships (*Gemeinder.*) whose total population— without regard to the fact of agglomeration—exceeds the boundary limit adopted. This objection, however, has much less weight when the minimum limit of an urban commune is placed at 10,000, for against so large a number, the scattered population or even a hamlet or two counts relatively little.

Finally, one has to consider whether the population of a single city, or of a number of cities, shall be employed as it is returned at each census, or whether the population dwelling on a given territory, thus diffusing over a long period the increase that actually comes by annexations. And in order to ascertain the growth of an urban population, shall we use the contemporaneous figures of each census, or settle upon a fixed number of cities for the whole series of censuses, thus discounting the effect of new cities arising from

[1] Supan, 58.

[2] Only 7 square kilometers; cf. table in ch. ii. sec. 20, *infra.*

the villages and towns? As will be pointed out in the course of the investigation, both methods have their advantages. For studying the gradual growth of urban population it is usually better to take a fixed territory and a definite number of cities and avoid accidental additions.[1] But to compare the distribution of population at long intervals such refinement would be both superfluous and incorrect. The relative growth of different cities is one thing; the concentration of population is another.[2]

As the first condition of an analytical study is, of course, an exact knowledge of facts, our plan will be to sketch the movement toward the concentration of population during the present century in the leading industrial states of the world and correlate the stages in this movement with industrial changes; then to present the statistics of other countries in less detail, and finally to bring the results together in comparative tables. Not till then may general causes be intelligently discussed. After that, some consideration will be given to the structure of city populations (their pecularities as distinguished from the rural populations), and the consequences of the movement from country to city. In conclusion, remedies will be discussed and some attempt made at forecasting the distribution of population in the near future.

---

[1] The statistical difficulties raised by the adventitious extension of the municipality or the political city have been pointed out anew by Prof. E. J. James in a brief article upon "The Growth of Great Cities" in the *Annals of the American Academy of Political and Social Science* (Jan., 1899), xiii, 1 *seq.*

[2] On the question of method it will suffice to refer the reader to the bibliographies appended to Sections 24–27 of G. von Mayr's *Bevölkerungsstatistik* (*Statistik und Gesellschaftslehre*, vol. ii; Freiburg i B. 1897), in addition to the references already given.

CHAPTER II

HISTORY AND STATISTICS OF URBAN GROWTH

I. THE UNITED STATES

IN a new country the rapid growth of cities is both natural and necessary, for no efficient industrial organization of a new settlement is possible without industrial centres to carry on the necessary work of assembling and distributing goods. A Mississippi Valley empire rising suddenly into being without its Chicago and its smaller centres of distribution is almost inconceivable to the nineteenth-century economist. That America is the " land of mushroom cities " is therefore not at all surprising.

But, on the other hand, it is astonishing that the development of the cities in a new country should outstrip that of the rural districts which they serve. The natural presumption would be that so long as land remains open to settlement, the superfluous population of the older States or of Europe would seek the fundamental, or food-producing, industry of agriculture, and build up cities only in a corresponding degree. Yet in the great cereal regions of the West, the cities have grown entirely out of proportion to the rural parts, resulting there, as in the East and in Europe, in an increasing concentration of the population. The only States [1] where the urban population has in recent years proportionately diminished or remained stationary are Louisiana, South Carolina, Vermont, Mississippi, and one or two

[1] Cf. the historical diagram illustrating the proportion of urban to total population by States and Territories in the *11th Cen., Pop.*, pt. i, p. lxv.

20

others. These are the commonwealths where industry is less progressive and up-to-date than elsewhere; the population is not economically organized, or there would be a more pronounced growth of centres of industry and commerce.

In tracing the historical causes of the concentration of population in the United States, it is needful to remember that internal migration here has not been of one kind exclusively, as in Europe. We have not only the migration cityward, but also the migration westward. Hence in a period when the western movement is particularly strong, the growth of cities is likely to diminish relatively.

The urban population is defined in the United States census reports as the population of cities or towns having at least 8,000 inhabitants. Table II, column 3, shows the growth of the urban population from 210,873 persons residing in six cities in 1800, to 18,284,385 inhabitants of 448 cities in 1890. That is, the urban population has increased eighty-seven fold in the century, while the population of the entire country has increased only twelve-fold. In 1800 the city population of this country was grouped as follows:[1]

Philadelphia	69,403
New York (county)	60,489
Baltimore	26,114
Boston	24,937
Charleston	20,473
Salem	9,457
Total	210,873

City life was practically unknown to the fathers of the Republic; their largest city held a smaller population than

---

[1] *Census of 1850*, p. lii. These are the figures used in the summaries of subsequent censuses. But in the table of cities, *11th Cen. Pop.*, i. 371, the population of Philadelphia is given as 41,220. The population of Philadelphia county or the present city, was 81,009.

TABLE II.

Date of Census. 1.	Population of United States. 2.	Cities 8,000 +. No.	Pop.	Per cent. of total pop. 3.	The great cities of 1890. No. 4.	Pop.	Other cities of 25,000 + in 1890. No. 5.	Pop.	Total of 124 cities. No. 6.	Pop.	Decennial percentage rates of increase of Col. 2.	Col. 3.	Rural pop.	Col. 4.	Col. 5.	Col. 6.
1790	3,929,214	6	131,472	3.35	6	127,046	13	51,844	19	178,890						
1800	5,308,483	6	210,873	3.97	9	208,075	25	103,851	34	311,926	35.10	60	34	63.8	100.3	74.4
1810	7,239,881	11	356,920	4.93	11	335,976	29	135,441	40	471,417	36.38	69	35	61.5	30.4	51.1
1820	9,633,822	13	475,135	4.93	17	469,848	35	171,422	52	641,270	33.07	33	33	39.9	26.6	36.4
1830	12,866,020	26	864,509	6.72	18	702,515	43	271,950	61	974,465	33.55	82	31	49.5	58.6	52.0
1840	17,069,453	44	1,453,994	8.52	22	1,149,438	53	425,683	75	1,575,121	32.67	68	30	63.6	56.5	61.6
1850	23,191,876	85	2,897,586	12.49	24	2,085,783	76	783,782	100	2,869,565	35.87	99	30	81.5	84.1	82.2
1860	31,443,321	141	5,072,256	16.13	24	3,350,108	87	1,264,540	115	4,614,648	35.58	75	30	60.6	61.4	60.8
1870	38,558,371	226	8,071,875	20.93	28	4,861,369	92	1,914,900	120	6,776,269	22.63	59	15	45.1	51.5	46.9
1880	50,155,783	286	11,318,547	22.57	28	6,694,636	96	2,710,727	124	9,405,363	30.08	40	27	37.7	41.1	38.8
1890	62,622,250	448	18,284,385	29.20	28	9,697,960	96	4,291,608	124	13,889,568	24.86	61	15	44.9	58.9	47.7

SOURCES.

For columns 2 and 3, the *Eleventh Census, Population*, pt. i, pages lxv, lxvii. Columns 4, 5 and 6 (the sum of 4 and 5) have been compiled from the data on pages 370–3 of the same volume, except that in the case of Philadelphia the population of the county has been taken throughout, although the actual consolidation of the city and county by law did not take place until 1854; the addition of nearly 300,000 persons in one census would seriously distort the real facts. The federal census does not report the population of San Francisco in 1850, and the population returned by the State census of 1852 (34,766) has therefore been used.

It will be observed that of the 124 cities which in 1890 had a population of 25,000 and upwards, only 19 were in existence, or within the territory of the United States, in 1790.

Cambridge, Massachusetts, in 1890, and but slightly larger than Atlanta. To-day it would rank forty-second among American cities. Not only have the cities increased in size and number, but they have absorbed a vastly larger proportion of the population. In 1790, out of 100 Americans only 3.35 were city dwellers; in 1890, the percentage was 29.2.

Table II also shows that this process of concentration has not been uniform in point of time. While the rural population has suffered a steady decline in the rate of increase from 35 per cent. in the decade 1800–10 to 15 per cent. in 1860–70 and 1880–90, the rate of growth of the urban population fluctuated enormously. In 1810–20 it was 33 per cent.; in 1840–50, 99 per cent. or three times as great. The causes of these fluctuations are to be sought in the economic conditions of the country.

Before 1820 the phenomenon of concentration of population was not to be found in the United States as a whole. In Maryland and Massachusetts, indeed, the urban population was gaining slightly upon the rural population, but in the other commonwealths, including New York, Pennsylvania, Rhode Island, where the largest proportions of urban residents were to be found, there was no such increase. In fact, the decade 1810–20 showed a relative decline of the cities in nearly all the States, and the urban population of the whole country held its own and no more. This was a consequence chiefly of the destruction wrought to American commerce by the War of 1812, the resulting stagnation of the commercial cities and a movement toward agricultural pursuits.

But early in the next decade there opened the era of canals, followed closely by the era of railways, which not only built up great commercial centres, but stimulated the industrial cities by immensely extending their market. The rate of increase goes up from 33, the country's average in

1810–20, to 82, two and a half times the country's average in 1820–30. In order to indicate clearly the rate of increase of the urban population as compared with the general rate, the following table is presented.[1] It is constructed from Table II by regarding the percentage rates of increase of the population of the United States as a standard, or 100, and calculating the ratio which the other decennial rates bear thereto; thus for the decade 1800–10, 35.10 is to 60 as 100 is to 190, etc.

TABLE III.

	United States.	Urban population.	124 large cities of 1890.	Rural population.
1800–10	100	190	140	91
1810–20	100	100	110	99
1820–30	100	244	155	93
1830–40	100	208	188	92
1840–50	100	276	226	84
1850–60	100	213	171	85
1860–70	100	261	207	66
1870–80	100	134	129	90
1880–90	100	246	196	60

Whether one considers the total urban population with the annual additions to the number of cities, or the fixed number of cities, one finds the periods of maximum concentration, in order, to be 1840–50, 1860–70, and 1880–90, while 1870–80 and 1850–60 are in both cases minima. The connection with the country's industrial development may be traced out as follows: The immediate result of the opening of the Erie canal in 1821 was the rapid expansion of commercial centres

[1] The urban population increases by the growth of villages into towns and cities as well as by the increase of city populations, thus bringing in a possible factor of disturbance much like large annexations to a single city. In order to avoid violent fluctuations that might be caused by large additions to the number of cities at any particular census, the writer has summarized in Table II the population at each census of all the cities (124) which in 1890 contained not less than 25,000 inhabitants, thus securing a comparatively fixed territory for the entire period.

in New York State. New York City started on its amazing development, and before 1830 had wrested from Philadelphia the position of metropolis of the New World. Buffalo and Rochester in the same decade passed from the village to the urban stage, soon to be followed by Syracuse, Rome, Utica and other towns along the route of the canal. Simultaneously began the expansion of manufactures in the New England States, causing a considerable concentration of population there. In the following decade 1830–40, the work begun by the canals was continued by the railways [1] and the cities grew apace, [2] attaining their maximum rate in 1840–50.

Thus far the railways had been confined chiefly to the Eastern States, and by opening up large markets for Eastern manufactures had caused a concentration of population which appears in all the figures of Table II. But after 1850 the railway system was extended into the West, where it became rather an instrument for the dispersion of population by permitting the settlement of the Western lands and furnishing an outlet for their products. It was in the decade of 1850–60 that the Mississippi Valley was peopled; [3] and as this was an agricultural or rural movement, the urban population of the country increased less rapidly than in 1840–50.

[1] The railway mileage in the United States (*11th Cen., Trans.,* i, 6) was:

1830	39.8
1840	2,755.2
1850	8,571.5
1860	29,919.8
1870	49,168.3
1880	87,724.1
1890	163,562.1

[2] According to Table II, the urban population had a larger relative increase in 1820–30 than in 1830–40. This may be due to a larger addition to the number of cities in the former period. Between 1820–30 the number of cities doubled; between 1830–40 they increased from 26 to 44. If only a definite number of cities be considered, the larger increase is in 1830–40 (Table III).

[3] Cf. the *Census Reports;* also the standard histories.

But the next decade 1860–80 showed another large urban increase, second only to that of 1840–50. This may be partly accounted for by the defects of the census of 1870, which admittedly left uncounted thousands of negroes belonging to the rural population of the South; but the chief explanation is the check imposed by the Civil War upon the settlement of the West, and the large numbers of the population that devoted themselves to manufactures during and following the war. The following table gives the rates of increase per cent. in the sections indicated: [1]

TABLE IV.

	North Central States.	South Central States.	Western States.
1840–50	61.23	42.24	115.12
1850–60	68.35	34.05	246.15
1860–70	42.70	11.54	60.02
1870–80	35.76	38.62	78.46
1880–90	28.78	23.02	71.27

This shows how the great movement toward settlement in 1850–60 was followed by a slackening in 1860–70, and by a renewal of the migration westward in 1870–80, thus bringing about a large increase in the rural population and a corresponding decrease in the urban percentage of growth as appears in Table III. The fact is even more distinctly brought into light by the following figures respecting the increase in the number of farms [2] and in cereal crops: [3]

TABLE V.

	FARMS IN UNITED STATES.		PRODUCTION OF CEREALS.		
	Number.	Increase per cent.	Total bushels (000,000 omitted).	Increase per cent.	Per capita.
1840	....	..	616	..	36.1
1850	1,449,073	..	867	41	37.4
1860	2,044,077	41	1,239	43	39.4
1870	2,659,985	25	1,387	12	35.9
1880	4,008,907	51	2,698	94	53.8
1890	4,564,641	14	3,519	30	56.2

[1] *11th Cen. Pop.*, i, 4, 5. [2] *11th Cen., Agr.*, p. 1. [3] *Ibid.*, p. 6.

The remarkable increase of the agricultural population in 1870–80, as set forth in this table, connected with the industrial paralysis after the panic of 1873,[1] fully explains why the urban growth was relatively smaller than it had been in any decade since 1820.[2]

In the latest decade, 1880–90, the development of the United States was industrial rather than agricultural, and the migration was cityward instead of westward. While the number of farms and the cereal production have increased but little, the manufacturing interests have prospered as never before.

TABLE VI.

MANUFACTURES; PERCENTAGE OF INCREASE.[3]

	Capital.	Average number of employees.	Net value of product.
1850–60	89.38	37.01	84.11
1860–70	67.80	56.64	63.31
1870–80	64.10	31.49	40.01
1880–90	120.78	65.77	106.59

It is thus clearly shown that the decade 1880–90 saw an exceptionally rapid development of the manufacturing industries. The result is that the number of towns of 8,000+ population rose from 286 to 448, an increase of 162, as compared with an increase of 60 in 1870–80; and the increase

---

[1] The principal manufacturing States, Rhode Island, Massachusetts, New Jersey, Pennsylvania, as well as Ohio, Maryland and other Eastern States, show a marked decrease in urban growth; and Missouri, Nebraska, Louisiana, Utah, etc., show an actual decline in the urban population.

[2] Nevertheless, it is probably true that the census of 1880 gives too small a number for the urban population. In New England, where the local unit, the township, includes a rural as well as urban population, the *Tenth Census* attempts to eliminate the rural population, whereas other censuses count the entire population of the township as urban. In Massachusetts, the *Tenth Census* finds an urban population of 1,042,039 in 33 cities; with the methods of the *Eleventh Census* there would be 36 towns with a population of 1,098,004. For all New England the difference would be about 100,000.

[3] *11th Cen., Mfs.,* i, 4.

in the urban population very nearly reached the maximum
of 1840–50.

Considering the close connection thus far shown to exist
between manufactures and concentration of population, one
would expect to find the bulk of city-dwellers in the North,
as is indeed the case:[1]

TABLE VII.

Divisions.	Urban population, 1890.	Proportion in each division.
North Atlantic	9,015,383	49.31
South Atlantic	1,419,964	7.76
North Central	5,793,896	31.69
South Central	1,147,089	6.27
Western	908,053	4.97
Total	18,284,385	100.00

One-half the entire urban population of the United States
is in the North Atlantic States and four-fifths in the territory
north of the Ohio and Missouri rivers,[2] a fact of considerable social, political and economic significance, and one that
will help to explain the results of election contests and legislative battles where the economic interests of different communities come into conflict. More than one-half of the
urban population, again, is concentrated in five commonwealths, as follows:

New York	3,599,877
Pennsylvania	2,152,051
Massachusetts	1,564,931
Illinois	1,485,955
Ohio	1,159,342
Total	9,962,156

Missouri, which ranks above Massachusetts in total population, has less that half the number of urban dwellers

[1] *11th Cen., Pop.*, pt. i, p. lxv.

[2] Approximately but not absolutely true, as parts of Missouri and South Dakota
and all of Kansas and Nebraska are south of the Missouri river.

(703,743), and in the present list follows after the little commonwealth of New Jersey (780,912 urban population). After Missouri, Michigan is the only State that has more than half a million city dwellers, although California lacks very little (about 5,000) of reaching the mark.

Thus far, the definition of urban population has been the one formulated by the census reports, the requirement being a population of 8,000. If, however, the line be drawn higher, the Eastern States will have a still larger proportion of the urban population; and *vice versa*. But the difference is not so great as might be expected.

TABLE VIII.[1]

PERCENTAGE OF POPULATION IN THE SPECIFIED DIVISIONS FOR PLACES

	Over 25,000.	8,000 to 25,000.	4,000 to 8,000.	2,500 to 4,000.	1,000 to 2,500.	Total over 1,000.
North Atlantic	51.03	43.70	44.15	39.23	38.04	46.61
South Atlantic	7.68	8.05	5.34	9.20	6.95	7.53
North Central	30.38	35.95	37.80	34.80	37.96	33.32
South Central	5.90	7.48	7.64	10.43	11.14	7.34
Western	5.01	4.82	5.07	6.34	5.91	5.20
United States	100.	100.	100.	100.	100.	100.

It appears from this table that the North Atlantic States have, in their urban population, a large proportion of the great-city dwellers and fewer villagers. The Western States are about equally represented in all the groups, while the remaining commonwealths are much stronger in villages and small towns than in large cities. The contrast between the North Atlantic and the North Central States is noteworthy, as the two sections contain the bulk of the urban population. In the North Atlantic States the urban population is essentially of the large-city type, and in the North Central States of the town or small-city type.[2]

[1] *Census Bulletin*, No. 165.

[2] These facts are made the basis of an interesting study of the "Distribution of our Urban Population," which appeared in the *American Statistical Association's*

While the eastern and northern States contain the vast majority of the townsmen of the country, it does not follow that they contain the greatest proportionate number of city dwellers. On the contrary, the large urban population of the Mississippi Valley is counterbalanced by a large rural population, while the Western States have a comparatively small rural population. The result is that in the Western States a larger percentage of the people dwell in cities than do the people of the North Central States, as will be seen in the following table : [1]

TABLE X.

PERCENTAGE OF POPULATION RESIDING IN TOWNS OF

	10,000+.	8,000+.	1,000+.
North Atlantic division	48.68	51.58	70.0
South " "	15.05	16.04	22.2
North Central "	24.59	25.90	38.9
South " "	9.82	10.45	17.5
Western "	29.71	29.74	44.8
United States	27.59	29.20	41.69

It is somewhat surprising thus to find so large a proportionate number of town-dwellers in the far West, as compared with the middle West. The probable explanation is

Publications (iv, 113–6), and showed how the large percentages of urban population in the East are due to the presence of great cities. New York and New Jersey afford a striking contrast, as do Missouri and Indiana. In the one case, the vast majority of the urban population is found in the commercial centres of New York City and St. Louis, while in the second case the urban population is scattered in manufacturing towns :

TABLE IX.

PERCENTAGE OF TOTAL POPULATION.

	New York.	New Jersey.	Missouri.	Indiana.
In all places of 1,000+	68.79	64.58	36.69	32.12
" places of 1,000-25,0co	16.21	21.66	12.86	21.98
" " " 25,000–100,0co	7.37	19.c6	1.99	5.30
" " " 100,0co+	45.20	23.86	21.82	4.84

[1] *11th Cen., Soc. Stat. of Cities*, pp. 1, 2; *Pop.*, pt. i, p. lxv; *Census Bulletin*, No. 165, pp. 2, 3.

the difference in the physical features of the two regions. While in the central States agriculture is the staple industry and is prosecuted by small farmers, in the Pacific States commerce brings men together in towns, and agriculture does not call for a dense population, as it is carried on so largely on large estates or ranches; the average size of a farm in the Western States, according to the census of 1890, being 324 acres as compared with 133 acres in the North Central States and 144 acres in the South Central States.

The following table arranges the States and Territories by groups according to the proportion of their population living in cities of 10,000 and upward:[1]

TABLE XI.

CLASS I. MORE THAN ONE-HALF URBAN.

1.	District of Columbia	88.10
2.	Massachusetts	65.88
3.	Rhode Island	57.91
4.	New York	57.66
5.	New Jersey	50.91

CLASS II. MORE THAN ONE-QUARTER URBAN.

6.	Maryland	43.87
7.	Connecticut	41.86
8.	California	40.98
9.	Pennsylvania	39.10
10.	Illinois	38.08
11.	Colorado	37.07
12.	Delaware	36.46
13.	Ohio	30.15
14.	Utah	28.73
15.	Washington	28.27
16.	Minnesota	27.69
	UNITED STATES	27.59
17.	Missouri	25.59

CLASS III. MORE THAN ONE-TENTH URBAN.

18.	New Hampshire	24.76
19.	Michigan	23.90

[1] *11th Cen., Stat. of Cities*, pp. 1, 2.

20. Louisiana 23.65
21. Wisconsin.. 22.46
22. Nebraska 22.15
23. Wyoming 19.26
24. Montana.. 18.58
25. Oregon 18.14
26. Maine 17.16
27. Indiana.. 16.68
28. Kentucky 13.87
29. Iowa 13.62
30. Virginia 12.85
31. Florida 12.02
32. Tennessee.. 10.65

CLASS IV. LESS THAN ONE-TENTH URBAN.

33. Georgia 9.91
34. Kansas 9.73
35. Texas 9.71
36. Vermont 7.93
37. South Carolina 6.11
38. West Virginia 5.85
39. Alabama 5.23
40. North Carolina 3.37
41. Arkansas 3.30
42. South Dakota 3.10
43. Mississippi 2.64

CLASS V. NO URBAN POPULATION.

44. North Dakota.
45. Idaho.
46. Nevada.
47. Arizona.
48. New Mexico.
49. Oklahoma.
50. Indian Territory.

The cartogram prepared by Dr. Billings, the census agent, to illustrate these figures emphasizes one or two facts of exceptional interest. First, all the Northern States (*i. e.,* the North Atlantic and North Central States together with Delaware and Maryland) have more than 15 per cent. of urban population, except the Dakotas, Kansas, Iowa, and Vermont. The Dakotas are recently settled agricultural

States and cannot be expected to have cities; Kansas is in the cattle-raising belt, with Texas and Oklahoma; Vermont has no sea-board and no manufacturing centres, and so falls below Maine and New Hampshire; but the position of Iowa is peculiar. Iowa stands in a position of isolation in the Middle West; Minnesota has 27.7 per cent. urban population, Missouri 25.6, Illinois 38.1, Wisconsin 22.5 and Nebraska 22.15, but Iowa has only 13.62 per cent. The Iowa people believe that the growth of their cities has been checked by railway discriminations which have favored Chicago, St. Paul, St. Louis and Omaha, as against their own commercial centres, and this is indeed the only adequate explanation.

Among the Southern States, on the other hand, Louisiana (23.65 per cent.) stands in isolation, for it is the only commonwealth whose urban population exceeds fifteen per cent. It is commerce rather than manufacturing that explains this, for Georgia is far more of a manufacturing State than Louisiana. The presence of a great commercial centre, New Orleans, is what gives Louisiana its prominence.

The Western States seem to go to extremes. Four of these are in the second group, and three in the third, while the remainder are in the fifth. None of them are in the fourth group, which is almost entirely Southern. The second group, it may be noticed, contains six States west and six States east of the Mississippi; but the Western States (except California and Colorado) fall in the second half of the group, while most of the Eastern States are in the first half. The striking feature is that California should outrank Pennsylvania. The commercial importance of San Francisco, fruit-growing and agriculture carried on in large estates, must be regarded as the causes of the high proportion of Californians who live in cities.

It was earlier shown that the historical tendency in the

distribution of population in the United States is for an ever-increasing proportion of the people to dwell in towns. A question of considerable importance is whether the tendency is toward great or small cities. The only careful investigation of this question is a part by Mr. Carl Boyd in the *Publications of the American Statistical Association.*[1] His classification of the cities rests upon the mean population of 1880 and 1890; thus Milwaukee, which had a population of 204,468 in 1890, is not included in the class of 200,000 and upwards because its population in 1880 was 115,587 and the mean would be 160,000. The result of the analysis is as follows:

TABLE XII.

	No. of Cities.	Percentage increase of population, 1880–90.
200,000 or more	12	36.87
60,000–200,000	28	63.07
30,000–60,000	40	52.45
17,000–30,000	81	53.72
11,000–17,000	93	53.74
8,000–11,000	102	47.30
	356	

This apparently demonstrates that the great cities of America are growing less rapidly than the smaller ones. But the evidence is inconclusive, for the class of cities 200,000 and upwards happens to include the cities of the settled East where population is increasing less rapidly than in the West; only two of the 12 cities in this group (St. Louis and San Francisco) are west of the Mississippi. On the other hand the second group, which shows the largest increase of all, includes the most rapidly growing cities of the new West; Minneapolis with an increase of 251 per cent; Omaha, 360 per cent; St. Paul 221 per cent; Kansas City 138 per cent; Denver 200 per cent; etc. The only

---

[1] " Growth of Cities in the United States during the Decade 1880–90," iii, 416 *ff.*

inference to be drawn from these figures is that in an era of rapid colonization the growth of the new centres of distribution may overshadow the development of the older commercial centres. We are still left in doubt as to the relative growth of large and small cities in settled communities. It is unfortunate that the American census authorities do not emulate the European official statisticians in making useful tabulations of the facts they gather; it is too much to ask of the individual investigator to classify the cities and compute their population for all the censuses. In Table II, however, the 124 cities of 25,000+ in 1890 have been divided into two classes, the line being drawn at 1,100,000, and the aggregate population of the four principal cities has also been computed. A comparison of the rates of growth of the three groups with the rate for the United States entire is as follows, the latter rate being represented as 100 as in Table III:

TABLE XIII.

	New York, Chicago, Philadelphia and Brooklyn.	Cities of 100,000+ in 1890.	Cities 25,000–100,000 in 1890.
1800–10	130	169	84
1810–20	80	120	80
1820–30	145	148	175
1830–40	165	195	173
1840–50	200	227	238
1850–60	186	170	173
1860–70	143	194	228
1870–80	117	125	137
1880–90	173	180	236

In only three of the nine decades (1800–10, 1810–20, 1830–40) did the great cities grow as rapidly as the middle-sized cities, while the four great centres were distanced in every decade except 1850–60. Since 1840, at least, it would appear as if there had been no movement toward centralization, such as exists in France with its one great metropolis ever distancing the other cities in growth. But some individual cities do, nevertheless, exert something of the power of attraction possessed by Paris. Take for example the cities of New York State. In 1890 there were 13 of 25,000 or more inhabitants; three of which, New York, Brooklyn and Long Island City, belong to the metropolis. The population of these three cities in 1890 was 3.8 times as great as in 1850; the population of the other ten cities 3.6 times as great, thus indicating the more rapid growth of New York city than the interior cities, some of which, however, notably Buffalo and Yonkers, outstripped New York. But Yonkers is itself a New York suburb, and if we were to add the parts of industrial New York that lie in New Jersey, we should find that the metropolis heads the list. While our evidence is by no means conclusive, it points to the inference that New York like Paris, grows at a more rapid rate than the smaller cities in the settled parts of the country. Of course, New York has been outdone by the commerical centres of the new West, and will continue to be outdone by them until their dependent territory is in a measure filled up.

The great difficulty in the statistical method here lies in its failure to take account of the great city's growth outside its own boundaries. The movement toward the suburbs, which is stronger in America than elsewhere with the exception of Australia, not only necessitates frequent annexations of territory, but even then baffles the statistician. This may be illustrated by studying historically the distribution of population in Massachusetts. And first as to annexations.

In 1890 Massachusetts contained sixteen cities whose population individually exceeded 25,000. Computing their aggregate population at each census and calculating the rates of increase, the following result is reached: [1]

---

[1] *11th Cen. Pop.*, i, 370-3.

TABLE XIV.

DECENNIAL RATES OF INCREASE.			PROPORTIONATE RATES OF INCREASE BOSTON.[1]			
	Mass.	16 cities.	Boston.	Mass.	16 cities.	a.	b.
1800–10....	11.63	27.8	33.24	100	238	283	344
1810–20....	10 83	15.9	30.22	100	147	280	250
1820–30....	16.68	55.6	41.79	100	332	250	228
1830–40....	20.85	55.7	52.11	100	268	250	240
1840–50....	34.81	63.9	46.58	100	183	134	149
1850–60....	23.79	33.0	29.92	100	139	126	147
1860–70....	18.38	39.6	40.87	100	215	222	98
1870–80....	22.35	42.1	44.83	100	189	201	107
1880–90....	25.57	32.9	23.60	100	129	92	90

The historical changes in the rate are not difficult of explanation. The impetus to city growth in 1820–30 was given by the cotton trade; Lowell was founded in 1826 and appears in the census of 1830 with a population of 6,474. The high rate of increase of the sixteen cities in 1840–50 is without doubt due to the fact that Lawrence, Somerville and Holyoke appeared for the first time in the census of 1850, completing the list. Since then the rate, especially as compared with the average for Massachusetts, has steadily declined. But this is also true of Boston, so that one feels warranted in drawing the conclusion that the abnormal growth of cities is a matter of the past rather than the future. This inference would seem to be more strongly justified, moreover, when one considers the rate of increase for the Boston of to-day, as given in the last column of the table. Here the disturbing influence of the annexations of 1867–1873[2] have been removed and it is now seen not only

[1] Column *a* corresponds to the rates given above, and is based on the population of Boston as returned at each census; column *b* is based on the population, at each census, of the present area of Boston, thus including all annexed territory.

[2] The annexed districts with population at federal census of 1870 were:

1867, Roxbury 34,753
1869, Dorchester 12,261
1873, West Roxbury 8,686
1873, Brighton 4,967
1873, Charlestown 28,323

Cf. *Census of Mass.*, 1895, i, 221.

that Boston's proportionate rate of growth has been diminishing throughout the century, but that, since 1820, it has
fallen below that of the sixteen cities, and in 1860–70 and
1880–90 below the average of Massachusetts.

But all such calculations are upset by the lack of agreement between the urban centre proper (the economic city)
and the legal city or municipality of the time being. The
recent State census of Massachusetts shows that the most
rapidly growing towns are the suburbs of Boston. As follows was the percentage increase of population in 1885–95,[1]
the suburban cities being indicated thus * :

*Everett 218.85
*Malden 81.07
*Somerville 74.17
Fitchburg 71.77
*Quincy 70.54
New Bedford 65.46
*Medford 60.08
Brockton 59.58
Fall River 56.85
North Adams 52.59
MASSACHUSETTS 28.73
Boston 27.29
    "   (within 8 miles of the State House) 37.19
    "   "   12 "   "   "   "   " 37.26
All incorporated cities (32) 38.05
Rural remainder 14.15

While, therefore, the capital city with its environs is con-
tinuing to absorb the population of the state, so that to-day
the " Greater Boston " contains 39.4 per cent.[2] of the population of Massachusetts as against 5.9 per cent. in the Boston
of 1800 and 13.7 per cent. in the Boston of 1850, its relative

---

[1] *Census of 1895*, i, 46–9. The list includes all cities whose rate of increase in
the decade exceeded 50 per cent.

[2] The so-called Metropolitan district includes virtually all towns within a radius
of ten miles of the State house. With a twelve-mile radius, the percentage in
Boston would be 40.17. Cf. *op. cit.*. i, 47.

growth is less rapid than it was during the first half of the
century. The proportion $28.75 : 37.26 = 100 : x$ yields 130,
whereas the proportionate rate did not fall below 147 until
1870.

But even at this rate the cities would gain upon the population of the country at large, and one may look for still
more profound changes in the distribution of population
than those indicated in the following table, which is based on
Table XVI:

TABLE XV.

PERCENTAGE OF POPULATION OF THE UNITED STATES RESIDING IN SPECIFIED
CITIES IN THE YEARS:

	1800.	1850.	1890.
100,000 + ...	0	6.0	15.5
20,000–100,000	3.8	3.8	8.3
10,000–20,000	0	2.2	3.8
Total 10,000 + ...	3.8	12.0	27.6

The present indications are that before 1910 one-half of
the American people will be residents of cities of 8,000.
This condition would be reached about 1920 if the rate of
concentration from 1820 to 1890 should prevail; in about
1915 if the rate of 1850–90 should be maintained; and soon
after 1905 if the rate of 1880–90 should continue.

Changes in the position of the different commonwealths
with reference to the proportion of urban population may be
expected. Concentration began in Massachusetts and
Rhode Island, Connecticut and Maryland.[1] The era of railways with the accompanying expansion of commerce on the
one hand and of the iron industry on the other, caused a
rapid growth of cities in New York and Pennsylvania. In
1830 and again in 1860, New York and Massachusetts had
an equal proportion of urban population; but now Massachusetts has a percentage of 70 per cent. of its population
in towns of 8,000+ and New York 60 per cent. New Jersey

---

[1] Cf. Diagram in *11th Cen., Pop.*, pt. i, p. lxv.

and Connecticut are overtaking New York, as a result of the development of small manufacturing cities. Both passed Maryland and Pennsylvania in the decade 1860–70, when the war gave life to so many machine industries. Illinois, now the ninth State on the census chart showing proportion of urban to total population, betrays the most uniform and consistent increase of any of the States. With the continual development of manufactures in Illinois and the continued growth of Chicago, there can be no doubt that by 1900 Illinois will have passed Pennsylvania, California and Maryland and have taken place close after New Jersey and Connecticut.

A summary of the urban statistics of the United States is given in

TABLE XVI.

Classes of cities.	No.	1800 Population.	No.	1850 Population.	No.	1890 Population
100,000+	..	......	6	1,393,338	28	9,697,960
20,000–100,000....	5	201,416	24	878,342	137	5,202,007
10,000–20,000.....	..	......	36	495,190	180	2,380,110
Total 10,000+ ...	5	201,416	66	2,766,870	345	17,280,077
" 2,000+......				18% est.	1,916	23,593,605

AUTHORITIES.

For 1800, see p. 21.

For 1850, the *Census of 1850*, p. lii and full tables. To the 22 cities of 20,000–100,000 in the lists on p. lii are added Allegheny City (21,262) and Chicago (29,963). Only 27 cities of the third group are given in the lists of principal cities (p. lii), their aggregate population being 372,584; to this number may be added Manchester, N. H., New Bedford and Charlestown, Mass., Norwich, Conn., Oswego, N. Y., New Brunswick, N. J., Norfolk and Petersburg, Va., and Lafayette, Ind., whose population was found in the tables for the separate States. The estimate of towns of 2,000+ is derived from a comparison of Tucker (*Progress of the United States*, 132), who gives the total for 1840 (2,321,527, or 13.6 per cent. of the total population) with the census figures of 1840 and 1860 for towns of 8,000+.

For 1890, the *Census Report on Social Statistics of Cities*, p. l, gives the total of cities 10,000+. The population of towns of 2,000+ is derived from *Census Bulletin*, No. 165, and the other totals are summaries from the *Report on Population*, pt. i, pages 370–3.

II. THE UNITED KINGDOM

§ 1. *England and Wales.*—From many points of view, England offers superior advantages for the study of the distribution of population and the causes affecting the same.

England was the pioneer in the modern industrial movement and is even now the typical industrial country. For while the aggregate output of machine or factory-made products in the United States exceeds that of England, it does not constitute so large a proportion of the entire national product. A smaller percentage of Englishmen and Scotchmen are devoted to agricultural pursuits than of any other nation of the world. The latter being the only workers who are of necessity resident in scattered habitations, it will be worth while to ascertain under what conditions the remainder of the population has dwelt.

Unfortunately, the English statistics present serious difficulties to the classification of dwelling-centres. This is chiefly the fault of the historical English method of local government, distributing the various functions to a variety of independent authorities over different areas and thus producing a chaos of boundaries and officials. In 1871, the 938[1] dwelling-centres which were taken to represent the urban population of England and Wales were thus classified: Municipal boroughs, comprising cities and towns to which charters of incorporation had been granted and were later governed by the Municipal Corporations Reform Act, 224; local board districts established either under the Public Health Act of 1848 or under the Local Government Act of 1858, 721 (including 146 municipal boroughs); places which had improvement, paving, lighting or other commissions under (special) local Acts, 88 (including 37 municipal boroughs); other "towns" of some 21,000 population, 96. But these "towns" not under a regular municipal authority had no recognized boundaries, and "the Superintendent Registrar of the District in each case distinguished the houses which in his opinion might properly be considered within the limits of the town."

[1] Or 946, if London be counted in its parts instead of a unit.

Such was the condition of affairs in 1871. In the earlier censuses there were still fewer places which had definite and recognized boundaries; such being the boroughs alone. But a borough might be either municipal or parliamentary. And sometimes there was a vast difference between the limits of the two; for example, Wolverhampton, the municipal borough, had a population of 49,985 in 1851, but a population of 119,748 dwelt within its parliamentary boundaries. All of which tended to confuse the statistician.

In 1872, however, legislation simplified matters considerably. By the Public Health Act of 1872,[1] it was enacted that all municipal boroughs, local board districts and towns with improvement commissions, should henceforth be termed " urban sanitary districts," and to these authorities were transferred all the powers and duties previously exercised by any other authority in the districts under the provisions of acts relating to local government, the utilization of sewage, the removal of nuisances, the regulation of common lodging houses, baths and wash houses and the prevention of disease. These powers connected with sanitation, which have since been augmented, are so important and, in fact, so essential a part of city government, that the English urban sanitary district may well be considered the typical urban community. To the original urban sanitary districts of 1872, others have been added from year to year, being carved out of the great area comprised in the rural sanitary districts as rapidly as an agglomeration of peoples becomes of sufficient magnitude to require urban sanitary regulations. The number of urban sanitary districts in the Census of 1891 was 1,011, of which only 194 had less than 3,000 inhabitants. Their aggregate population constituted 71.7 per cent. of the entire population of England and Wales; only 1.3 per cent.

[1] 35 and 36 Vict., cap. 79.

of the population dwelt in urban districts smaller than 3,000.[1]

With these explanations, the following summary table is put forward to show the degree in which the population was concentrated at the different periods in the present century:

TABLE XVII.

Classes of cities.	No.	1801. Population.	No.	1851. Population.	No.	1891. Population.
Over 20,000	15	1,506,176	63	6,265,011	185	15,563,834
10,000–20,000	31	389,624	60	800,000	175	2,362,376
5,000–10,000	60	418,715	140	963,000	262	1,837,054
Total 5,000+	106	2,314,515	263	8,028,011	622	19,763,264
" under 5,000	...	6,578,021	...	9,899,598	...	9,239,261
Grand total	...	8,892,536	...	17,927,609	...	29,002,525

SOURCES.

The population of cities of 20,000 and upwards is derived from Table XVIII, where the sources are named. For the smaller cities and towns, the data were derived as follows:

For 1801, a list of cities and towns containing upwards of 5,000 inhabitants in the *Annual Register* for 1801, pp. 171–3. A compilation from the data in the *Census of 1841* (Introductory Volume, p. 10) gives approximately equal results, *e. g.*, 46 cities of 10,000 with total population of 1,882,667 in the *Annual Register*.

For 1851, only the aggregate urban and rural populations are given in the census volume (I, p. xlvi, Table XXIII). The summaries of cities above 20,000 are exact, and are based on table 42 (p. cxxvi of the *1851 Census*, vol. I); of the smaller cities they are only approximately correct (Table VII, p. cciv ff).

For 1891, *Census of 1891*, iv, 10, *General Report*. The numbers relate to urban sanitary districts, and the administrative county of London is reckoned as one district.

In the ninety years covered by the table, over twenty millions of people were added to the population of England and Wales; but while the rural inhabitants (those dwelling in places of less than 5,000) increased from 6,600,000 to 9,200,000, the town-dwellers increased from 2,300,000 to 19,800,000. That is, of the total increase of twenty millions, about 17,400,000, or 80 per cent., fell to the towns and cities. It is, moreover, noticeable that the increase of the rural population took place entirely in the first half of the century, and later turned into an actual decrease. Some 800,000 more people are classed as belonging to the rural

[1] That some rural sanitary districts contain a population of 50,000 or more signifies nothing, since this is scattered population contained within a large area.

population in 1851 than in 1891; so that while in some countries much is said of a rapid growth of cities, causing the rural population to suffer a *relative* decline, in England there is a decrease in the absolute numbers of the rural inhabitants. The decline began in 1861, as may be seen in the following percentages of decennial increase or decrease calculated from the figures of Table XVIII:

	Urban.	Rural.
1851–61	21.9	+1.88
1861–71	28.1	—5.86
1871–81	25.6	—3.84
1881–91	18.5	—2.76

In does not follow from this that there has been a rural depopulation in England in the strict sense of the term; for the aggregate rural population of a country may diminish either as a result of emigration or as the result of the growth of hamlets and villages into towns and cities. The increase in the mere number of cities is remarkable. In 1891 England and Wales contained 360 urban sanitary districts, or towns, of 10,000 and more inhabitants; in 1881 there were 123; in 1801, 45, and in 1377, with a population nearly one-fourth as great as that of 1801, only two cities, London with almost 35,000 inhabitants and York with about 11,000. Nine towns are believed to have had a population of 5,000 or more, and 18 a population of not less than 3,000[1] in lieu of the present number of 817 in a population about fourteen times as large. In 1377 the population of these 18 towns, formed eight per cent. of the entire population[2] In 1688 the towns, according to Gregory King,[3] contained one-

[1] Based on an enumeration for the poll tax. For the list of cities, see Jas. Lowe, *The Present State of England*, London, 1822, appendix, p. 74. Cf. also the economic histories.

[2] The ratio of urban to rural population was as 1 : 12.34.—Rogers, *Six Centuries of Work and Wages*, 129.

[3] *National and Political Observations upon the State and Condition of England*, 36.

fourth of the population. But such estimates are extremely crude, as appears from Arthur Young's observation in 1770 that half the population was urban;[1] whereas Table XVII shows that not more than one-third of the population could properly be called urban even in 1801.

The question of rural depopulation in England has been frequently discussed by the English statisticians and will not be entered into here, at any length, since this paper is concerned with the relative increase or decrease of the country as compared with the city. Dr. Ogle's investigation[2] covered the seventeen registration counties in which more than ten per cent. of the population were devoted to agricultural pursuits, with the exception of the two mining counties of Cornwall and Shropshire. Defining as the rural population the inhabitants of all districts in these counties except urban sanitary districts of 10,000 and upwards, he found that it aggregated 2,381,104 in 1851 and 2,358,303 in 1881. The loss is scarcely perceptible. And even if the rural population be restricted to sanitary districts of less than 5,000, it shows a decrease of only 2.1 per cent. in the entire period.

There are fifteen English counties which reached their maximum population in 1841 or at some other census prior to 1891. Their aggregate loss from the year of maximum to 1891 is 133,600, and of this loss 46,570 or over one-third is found in Cornwall, where the cause is not agricultural depression, but failure of the tin mines.[3] All this does not imply a rural depopulation, which connotes a great

[1] *Travels in France* (2d ed.), i, 480. Cf. Toynbee's criticism, *Industrial Revolution* (Humboldt ed.), p. 37, foot-note 3.

[2] Ogle, " The Alleged Depopulation of the Rural Districts," in *Jour. of Stat. Soc.* (1889), 52: 205 *ff.* Cf. also Longstaff, *loc. cit.* (1893), 56: 380, and *Census of 1891*, iv, 12 (*Parliamentary Papers*, 1893, cvi).

[3] Cf. Longstaff, *Studies in Statistics*, ch. v, where similar results are given for the census of 1881.

TABLE XVIII.

DISTRIBUTION OF POPULATION IN ENGLAND AND WALES.

	London.	Other cities of 100,000 +.		Cities of from 20,000 to 100,000.		All cities 20,000 +.		Aggregate urban population.		Aggregate rural population.	Total population.	Official Sources.
								Towns.	Population.			
1801	864,845		....	14	641,331	15	1,506,176		....	....	8,892,536	Census of 1841, Introd., p. 10.
1811	1,009,546	2	210,484	15	619,370	18	1,839,400		....	....	10,164,256	" " " "
1821	1,225,694	3	393,330	24	870,242	28	2,489,266		....	....	12,000,236	" " " "
1831	1,471,941	5	791,315	37	1,203,624	43	3,466,880		....	....	13,896,797	" " " "
1841	1,873,676	8	1,039,942	48	1,695,045	54	4,608,663		....	....	15,914,148	" " " "
1851	2,362,236	11	1,678,551	54	2,224,224	63	6,265,011	580	8,990,809	8,936,800	17,927,609	1851, I : cxxvi, cciv.
1861	2,803,989	12	2,211,075	60	2,652,558	72	7,667,622	781	10,960,998	9,105,226	20,066,224	1861, I : 102–104.
1871	3,254,260	12	2,617,726	90	3,671,982	103	9,543,968	938	14,041,404	8,670,862	22,712,266	1871, 4 : 34, xxxi.
1881	3,834,354	19	3,864,321	125	4,754,326	145	12,453,501	967	17,636,646	8,337,793	25,974,439	1881, 4 : 9.
1891	4,232,118	23	5,021,856	161	6,309,860	185	15,563,834	1,011	20,895,504	8,107,021	29,002,525	1891, 4 : 10.

EXPLANATORY.

The population of London here given will not be found to correspond with the figures of the recent censuses, because the latter cover the area of the present Registration London. At the census of 1801, the metropolitan area consisted of 30,002 acres, and the foregoing data relate to this area from 1801 to 1831. In 1841, the metropolitan limits were enlarged to 44,816 acres by the addition of several outlying parishes; with the old limits, the population in 1841 was 1,690,684. In 1844 and 1846, further additions were made, raising the area to 75,362 acres, but increasing the population in a very slight degree: this is the area for 1851, 1861 and 1871. For 1881 and 1891, the figures above refer not to Registration London, but to the administrative county, whose boundaries include one or two additional parishes—a matter of about 20,000 population. (Cf. *Digest of the Census of 1871*, by James Lewis, p. 28.)

Salford is included in the columns of cities of 100,000 +, at first as a suburb of Manchester, and independently since 1861, when its population was 102,-449. . . . In the tables of the census of 1861, the parliamentary boroughs of Stoke-upon-Trent and Wolverhampton exceed 100,000, and are reckoned in the second column; but in the census of 1871 they are replaced by the municipal boroughs of Hanley and Wolverhampton, and fall in the third column.

The urban population from 1851 to 1871 consists of "municipal boroughs, towns of improvement acts, and towns of some 2,000 or more inhabitants, without any organization other than the parish vestry." (*Census of 1871*, Introd., p. xxxi. In 1881 and 1891 it consisted of the urban sanitary districts.

The aggregate population of England and Wales is that uniformly given in the recent censuses, as the earlier censuses vary according to the treatment of army, marine, isles of the sea, etc.

scarcity of farm labor. Nevertheless, it is somewhat start-
ling to read in the preliminary census report of 1891 (p. vi)
that in the preceding decade there was a decline of population in 271 out of the 632 registration districts in England
and Wales; and that in 202 of the 271 there had also been
a decline in the decade 1871–81. And even Dr. Ogle admits
that hard times, the use of labor-saving machinery and the
conversion of arable into pasture land have caused the
farmers to reduce their labor force.

But the decrease of the rural population in England is less
significant than the great urban increase already indicated in
Table XVII and set forth in greater detail in Table XVIII.
Looking at the movement of population as a whole it is seen
what a considerable change in the conditions of life has taken
place during the century. The population of cities of 20,000
or more inhabitants has multiplied tenfold, while the remainder of the population has not quite doubled. A table
of percentages will present the facts embodied in Table
XVIII more graphically:

TABLE XIX.

PERCENTAGE OF POPULATION OF ENGLAND AND WALES IN

	London.	Other great cities.	Cities 20,-000–100,000.	All cities 20,000+.	Urban districts.	Rural districts.
1801	9.73	0.	7.21	16.94	....	....
1811	9.93	2.08	6.10	18.11	....	....
1821	10.20	3.27	7.35	20.82	....	....
1831	10.64	5.71	8.70	25.05	....	....
1841	11.75	6.52	10.63	28.90	....	....
1851	13.18	9.40	12.42	35.00	50.08	49.92
1861	13.97	11.02	13.22	38.21	54.60	44.40
1871	14.33	11.50	16.20	42.00	61.80	38.20
1881	14.69	14.91	18.40	48.00	67.90	32.10
1891	14.52	17.30	21.76	53.58	72.05	27.95

In 1851 the urban population constituted 50 per cent. of
the whole; in 1891, 72 per cent. This increase, moreover,
was not in the smaller cities, since the cities of 20,000 and

over account for 18.5 of the 22 per cent. increase. The increase has not been divided equally among the three classes of cities over 20,000 shown in the table, for London has gained only 2.34 per cent., while the other "great cities" have gained 7.9 per cent. and the middle-sized cities 9.34 per cent. London, in fact, grew no more rapidly than the small cities, i. e., those having between 2,000 and 20,000 inhabitants. While, then, there has been a concentration of population in cities of at least 20,000 population, it is not a form of concentration carried to the extreme; for London's population is barely holding its own in the general growth of population, and is dropping behind the population of provincial and middle-sized cities. These latter cities are indeed constantly recruited from the next lower order of cities, but even when such manner of growth is excluded and the comparison confined to a fixed number of towns, it will not be found that population is concentrating in one great metropolis very rapidly. An English statistician, Mr. R. Price Williams, has, happily, summarized the population in a certain number of towns at each census from 1801 to 1871, using, in nearly all cases, the same territorial limits. While many considerable cities of 1871 were mere villages in 1801, and therefore a part of the rural population, for present purposes this fact may be neglected. Taking the rate of increase as given in Mr. Williams's brilliant paper in the *Journal of the Royal Statistical Society*,[1] and comparing them with the rate of increase for the entire country as the average or standard (100), the following interesting results are obtained:

[1] Vol. xliii (1880), 462–496.

TABLE XX.

PROPORTIONATE DECENNIAL INCREASE.

	London.	Other great cities.	All cities of 20,000+ exc. London.	Small towns.	Total urban population.	Total rural population.	Pop. of England and Wales.
1801–11	131	150	140	91	122	84	100
1811–21	117	163	147	105	126	81	100
1821–31	126	239	190	95	143	66	100
1831–41	122	202	182	86	138	67	100
1841–51	167	209	195	82	158	46	100
1841–61	157	172	165	61	137	61	100
1861–71	121	131	152	83	132	64	100

EXPLANATIONS.

London—the registration district.
" Other great cities "—the 16 cities which, in addition to London, had over 100,000 inhabitants in 1871.
" Small towns "—places which contained, in 1871, a population of 2,000–20,000.
Urban population—the population at the various censuses of all towns with 2,000 or more inhabitants in 1871.
Rural population—the remainder.
Some of these figures agree with the calculations of Sir Rawson W. Rawson, in the *J. of Stat. Soc.*, 43; 500.

It will be noticed that the urban population of Mr. Williams's calculations has uniformly exceeded in its rate of increase the average of the entire country; while the rural population, being the complement of the urban population in the general total, has of course fallen below the average. The smaller towns, it is worth noting, have also grown less rapidly than the population of England and Wales in its entirety, except in the single decade 1811–21. The 98 cities other than London which had a population in excess of 20,000 in 1871, have far outstripped the small towns and rural districts; but even their rapid growth is inferior to the expansion of the sixteen "great cities," in every decade except the last. There is therefore a regular progression in the rate of growth, beginning with the villages and scattered population in the country districts and proceeding through the several classes of towns to the largest cities.

Levasseur[1], observing a similar phenomenon in France, formulated the law that "the force of attraction in human

[1] Following Legoyt. Cf. *La France et l' Étranger* (1865), pp. 50, 262, etc.

groups, like that of matter, is in general proportionate to the mass."[1] If London be classed with the other English cities of 100,000, Levasseur's rule will hold good for England. But London's population is properly a class by itself and is so treated in the tables. London might be expected to grow more rapidly than the provincial cities, just as Paris does. But such is not the case in a single decade of the century. Moreover, in the last decade represented by Mr. Williams's figures, the great cities were outstripped by the middle-sized cities. This tendency has become even more manifest in the subsequent periods, as appears in the following table[2] for 1881–91 :

TABLE XXI.

URBAN SANITARY DISTRICTS.

Population.	No.	Mean percentage of increase of population.
London	I	10.4
250,000–600,000	5	7.2
100,000–250,000	18	19.9
50,000–100,000	38	22.8
20,000–50,000	123	22.1
10,000–20,000	175	18.9
5,000-10,000	262	11.5
3,000–5,000	195	6.6
Under 3,000	194	3.6
Total urban	1,011	15.4
" rural	....	3.0

It thus appears that the largest growth is in the cities of from 20,000 to 100,000 inhabitants, with the classes 100,000 to 250,000 and 10,000–20,000 in close company. The urban districts under 3,000 have gained little more than the rural districts and the small towns (3,000–10,000) and the six great cities have increased less than the general population. That the villages should be falling behind is not surprising,

---

[1] *La population française*, ii, 355.

[2] *Census of 1891*, iv, 10.

but it at first seems strange that the very largest cities should manifest so slow a growth.   The six cities are:

	Increase or decrease per cent.
London	10.4
Liverpool	—6.2[1]
Manchester	9.3
Birmingham	9.4
Leeds	18.9
Sheffield	14.0

Leeds and Sheffield alone rise above the general rate (11.65) for England, while Liverpool has actually lost! Yet nobody believes that Liverpool is decaying; the explanation of the matter is simple enough: the growing business of the city requires the transformation of dwellings into stores and the dispossessed persons move away from the centre of business.   As there is little more room within the municipal limits most of these people live in the environs, but are no longer counted in Liverpool.[1]   This process is going on in nearly all the great cities, as will appear later. But as it is comparatively recent that such cities as London have reached " the point of saturation," it does not affect the conclusion that in England the largest urban aggregation has exerted a weaker power of attraction than the class of " great cities."   The concentration of population has not been carried to its utmost point in the England of the nineteenth century.

There now arises the question of the causes that influenced the distribution of population in England and Wales in the direction shown by the preceding analysis.   The tables of Mr. Price Williams[3] show that the maximum urban increase was in 1811–21; but this was balanced by a sim-

---

[1] Decrease.

[2] Cf. E. Cannan, " Growth of Manchester and Liverpool " in *Economic Journal*, iv, 111–114.

[3] *J. of St. Soc.*, 43 : 462 *seq.*

ilarly large increase in the rural districts, so that the concentration was not so great then as later. Table XIX shows that the entire period of 1821 to 1851 was a period of concentration in cities, and in this period the two decades 1821–31 and 1841–51 are especially marked. The earlier decade saw the rise of the sixteen " great cities; " the second decade, the expansion of London.

The charts accompanying the article of Price Williams already referred to clearly show that most of the great English cities attained their maximum rate of growth in 1821–31, which was in some cases phenomenal. Brighton's increase, for example, was 69.7 per cent., Bradford's 65.5, Salford's 55.9, Leed's 47.3, Liverpool's 45.8, Manchester's 44.9, Birmingham's 41.5, Sheffield's 40.5. Thus eight of the twelve [1] " great cities " of 1871 owe their largest decennial increase to the causes at work in 1821–31. With the exception of Bristol, all the eight cities are in the manufacturing district in the North; and Bristol is a port in an adjacent county. It may therefore be conjectured that the period was marked by a great expansion of the manufacturing industries; and it was indeed at this time that the cotton trade began to assume large dimensions. The number of pounds of cotton imported [2] was in—

1781	5,198,775
1785	18,400,384
1792	34,907,497
1813	51,000,000
1832	287,800,000
1841	489,900,000

" Though 1800 marks the beginning of a continuous expansion in both cotton and woolen manufactures, it was not until about 1817, when the new motor had established itself

[1] The four other cities were Hull, Nottingham, London, and its suburb West Ham.

[2] Hobson, *Evolution of Modern Capitalism*, 60.

generally in the large centers of industry and the energy of
the nation was called back to the arts of peace that the new
forces began fully to manifest their power." [1]   It must therefore be clear to every mind that the decade under discussion
(1821–31) presents in England a typical instance of the
effect which the growth of manufactures and the development of the factory system, or system of centralized industry,
has upon the distribution of population. [2]

The marked concentration of population in 1821–31 was,
then, produced by the industrial changes affecting the cities
of northern England.   In the succeeding decade the concentration continued, at a somewhat diminished rate, under the
same influences.   But in 1841–51 was reached the most
notable period of concentration in the century.   Table XX
shows that London's rate of increase reached its maximum
at this time, but that alone does not fully account for the
effect.   A more detailed analysis, as follows, shows that the

---

[1] Hobson, *op. cit.*, 64.

[2] The influence of the above-mentioned forces on the movement of population
in a small area may be studied with profit in Lancashire, the seat of the cotton
trade.   Price Williams (*loc. cit.*, p. 476 ff) gives these figures:

TABLE XXII.

DECENNIAL INCREASE OF POPULATION IN

	Lancashire.	Rural districts.	Urban districts.	Small towns. (2,000–20,000.)	Large towns. (20,000+.)
1801–11	23.02	20.44	25.07	19.40	26.37
1811–21	27.09	20.20	32.37	25.44	33.08
1821–31	26.97	13.29	36.46	19.44	39.95
1831–41	24.70	12.51	31.73	19.07	33.94
1841–51	21.84	12.67	26.37	14.35	28.23
1851–61	19.61	20.46	19.23	20.77	19.01
1861–71	16.06	14.86	16.58	19.91	16.12

The noteworthy feature of Lancashire's growth is the concentration of population in the large cities which was going on throughout the period 1801–51, and
especially in the decade 1821–31, when the great expansion of the textile industry
took place.

middle-sized cities were even more influential in their action
on the general result:

	Average Eng. and Wales.	London.	Other great cities (100,000+).	82 cities 20,000-100,000.	Towns 2,000- 20,000.	Total urban.
1821–31....	100	126	239	150	95	143
1841–51....	100	167	209	182	82	158

The bounties in which the urban population (*i. e.*, cities of
20,000 and upwards) increased most in 1841–51 are as
follows:

	Per cent.
Monmouth	78.7
Bedford	65.0
Chester	48.8
Glamorgan	45.3
Lincoln	44.7
Average of the 82 cities	23.2

As to the influences on the growth of the city population
of Monmouth and Glamorgan counties there can be no doubt.
Glamorganshire contains the great coal-fields and iron-mines
of South Wales, and it was the iron industry that built up its
three largest cities, Merthyr Tydvil, Cardiff, Swansea, and
the iron-smelting seat, Newport in Monmouth. It is to be
regretted that the development of the iron industry in the
North cannot also be traced; but the iron deposits and the
smelting-centres there are mainly in Yorkshire and Lancashire, where the other factors of previously established
manufactures complicate the study.

Outside the iron districts the cities that showed the
highest rates of increase in this period were ports. Thus in
Lincolnshire, the growth was mainly in Grimsby, a rival of
Hull;[1] Cheshire's high rate is due almost wholly to Birkenhead, a port on the Mersey opposite Liverpool. Of the ten

---

[1] Chisholm (*Handbook of Commercial Geography*), speaking of Hull, says that
"since the introduction of railways it has had a growing rival in Grimsby"
(p. 231).

cities that grew most rapidly in 1841–51, seven were seaports.[1]

Now commercial statistics show that English trade experienced a very considerable impetus about this time,[2] and the stimulus came from the opening of railways, which was of course accompanied by a great expansion of the iron industry. The first railroad, the Liverpool and Manchester line built by George Stephenson, was opened in September, 1830. Its effect on the distribution of population was not immediate, owing to the slowness with which the system developed. But by 1840 the United Kingdom possessed 800 miles of railways, and construction was then going on so rapidly that by 1850 the number of miles had risen to

[1] Birkenhead (port), Hanley in Staffordshire, Torquay (p), Grimsby (p), Cardiff (p), Newport (p), Southport (p), Luton in Bedfordshire, Hythe (p), Merthyr Tydvil. Bradford is excluded as being one of the sixteen " great cities."

[2] The following are the statistics of imports and exports in million pounds sterling:

	Imports.	Exports.
1785	14.27	13.66
1795	20.10	22.23
1810	39.30	43.57
1825	44.21	56.32
1830	46.30	69.70
1835	49.03	91.16
1840	67.49	116.48
1845	85.30	150.88
1850	100.47	197.31
1855	123.60	116.70
1860	210.53	164.52

These figures are not to be depended on absolutely; and in 1854 the method of valuation was changed, which probably had some effect. Up to 1800 the data refer to Great Britain; thereafter to the United Kingdom. But making allowance for all uncertainties, it would still appear that a great expansion of trade began about 1835–40. Between 1835 and 1850 the imports doubled in value, and the exports more than doubled; and this was in a period of falling prices. The repeal of the Corn Laws and adoption of a free trade policy in 1846, favored a larger foreign trade.

6,600.[1] The census of 1851 is therefore the first one to show the effects of the new transportation methods on the distribution of population. Contemporaneously with the beginnings of railway enterprise occurred the establishment of the iron industry, the leading events of which were the substitution of hot for cold blast in 1829 and the adoption of raw coal in place of coke in 1833,[2] so that it was not much before 1840 that the production of iron assumed large dimensions.[3]

The conclusion is therefore unavoidable that it was the opening of railways, with the concomitant development of the iron industry, and expansion of domestic and foreign commerce under free trade, which occasioned the great concentration of population in the decade 1841–51, in the seaports and iron producing districts. This explains why London, Wolverhampton and Portsmouth, alone of the seventeen great cities attained a higher rate of growth in 1841–51 than in 1821–31. Wolverhampton was a centre of the Staffordshire iron manufacturing district, and the three other cities were great seaports. It has already been shown that the middle sized cities whose growth contributed so much to the high degree of concentration in 1841–51 were either seaports or iron-centres.

[1] Hobson, *op. cit.*, 82.   [2] *Ibid.*, 65.

[3] The following are the statistics of the pig iron production in Great Britain and Ireland:

1790	68,000 Tons..
1800	158,000 "
1810	305,000 "
1820	400,000 "
1830	700,000 "
1840	1,396,000 "
1850	2,250,000 "
1860	3,827,000 "

[4] The *Census of 1851* classified 212 cities, and computed their rate of growth

Since 1851 the process of concentration has sensibly diminished. As already indicated, this is due in part to the overflow of municipal boundaries in the greater cities where a small area was already filled. This movement and the growth of small suburban towns account for the recent tendency of city-growth to center in the smaller cities. Cf. Table XXI.

§2. *Scotland.*—Like England and Wales, Scotland is preeminently a manufacturing and commercial country. A mountainous country, with comparatively little arable land, Scotland could not maintain its population with the products of its own soil, and, as in the case of England, the agricultural population attained its maximum number some years ago, in 1861, as appears from Table XXIV.

Since then the entire addition to the number of inhabitants, amounting to the number of one million souls, has found shelter in the towns, where by pursuing commerce or industry it obtains the wealth needed to import food-products for its own sustenance. The rural population has lost some 50,000 persons since 1861 and indeed is now fairly equal to the number in 1851, the earliest year for which we have an official classification of the people into urban (towns of 2,000+) and rural populations. But the tendency toward concentration may be perceived at a much earlier date;

during the half century 1801–51. It is interesting to note that the highest rate was that of the watering places, as appears below (*op. cit.*, vol. i, p. xlix):

TABLE XXIII.

No.	Class.	Increase per cent., 1801–51.
15	Watering places	254.1
51	Manufacturing places	224.2
28	Mining and hardware places	217.3
26	Seaports (exc. London)	195.6
1	London	146.4
99	County towns (exc. London)	122.1
212	Cities	176.1

TABLE XXIV.

NUMBER AND POPULATION OF CITIES IN SCOTLAND.

	Great cities.		Cities 20,000-100,000.		Cities 10,000-20,000.		All cities 10,000+.		Urban.	Rural.	Total.	Per cent. of population. Urban.	Rural.
1801	....	....	5	223,792	3	48,850	8	272,642	....	....	1,608,420		
1811	1	103,224	5	196,651	5	67,868	11	367,743	....	....	1,805,864		
1821	2	250,783	5	161,768	7	89,837	14	502,388	....	....	2,091,521		
1831	2	329,324	5	203,866	7	105,127	14	638,317	....	....	2,364,386		
1841	2	399,186	6	258,740	9	124,028	17	781,954	....	....	2,620,184		
1851	2	489,399	7	311,742	9	127,390	18	928,531	1,497,979	1,391,663	2,888,742	51.80	48.20
1861	2	562,985	7	335,223	11	149,426	20	1,047,634	1,616,314	1,446,160	3,062,294	52.78	47.22
1871	3	793,112	6	286,322	16	235,428	25	1,314,862	1,951,704	1,408,314	3,360,018	58.09	41.91
1881	4	1,059,957	11	405,849	19	275,247	34	1,741,053	2,306,852	1,428,721	3,735,573	61.75	38.25
1891	4	1,200,374	13	508,021	20	304,086	37	2,012,481	2,631,298	1,394,349	4,025,647	65.37	34.63

EXPLANATORY.

Since the Scotch censuses began to be published separately from the English (1861), they have summarized the population in towns of 2,000 + as the urban population. The summary may always be found in the Appendix Tables of the general report (vol. i of the census: cf. *Census of 1891*, vol. i, p. xviii). In 1851 the urban population embraced some towns with less than 2,000 inhabitants (Cf. *Census of Great Britain, 1851*, vol. i, sec. i, p. xlvi). The summaries of the larger cities, by classes, are compiled from the various censuses, but the following have afforded most of the data: For the great cities (100,000+), and cities of 20,000+, 1801-51, *Census of Great Britain, 1851*, vol. i, sec. i, p. cxxvii, and sec. ii, tables; 1861-71, a *Return to the House of Commons Showing the Population of Scotland* at the decennial censuses, 1801-81. The boundaries are always those of the parliamentary boroughs. For the smaller cities, down to and including 1831, the boundaries are usually those of the parish, and are therefore unduly extended. From 1841 to 1871, the parliamentary Return of 1883, above mentioned, is the authority. The summaries for 1881 and 1891 are made from the list of towns given in Wagner-Supan's *Bevölkerung der Erde*, ix, p. 48, the boundaries being generally those of the municipal borough and the population including shipping, which is not embraced in the parliamentary boroughs (Cf. Table XXVI); Glasgow's population is here given as 577,419 in 1881 and 658,198 in 1891, the area being that of the new parliamentary borough. (See foot-note, Table XXVII.)

Table XXIV indeed shows that whereas the population in towns of 10,000+ doubled in the forty years 1851–91, it nearly tripled in the forty years 1811–51. And there was a long period in which the statisticians of the British government announced in each census that the " tendency toward agglomeration in towns is even stronger in Scotland than in England." This appears to be true, however, only of the larger cities and especially of Glasgow, as appears from the following comparisons:

TABLE XXV.

Percentage of population constituted by:	1801.	1851.	1891.
(a) the cities of 10,000+.			
England	21.3	39.5	61.7
Scotland	17.0	32.2	49.9
(b) the towns of 2,000+.			
England	...	50.1	72.1
Scotland	...	51.8	65.4
(c) the metropolis of			
England	9.7	13.2	14.5
Scotland	5.1	11.5	19.4

From (b) it is clear that since the middle of the century the tendency toward concentration has been far less pronounced in Scotland than in England; indeed, in 1851 Scotland had a relatively larger urban population than England, but by 1891 there was a considerable difference in England's favor. The preceding comparison (a) shows that between 1801 and 1851 the process of concentration went forward at an equal rate in the two countries; it is even possible that Scotland's increase is here made to appear too small as a result of the necessity of counting in the population of an entire parish, or township, in 1801, when only the agglomeration should be reckoned. This would make 17 per cent. an unduly large percentage for 1801.

But when the comparison is turned toward London and Glasgow (c), it is easy to realize why the statisticians so often spoke of the "stronger tendency of the Scotch people toward agglomeration in large towns." In 1801 the English metropolis contained nearly one-tenth of the population of England and Wales; the Scotch metropolis little more than one-twentieth of the population of Scotland. In 1851 the two were on almost equal footing, and in 1861 Glasgow had taken the lead in the movement toward concentration, so that in 1891 it counted for considerably more in Scotland, in point of numbers, than London did in England.

The explanation of Glasgow's exceptional growth lies in the extent and variety of its natural resources. It occupies the position of a great commercial centre like London; it has a climate peculiarly favorable to the textile industry like Manchester; and it is situated in the midst of a great coal and iron district like Birmingham. The city's growth in numbers is shown in the following table, which also includes the aggregate population of the seven next largest cities (Edinburgh, Dundee, Aberdeen, Leith, Paisley, Greenock and Perth; Govan, a suburb of Glasgow, being excluded):

TABLE XXVI.

| | Parliamentary. | | Glasgow. City and Suburbs. | | | Seven Cities. | |
	Population.	Percentage increase.	Population.	Percentage increase.	Ratio to population of Scotland.	Population.	Percentage increase.
1801	77,058	....	81,048	....	5.1	194,428	....
1811	103,224	34	108,788	34.2	6.0	231,965	19.3
1821	140,432	36	147,043	35.2	7.0	290,316	25.1
1831	193,030	37.6	202,426	37.7	8.6	356,981	23.0
1841	261,004	35.2	274,533	35.6	10.0	396,930	11.2
1851	329,097	26	344,986	25.7	11.5	450,601	13.5
1861	394,864	20	436,432	23.6	14.2	480,725	6.7
1871	477,156	20.8	547,538	25.5	16.3	579,315	20.5
1881	487,985	2.3	674,095	23.1	18.3	680,097	17.4
1891	564,981	15.7	782,445	16.1	19.4	763,012	12.2

Sources.—*Census of Great Britain, 1851*, vol. i, p. cxxvii, and tables of Section II, for 1801-51; for 1861-1881, the *Parliamentary Return of 1883, op. cit.; Census of Scotland, 1891*. 172. The population of suburban Glasgow as given here for 1891 is based on the area assumed by the census in 1881. The parliamentary limits serve for the seven cities throughout.

In the earlier half of the century Glasgow's rate of growth closely agrees with Lancashire's (Table XXII *supra*), both being due to the development of the cotton trade after 1817. But since 1841, Glasgow has felt the influence of a vast expansion of the iron industry,[1] and of commerce also,[2] so that the falling off in the rate of increase is much less marked than it is in the case of Lancashire. Indeed, when compared with the rate of increase for the entire country, whose population began to be seriously diminished by the emigration in 1850,[3] Glasgow is shown to have exercised greater powers of attraction in 1851–61 than in any other decade. This is brought out in the following table, constructed on the same lines with Table XX, so as to permit of comparison with the English cities:

[1] The production of pig iron in Scotland, according to the Encyclopœdia Britannica, Art. " Scotland," was as follows:

1796	18,640 tons	
1830	37,500 "	
1840	241,000 "	
1845	475,000 "	
1865	1,164,000 "	
1870	1,206,000 "	(maximum)
1884	988,000 "	

In 1859 Scotland produced one-third of the entire British output. The influence of railway building may be noted here as in the case of England.

[2] According to the same article, the total exports and imports of Scotland amounted to about eleven million pounds sterling in 1825, fourteen million in 1851, and fifty million in 1874.

[3] Before 1850, the number of Scotch immigrants to the United States did not, in any single decade, reach 4,000 (in 1841–50 it was 3,712); but in 1851–60, the number leaped to 38,331.

TABLE XXVII.

Decennial increase per cent. of the population of Scotland.		Scot-land.	Proportionate Decennial Increase:		
			Seven cities.	Glasgow, including suburbs.	The eight cities.[1]
1801–11	12.27	100	158	278	191
1811–21	15.82	100	158	222	180
1821–31	13.04	100	176	289	211
1831–41	10.82	100	103	329	181
1841–51	10.25	100	132	249	181
1851–61	6.00	100	112	340	205
1861–71	9.72	100	211	263	212
1871–81	11.18	100	148	207	170
1881–91	7.77	100	157	208	167

Of the eight cities here considered, only four (Glasgow, Edinburgh, Dundee, and Aberdeen) have a population in excess of 100,000. But the others exceed 60,000 except Perth (30,000). The influence of Glasgow on the aggregate is seen particularly in the decade 1851–61. The maximum in 1861–71 is to be explained by the vast increase of commerce consequent upon the annihilation of the American carrying-trade in the Civil War; Glasgow, it may be surmised, here lagged behind the other cities chiefly because of the cotton famine, which did not affect them.

In general there is an agreement with the facts brought out in Table XX for the English cities, except that the falling off in the rate of concentration occurs later. This is undoubtedly due to the fact that the boundaries of the Scotch cities except Glasgow have been so broad that population has not found it necessary to cross the city limits as business encroached upon the resident districts. While in the last two decades the increase of the urban population as a whole (20.2 per cent. in 1871–81 and 14.1 per cent. in 1881–91, in towns of 20,000+) exceeded the increase of the

[1] In this summary, Glasgow's population is that of the parliamentary borough, except in 1881 and 1891, where the area is that adopted for the parliamentary borough after Nov. 1, 1891; the numbers being 577,419 and 658,198 respectively (*Census of 1891*, i, 149, 152, 155).

seven cities considered, this is caused partly by the accession
of new towns from among the villages and partly by Glasgow's higher rate (including suburbs). Speaking broadly,
the force of attraction among the population centres of Scotland is proportional to the mass, *i. e.*, in rapidity of growth
the order is (1) Glasgow, (2) the other large cities, (3) urban
population, (4) rural population, which is declining.

The absolute and relative decrease of the rural population
presented in Table XXIV is due almost entirely to a diminution of the agriculturists, caused by deep-seated industrial
movements which have brought more fertile land into competition with the old-world soil.   In Scotland much complaint
is made of the enclosure of land in forest preserves,[1] but it
is obvious that this is merely the immediate occasion of a
re-distribution of population caused by changes in the
world's industry.   That it is the scattered agricultural population and not the village population that is declining, is witnessed by the following percentages of increase and decrease:

TABLE XXVIII.

	1861-71.	1871-81.	1881-91.
Towns (2,000 +)	+20.76	+18.20	+14.06
Villages (300–2,000)	+13.90	+15.73	+ 4.01
Rural districts (300–)	— 7.69	— 3.96	— 5.33

In the last decade the village population failed to hold its
own, denoting either an exceptional accession of villages to
the rank of towns, or a real falling off in the growth of villages.   In 1861 the village population constituted 11.1 per
cent. of the population of Scotland; in 1871, 11.5 per cent.;
in 1881, 12 per cent.; in 1891, only 11.6 per cent.

Taking a wider view of the distribution of population in
Scotland, it will be observed that the smaller cities have
only maintained their ground while the great increase in the

---

[1] Cf. Longstaff's article on " Depopulation " in Palgrave's *Dictionary of Political Economy*.

urban population has been concentrated in the largest cities, thus:

TABLE XXIX.

PERCENTAGE OF POPULATION RESIDENT IN

	1801.	1851.	1891.
Glasgow	5.1	11.5	19.4
Other "great cities"................	0.	5.4	10.0
Cities 20,000–100,000	8.8	10.8	12.6
" 10,000–20,000	3.1	4.5	7.5
Total 10,000+...................	17.0	32.2	49.9
Towns 2,000–10,000................	...	19.6	15.0
Total 2,000+.....................	...	51.8	95.4

§3. *Ireland.*—Ireland is the one country of the Western world that has suffered a decline in population in the present century; but it nevertheless shows the general tendency toward concentration. The following table shows a steady increase down to 1851, followed by as steady a decrease:

TABLE XXX.[1]

	Population of Ireland.	Urban Population.
1801...............................	5,216,331	
1811...............................	5,956,460	
1821...............................	6,801,827	
1831...............................	7,767,401	
1841...............................	8,196,597	1,143,674
1851...............................	6,574,278	1,226,661
1861...............................	5,798,967	1,140,771
1871...............................	5,412,377	1,201,344
1881...............................	5,174,836	1,245,503
1891...............................	4,704,750	1,244,113

In the decade 1841–51 occurred the great potato famine (1846), which carried off by death over 700,000 individuals and caused nearly a million more to depart from the country. Now it appears that this entire loss fell on the

[1] The first census of Ireland was taken in 1821, and the earlier figures are substantially estimates. The later figures agree with those given in the latest census (1891, pt. ii, *General Report*, p. 107), except in the years 1841 and 1851, which here include the military, and therefore exceed those of the 1891 census by about 20,000. The urban population in the last three or four censuses has included the population of all places exceeding 2,000; the data have been found in the various census reports, detailed reference to which is unnecessary.

rural districts, for the towns not only did not lose in population, but made gains in many cases, amounting in the aggregate to 83,000. Further, the Irish population has been decreasing ever since the famine, but the urban population remains practically stationary; the result being that we have in Ireland the universal phenomenon of relative growth of the cities (as compared with the country). Thus the proportion of urban and rural population was:

	1841.	1851.	1861.	1871.	1881.	1891.
Urban	13.9	18.7	19.7	22.2	24.1	26.4
Rural	86.1	81.3	80.3	77.8	75.9	73.6

In the last half-century the urban population has nearly doubled its proportion of the aggregate, but it is to be noted that this increase is not general among all the places counted as "urban" by the census. The villages and small towns have, in fact, decayed in sympathy with the emigration of the rural population; but this loss is fully made up by the rapid growth of Dublin and Belfast. Comparing the aggregate population of the nineteen cities of 10,000 and upwards in 1841 and 1891, it will be found that they gained about 237,000; but Dublin (inclusive of suburbs) and Belfast in the same period gained 257,000, thus showing a net loss for the remaining urban population.[1] Broadly speak-

[1] The following table, based on statistics furnished by Dr. Longstaff in his article on "Rural Depopulation" (*J. of St. Soc.*, 58 : 429), includes the cities which had a population of 10,000 + in either 1841 or 1891:

TABLE XXXI.

POPULATION (IN THOUSANDS).

	1841.	1891.	Increase or Decrease per cent.
19 cities (10,000+)	671.1	908.5	+ 35
Dublin City	232.7	245.	+ 5
" suburbs	33.6	97.3	+189
Total Dublin	266.4	342.3	+ 28
Belfast	75.3	255.9	+240
Dublin and Belfast	341.7	598.3	+ 75
4 cities with 20,000 to 100,000 in 1891	167.5	166.5	— 0.6
13 remaining cities having less than 20,000.	161.9	143.6	— 12.

ing, the growth of population in Ireland is confined to Belfast and the suburbs of Dublin; Dublin itself attained its maximum numbers in 1851 and has since steadily declined. Even in the most recent decade no other cities showed any substantial progress, although Londonderry, Lisburn and Lurgan and Dundalk increased slightly.[1] Hence in Table XXXII the smaller cities are shown to have lost population in 1881–91; the class of cities between 20,000 and 100,000 betrays a small gain, which, however, is due to the inclusion of the larger Dublin suburbs. The gain in Dublin and Belfast is 43,000, which would be increased to 62,000 with the inclusion of the former's suburban population.

TABLE XXXII.

Cities.	1800.		1851.		1881.		1891.	
	No.	Pop.	No.	Pop.	No.	Pop.	No.	Pop.
100,000 + ...	1	167,900	1	261,700	2	457,724	2	500,951
20,000–100,000	4	186,000	6	313,060	6	217,897	6	218,617
10,000–20,000	5	64,500	7	96,930	12	149,314	10	124,981
Total, 10,000+	10	418,400	14	671,690	20	824,935	18	844,549

SOURCES.

This summary is compiled from a variety of sources, the official documents not always being at hand. For 1891, the *Census of Ireland*, Part II, General Report, p. 327-9. For 1881, the *Census of 1881*. For 1851, the *Census of 1851*, supplemented by *British Almanac* 1852, and *Harper's Statistical Gazeteer*, 1855. For 1800 there are no official statistics. Those used in this table are mainly derived from Hassel, 1809, and relate to the period 1800-09. The actual figures follow;

	1880.	1851.			1800.	1851.
1. Dublin	167,900	261,700	8. Londonderry		11,000	19,604
2. Belfast...........	50,000	99,660	9. Drogheda...........		10,000	16,876
3. Cork	67,000	86,485	10. Newry.......		15,000	13,327
4. Limerick	39,000	55,268	11. Wexford...........		......	12,471
5. Waterford........	30,000	26,667	12. Clonmel		......	12,386
6. Galway	12,000	24,697	13. Sligo		......	11,411
7. Kilkenny	16,500	20,283	14. Carlow		......	10,995

[1] *Cf.* Supan, ix, 49.

Probably no other country in Europe exhibits so clearly as does Ireland the influence which modern economic changes have brought about in the distribution of population. The re-organization of industry founded on international specialization has almost destroyed Irish agriculture and depopulated the rural districts and small towns of Ireland; on the other hand it has built up the one industry wherein Irish producers work advantageously—the linen manufacture—and has moreover concentrated this industry in one city. The result is that the growth of Belfast in this century is equaled by very few cities in Europe; while Dublin, a manufacturing and commercial city, and Londonderry, a seaport, are the only other cities of importance that have grown at all since 1841.

III. FRANCE.

French statistics of urban population are exceptionally instructive for two reasons: (1) they have been kept for a longer period and with greater scientific accuracy than those of other European nations, and (2) they concern the one great country of the nineteenth century whose population has reached a stationary condition. Elsewhere in Europe the rural populations, by reason of their continuous increase, produce a surplus which must migrate either to the cities or to foreign lands; but in France this rural excess has been very small. That the cities of France have nevertheless enjoyed a rapid growth demonstrates the existence of world-wide influences upon the distribution of population.

Since 1846 the French census reports have grouped together as urban communes all the communes which contain a population of 2,000 or more, living in contiguous houses.[1] A commune might not contain any one community of 1,000 or even 500 people; but so long as it included within

---

[1] An urban commune—"celle dont la population agglomerée dépasse 2,000 habitants;" agglomerée—"celle qui se groupe immédiatement autour du clocher."

its borders 2,000 persons living in communities or groups
and not entirely scattered, it would be classed among the
urban communes, and its total population—the scattered as
well as the agglomerated—would be added to the urban
population.

TABLE XXXIII [1]

	Population.			Percentage of urban in total population.
	France.	Rural.	Urban.	
1846...........	35,400,486 [2]	26,753,743	8,646,743	24.4
1851...........	35,783,170	26,647,711	9,135,459	25.5
1856...........	36,139,364	26,244,536	9,844,828	27.3
1861...........	37,386,313	26,596,547	10,789,766	28.9
1866...........	38,067,064	26,471,716	11,595,348	30.5
1872...........	36,102,921 [3]	24,868,022	11,234,899	31.1
1876...........	36,905,788	24,928,392	11,977,396	32.4
1881...........	37,672,048	24,575,506	13,096,542	34.8
1886...........	38,218,903	24,452,395	13,766,508	35.9
1891...........	38,343,192	24,031,900	14,311,292	37.4

The table shows the rapid increase in the proportion of the
French population classed as urban, starting from 24.4 per
cent. in 1846 and reaching 37.4 per cent. in 1891. This is
an increase of 50 per cent., which is as much as England's
increase in the same period. It is calculated that in 1920
one-half of the population of France will be urban.[4]

In France, the decline of the rural population is not only
relative but absolute, thus being in effect a rural depopulation, except in so far as the rural loss is caused by the
growth of villages into towns which thereby pass from the
rural to the urban group. In 1846 the rural population

---

[1] *Résultats statistiques du dénombrement de 1891.* Paris, 1894, p. 32 and p. 65.

[2] As finally corrected, 35,401,761.

[3] Decrease due to loss of Alsace-Lorraine in the war of 1870–1.

[4] *Op. cit.,* p. 66.

amounted to 26,753,743; in 1890 to 24,031,900. The decrease is noticeable in all but two inter-censal periods, 1856–61 and 1872–76. The former exception is accounted for by the annexation of Nice and Savoy in 1859, with a population of about 669,000. The latter increase, which is only 60,000, is very probably due to the dislocation of population in 1872 (concentration of troops) as a result of the war with Germany. Since 1876, the rural depopulation has continued unceasingly and has given the French sociologists a real problem to investigate.

That the growth of the urban population and the decline of the rural population are not caused by differences in the natural movement of population is clearly shown by the vital statistics:

TABLE XXXIV.

	1881–86.		1886–91.	
	Rural.	Urban.	Rural.	Urban.
Births............	2,587,437	1,543,112	2,609,250	1,692,719
Deaths	2,254,994	1,499,447	2,417,506	1,693,848
Natural increase	+332,443	+ 43,665	+191,744	− 1,129
Total increase or decrease	−123,111	+669,966	−393,479	+517,768
Gain or loss by Migration	−455,554	+626,301	−585,223	+518,897

In the five-year period 1886–91, the urban population increased by 544,784 persons. Of this increase 27,014 were added by the growth of rural into urban communes; but all of the remainder (517,768) and 1,129 persons in addition (the deficit of births) came from the rural districts which had an emigration of 585,223. This number is thrice as large as the excess of births over deaths. The increase of the urban population is due, not to a high birth-rate, but to

---

[1] *Op. cit.*, p. 72. The influence of villages growing into cities is here discounted by considering the same number of cities in 1886 and 1891, thus giving different results from those in Table CXX.

migration from the country. Perhaps this rural depopulation is most forcibly recalled by the fact that the number of small communes has been constantly increasing. As people leave the rural villages, these latter sink into the grade of hamlets; thus the number of communes containing less than 500 inhabitants has increased as follows:

1851	15,684
1861	16,547
1876	16,442 [1]
1891	17,590
1896	18,054

A question of interest and importance now arises: Is the urban increase a village growth or a large-city growth? And Table XXXV gives the answer. Throughout the century the proportion of Frenchmen residing in villages (2,000–10,000) has scarcely varied from 11 per cent. Nor has the proportion in the smaller cities (10,000–20,000) appreciably increased. The middle-sized cities, and more particularly the great cities, are the places that have really gained from the re-distribution of the population.

It is also interesting to find that the class of large cities increases not only by the continual recruitment from below but also by its own rapidity of growth. Thus, Levasseur tabulated for 1801 the cities which in 1881 had a population of at least 20,000.[1] His results may be arranged thus:

	Increase per cent. 1801–1881.
France	40.
Cities of 20,000+ (excluding Paris)	145.
9 cities of 100,000+ (excluding Paris)	185.
Paris	134.

[1] 1,689 communes lost in the war with Prussia.

[2] *Les Populations Urbaines*, pages 11-14; reproduced in *La Population Française.*

TABLE XXXV.

DISTRIBUTION OF POPULATION OF FRANCE IN SPECIFIED YEARS.

Communes.	1801.		1851.		1891.		Per cent. of total population.				
	No.	Population.	No.	Population.	No.	Population.	4. 1801.	5. 1836.	6. 1851.	7. 1872.	8. 1891.
100,000+	3	767,386	5	1,656,900	12	4,597,217	2.8	3.6	4.6	9.1	12.0
20,000–100,000	31	1,073,000	58	2,154,600	93	3,499,072	3.9	4.5	6.0	6.7	9.1
10,000–20,000	56	760,000	102	1,362,000	127	1,843,563	2.8	3.1	3.8	4.4	4.8
Total, 10,000+	90	2,600,000	165	5,173,500	232	9,939,852	9.5	11.2	14.4	20.2	25.9
Towns 2,000–10,000	......	......	......	......	......	......	[11.0]	[11.0]	11.1	11.0	11.5
Total urban	......	......	......	9,135,459	......	14,311,292	[20.5]	[22.2]	25.5	31.1	37.4
" rural	......	......	......	......	......	......	[79.5]	[77.8]	74.5	68.9	62.6

AUTHORITIES.

The aggregate urban population has been given in each quinquennial census since 1846 (Cf. Table XXXIII). The remaining totals have been compiled from the following sources:

1801—*Statistique de la France, Première Série, Territoire et Population*, Paris, 1837, and Levasseur, *La France et ses Colonies*, ii, 346.
1836—From the figures in *Journal des Économistes*, 1857, 2d series, xiii, p. 368.
1851—*Annuaire de l'Économie Politique et de la Statistique*, 1853, pages 17-19.
1872—Census. Cf. *Annuaire de l'Économie Politique*, 1874. The totals are 3,296,808, 2,402,057 and 1,576,950, a grand total for cities (10,000+) of 7,275,905.
1891—*Résultats statistiques du dénombrement de 1891*, Paris, 1894, pp. 362–6, 541.
The percentages in brackets are approximate, exact figures not being obtainable.

Taking the first 80 years of the present century, it is thus clearly demonstrated that the most rapid growth has been in the large cities; and while in England London's rate of increase was invariably lower than that of other great cities, or even the middle-sized cities, in France the capital leads the other cities by a wide margin.

Table XXXVI will help to carry out the analysis more thoroughly; it is based on the principle of a fixed area or number of cities, which does away with the disturbing element of new cities arising from towns. And as the cities considered throughout are those of the France of to-day, we must take the population of France on its present territory in order to exclude Strasburg and other cities of Alsace-Lorraine. The table relates to four classes of cities. In default of better statistics, the *chefs-lieux* or chief towns of the several *arrondissements*, which of course remain fixed in number,[1] will represent the smaller cities. To show how misleading it would be in this analysis to classify the cities at each census, column 11 has been added, which may be compared with column 9. The latter is concerned throughout with 12 cities, while the former starts with 2 and ends with 12. Obviously, any deductions as to the rate of increase of an average large city would be misleading if based on the high rate of column 11.

---

[1] In this case no deduction is made for Alsace-Lorraine; but as there was no change until 1871, the only years affected are 1886 and 1891, whose ratios are somewhat lower than they should be. The average population of the chefs-lieux in 1801 was 10,618, and they were graded as follows:

	1801.	1836.
Under 5,000 population	153	121
From 5,000 to 10,000	124	136
From 10,000 to 20,000	52	65
From 20,000 to 100,000	31	38
Over 100,000	3	3
	363	363

TABLE XXXVI.

	Actual population.					Relative to population in 1801.					
	France (present territory).	Chefs-lieux.	Cities of 20,000+ (in 1886).	The twelve great cities of 1891.	Paris.	France.	Chefs-lieux.	Cities of 20,000+.	Twelve large cities.[1]	Paris.	Cities of 100,000+ at each census
	1.	2.	3.	4.	5.	6.	7.	8.	9.	10.	11.
1801	26,930,756	3,854,202	2457.331	1,184,838	547,756	1000	1000	1000	1000	1000	1000
1811	....	4,063,110	....	1,281,214	622,636	......	1054	......	1081	......	1082
1821	29,871,176	4,321,039	....	1,423,082	713,966	1102	1121	......	1201	1300	1267
1831	31,787,900	4,619,136	....	1,558,562	774,338	1178	1198	......	1315	1410	1372
1836	32,759,829	4,951,684	3,098,326	1,747,205	909,126	1216	1285	1261	1475	1670	1571
1841	33,400,864	....	....	1,833,503	935,261	1240	......	......	1547	1710	1759
1846	34,546,975	5,688,375	....	2,059,637	1,053,897	1281	1476	......	1738	1930	2007
1851	34,901,938	5,852,995	....	2,087,846	1,053,262	1300	1519	......	1762	1930	2159
1856	35,174,124	6,230,995	....	2,494,089	1,174,346	1307	1617	......	2105	2040	2822
1861	35,844,902	....	....	3,173,602	1,696,741	1332	......	......	2678	3060	3781
1866	36,495,489	....	5,912,702	3,435,257	1,825,274	1355	......	2406	2900	3330	4084
1872	36,102,921	....	....	3,531,724	1,851,792	1342	......	......	2981	3380	4296
1876	36,905,788	....	....	3,770,269	1,988,806	1372	......	......	3182	3630	4578
1881	37,672,048	....	....	4,190,958	2,269,023	1396	......	......	3537	4140	5219
1886	38,218,903	9,143,000	7,484,196	4,361,890	2,344,550	1420	2372	3048	3682	4260	5556
1891	38,343,192	9,642,000	....	4,597,217	2,447,957	1425	2502	......	3880	4460	
1896	38,517,975	....	....	4,793,491	2,536,834	1430	......	......	4050	4630	5990

¹ If territory annexed to Paris, Lyons, Lillie and Havre in 1852–65 were included in the earlier censuses, the ratios would stand as follows:

1831......1389   1836......1591   1841......1695   1846......1936   1851......2019   1856......2378   1861......2696

AUTHORITIES.

Column 1.—*Résultats statistiques du dénombrement de 1801*, p. 33; except for 1896 and 1866, which are from Conrad's *Hdwbh*. ii, 420.

Column 2.—*Statistique de la France* (publiée par le ministre des travaux publics, de l'agriculture et du commerce, Paris. Imprimerie Royale, MDCCCXXXVII. *Territoire et Population*) for years 1801–36, inclusive; Block, *Statistique de la France*, i, 57, for years 1846–56; for 1886 and 1891, personal computations from the censuses.

Column 3.—Levasseur, *La Population Française*, ii, 345–6   Column 4.—Author's computations from the official statistics.

Column 5.—*Annuaire Statistique de la Ville de Paris*, supplemented by *Statistique générale de la France—Territoire et Population* (figures for 1801, 1831, 1836) and later censuses (since 1876). Annexation of suburbs, 16 June, 1859, added nearly half a million people.

The table shows at once that the French cities have been growing at a rate proportionate to their size; Paris leads off and is followed by the twelve large cities, the middle-sized cities, the smaller cities, and finally by France. And it is to be remembered that each of the lower rates gets the benefit of the higher rate, inasmuch as Paris is included among the large cities, the large cities in the class of cities above 20,000 population, and so on. Thus there seems to be no exception to the rule that the larger the city the faster the growth.[1] A graphical presentation of the facts of Table XXXVI would show that in the decade 1846–56 the great cities outstripped Paris; but in 1859 Paris annexed all the suburbs as far as the fortifications, and her curve of growth therefore takes a sharp upward bend in 1856–61. Since then Paris has on the whole kept ahead of the great-cities' class, although in certain periods, *e. g.*, 1866–72, she fell somewhat behind. The third class of cities follow at a slower rate, although since 1840 they have distanced the *chefs-lieuz*. The curve for the general population of France drags along at the bottom.

Recent figures tend to show that the most rapid growth is in the middle-sized cities, as in England.[2] Thus the following table shows an increase of 47 per cent. for all cities of

[1] The proof will be strengthened by the following figures giving the sum of all the *chefs-lieux* and of other cities with more than 10,000 inhabitants (a class midway between the *chefs-lieux* and cities of 20,000—columns 7 and 8):

1801	3,894,000	1,000
1836	5,135,000	1,319
1846	6,179,057	1,587
1851	6,406,557	1,645
1861	7,099,975	1,823
1866	7,769,906	1,995
1886	10,202,000	2,620
1891	11,055,401	2,838

Cf. Block, *op. cit.*, i, 57, and Levasseur, ii, 343.

[2] *Supra*, Table XX.

more than 10,000 population: the great cities (*i. e.*, those with 100,000+) show precisely the same gain; the small cities (10,000-20,000) fall considerably below, and the middle-sized cities (20,000–100,000) rank somewhat above the average:

TABLE XXXVII.

Groups of Communes having......in-habitants *agglomerés*	Total population in thousands. 1861.	1891.	Percentage increase.
From 10,000 to 20,000	1,290.4	1,828.7	42
From 20,000 to 100,000	1,941.7	2,914.5	50
100,000+	3,066.5	4,943.0	47
Total 10,000+	6,298.6	9,236.2	47

Closer analysis (as given in the census of 1891, p. 59, and reprinted in Table XXXVIII) shows that the largest increase in the middle-sized cities falls in the class of cities having a population of from 15,000 to 50,000.

TABLE XXXVIII.

	1861.	1891.	Increase per cent.
10,000–15,000	751,121	988,810	33.
15,000–20,000	539,292	839,863	56.
20,000–30,000	619,074	932,536	51.
30,000–50,000	595,105	936,009	57.5
50,000–100,000.............	727,525	1,045,969	44.
100,000+	3,066,520	4,493,031	47.
	6,298,637	9,236,218	47.

Judging from the recent development of suburbs everywhere, the increase of the middle-class cities simply means a movement from the centre of the great city to its environs; and the gains in the third-class cities will be swept away with the absorption of suburbs in the large cities. Such was the actual course of events in the period 1836–51.

---

[1] Comte De Chastellux, "Accroissement de la population urbaine en France," *Journal des Économistes*, 1857, 2d series, xiii, 372.

Figures like the above were published[1] to show that the great cities were falling behind, thus:

TABLE XXXIX.

	No. in 1836.	Percentage increase of population, 1836-51.
100,000+	3	10.87
50,000–100,000	6	10.77
30,000–50,000	14	10.67
20,000–30,000	20	11.60
10,000–20,000	76	13.77
5,000–10,000	273	6.61
	392	10.02

The inferences from these figures are supported by the diagrams of Levasseur and Meuriot, which show a falling off in the rate of increase in the great cities; but with the incorporation of their rapidly growing suburbs, which had contributed to the high rate for the smaller cities, the great cities again distanced the small ones. Our figures incontrovertibly establish the fact that over a long period (1801–81) the French cities have grown in this order:

1. Paris.
2. The great cities.
3. Middle-sized cities (20,000+).

And, though the data cannot claim entire accuracy, it is reasonably certain that the small cities rank below the above classes in rate of increase.

The connection of urban growth with industrial development in France is very close and may be easily shown with the aid of the commercial statistics at hand. M. Levasseur has graphically indicated in several diagrams in *La Population Française*[1] the progress of the great cities in France. Their growth does not fairly begin until 1831; in 1851 it is redoubled and continued until the war of 1870–1, since which, as a general rule, it has fallen off very considerably.

[1] Vol. ii, 347, 348.

The following percentage, based on Table XXXVI, illustrate the course of development already portrayed by M. Levasseur:

TABLE XL.

PERCENTAGE INCREASE OF POPULATION IN

	France.	Twelve great cities.	Ratio.
	1.	2.	2:1.
1801–21	10.95	21.2	193.
1821–31	6.43	9.5	148.
1831–41	5.1	17.7	349.
1841–51	4.5	13.9	310.
1851–61	2.7	51.9	1880.
1861–72	1.0	11.3	1130.
1872–81	4.4	18.7	425.
1881–91	1.8	9.7	535.

The vast increase of population in the cities in 1851–61 is in part due to large annexations by Paris (about 500,000 in 1859), Lyons (1852), Lille (1858) and Havre. But if this annexed territory be included in the earlier census there will remain an unprecedented increase in the years 1851–72; thus the corrected rate of increase and the ratio to the rate of entire France are:

1831–41	22.0	432
1841–51	19.0	424
1851–61	33.0	1220
1861–72	10.0	1000

The Industrial Revolution, the effects of which on the distribution of population culminated in England in the decade 1821–31, began shortly after the Revolution of 1830 in France and was only fairly under way when Stephenson's invention of the railway locomotive revolutionized systems of communication. The full influence of both these revolutionary changes in industry did not make itself felt in France until the middle of the century, as appears from statistics respecting the consumption of coal and cotton, the number of steam engines and the production of iron:

TABLE XLI.

	Cotton consumed [1] (million kilos).	Stationary steam engines [2] (horse-power).	Coal consumed [3] (thousand tons).	Production of pig and bar iron [4] (thousand tons).
1789	....	....	450	69
1802	....	....	935	....
1810	....	....	....	112
1811	....	....	864	....
1815	....	....	1,112	....
1816	12	....	....	....
1817	13	....	....	....
1820	20	....	1,348	....
1825	....	....	1,994	199
1830	29	....	2,494	266
1835	....	....	3,288	295
1840	53	34,350	4,257	348
1845	....	....	6,343	439
1850	59	66,642	7,225	416
1855	....	....	12,294	849
1860	123	180,555	14,270	898
1865	....	....	18,522	1,204
1869	132	320,447	21,400	1,381
1870	....	....	18,880	....
1871	....	315,884	....	....
1875	....	....	24,558	1,448
1880	....	544,152	28,846	1,725
1885	....	....	30,035	1,631
1890	....	863,007	32,318	....

The consumption of cotton is a fair index of the state of the textile industry, and it will be noticed that the first marked increase occurs in the decade 1830–40. The figures for 1850 are hardly representative of the latter decade, since industry had not then recovered from the destruction and dislocation produced by the Revolution of 1838; but it is clear that the period 1840–60 was one of great growth in the cotton trade.

Steam-power was evidently utilized to only a small extent in France before 1840. Its rapid increase in 1840–60 will be perceived.

[1] Block, in Lalor's *Cyclopedia of Political Science*, ii, 274.

[2] A. de Foville, *La France Économique, année* 1889, p. 194.

[3] Foville, *op. cit.*, 208.

[4] *Ibid.*, 214, and Block, *Statistique de la France*, ii, 200.

The consumption of coal does not take on imposing dimensions before 1825; and once more the period 1840–60 (together with 1872–85) is seen to be one of unusually rapid expansion.

Inferences of a similar character may be drawn from the statistics of iron production. Taken all together, they demonstrate the importance of the period 1840–60 in the industrial history of France. Hand in hand with this industrial development went a commercial development. A diagram [1] representing the total foreign commerce (imports and exports, excluding goods *in transitu*) would show that steady growth began about 1834 and continued slowly until 1846. But after the February Revolution the curve rises more rapidly and reaches maxima in 1856, 1864 and 1872. The internal commerce passed through similar stages of growth. As is generally known, the era of railway building opened in France several years later than it did in England and the United States; the legislation of 1842 may fairly be said to denote a serious purpose on the part of the country to develop the new system of transportation.[2] Hence, it

---

[1] Based on the statistics given by Block, *op. cit.*, ii, 286, and Foville, *op. cit.* 271–2.

[2] Cf. Hadley, *Railroad Transportation*, 190. The following table (compiled from Block, ii, 322, and Foville, 307) indicates its subsequent progress:

	Railways opened. (Kilometers.)	Total length of railway in operation.		Railways opened. (Kilometers.)	Total length of railway in operation.
1835......	...	149	1853......	190	
1842......	27	593	1854......	596	
1843......	229		1855......	886	5,527
1844......	2		1856......	664	
1845......	52		1857......	1,262	
1846......	438		1858......	1,222	
1847......	509		1859......	393	
1848......	390		1860......	365	9,433
1849......	628		1865......	515	13,585
1850......	151	3,002	1875......	...	21,770
1851......	544		1880......	...	26,190
1852......	316		1885......	...	32,497

was not until the middle of the century that the changes in the distribution of population began on a large scale in France, while they took place in the two Anglo-Saxon countries in 1840–50. The merchandise traffic of the French railways amounted to 200,000 tons (metric) in 1847; in 1854, it had reached a million tons; in 1857, two million tons; in 1860, three million tons, and thereafter increased at the rate of about one million tons each three years, aggregating in 1883, eleven million tons, and since then increasing very slowly.[1]

The connection between industry and distribution of population is thus seen to be too direct in France to demand extended exposition.

IV. GERMANY.

The German Empire has done much for the improvement of statistics, and its own statistical publications are of the highest rank. But as the Empire itself is a comparatively recent creation, its statistics do not suffice for a study of the concentration of population in its historical development. For the greater part of the century, therefore, the investigation will be based on the statistics of Prussia, the predominating and typical state of the Empire. Saxony is more advanced industrially than Prussia, but is too small to serve as the typical German state.

Table XLII shows the urban and rural populations at the several censuses. The definition of urban population, it should be remarked, is here a legal rather than a statistical one, and includes only such places as possess certain rights and privileges. The legal distinction between *Stadtgemeinden* and *Landgemeinden* had a real basis in fact earlier in the

---

[1] *Album de statistique graphique de 1893* (published by the Bureau de la Statistique générale de la France), Table 20.

century, but it is now lost. Many *Landgemeinden* have become cities in every sense of the word except the legal one. Thus in 1895, according to the preliminary census returns, there were 52 towns classed in the rural population although they contained a population of more than 10,000 in each case, some of them being large cities. The distribution of the rural population according to the size of the dwelling place was as follows:

Places containing	No.	Aggregate population.
50,000+ inhabitants................	2	122,615
20,000–50,000 "	6	172,788
10,000–20,000 "	44	598,413
5,000–10,000 "	140	922,038
2,000–5,000 "	700	2,048,191
Total 2,000+	892	3,864,045
Less than 2,000	51,570	15,031,976
		18,896,021

Here is a population of 3,864,045 which should be reckoned as urban; on the other hand, there were 317 urban *Gemeinden* containing less than 2,000 inhabitants with an aggregate of 435,761. If the population be distributed on the usual basis of division we shall have this contrast:

	Urban.	Per cent.	Rural.	Per cent.
Legal	12,953,774 =	40.66	18,896,021 =	59.34
Statistical	16,382,058 =	51.41	15,467,737 =	48.59

Prussia's population is now more than half urban according to the statistical definition, whereas only 40.7 per cent. is urban according to the legal distinction. But in 1867, the earliest year in which the statistical distinction between urban and rural population can be drawn, the difference was

TABLE XLII.

GROWTH OF POPULATION IN PRUSSIA.

	Cities of 100,000 +			All Cities.			Rural		Total Pop.
	No.	Pop.	Per cent.	No.	Pop.	Per cent.	Pop.	Per cent.	of Prussia.
1816	1	197,817	= 1.91	935	2,627,655	= 25.46	7,438,460	= 73.50	10,349,031
1834	1	257,336	= 1.90	972	3,464,587	= 25.64	9,825,256	= 72.73	13,507,999
1837	1	265,394	= 1.88	972	3,639,983	= 25.82	10,244,353	= 72 67	14,098,125
1840	1	311,491	= 2 09	973	3,861,017	= 25.87	10,863,337	= 72 77	14,928,503
1843	1	333.990	= 2.16	979	4,059 840	= 26.25	11,208,376	= 72.45	15,471,084
1846	2	495.995	= 3.08	980	4.308,065	= 26.73	11,603,990	= 72.02	16,112,938
1849	2	505,376	= 3.09	980	4,370,863	= 26.76	11,714,275	= 71.73	16,331,187
1852	2	535.990	= 3.16	981	4,438,377	= 27.38	12,120,211	= 71.57	16,935,420
1855	3	648.415	= 3.78	986	4,750,144	= 27.71	12,181,391	= 71.11	17,202,013
1858	3	577,443	= 3.84	987	5,038,812	= 28 53	12,436,610	= 70.41	17,739,913
1861	3	776,679	= 4 28	992	5,351,219	= 29.41	12,810,719	= 69.28	18,491,220
1864	3	883,377	= 4 61	994	5,717,586	= 29.84	13,191,943	= 68.85	19,255,139
1867	4	1,105,831	= 4 61	1273	7,456,160	= 31.10	16.515,177	= 68.90	23,971,337
1871	4	1,275,663	= 5.18	1200	8.000 931	= 32.46	16,605,253	= 67.54	24,641,539
1875	6	1,673,728	= 6.50	1286	8,780,267	= 34.18	16,913,367	= 65.82	25,693,634
1880	7	2,049,136	= 7.51	1287	9,707,802	= 35.58	17,571,309	= 64.42	27,279,111
1885	12	2,880,293	= 10.17	1287	10,554,596	= 37.27	17,763 874	= 62.73	28,318,470
1890	16	3,979,886	= 13.29	1263	11,786,061	= 39.38	18,169,220	= 60.62	29,955,281
1895	18	4,632,731	= 14 55	1266	12,953,774	= 40.66	18,896,021	= 59.34	31,849,795

SOURCES.—From 1816 to 1864, inclusive, Dr. H Schwabe "Ueber die Quellen für das Wachstum der grossen Städten im preussischen Staate," *Berliner Stadt und Gemeinde-Kalendaar und Statistisches Jahrbuch für 1867, Erster Jahrgang*.

From 1871 to 1895, inclusive, *Vorläufige Ergebnis e der Volkszählung vom 2 Dezember, 1805, im Königreich Preussen;* and Jannasch, "Das Wachsthum und die Concentration der Bevölkerung des preussischen Staates," *Zeitschrift des königlich preussischen statistischen Bureaus*, 1878, xviii, 263–284.

The official Volkszählungen.

Up to 1854 the military population is excluded from the urban and rural classification while appearing in the general total for Prussia: hence the sum of the urban and rural is not equal to the total in the last column. In 1871 there were 35,355 troops in France, which are similarly treated; 1816, similarly 29,038; 1849, 34,704.

While the passing of towns from one category to another by their growth has important effects on the percentages, it plays no considerable part in the rural population; the latter lost thus only some 17,000 inhabitants in the period 1840–55.

The lack of figures antecedent to 1816 is of no consequence, as the fifteen years of war left the country practically where it was in the first year of the century. The figures are not absolutely exact owing to frequent annexations, and to the varying treatment of the military by the different authorities. In the general total, the aim has been to include the whole population even when some Prussian troops were on foreign soil. The authority mainly relied upon for this was the *Statistisches Handbuch für den preussischen Staat*, 1893 (vol. ii). Another set of figures was given by Dr. Engel, the director of the Prussian bureau of statistics, in the bureau's *Zeitschrift* for 1861, i, 25:

	Cities.	Country.	Total.	Military in city	in country
1816	2,881,533	7,838,460	10.319,993	150,094	
1822	3,167,933	8,496,200	11,664,133	169,960	
1831	3.599,635	9.439.335	13,038,970	258,215	
1840	4,066,266	10,862,237	14,928,503	205,247	
1849	4,582,198	11,714,285	16,296,483	257,385	3,451
1858	5,235,999	12,436,610	17,672,609	195,966	4,273

In these statements are excluded 29,038 Prussian troops stationed in France in 1816; 34,704 military in 1849; 67,304 persons in 1858, most of whom were residents of the principality of Hohenzollern annexed in 1849. As between this date and Table XLII, the principal difference that exists relates to the urban population, and is due to the inclusion of the military in the former case and its exclusion in the latter.

The military constituted the following proportion of every 100 inhabitants in the years

1834.	1837.	1840.	1843.	1846.	1849.	1852.	1855.	1858.	1861.	1864.
1.63	1.51	1.36	1.30	1.25	1.51	1.05	1.18	1.06	1.31	1.31

less important,[1] and it is safe to neglect it altogether for the first half of the century.

Down to 1852 the concentration of population can scarcely be observed in Prussia. Table XLII shows, indeed, a very small and gradual increase in the percentage of the population reckoned as urban, but this would almost disappear if the military were added to the urban population—where it mostly belongs.[2] The figures of Dr. Engel therefore indicate that the urban increase was actually slower than the rural increase down to 1843. His figures[2] end with 1858, but the ratios for 1895 have been appended:

	1816.	1822.	1831.	1840.	1849.	1858.	1895.
Prussia	1000	1130	1263	1447	1579	1702	3086
Urban	1000	1099	1249	1411	1590	1817	4500
Rural	1000	1142	1269	1461	1575	1672	2540

It may be regarded as sufficiently established that the modern tendency toward a preponderance of the urban population was not manifested in Prussia before the middle of the century. Then came suddenly a period of rapid concentration, which is shown below in a comparison of the rates of increase of the entire population. For an increase

---

[1] The percentages were 35.8 and 31.1. Taking all townships (*Gemeinden*) of 2,000 + population:

TABLE XLIII.

	Number.	Population.	Percentage of total population.	Rural population.
1867	1,400	8,585,954	35.81	15,385,383
1871	1,406	9,176,258	37.29	15,429,926
1875	1,514	10,343,618	40.26	15,350,016
1880	1,615	11,614,385	42.60	15,664,726
1885	1,648	12,754,674	45.00	15,563,796
1890	1,726	14,529,598	48.50	15,425,683
1895	1,841	16,382,058	51.43	15,467,737

The principal source of information is Jannasch, *loc. cit.*, xviii, 275; with subsequent censuses.

[2] *Cf.* Remarks under Table XLII.

TABLE XLIV.

GROWTH OF POPULATION OF GERMANY, THE GREAT CITIES AND BERLIN.

Present territory of the German Empire.	25 great cities of 1890.		Of total population, the following numbers per 1,000 were in the 25 cities.	Berlin's proportion of the 25 cities.
	With suburbs.	Berlin.		
1.	2.	3.	4.	5.	6.
1819..	25,917,010	1,239,700	....	201,138	47.	16.2
1837..	31,589,547	1,527,400	....	283,722	48.	18.5
1840..	32,785,150	1,636,500	....	328,692	50.	20.0
1849..	35,128,398	1,867,600	....	378,204	53.1	20.3
1852..	35,929,691	2,050,400	....	438,958	57.1	21.4
1855..	36,111,644	2,153,000	....	447,483	59.5	20.8
1858..	36,960,742	2,295,800	....	458,637	62.1	20.0
1861..	38,137,410	2,484,748	....	547,571	65.2	22.0
1864..	39,389,904	2,766,138	....	632,749	70.4	22.9
1867..	40,088,621	2,994,645	3,432,261	702,437	74.9	23.4
1871..	41,058,792	3,352,181	3,883,923	826,341	81.6	24.6
1875..	42,727,360	3,812,144	4,538,900	966,858	89.2	25.3
1880..	45,234,061	4,325,952	5,211,366	1,122,330	95.6	25.9
1885..	46,855,704	4,844,240	5,969,089	1,315,287	104.3	26.9
1890..	49,428,470	5,970,000	7,077,476	1,578,794	120.7 [1]	26.4

[1] Or, including annexations made since the census of 1890, 128.8.

SOURCES.

The data of column 1 refer to the "resident" population down to the year 1864. In 1867 the "resident" population of Germany was 40,180,825, which is about 100,000 more than the "actual population" as given in the table. Cf. *Monatshefte zur Statistik des Deutschen Reichs,* ii, Heft vii, 54, 1879 (*Statistik des Deutschen Reichs, Erste Reihe,* Bd. 37) and recent numbers of *Statistisches Jahrbuch für das Deutsche Reich.*

1890. Data from *Vierteljahrshefte zur Statistik des Deutschen Reichs,* 1892, ii: "Gemeinden und Wohnplätzen vom mindestens 2,000 Einwohnern nach dem Ergebniss der Volkszählung vom 1 Dezember, 1890." . . . . The population of Munich was there given as 349,024, but was afterwards corrected.

1885. Data from *Statistik des Deutschen Reichs, Neue Folge, Bd. 32.*
1880.   "   "   "   "   " *Erste Reihe, Bd. 57.*
1875.   "   "   "   "   "   " *Bd. 25,* ii, p. 88.
1871.   "   "   "   "   "
1867.   "   " *Monatshefte zur Statistik des Deutschen Reiches,* 1884, v (except Breslau, which has been allowed to stand).
1864 and 1861. Data for the Prussian cities: *Jahrbuch der amtlichen Statistik des preussischen Staats,* i, 1876. For the other cites, see below.

For the years 1840-1858: The Prussian cities as above for 1861-64; the other cities as below.
For 1837 and 1819: (1) Hoffman, *Beiträge zur Statistik des preussischen Staats,* Berlin, 1821. (2 Hoffman, *Die Bevölkerung des preussischen Staats,* Berlin, 1839.
The other sources mentioned are as follows:

Altona, (a) Tabellen über die, in den Herzogthümern Schleswig und Holstein am 1 Feb., 1835, vorgenommene Volkszählung, Kopenhagen, 1836; containing 1803 and 1805. (b) Einleitung zu dem statistischen Tabellenwerk, neue Reihenfolge, 12 Band, über die Volksmenge in Königreich Denmark, etc., Kopenhagen, 1857; for 1845 and 1855. (c) Ergebnisse der am 3 Dez. 1864 in Herzogthum Holstein vorgenommenen Volkszählung, Kiel, 1867; for 1860 and 1864.

Brunswick, Beiträge zur Statistik des Herzogthums Braunschweig, Heft xii, 1895, and Heft ii, Völkszählung für 1871.

Bremen, Jahrbuch für die amtliche Statistik des Bremischen Staates, V. Jahrgang (1871) 2te Heft, p. 10.

Chemnitz, M. Flinger (sometime director of the municipal statistical bureau), Die Bewegung der Bevölkerung in Chemnitz von 1730 to 1870. Chemnitz, 1872.

of 100 in the Prussian population there was an increase in the urban population of

1816–34	103	
1834–52	111	
1852–61	234	(From Table XLII.)
1861–71	146	
1867–71	233	
1867–71	233	
1871–80	253	
1880–90	253	(From Table XLIII.)
1890–95	196	

That the inferences drawn from this investigation of the Prussian population also hold good of Germany at large may be concluded from a comparison of the growth of the larger German cities with that of the whole country. In Table XLIV such a comparison is made for Berlin and the 25 cities which in 1890 severally contained 100,000+ inhabitants. As might be expected, the great cities have developed more rapidly than the entire urban population, but down to 1849 their rate of increase was comparatively slow (cf. col. 5) ; and Dr. Brückner in his brilliant statistical study of these great cities does not go back of 1861.[1] Their increase compared with Germany is—

1819–37	108
1837–52	244
1852–61	345

The great cities began their career a little earlier than the

---

Dresden, Mitteilungen des statistischen Bureaus der Stadt Dresden. Heft ii. Dresden, 1875.
Frankfurt, Beiträge zur Statistik der Stadt Frankfurt a M. Neue Folge. 1te Heft.
Hamburg, Statistisches Handbuch für den Hamburgischen Staat. 4te Ausgabe, 1891, p. 17.
Hannover, Zur Statistik des Königreichs Hannover, Heft 2 (for 1833 and 1848), Heft 4 (for 1852): Sonne, Beschreibung des Königr. Hannover. Bd. 4, p. 339 (for 1813 24).
Leipzig. Mitteilungen des statistischen Bureaus der Stadt Leipzig. Heft 6.
Munich, Mitteilungen des statistischen Bureaus der Stadt München. Bd. ii.
Strassburg, Statistique de la France, Territoire et Population, Paris, 1837 (covering 1789 to 1836); Résultats généraux du dénombrement de 1861, etc. Strasbourg, 1864 (covering 1836 1861).
Stuttgart, Beschreibung von Würtemburg (publ. by the royal statistical-topographical bureau). Heft 36. Stuttgart, 1856.
The suburban population statistics are from Brückner's article in *Allg. Stat. Archiv.*, vol. i, p. 149. In making out his list of suburbs, Dr. Brückner followed the suggestions of local authorities.

[1] " Die Entwickelung der grossstädtischen Bevölkerung im Gebiete des Deutschen Reiches," in Allg. Stat. Archiv., vol. i.

urban population as a whole, as will appear in a closer
analysis of the ratios just given:

	25 cities.	Prussian urban population.
1849–52	410	
1852–55	150	354
1855–58	300	193
1858–61	270	152

While entire accuracy cannot be claimed for these figures,
it is to be remarked that it is only natural for the impulse
toward concentration to make itself felt first in the great
cities. The subsequent development is to be seen in Dr.
Brückner's figures [1] which express the average annual increase for each 1,000 of the mean population:

TABLE XLV.

	Ger-many.	The 25 large cities. Excluding, Including suburbs.		Berlin.	Relative rates. Average for Germany.	25 cities.	25 cities with suburbs.	Berlin.
1861–64..	10.8	35.7	....	48.4	100	330	....	448
1864–67..	6.6	22.0	....	34.5	100	333	....	523
1867–71..	5.9	28.2	30.9	40.5	100	495	524	686
1871–75..	10.0	32.1	38.9	39.2	100	321	389	392
1875–80..	11.4	25.3	27.6	29.3	100	222	242	257
1880–85..	7.0	24.2	27.1	31.7	100	346	387	453
1885–90..	10.7	30.8	35.5	36.5	100	288	332	341

Brückner has avoided the disturbances caused by annexations by carrying back his calculations on the basis of the
territory of each city at the latest census. But he wrote
originally before the census of 1890, and to avoid an unusually high rate as a result of suburban annexations, he

---

[1] *Loc. cit.*, 151, 169.

subtracts these.[1] Otherwise the ratio for 1885–90 would be 425 instead of 288. In any event it is clear that the concentration of population in Germany continued with undiminished force to 1890.

With this exception, the period in which the cities grew most rapidly was 1861–4, but in 1867–71 with a smaller rate of gain the process of concentration reached its height, the increase of the 25 cities being five times as large as that of Germany; Berlin's increase being at the same time nearly seven times as large. In the other inter-censal periods, the rate of growth of the cities remains three times as high as that of the Empire, except in 1875–80, when it fell to 2.22.

The causes of this movement of population will be found in the industrial history of Germany. Prior to 1840, Germany was a land of local industries producing for local markets. The English factory system, with its vastly increased production, was unknown in Germany. Professor Schmoller, who is wont to see the brighter side of the system of domestic industry and small employers, characterizes the years 1830–40 as the happiest decade of the nineteenth century for German workingmen. But in 1835 the first railway line in Germany had been opened[2] and in its

[1] Namely :

Elberfeld	2,719
Altona	21,589
Cologne	78,036
Munich	18,392
Leipzig	119,472
Total	240,208

If this sum were subtracted from the aggregate population of the cities in Table XLIV, their proportion would be reduced from 120.7 to 115 per thousand (col. 5).

[2] From this time on railways were rapidly extended, as shown by the following figures from Conrad's *Hdwbh.* (Art. " Eisenbahnen ") :

	Kilometers.
1840	469
1850	5,856
1860	11,088
1870	18,450
1880	33,411
1890	41,793

wake came all those fundamental changes in the organization of industry which had been made in England earlier in the century.

The new technique was admitted and industry transformed; " Grossindustrie " or production on a large scale slowly superseded " Kleinindustrie ;" banks and the apparatus of a credit system were established ; it was a period of economic and political ferment. By 1848 the industrial transformation had been to a considerable extent accomplished and the Revolution of that year, its natural outcome, carried the political changes as far as they were destined to go for some time. About the same time industry was stimulated by the inflow of new gold from California and Australia, and there came to Germany a period of unparalleled industrial expansion. It was then that the growth of cities began, which has already been described. This continued, with increasing rapidity, until the maximum rate of concentration was reached in 1867–71 (Table XLV), partly as a result of an increased emigration to America [1] (from the rural population), partly as a result of military operations in the wars against Austria and France, which not only checked the increase in the population of the country as a whole (thereby emphasizing the relative progress of the cities), but drafted soldiers from the rural districts to strategic points, and also, as in the United States, in 1860–70, greatly stimulated manufactures for the supply of war needs and new wants arising in a rejuvenated and triumphant people.

---

[1] After 1854 emigration steadily decreased for a decade, *e. g.*, 215,000 in 1854, 27,559 in 1862. After that, emigration to the United States increased (Philippovich, in Conrad's *Hdwbh.*, i, 1019) :

1862–64	117,961
1865–67	332,742
1868–70	339,637

Poor harvests in 1867 and 1868 also had some effect on the movement of population.

While the rate of increase of the whole German population was greatly reduced in 1867–71, Berlin nearly maintained its high rate of 1858–64 and contributed largely to the concentration noticeable in Table XLV. The table shows the effects of the crisis of '77 in checking agglomeration. The industrial depression following this crisis was even more severe in Germany than in the United States, as it brought to an end the period of unprecedented speculation following the successful termination of the French war and the payment of the French indemnity. All this time emigration was declining [1] as a result of the hard times in the United States after 1873, thus depressing the general rate of increase. Since 1880 Germany has been rapidly advancing along healthy lines in both commerce and manufactures, and her city populations have increased amazingly. Since 1880 the rural population has apparently been declining (Table XLVI), but this is in no sense a rural depopulation. Between 1880 and 1890 the number of towns having at least 2,000 inhabitants increased from 2,707 to 2,891, thus involving a minimum rural decrease of 368,000. But the total rural decrease in 1880–90 was only 328,290.

As may be inferred from Tables XLIV and XLV, the tendency toward agglomeration in Germany has been a centralizing one, that is, a concentration in the largest cities. The great cities have increased more rapidly than the urban

---

[1] The total immigration to all foreign countries was as follows (*Ibid.*, i, 1019):

1871	75,912
1872	128,152
1873	110,438
1874	47,671
1875	32,329
1876	29,644
1877	22,898
1878	25,627
1879	35,888
1880	117,097

TABLE XLVI.

Population of *Gemeinden* having in the year specified

	2,000–5,000 inhabitants			5,–20,000 inhabitants			20,–100,000 inhabitants			More than 100,000 inhabitants			Total Urban.			Rural (*Gemeinden* under 2,000 population).		Germany.
	Population	No. of towns.	Per cent. of total pop. of Germany.	Population	No. of towns.	% of total pop.	Population	No. of towns.	% of total pop.	Population	No. of towns.	% of total pop.	Population	No. of towns.	% of total pop.	Population	% of total pop.	
1871	5,086,625	1,716	12.4	4,588,364	529	11.2	3,147,272	75	7.7	1,968,537	8	4.8	14,790,798	2,328	36.1	26,219,352	63.9	41,058,792
1875	5,379,357	1,837	12.6	5,124,044	591	12.0	3,487,587	88	8.2	2,665,914	12	6.2	16,657,172	2,528	39.	26,070,188	61.	42,727,360
1880	5,748,976	1,950	12.7	5,671,325	641	12.6	4,027,085	102	8.9	3,373,144	14	7.2	18,720,530	2,707	41.4	26,513,531	58.6	45,234,061
1885	5,805,893	1,951	12.4	6,054,629	683	12.9	4,171,874	116	8.9	4,440,381	21	9.5	20,478,777	2,771	43.7	26,376,927	56.3	46,855,704
1890	5,935,012	......	12.0	6,481,473	......	13.1	4,829,202	......	9.8	5,997,542	26	12.1	23,243,229	2,891	47.	26,185,241	53.	49,428,470

AUTHORITY.—*Statistik des Deutschen Reiches, Neue Folge, Band 68, Die Volkszählung am 1 Dezember, 1890, im Deutschen Reiche.*
EXPLANATION.—The troops garrisoned in France in 1871 (48,642) appear in the total, but not in the urban or rural categories.
In 1890 the totals were also prepared on the basis of the *Wohnplatz*, or town, as a unit, which naturally reduced the urban percentage. The urban population then constitutes 42.5 per cent, the rural 57.5 per cent. of the entire population.

population, and Berlin faster than either. This conclusion appears with overwhelming force in the following statistics from the German census of 1885:

TABLE XLVII.

ANNUAL INCREASE PER THOUSAND OF THE MEAN POPULATION.

	1867–71.	1871–75.	1875–80.	1880–85.	1867–85.
Gemeinden of less than 2,000 in '85.	0.6	1.1	6.0	—0.2	2.0
" 2,000–5,000 " "	6.4	12.4	12.4	8.4	9.9
" 5,000–20,000 " "	12.4	25.5	19.7	16.4	18.3
" 20,000–100,000 " "	22.0	30.3	22.9	21.7	23.6
" 100,000+ " "	26.9	33.2	25.3	24.1	26.6
Germany......................	5.9	10.0	11.4	7.0	8.6

In this table, the irregularities occasioned by the passing of towns from one group to another between censuses are avoided by classifying all the towns as returned in the census of 1885 and then computing their population at the previous censuses. The result is singularly striking. In each inter-censal period the percentage of growth increases with the size of the agglomeration. If the several rates be compared with Germany's for the entire period 1867–85, the following result will be obtained:

Germany	100
Towns of less than 2,000...	23
" " 2,000–5,000	115
" " 5,000–20,000	213
" " 20,000–100,000	275
" " 100,000 and more..	310

And as has already been shown (in Table XLIV), the class of great cities has itself been outstripped by Berlin. In 1819, of the residents of the 25 cities under consideration, one in six was a Berliner, but in 1890, one out of every four.

If now we take account of the increase in population in cities not only through the tendency of people to migrate thither, but also through additions to the number of cities, we shall see the concentration of population in cities considerably intensified. Table XLVI shows that the smaller towns and cities have held their own in the general increase, while the middle-sized cities (20,000–100,000) made only a moderate gain. Almost the entire increase of population has been absorbed by the great cities.

To indicate the development at wider intervals, it is necessary to recur to the data for Prussia. Tables XLII and XLIII yield the following percentages: [1]

TABLE XLVIII.

PERCENTAGE OF POPULATION OF PRUSSIA IN

Towns of	1816.	1849.	1890.
100,000+	1.8	3.1	12.9
20,000–100,000	4.2	4.7	10.1
10,000–20,000........................	1.25	2.83	7.0
Total 10,000+.....................	7.25	10.63	30.0
2,000–10,000	19.25	17.67	18.5
Total 2,000+.......................	26.50	28.30	48.5

Saxony's urban growth has surpassed that of Prussia, the reason being that Saxony is more exclusively a manufacturing state. For Saxony the following summary is presented:

[1] As previously remarked, the legal definition of "Stadtgemeinde" corresponds closely to the statistical definition down to about 1850, and is therefore used in these totals for 1816 and 1849. There are no statistics earlier than 1816, but it has been found that few changes took place between 1800 and 1816, the gains in population having been wiped out in the Napoleonic wars. That the distribution of population in Prussia may be regarded as fairly typical of Germany may be shown by comparing Tables XLVII and XLVIII:

	Prussia.	Germany.
Cities of 100,000+	12.9	12.1
" " 20,000–100,000	10.1	9.8
" " 2,000–20,000	25.5	25.1
Total......................	48.5	47.0

TABLE XLIX.

	1815.		1834.		1849.		1890.		
	No.	Pop.	No.	Pop.	No.	Pop.	No.	Pop.	%.
Cities of 100,000+	0	......	0	......	0	......	3	792,318	22.6
" " 20,000-100,000	2	88,700	3	132,072	3	187,219	9	259,559	7.4
" " 10,000-20,000	1	13,623	1	11,279	6	69,667		165,461	4.7
Cities of 10,000+	3	102,300	4	143,351	9	256,886		1,217,338	34.7
Towns of 2,000-10,000 (by subtraction).	(72	281,729)	(92	354,984)				(1,043,445)	
Total 2,000+	..	......	76	425,080	101	611,870		2,260,783	64.53
Saxony	1,148,802		1,595,668		1,894,431			3,502,684	100.

AUTHORITIES.

Statistische Mittheilungen aus dem Königreich Sachsen, i, 1851, for period 1834-40.

" Stadt und Land in Königreich Sachsen von 1834 bis 1875," in *Zeitschrift des Königl. sächs. statis. Bureaus*, xxii, 296-306 (1876).

G. Lommatzch, *Die Bewegung des Bevölkerungsstandes im Königreich Sachsen* 1871-90. Dresden, 1894.

Hauptergebnisse der sächsischen Statistik. A. *Bevölkerungsstatistik*, 1834-90, in *Zeitschrift*, etc., 36: 51-63 (1890).

Results of the census of 1890 in *Zeitschrift*, etc., 37: 51 (1891).

Cf. also *Repertorium der in sämmtlichen Publicationen des König. sächs. statis. Bureaus von 1831-86 behandelten Gegenständen.*

Bavaria has a smaller urban population, especially as regards great cities. The earlier statistics are wanting :

TABLE L.

	1818.		1852.			1890.		
Cities.	No.	Pop.	No.	Pop.	Per cent.	No.	Pop.	Per cent
100,000+	0	....	1	109,574	2.4	2	493,184	8.8
20,000-100,000	4	136,800	5	169,318	3.72	10	393,938	7.0
10,000-20,000	..	....	..	......	...	17	240,184	4.7
Total 10,000+ ..	..	....	..	....	...	29	1,127,306	20.5
Urban (2,000+)	..	....	..	....	...	...	1,782,463	31.9
Urban (official)	..	......	52	611,122	13.4	52	1,287,704	20.5
Bavaria	..	3,707,966	..	4,559,452	...	..	5,594,982	

AUTHORITIES.

Beiträge zur Statistik des Königreichs Bayerns, Heft 1 (1850); *Heft* 13 (1865); *Hefte* 28, 31, 82 (1871); *Hefte* 36, 42 (1875); *Heft* 46 (1880); *Heft* 58 (1890). Also *Zeitschrift des Königl. bäyerischen statis. Bureaus*, vols. 8, 9, 13, 14, 22, 23, 24. And the Bavarian statistical *Jahrbuch*, ii (1895).

For index of Bavarian official statistical documents *cf. Geschichte und Einrichtung der amtlichen Statistik im Königr. Bayern*, München, 1895 (p. 309 *ff*).

The " official " urban population consists of 52 towns (see note 1, p. 94).

The census of 1890 showed that the concentration was in the direction of the larger cities :

TABLE LI.

INCREASE PER CENT.

	1840-52.	1852-71.	1871-80.	1880-90.	1840-90.
Bavaria	4.31	6.42	8.92	5.87	28.
Rural	3.32	2.52	5.59.	.78	12.71
Urban [1]	11.24	31.60	25.67	27.41	134.39
12 cities of 20,000+ in 1890	12.97	45.42	30.03	34.40	187.09
Munich	14.55	55.14	19.60	43.28	204.52

V. AUSTRIA.

The Austrian census of 1890 is a model work. A combination of American ingenuity in the way of electrical tabulating machines, and of German thoroughness and completeness in working up the results, produced a statistical document far and away superior to any other census. It is especially valuable for its classification of dwelling-centres, with the presentation of all the essential data in accordance with this classification; thus encouraging investigations into the structure and composition of town-populations of varying size.

At the present time there exists in Austria a strong tendency toward agglomeration. Thus, between 1880 and 1890 the percentage increase was as follows [2] in

Places of less than 500 inhabitants	4.83
" " 500–2,000 "	2.30
" " 2,000–5,000 "	7.34
" " 5,000–10,000 "	6.93
" " more than 10,000 "	33.06
Austria	7.91

The Austrian population increased 7.91 per cent. in the decade, but none of the towns under 10,000 population reached this rate, while the exceptionally high rate of in-

---

[1] Urban: the "unmittelbaren Städte" 41 in number, and the 11 larger towns in the Pfalz.

[2] Rauchberg, "Der Zug nach der Stadt," in *Statistische Monatschrift* (Vienna), xix. 127 (1893).

TABLE LII.

SHOWING GROWTH OF POPULATION IN

	Austria.	Towns 10,000+. No.	Towns 10,000+. Aggregate Per cent. of total pop.	Vienna.	Other cities of 100,000+ in 1890.	Cities 50,000–100,000 in 1890.	Eight small cities.	Sixteen Vienna suburbs.	Total of Cols. 3, 4, 5, 6, 7.	Austria. Annual (geometrical) increase per cent.
	1.	2.	2.	3.	4.	5.	6.	7.	8.	9.
1786	11,875,000	14	551,000 = 4.4	232,000	[193,600]					
1800	[12,600,000]	14	614,000 = 4.4	260,224	[200,000]					
1818	13,330,640									
1821	13,904,341									1.433
1824	14,518,749									1.306
1827	15,130,762									1.386
1830	15,588,142			317,768	239,750	95,000 ca	37,000 ca	[35,000]	[712,000]	.998
1834	15,713,952	21	831,127 = 5.1	326,353	242,190	100,000 ca	42,800 ca	55,000 ca	830,300	.201
1837	16,083,046			333,582	250,641					.777
1840	16,575,118	28	984,600 = 5.8	356,869	275,845					1.010
1843	17,073,231	35	1,128,137 = 6.4	373,236	279,868					.992
1846	17,613,406			407,980	293,065					1.044
1850	17,534,950	48	1,551,494 = 8.5	431,147	309,808	129,581	52,400	80,000 ca	1,019,849	–.112[1]
1857	18,224,500	53	1,808,000 = 9.3	476,222	342,220	139,000 ca	71,339	117,000 ca	1,177,893	.553
1869	20,217,531			607,514	396,215	191,171	108,305	207,400	1,549,753	.869
1880	21,981,821		2,836,457 = 12.8	725,402	424,465	223,530	149,139	344,400	1,952,609	.764
1890	23,707,906	100	3,789,365 = 15.8	{ 798,719 1,341,897 }	521,531	264,229	181,300	464,110	2,481,008	.759

[1] Decrease.

AUTHORITIES.

Col. 1.—Rauchberg, *Die Bevölkerung Oesterreichs*, p. 24, since 1818. For 1786, J. V. Göhlert, *Die Ergebnisse der in Oesterreich im vorigen Jahrhundert ausgeführten Volkszählungen*, etc., in vol. xiv. of the *Sitzungsberichten* of the Vienna Akademie der Wiss. Phil.-hist. Classe, pp. 52–73.

Col. 2.—Computed from various sources: For the first quarter of the century, J. M. Lichtenstein, *Vollständiger Umriss des Oest. reichischen Kaisertums*, 1820; Hassel, *Statistische Uebersichtstabellen der sämmtlichen Europäischen Staaten* 1809, and later editions or similar works under other titles: for 1837, S. Becher, *Statistische Uebersichten der Bevölkerung der Oesterreichischen Monarchi.* 1841, and J. Springer, *Statistik des Oesterreichischen Kaisertums*, 1840; the earliest official data = *Tafeln zur Statistik der Oesterreichischen Monarchie für das Jahr 1846,* Wien, 1850, while the first trustworthy census is *Statistische Uebersichten über die Bevölkerung von Oesterreich nach der Zählung von 1857,* Wien, 1859. The remaining figures are drawn from the more recent censuses, or from Rauchberg's articles in *Statistische Monatschrift*.

Cols. 3, 4, 5, 6, 7, 8.—Chiefly from Rauchberg, in *Statistische Monatsschrift,* xix (1893).

Figures enclosed in brackets are estimates.

Until 1850, the date of the censuses is January 1; in 1850 and 1857, October, and since 1857, December 31.

The above figures refer to the *civil* population, except in the towns of 10,000 and upwards, in the years 1880 and 1890, when the "actual" or "present" population (military as well as civil) is given. The enumerated population of Austria was 20,394,980 in 1869: 22,144,244 in 1880, and 23,895,413 in 1890.

By the law of Dec. 19, 1890, Vienna incorporated numerous suburbs (including those in column 7), and if these were included in the city at the census of 1880, the total (civil) population would be increased to 1,341,897. The "actual" population of Vienna was 725,459 in 1880 and 1,364,548 (the new territory) in 1890.

Col. 4.—The four great cities are Prague, Lemberg, Triest and Graz.
Col. 5.—These cities are Brünn, Cracow Czernowitz and Pilsen.
Col. 6.—The eight small cities are Marburg, Aussig, Brüx, Budweis, Reichenberg, Teplitz, Mährisch-Ostrau and Tarnow.
Col. 8.—Includes also Prague's suburbs.

crease in the urban population indicates a widespread movement from the country to the city. How long this movement has been in progress it is not easy to determine, owing
to the scantiness of Austrian statistics prior to the recent
model census. But from a multiplicity of sources of varying
value, Table LII has been constructed. The civil population in the present territory of the kingdom of Austria is
there given at different periods together with some data concerning the population of cities.[1] The figures for towns of
10,000 population and upwards are not thoroughly trustworthy guides, but, as the following table will indicate, they
are in agreement with other figures which are more accurate
although less complete :

TABLE LIII.

PROPORTIONATE RATES OF INCREASE.

	Austria.	Cities of 10,000+.	Vienna.		Vienna and suburbs.	17 leading cities.[2]
1800–21....	100	106	112			
1821–37....	100	232	186			
1837–43....	100	298	192	1830–40	262	272
1843–46....	100	456	290	1840–50	402	377
1846–57....	100	1,071	480	1850–57	403	388
1857–69....	100	206	253	1857–69	342	285
1869–80....	100	563	183	1869–80	339	298
1880–90....	100	425	167	1880–90	258	318

It is to be observed, first, that in all four classes of urban
population in this table the rate of increase, compared with
that for the entire country, is low during the earlier half of
the century; but it is constantly increasing and in the period
1846–57 reaches its maximum. A variety of causes contributed to this result. The great famine of 1847 and 1848
carried off thousands of Austrians, and, combined with the
Hungarian revolt of 1848 and the political troubles at home,
resulted in a serious loss of population, as shown by the

[1] Chiefly from Rauchberg's article, *loc. cit.*, xix, 138–41.
[2] Cf. Table LII, col. 8.

census of 1850.[1] The famine naturally affected most seriously the scattered population of the rural districts away from the transportation routes, while the shifting of population caused by military movements doubtless drew additional persons from the rural districts. But both these factors may be discounted, for the table also shows that the years 1850–57, which exclude them, have a maximum rate for Greater Vienna and 17 of the principal cities. It is beyond question the influence of railway building which accounts for the shifting of population made manifest in 1857. The railway era fairly opened in 1840, but for some years brought advantage only, or chiefly, to Vienna. The development is set forth in the column headed "Vienna and suburbs," which is practically the Vienna created by law December 19, 1890. Compared with the general rate of increase for Austria, Vienna attained its highest rate in 1840–50 and 1850–57, since which it has regularly declined. Vienna's high rate in 1840–50 acts decisively on that of the 17 leading cities, but in the last decade they manifest an independent growth, and one larger than Vienna's. This again may be referred to the influence of railways, for it was in the decade 1865–75 that the largest extensions were carried out.[2]

[1] Cf. Table LII, first and last columns; also Rauchberg, *Die Bevölkerung Oesterreichs*, p. 27, and diagram.

[2] The following figures are from Neumann-Spallart's *Uebersichten der Weltwirthschaft*, and Conrad's *Hdwbh.*, iii, 214:

	Length of railways (kilometers) in Austro-Hungary.
1830	121
1840	475
1845	1,058
1850	2,240
1855	2,829
1860	5,160
1865	6,397
1870	9,761
1875	16,766
1880	18,476
1885	22,341
1889	26,501

The apparent decrease of agglomeration in 1857–69 must be explained by a visitation of the cholera and the war with Prussia in 1866. Nearly all the cities of Bohemia, where the war was fought, show an unusually low rate of increase in 1857–69.[1]

The effect of the different modes of reckoning in Table LIII appears in the proportionate rates for 1880–90 of the class of cities of 10,000+ and of a definite number of cities (17). Still, both show a very considerable tendency toward agglomeration in the last decade. But does agglomeration in Austria mean concentration in a few great cities?

TABLE LIV.

SHOWING THE DISTRIBUTION OF POPULATION.

	Number and population of Gemeinden.						Proportions of total population.			
	1880.		1843.		1890.		1800.	1843.	1880.	1890.
Austria.......	12,600,000	47,438	17,073,231	58,891	23,895,413		100.	100.	100.	100.
Under 2,000 ..	....	46,713	13,852,766	57.578	16,128,205		....	81.1	70 4	67.5
Over 2,000	....	725	3,220,465	1,313	7,767,208		....	18.9	29.6	32.5
2,000–10,000 ..	....	697	2,235,865	1,212	3,977,843		....	13.1	16.8	16.7
10,000–20,000.	8 102,000	21	264,054	69	919,106		0.81	1.6	} 8.2	{ 3.8
20,000–100,000.	5 217,000	5	235,606	27	962,836		0.93	1.4	}	{ 4.
100,000+	1 232,000	2	484,942	5	1,907,423		2.63	2.8	4.6	8.

AUTHORITIES.

Compiled chiefly from Rauchberg's article already cited (Table LII). The figures for 1800 are gathered from various statistical hand-books (*Staatenkunde*) of the early part of the century.

It should be noticed that the figures for 1880–90 refer to the "actually present" (*ortsanwesend*) instead of the civil population (cf. Table LII, Explanations).

In 1846 the city republic of Cracow was annexed, adding some 50,000 to the middle-sized cities.

It will be seen from Table LIV that the urban population (towns of 2,000 +) increased from 18.9 per cent. of the total population in 1843 to 32.5 per cent. in 1890, and that while the increase was divided among the several classes of cities, a disproportionately large part fell to the "great

[1] Cf. *St. Mon.*, xix, 138. It is possible that the urban population of 1857 is estimated too high in the tables, for in the census of 1857 the population of towns is given on the basis of the entire township. If this is so, the rate for 1850–57 would be somewhat reduced, and that for 1857–69 increased.

cities." While, however, the great cities are absorbing an ever increasing proportion of the population, it will be interesting to know whether the average great city grows more rapidly than the average small city,—whether Levasseur's hypothesis regarding the attractive power of cities according to size holds good of Austria. The following table[1] shows roughly the percentages of increase in several groups of cities classified according to their population in 1890:

TABLE LV.

| | 1831-40. | 1841-50. | 1851-57. | 1858 69. | 1870-80. | 1880-90. | Increase from 1,000. | |
							1870 90.	1831-90.
Vienna	12.4	21.	16.	23.	16.1	13.2	1,313	2,512
Four " great cities "	15.	12.	14.	13.	7.	23.	1,317	2,173
Four " large cities "	5.	29.	10.	25.	23.	18.	1,460	2,781
Above nine chief cities	12.	19.	14.	20.	14.	17.	1,340	2,448
Eight small cities	16.	22.	51.	43.	38.	22.	1,680	4,846
Vienna suburbs—16	57.	45.	66.	66.	66.	26.	2,238	13,260
Prague suburbs—9	..	22.	67.	43.	115.	63.	3,442	
Austria	6.2	6.	5.7	9.2	8.	7.9	1,172	1,508

Throughout the entire sixty years the eight small cities have grown more rapidly than the chief cities; and of the nine chief cities, the four great cities (those of 100,000 + in 1890) have been outstripped by the smaller ones. Vienna's growth is exceeded by that of the small cities and middle-sized cities.

But account has to be taken of extra-municipal or suburban growth, and the table shows that of the classes of towns, the suburbs of Vienna and Prague have had the most rapid growth. It is therefore necessary to compute the population of the city and suburbs as an industrial unit. In Table LIII, it has already been seen that the enlarged

[1] Based on Table I.II. The percentages of 1851-7 and 1858-69 have, for the sake of comparison, been reduced to ten-year periods. . . . The suburbs of Prague increased in population from 18,000 in 1840 to 172,000 in 1890. . . . The ratios for Vienna are based on the ancient limits of the city; making the present limits the basis for 1830 and 1869, as well as 1890, the ratios in the last two columns would be 1,550 and 3,728 instead of 1,313 and 2,512.

Vienna outstripped the other cities in every decade except 1830–40 and 1880–90.[1] A more complete analysis is made in

TABLE LVI.

	1857.	1890.	Increase per cent.
Vienna (present limits)	593,000	1,341,900	126
Eight cities 50,000+ in 1890	481,000	785,700	63
Twenty cities, 20,000–50,000 in 1890.	295,000	634,600	115
Three suburbs of Prague 20,000+ ..	11,000	108,000	873
Total cities of 20,000+ in 1890..	1,380,000	2,870,200	108
Eight large cities including suburbs..	513,000	937,900	83
Eight selected small cities	71,000	181,300	154

These figures show that the eight smaller cities heretofore considered are not quite typical of their class, for in the period 1857–90 they increased 154 per cent., and the class 20,000–50,000 (averaging about the same in population) only 115 per cent.   The rank of the cities as regards growth is now: Vienna, 126; middle-sized cities, 115; large cities, 83; Austria, 30.   In the last decade, as we have seen in Table LV, the four great cities in addition to Vienna increased at a somewhat higher rate than the eight small cities which in turn have grown more rapidly than their class; so that the present tendency in Austria seems to be toward centralization, although not so marked as in France.

VI. HUNGARY.

In Hungary the mediæval distinction between town and country, based chiefly on political status, still holds good, and the statistical distinction would in any event be invalidated for the smaller classes of towns on account of their unusual extent of territory.   In Hungary the township or primary political unit has an average area of 22 square

---

[1] The diminished rate of increase in the Vienna suburbs in 1880–90 is due to the spread of population into new territory; and indeed these figures include only about two thirds of all the suburban inhabitants taken into the city in 1890.

TABLE LVII.

SHOWING GROWTH OF POPULATION IN HUNGARY.

	Hungarian Monarchy.	Hungary Proper.	Free Cities.	Small Cities.	Remainder of Hungary = Rural.	Seven largest cities of 1890.	Buda-Pest.	131 towns (cols. 4·5 — Per cent of total pop.)
	2.	3.	4.	5.	6.	7.	8.	9.
1800	......	9,859,000	......	......	......	220,400	61,000	......
1820	......	11,340,900	......	......	......	254,400	85,000	......
1831	......	[11,450,000]	......	......	......	308,900	104,600	......
1850	13,191,553	11,554,377	660,609	744,547	10,140,221	392,832	156,506	12.2
1857	13,768,513	12,067,183	788,417	844,388	10,434,378	465,226	186,945	13.5
1869	15,417,327	13,561,245	946,793	945,524	11,668,928	563,975	254,476	14.0
1880	15,642,102	13,728,622	1,112,822	1,008,653	11,607,147	692,032	360,551	15.4
1890	17,349,398	15,133,494	1,331,067	1,118,317	12,684,110	863,563	491,938	16.1

PERCENTAGE INCREASE.

	Hungarian Monarchy.	Hungary Proper.	Free Cities.	Small Cities.	Remainder of Hungary = Rural.	Seven largest cities of 1890.	Buda-Pest.	131 towns
1800–20	......	[9.6]	......	......	......	15.4	23.	......
1820–31	......	[9.1]	......	......	......	21.4	40.	......
1831–50	......	4.44	......	......	......	27.1	50.	......
1850–57	4.37	12.38	17.74	13.41	2.90	18.4	19.45	15.46
1857–69	11.98	1.23	20.09	11.98	11.83	21.2	36.12	15.89
1869–80	1.46	10.23	17.54	6.68	—.52	22.7	41.68	12.11
1880–90	10.91		19.61	10.87	9.29	24.7	36.44	15.46

AUTHORITIES.

The data for the first half-century are mere estimates, derived chiefly from *Staatenkunden* of the period. All the figures since 1850 are taken directly from the 1890 census, except column 7, where they have been computed from the same source (*Ungarische Statistische Mittheilungen, Neue Folge, Bd I.: Ergebnisse der in den Ländern der ungarischen Krone am Anfange des Jahres 1891 durchgeführten Volkszählung, I. Theil*, Buda-Pest 1893. In Magyar and German. Esp. pages 50*, 67*, 85*.)

EXPLANATIONS.

Col. 2.—Including Fiume (29,494 in 1890) and Croatia-Slavonia (2,186,410 in 1890).   Col. 4.—"Stadte mit municipium," 25 in number.
Col. 5.—"Stadte mit geordnetem Magisirat," 106 in number (1890).   Col. 7.—The six cities besides Buda-Pest, with their population in 1890, are:
   Szegedin 85,569   Debreczin 56,940   Pressburg................52,411
   Maria-Theresiopol 72,737   Hód-Mezö-Vásárhely 55,475   Kecskemet 48,493

kilometres, while in Austria it is 11 and in Germany 7.
Obviously, such a township might contain a population of
more than 2,000, which should be so scattered as to deprive
it of any urban character. The Hungarian statistics, therefore, regard as urban the population of 131 towns and cities
possessing special political privileges.[1] Twenty-five of the
cities are known as "towns with municipal charters " (*Städte
mit Municipium*), and contain in each case upwards of
10,000 inhabitants, their average population being, in 1880,
44,513, and in 1890, 53,243. They appear in Table LVII
as "free cities" and will represent the middle-sized cities.
The other class of cities embraced in the urban population
consists of the towns with magistrate appointed by the crown
(*Städte mit geordnetem Magistrat*), numbering 106 in 1890
and 118 in 1880; their average population in 1880 was
8,743, and in 1890, 10,550. They will represent the class of
smaller cities and appear in the table under that heading.

These two groups together may be taken as constituting
the urban population of Hungary. In the forty years
1850–90, they have increased much more rapidly than the
rural remainder. Indeed, in one period (1869–80), which
includes years of severe famine, the rural population actually
declined. In the other periods its rate was subject to great
fluctuations, while the cities progressed at a more uniform
rate. As the periods covered by the percentages in Table
LVII are not of equal length, it is necessary to compute the
percentage increase per annum, thus:

TABLE LVIII.

YEARLY AVERAGE INCREASE.

	Hungary.	131 cities.
1850–57	.63	2.075
1858–69	.98	1.235
1870–80	.11	1.044
1881 90	.68	1.447

[1] The justification of this classification is stated in the census of 1890, Part I.,
p. 66 * (Cf. Table LVII for full title of the census).

It is here shown that the most rapid urban growth took place in the years 1850–7, as is the case in Austria. And while the figures are not at hand to prove it, it may well be surmised that this period of urban expansion began, as in Austria, in 1840–50. Thus the first real impetus to the growth of the capital city Budapest came in 1840;[1] between 1830 and 1840 its population was stationary, so that between 1840 and 1850 its growth was fully 50 per cent., as may be observed in Table LVII, and this is a higher rate than has since obtained. But Budapest's development then was exceptional, and it apparently had little influence on the rate of growth of the seven leading cities (those now exceeding 50,000 population), in which the annual average (geometrical) increase was

1800–20	.72 ca
1820–31	1.96 ca
1831–50	1.21 ca
1850–57	2.446
1857–69	1.617
1869–80	1.878
1880–90	2.239

These figures are not of course entirely trustworthy, but they indicate that the growth of cities, while increasing from year to year, has not reached the high rate attained in 1850–7, which may be attributed in part to political and social causes, but chiefly to the establishment of railway communication between Budapest and the country population.

Considerable interest attaches to the relative rates of increase of large and small cities. In Hungary there is not the slightest doubt that the movement has been toward concentration and centralization. Even France gave no more

[1] Körösi, *Die Hauptstadt Budapest in 1881, Heft I.*

striking example than the following which indicates the
total increase per cent. in 1850–90:

1. Buda-Pest 214.33
2. Seven large cities 120.00
3. Free cities 98.78
4. Small cities 50.07
5. Rural districts 25.10
   HUNGARY... 30.88
6. Urban (cols. 4 and 5).. 73.13

An examination of the table shows that this is the order
of growth in every period, without exception, since 1850.
And as the number of cities is in each case nearly constant,
the evidence is conclusive that places are growing at a rate
proportionate to their size.

But the cities of Hungary are still too small for these indications of concentration to excite alarm. Budapest, the
only city that has reached the 100,000+ class, constitutes
but 3.2 per cent. of the Hungarian population. And the
entire urban population is relatively small, notwithstanding
the inclusion of towns which have a considerable population
residing in extended territory under rural rather than urban
conditions, as shown by

TABLE LIX.

GROWTH OF CITIES IN HUNGARY.

	1800–1808.			1850.			1890.		
	No.	Pop.	Per cent.	No.	Pop.	Per cent.	No.	Pop.	Per cent.
100,000+	0	0	....	1	156,506	1.35	1	491,938	3.23
20,000–100,000.	6	228,000	2.31	12	369,996	3.2	37	1,218,000	8.03
10,000–20,000..	24	300,000	3.04	..	(525,000	4.5)	67	961,520	6.34
Total 10,000+.	30	528,000	5.35	..	(1,050,000	9.1)	105	2,671,458	17.6
Total 2,000+.	..	....	....	..	....	...	435	7,413,387	49.

AUTHORITIES.

As in Table LVII for 1850 and 1890. The cities of 10,000–20,000 are estimated, as it is impossible to distinguish what is urban population in townships the size of those in Hungary. If the
urban population be defined as that resident in towns of 2,000+, Hungary would have, in 1890, a
percentage of 49, which is absurd. The real urban population of Hungary is comprised in the
131 cities of Table LVII, and amounts to 16.1 per cent. of the entire population. The figures
above for 1880–08 are derived from various hand-books of "Staatenkunde."

VII. RUSSIA.

The giant-nations that will struggle for world-supremacy in the twentieth century are the United States, the British Empire and Russia. In population, Russia ranks second, and if the vigor of an army depends upon a numerous peasantry, Russia may lay claim to the first place; for scarcely twelve per cent. of the Russian population dwell in "men-consuming" cities. It is open to doubt, however, whether Russia with its immense numbers of agriculturists, or the United States and Britain, with their centres of enlightenment and business enterprise, would be the more formidable military power.

Russia has made more progress in the manufacturing industries than is commonly supposed. It now imports but a small percentage of its woolen and cotton goods, and in all the fundamental industries except iron and steel is nearly as self-containing as the United States.[1] The factory industries are concentrated mainly in Poland and the region about Moscow, and in those districts a considerable urban population is found, which is rapidly growing. Perhaps the most extreme instance is the Polish city of Lodz, the "Manchester of Russia," which in 1860 had 31,500 inhabitants and in 1897, 314,780, a growth that would be regarded as phenomenal even in America.

But the factory system has to struggle against many disadvantages in Russia. Its great competitor, household or domestic industry, has almost entirely succumbed in the countries of the Western world; but in Russia, the winters are so long and severe that the agricultural population is largely left without work and obliged to follow other pursuits. Most of the peasants carry on manufacturing industry in their homes, but in some of the larger villages and pro-

[1] Cf. *The Industries of Russia* (5 vols., St. Petersburg, 1893), a series of governmental publications for the World's Fair. Translated by John M. Crawford.

vincial cities, they go into factories, which are thus either shut during the summer or kept in operation with a limited number of workmen. It is estimated that "at least half of the urban population are peasants coming and going, seeking and losing occupation."[1]

In 1886, the Russian Empire contained 555,990 settlements, of which 1,281 had municipal institutions. Their aggregate population is taken as the urban population; this mediæval distinction appearing to be substantially equivalent to the statistical limit of 2,000 population.[2] The preliminary results of the census of 1897[3] show the distribution of the urban population to be as follows:

TABLE LX.

	Total population.	In towns.	Percentage of urban pop. in total.
Russia proper	94,215,415	11,830,546	12.5
Poland....................	9,455,943	2,059,340	21.8
Caucasus	9,248,695	996,248	10.8
Siberia....	5,727,090	462,182	8.1
Central Asia..............	7,721,684	932,662	12.1
Total	126,368,827	16,280,978	12.9
Finland	2,527,801	est. [250,100]	10.
The Empire	128,896,628	16,531,000	12.8

Thus it appears that even in the most densely populated province of the Empire (Poland), the urban population constitutes only 21.8 per cent. of the total.

Considering the fact that serfdom was abolished only in 1861, and that the era of industrialism scarcely opened before the seventies, it is to be expected that the growth of the urban population has been comparatively recent. The statistics are scanty and not thoroughly trustworthy, for it was not until February 9, 1897, that a general census was taken of

[1] Crawford, *op. cit.*, iii, 59.

[2] While over 300 of the towns contained less than 2,000 inhabitants, their aggregate population is almost infinitesimal compared with the total. Cf. Tables LXIII, LXI.

[3] For title, see Table LXI.

the Empire, in the modern sense of the word. The earlier statistics of population rest on partial enumerations of males for military and fiscal purposes, combined with the records of births and deaths. Nevertheless, these estimates have some value, as is shown by the fact that the estimated population in 1895 was 129,545,000 as compared with an enumerated population at the beginning of 1897 of 129,000,000.[1]

The growth of population as calculated by the Central Commission in the "Revisions" and subsequent estimates, and the aggregate population of towns as computed by the writer from the best authorities, are shown in

TABLE LXI.

Year.	Authority.	Pop. of Russia.	Cities.	Authority.	Percentage in cities.
1722...	1st revision [1]	14,000,000			
1794...	....	....	2,279,412	Storch	6 5
1796...	5th revision	36,000,000	2,850,926	Herman......	7.
1811 ...	6th revision	41,000,000			
1815...	7th revision	45,000,000			
1825 ...	....	....	3,521,052	v. Olberg	7.
1835...	8th revision	59,000,000			
1838...	Köppen	59,042,866	4,745,632	Köppen	8.75
1856...	Official tables	71,243.616 / 63,862.000 [2]	5,684,000 [2]	v. Olberg. ...	8 96
1870...	Mitteilungen '82 .. / Jannasch	85,038,504 / 85,018,082	9,064,039	Jannasch	10.66
1885...	Annuaire...........	108,787,235	13.947.825	Annuaire.....	12.8
1890...	Kalendar	115,989,443	13,972,643	Kalendar	12.0
1897 ...	P. R.	126,368,827	16,280,978	P. R...... ...	12.9

[1] The several "Revisions" may be found in Schnitzler, *L'Empire des Tsars*, ii, 107. The other authorities mentioned are as follows:

Annuaire Statistique de la Russie, 1884 5. Publication du Comité Central de Statistique, Ministère de l'Intérieur. St. Petersburg, 1887 in Russian and French).

Statistical Tables of the Russian Empire, 1856. (Pub. in Russian, by the Statistical Central Com. Min. of Interior, St. Petersburg , 1858.

German trans. of above by E. v. Olberg, Berlin, 1859.

St. Petersburger Kalendar German).

Statistische und andere wissenschaftliche Mitteilungen aus Russland, 1868-83. St. Petersburg.

P von Köppen, *Russland's Gesammtbevölkerung im Jahre* 1838.

H. Storch, *Hist. statistische Gemälde des russ. Reiches* Riga-Leipzig, 1793 1803. 8 vols.

Thaddäus Bulgarius, *Russland: Statistik*. German trans. by von Brackel. Riga-Leipzig, 1839.

Fr. Fred W. von Reden, *Das Kaiserreich Russland*. Berlin, Posen and Bromberg, 1843.

A. von Buschen, *Bevölkerung des russ. Kaiserreichs*. Gotha, 1862.

Renseignements sur la population de Finlande. Helsingfors, 1869. (By the chief of the Bureau of Statistics.)

Jannasch, in *Zeitschrift des königl. preus. statis. Bureaus*, 1878. p. 283.

Premier Recensement général de la population de l'Empire de Russie, 1897. Livraison 1, pp 27-29. The foregoing figures exclude Finland. In Livraison 2, the urban population was corrected to read 16,504,085.

[2] Exclusive of Poland, Finland and Turkestan.

[1] The provisional results of the 1897 census may be found in *Statesman's Year Book* and *Almanac de Gotha*, 1898, and *J. of St. Soc.* 60: 774-5 (Dec., 1897).

The process of agglomeration in Russia is still slow, even though it has been quickened in the most recent decades. The apparent decline in 1885–90 is, however, likely to be due to some deficiency in the statistics. While Russia has important and rapidly growing " great cities," the rural population also increases so rapidly as to neutralize urban growth. This will appear from the following statistics of population of the thirteen cities that in 1885 ranked as " great cities " (100,-000+); the figures, which are of course little better than estimates, are based chiefly on the authorities of Table LXI :

TABLE LXII.

Year.	Russian Cities.	Percentage increase.	Per cent. of total pop.	Year.	French Cities.	Percentage increase.	Per cent. of total pop.
1815–25 .	827,000	..	1.8	1821.....	1,423,082	..	4.6
1856.....	1,583,300	94	2.2	1856.....	2,494,089	75	6.9
1870.....	2,383,000	50	2.8	1870.....	3,531,701	53	9.8
1885.....	3,541,865	68	3.2	1886.....`	4,190,958	10	12.0
1897.....	2,641,395	31	3.6	1896.....	4,793,491	16	12.4

While the Russian cities have grown rapidly, more so than the French, they have not greatly distanced the rural population, and consequently the part they play in the national life is relatively small. In the period 1885–97 the increase of the great cities was 31, that of Russia 19 per cent., the ratio of the former to the latter being 160 to 100. While this is a somewhat lower rate of concentration than prevails in some other countries, it shows that Russia has entered the circle of " Capitalism." The general result for the century is given in

[1] The 12 principal cities (100,000+) in 1891.

TABLE LXIII.

| | | 1820. | | | 1856. | | | 1885. | |
Towns.	No.	Pop.	Per cent.	No.	Pop.	Per cent.	No.	Pop.	Per cent.
100,000+ ··········	3	595,000	1.4	4	1,123,698	1.6	13	3,541,865	3.2
20,000–100,000 ······	17	493,000	1.0	42	1,407,266	1.9	116	4,301,508	4.0
10,000–20,000 ·· ····	45	571,000	1.39	41	250,178	1.8	164	2,293,344	2.1
Total 10,000+····	65	1,659,000	3.7	140	3,781,142	5.3	293	10,136,717	9.3
2,000–10,000 ·········	··	········	···	···	·········	···	656	3,215,878	3.0
Total 2,000+·····	··	·········	···	···	·········	···	949	13,352,595	12.3
Russia···········	··	45,000,000	100	···	71,200,000	100	···	108,800,000	100

So far as these figures have value, they indicate that the tendency in Russia is towards the growth of middle-sized cities (20,000–100,000) rather than great cities. But too much weight should not be attached to so small percentages.[1]

VIII. SWEDEN.

The following percentages, being the proportion of the Swedish population residing, at the various censuses, in the 19 cities that had more than 10,000 inhabitants each in 1890, show that the movement toward the cities did not begin until about 1850:

1805	6.3
1810	6.1
1820	6.4
1830	6.4
1840	6.3
1850	6.7
1860	7.6
1870	9.05
1880	10.7
1890	13.7

The same inference may be made from Table LXIV, where the term urban is used in the legal sense, over 40 "towns" having in 1890 less than 2,000 inhabitants. Stock-

[1] According to the preliminary results of the census of 1897, Russia contained 19 cities of the first class (100,000+), with an aggregate population of 5,718,738, or 4.43 per cent. of the total population of the Empire (exclusive of Finland).

holm since 1850 has been gaining on the rest of the population.

TABLE LXIV.

Year.	Population.	Rural.	Urban.	Proportion Rural.	Proportion Urban.	No. of Towns.	Stockholm Percentage.
1805....	2,412,772	2,380,715	232,057	90.39	9.61	86	3.01
1810....	2,377,851	2,155,116	222,735	90.63	9.37	86	2.75
1815....	2,465,066	2,223,894	241,172	90.18	9.82	..	2.96
1820....	2,584,690	2,330,798	253,892	90.18	9.82	86	2.93
1830....	2,888,082	2,607,124	280,958	90.27	9.73	..	2.79
1840....	3,138,887	2,835,204	303,683	90.33	9.67	..	2.68
1850....	3,482,541	3,131.463	351,078	89.91	10.09	..	2.67
1860....	3,859,728	3,425.209	434,519	88.74	11.26	..	2.90
1870....	4,168,525	3,628,876	539,649	87.05	12.95	..	3.27
1880....	4,565,668	3,875,237	690,431	84.88	15.12	90	3 70
1890....	4,784,981	3,885,283	899,698	81.20	18.80	92	5.15

It is worth while noting that the urban population failed to maintain its own for several decades early in the century, and that Stockholm itself participated in the relative decline. Since 1840, the urban population has had a rapid growth, as Stockholm has had since 1850.

The difference between the legal or official urban population, and the statistical one is brought out in the following table:

TABLE LXV.[1]

	1805. No.	1805. Pop.	1805. Per cent. of total.	1850. No.	1850. Pop.	1850. Per cent. of total.	1890. No.	1890. Pop.	1890. Per cent. of total.
100,000+	0	......	..	0	......	..	2	351,111	7.3
20,000-100,000	1	72,652	3.0	2	119,154	3 4	6	167.348	3.5
10,000-20,000	2	23,043	0.9	3	44,100	1.3	11	142.638	2.9
Total 10,000+	3	95,695	3.9	5	163,254	4.7	19	661,097	13.74
2,000-10,000	20	74,371	3.1	..	......	..	41	199,358	4.21
Total 2,000+........	23	170,066	7.0				60	860,455	18.
" urban (legal)..	86	232,057	9.6				92	899,698	18.8

[1] Most of the necessary data for the study of the subject may be found in the census of 1890; *Bidrag till Sveriges officiele Statistik. Befolknings-Statistik. Ny följd I.*, 2, etc.

IX. NORWAY.

The urban and rural growth in Norway appears in the following decimal rates of increase : [1]

TABLE LXVI.

	Rural.	Urban.	Christiania.	Proportion of Urban in 100 inhabitants.	
1801-15	0 3	1.1	12.3	1801	10.7
1815-25	17.7	25.9	52.8	1815	10.7
1825-35	13.7	13.0	32.2	1825	11.3
1835-45	9.9	21 7	35.8	1835	11.3
1845-55	10.5	24.1	25.0	1845	12.3
1855-65	11.6	31.0	39.0	1855	13.6
1865-75	3.2	24.8	36.0	1865	15.6
1875-91	3.1	42.6	96.0 [2]	1875	18.3
				1891	23.7
1801-91	93.4	406.7	1170.0		

TABLE LXVII.

Year.	Norway.	Rural.	Urban.	Christiania.
1801	883,038	789.469	93,569	11,923
1815	886,374	791,741	94,633	13,386
1825	1,051,318	932,219	119,099	20,759
1835	1,194,827	1,060,282	134,545	24,445
1845	1,328,471	1,164,745	163,726	33,177
1855	1,490,047	1,286,782	203,265	41,266
1865	1,701,756	1,435,464	266,292	57,382
1875	1,813,424	1,481,026	332,398	76,866
1891	2,000,917	1,526,788	474,129	151,239 [2]

Thus even in agricultural Norway the cities are growing rapidly, while the rural population has in the last quarter-century come almost to a standstill. The concentration since 1865 has been enormous. That the urban growth is

---

[1] Calculated on statistics given in *Statistik Aarbog for Kongeriget Norge*, 1893. The distinction between urban and rural is still the mediaeval one; in 1801 out of an " urban " population of 93,569, but 28.854 lived in towns of 10,000 or more, and 70,472 in towns of at least 2,000. In 1890, however, out of an urban population of 474,129, all but 30,570 lived in towns of 2,000 and more.

[2] Due to annexation of suburbs.

due mainly to the larger towns and cities, the following
table will demonstrate:

TABLE LXVIII.[1]

	1801.			1845.			1891.		
	No.	Pop.	Per cent.	No.	Pop.	Per cent.	No.	Pop.	Per cent.
100,000+	0	.....	...	0	.....	...	1	151,239	7.56
20,000–100,000 ..	0	.....	...	2	55,518	4.2	4	124,335	6.22
10,000–20,000 ...	2	28,854	3.27	1	14,778	1.1	5	58,123	2.90
2,000–10,000	10	41,618	4.7	17	68,154	5.1	24	109,862	5.49
Under 2,000	40	23,097	2.7	36	25,276	1.8	27	30,570	1.53
Total urban...	52	93,569	10.7	56	163,726	12.3	61	474,129	23.70
2,000+	12	70,472	7.9	20	138,450	10.4	34	443,559	22.17
10,000+	2	28,854	3.27	3	70,296	5.3	10	333,697	16.68

X. DENMARK.

The growth of the various categories of population is dis-
played in the following table. In order to show the effect
on classification of the modern growth of suburbs, two columns are given for the urban and rural classes; in the first
column the urban population includes Copenhagen with all
its suburbs and also the *Handelsplader* (seaports); in the
second column the *Handelsplader* are included in the rural
population and also the suburbs of Copenhagen, except
Frederiksburg, which is included in "Provincial towns."

TABLE LXIX.

AVERAGE ANNUAL INCREASE IN 10,000 OF MEAN POPULATION.[2]

	1834–40.		1850–60.		1870–80.		1880–90.		Population 1890.	
Denmark	84	84	111	111	102	102	99	99	2,172,380	
Rural	85	86	92	97	68	77	21	38	1,434,230	1,508,814
Urban	81	79	181	162	197	180	273	255	738,150	663,566
Copenhagen	51	46	156	126	247	209	323	291	375,719	312,859
Provincial towns.	111	112	201	192	155	157	223	224	362,431	350,707

[1] For index to the Norwegian censuses, cf. *Fortegnelse over Norges officielle
Statistik mit Flere Statistike Vaerker*, 1828–30. June, 1889. The following
have been most used: *Norges officielle Statistik, Aeldre Raekke C*, No. 1 (censuses of 1865 and 1875, and also of 1801–25; *Folkemaengdens Bevaegelse i
Aarene* 1856–65. Christiania, 1868–90.

[2] Cf. Danish censuses of 1890 and 1840.

From this it appears that early in the century suburban growth was relatively unimportant; the inclusion or exclusion of suburbs does not greatly effect the rural or urban rate, as may be seen by comparing the town columns for the period 1834–40. But in 1880–90, it makes a considerable difference where the suburbs are placed; without them, Copenhagen has an annual increase of 2.91 per cent., with them 3.23.

In the period of 1834–40, the rural increase was larger than the urban, which was depressed by the low rate for Copenhagen; the other towns and cities had the maximum rate. In 1850–60 the urban rate exceeded the rural, but the provincial towns still lead Copenhagen. In 1870–80 and 1880–90 there has been a great falling-off in the rural rate of growth, while the urban rate has been correspondingly increased, and Copenhagen has forged way ahead of the other cities. Additional information necessary to this study is given in Tables LXX, LXXI, LXXII.

TABLE LXX.

	Denmark.	Urban population. Actual	% of total.	Copenhagen = per cent of total .
1801	929,000	194,431	20.9	10.9
1834	1,223,797	251,502	20.5	9.7
1840	1,289,075	266,822	20.7	9.6
1860	1,608,362	381,662	23.7	10.4
1870	1,784,741	450,241	25.2	11.5
1880	1,969,039	563,930	28.6	13.9
1890	2,172,380	738,150	34.0	17.3

TABLE LXXI.

NUMBER OF TOWNS AND PROPORTION OF URBAN POPULATION IN EACH CLASS.

	1801.	%	1840.	%	1860.	%	1880.	%	1890.	%
Copenhagen	1	51.9	1	46.1	1	44.0	1	48.5	1	50.9
10,000–40,000	0	0	0	0	3	14.1	5	15.2	7	18.8
2,000–10,000	9	18.5	24	34.8	31	32.6	39	28.8	42	25.6
Under 2,000	62	29.6	46	19.1	39	9.3	29	7.5	23	4.8
Total	72	100.0	71	100.0	74	100.0	74	100.0	73	100.0

TABLE LXXII.

	1801.			1840.			1890.	
100,000+	1	100,975	10.9	1	123,123	9.6	1	375,719	17.3
20,000–100,000	0	......	...	0	......	..	2	63,574	2.9
10,000–20,000	0	......	...	0	......	..	5	74,528	3.4
Total 10,000+	1	100,000	10.9	1	123,123	9.6	8	513,821	23.6
Total 2,000+	10	136,967	14.8	25	215,962	16.8	50	702,679	32.4
Total " Urban "....	..	194,431	20.9	..	266,822	20.7	..	738,150	34.0

AUTHORITIES.

The principal source of information for all the tables is the Danish census of 1890: *Danmarks Statistik. Statistik Tabelvaerk, fjerde Raekke, Litra A*, Nr 8a, *Hovedresultaterne af Folketaellingen i Kongeriget Danmark den 1ste Feb., 1890.* Udgivet of det statistiske Bureau, Kjobenhavn, 1894. The census of 1840 (*Tabelvaerk, Siette Haefte*) has also been used to a considerable extent.

IX. THE NETHERLANDS.

The tendency toward agglomeration in the Netherlands is first noticeable about 1850; up to that time the rural population increased more rapidly than the urban. City growth has increased since 1850, and in the last decade was unprecedented, as shown in

TABLE LXXIII.

	Increase of population from 1829.[1]			Increase per 10,000 by decades.[3]			
	Total.	Urban.[2]	Rural.	General.	Urban.[4]	Rural.	Ratio of urban to general increase.
1829....	100.	100.	100.				
1839....	109.46	109.02	100.60	945	908	962	95
1849....	116.97	115.42	117.50	686	591	728	86
1859....	126.62	126.84	126.54	825	995	751	120
1869....	136.97	140.40	135.76	817	947	761	116
1879....	153.54	167.52	148.69	1210	1725	979	143
1889....	172.62	209.82	159.73	1240	2400		193

[1] *Overzicht von de Uitkomsten bewerkt door de Centrale Commissie voor de Statistik,* 1893.

[2] As urban is regarded the population at each census of the 21 *Gemeenten* (communes) whose population exceeded 20,000 in 1889.

[3] *Uitkomsten der zerde tienjarige Volkstelling in het Konigrijk der Nederlanden,* 31 Dec., 1879. 's. Gravenhage, 1881; *Résumé statistique pour la Royaume des Pays Bas,* 1850–83, published by La Société de Statistique des Pays-Bas, Le Haye, 1884.

[4] As urban is here regarded the population of 34 communes which severally had 10,000+ population in 1859.

The rapid increase in the urban population since 1869 is very largely due to the growth of the great cities, Amsterdam, Rotterdam and The Hague. Hence, in the Netherlands there exists a considerable concentration of the agglomerated population. The changes that have taken place in the distribution of population are shown in Table LXXIV. A difficulty with Dutch urban statistics is that they usually adopt as the unit the township (*Gemeente*), which includes a considerable rural population, owing to its territorial extent. The difference between the township population ànd the true urban population is brought out in the last two columns of

TABLE LXXIV.

POPULATION OF THE CITIES.

	1795.	1829.	1849.	1889.	1889.
100,000+	217,024	202,364	274,035	766,728	750,763
20,000–100,000 .	242,910	324,168	438,980	644,856	565,700
10,000–20,000 ..	94,986	151,517	221,919	527,899	187,400
Total 10,000+.	554,920	678,046	884,938	1,939,483	1,503,900
Holland	1,880,463	2,613,487	3,056,879	4,511,415	4,474,461

NUMBER OF CITIES AND PERCENTAGES IN TOTAL POPULATION.

100,000+	1	11.5	1	7.7	1	7.3	3	17.0	3	16.6
20,000–100,000 .	9	13.0	9	12.4	11	14.4	18	14.3	16	12.7
10,000–20,000 ..	7	5.0	11	5.9	16	7.3	..	11.7	15	4.2
Total 10,000....	17	29.5	21	26.0	28	29.0	..	43.0	33	33.5

Sources.—Compiled from the authorities of Table LXIII, except the last column, which is based on Supan for the cities, and for Holland the figures denote the " actually present " population.

XII. BELGIUM.

In Belgium the line between urban and rural population is drawn at 5,000. The growth of the urban population since 1846 is shown in

TABLE LXXV.[1]

	Belgium.	Rural.	No. of places.	Urban. Population.	Per cent. of total.
1846	4,337,196	2,921,329	112	1,415,867	32.6
1856	4,529,461	2,952,079	118	1,577,382	34.8
1866	4,827,833	3,046,460	131	1,781,373	36.9
1880	5,520,009	3,143,232	166	2,376,777	43.1
1890	6,069,321	3,174,627	191	2,894,694	47.7

In Belgium the tendency toward agglomeration has existed from the earliest date of the records, but it is more marked in recent years. The urban population, moreover, is largely concentrated in a few great cities and their suburbs. Table LXXVI indicates the importance of the suburbs of Brussels and Antwerp in any classification of the urban population. While the totals remain about the same, the distribution between large and small cities is vastly different when the suburbs of Brussels, Antwerp and Ghent are separately treated:

TABLE LXXVI.

	1802–15. Estimates.		1846. Exclusive of suburbs.		Inclusive of suburbs.		1890. Exclusive of suburbs.		Inclusive of suburbs.
Brussels........		66,297		123,874		188,458		176,138	465,517
Antwerp		56,318		88,487		97,948		224,012	268,397
Ghent..........		55,161		102,297		105,894		148,729	171,927
100,000+		0	2	226,851	2	294,352	2	696,530	..	1,053,591
20,000–100,000 ..	5	261,408	11	415,875	11	425,336	25	826,210	..	525,684
10,000–20,000 ...	11	145,135	18	234,224	14	181,131	44	573,687	..	526,251
Total 10,000+.	16	406,543	3·	876,950	27	900,819	73	2,096,436	61	2,105,436

PERCENTAGE OF POPULATION OF BELGIUM.

100,000+	0	5.2	6.8	11.4	17.4
20,000–100,000 ..	8.7	9.6	9.8	13.7	8.7
10,000–20,000 ...	4.8	5.4	4.2	9.4	8.7
Total 10,000+.	13.5	20.2	20.8	34.5	34.8

SOURCES—*Récensement de 1890*, and Supan. For 1880 the estimates are compiled from Hassel, 1809: the population of Belgium was then estimated at 3,411,082, but it included parts of Luxemburg, and Limburg afterward added to Holland; without them the population may be roughly estimated at 3,000,000.

[1] *Statistique de la Belgique, Récensement général du 31 Dec., 1890, Tome I.*, p. XV. Brussels, 1893. For 1846 and 1856 the population is *de fait*; for 1866, 1880, 1890 *de droit*.

XIII. SWITZERLAND.

Even in the little agricultural republic there has been in the present century a very noticeable tendency toward agglomeration. Compared with the entire population, the aggregate population at each census of the fifteen principal towns of 1888 (*i. e.*, those of 10,000+) has increased very rapidly:

	Switzerland.	Percentage in 15 towns.
1850	2,392,740	9.4
1860	2,510,494	11.4
1870	2,655,001	12.8
1880	2,831,787	14.5
1888	2,917,754	16.5

The periods 1850–60 and 1880–1888 show large gains for the towns. The urban growth is indeed for the most part in the larger towns, as appears from

TABLE LXXVII.

	1822.			1850.			1888.		
	No.	Pop.	Per cent. of total.	No.	Pop.	Per cent. of total.	No.	Pop.	Per cent. of total,
20,000–100,000	1	24,600	1.3	4	125,080	5.2	8	384,360	13.2
10,000–20,000	4	54,300	3.0	4	51,048	2.1	7	96,028	3.3
Total 10,000+	5	78,900	4.3	8	176,128	7.3	15	480,388	16.5
Switzerland		1,855,300							
Total 5,000+	11	120,000	6.5	18	301,538	12.7	52	726,060	24.7

SOURCES—*Schweizerische Statistik, Die Ergebnisse der Eidgenössischen Volkszählung vom 1 Dez. 1888.* (Esp. *Lieferungen* 84, 88, 97); M. Wirth, *Statistik der Schweiz*, Zürich 1871–3; S. Franscini, *Neue Statistik der Schweiz*, Bern, 1848; Hassel, 1822.

XIV. ITALY.

Like Germany, Italy is a new nation with few statistics of the national dominion, and it is very difficult to obtain statistics concerning the urban population prior to 1861. No census has been taken since 1881.

In Italy the mass of the population dwells in small towns; even the agriculturists dwell in villages and go out to their work in the fields.   The agglomerated population is therefore comparatively large.   Hence, it is customary in Italy to reckon with the urban population only the *centri* of 6,000 or more inhabitants; while the smaller *centri*, the *casali* or villages, and the scattered population are all combined in the rural population.   The percentages since 1861 were as follows:

TABLE LXXVIII.[1]

		1861.	1871.	1881.
Urban	..Centri of 6,000+	25.17	24.93	27.02
Rural	{ Centri of 6,000—..............	42.84	49.37	45.68
	{ Scattered pop.................	31.99	25.70	27.30
		100.	100.	100.

Italy's urban percentage therefore appears to be about 25, which is also the percentage of population dwelling in *capoluoghi*, or head communes of provinces and districts (*circondari*) in 1881—7,082,163 in a total population of 28,459,628. The urban population is apparently increasing but slowly; in the larger cities however there is a constant growth:

TABLE LXXIX.

AGGLOMERATED POPULATION.

Towns.	1871.	1881.
Under 2,000..	43.59	40.25
2,000–6,000	22.86	22.59
6,000–8,000	5.12	5.30
8,000–20,000	13.13	13.56
20,000–100,000	7.23	8.76
100,000+	8.07	9.54
	100.00	100.00

And throughout the century there can be traced a tendency to concentrate in the great cities:

[1] *Censimento della Populazione del Regno d' Italia al 31 dicembre*, 1881; same 1871 and 1861.

TABLE LXXX.[1]

NUMBER AND POPULATION OF ITALIAN CITIES.

	1800.		1847-8.		1881.	
Italy	18,124,000	100.	23,617,000	100.	29,459,628	100.
100,000 + ...	(4 800,000	4.4)	(8 1,425,000	6.)	9 1,974,394	6.9
20,000–100,000 ...	.. ..	....	.. ..	..	57 1,811,188	6.4
10,000–20,000	.. ..	....	.. ..	..	149 2,084,806	7.3
Total 10,000 +....	.. ..	....	.. ..	..	215 5,870,388	20.6
Total 2,000 + ...	.. ..	....	.. ..	..	 12,358,430	43.43

XV. OTHER EUROPEAN COUNTRIES.

The more important countries of Europe have been treated at length, but, in order to complete the study, statistical tables setting forth the development of urban populations in the remaining European countries are appended. Trustworthy data are usually lacking for these countries except in recent years, but the best authorities have been relied upon.

TABLE LXXXI. SPAIN.

	1800-10.	1820 ca.	1857.	Increase 1800-57.	1887.	Increase 1857 87.
Spain	10,836,000	11,411,924	15,464,430	42.5	17,565,632	13.6
15 cities..............	888,850	....	1,340,326	50.9	1,928,691	43.
5 great cities	495,332	....	778,214	56.5	1,190,725	53.
Madrid	156,670	167,607	281,170	79.0	470,283	62.

	1820 ca.			1857.			1887.		
	No.	Pop.	% of total.	No.	Pop.	% of total.	No.	Pop.	% of total.
Total 100,000 +..........	1	167,607	1.45	4	683,921	4.4	5	1,190,725	6.8
20,000–100,000	24	945,270	8.3	23	805,767	5.2	56	1,975,423	112.
20,000 + ...	25	1,112,877	9.75	27	1,489,688	9.6	61	3,166,148	18.
10,000–20,000 (estimated)	(36	476,530)	....	72	(1,080,000)	...	140	(2,100,000)	
10,000 + (estimated)......	61	(1,600,000	14.)	99	(2,570,000	16.2)	201	(5,200,000	29.6)

NOTE.—The five great cities are Madrid, Barcelona, Valencia, Sevilla, Malaga. The fifteen cities include these five and ten others exceeding 50,000 in population in 1887. The authority for 1800-10 is Hassel 1809; for 1820, Hassel 1823; for 1857, *Censo de la Poblacion de España, on 21 de Mayo de 1857*, and Kolb, 1868; for 1887, the Census. The statistics relate to the commune or township, which in Spain is exceedingly large and contains a rural population. The estimates for towns 10,000-20,000 are arithmetical (multiplying 15,000 by 72 and 140); but they probably approximate actual conditions. According to the *Nomenclator de Espagna*, 1888, the urban population was 4,851,903, and the rural 12,713,369, or 27.89 and 72.11 per cent. respectively.

[1] Estimates are enclosed in parentheses.

TABLE LXXXII. PORTUGAL.

	1801.	1857.	Increase per cent.	1878.	Increase per cent.	1890.	Increase per cent.
Portugal	3,661,809	3,908,861	6.5	4,550,699	16.4	5,082,247	11.1
Eight cities ...	115,600	195,600	64.0	208,099	6.2	253,050	12.6
Lisbon	350,000	275,286	21.4a	246,343	10.5a	307,661	12.4

	No.	Pop.	% of total.	No.	Pop.	1857. % of total.	No.	Pop.	% of total.
100,000+	1	350,000	9.5	1	275,286	7.2	2	447,517	8.8
20,000–100,000	1	30,000	.8	3	140,000	3.5	1	23,089	.4
10,000—20,000	7	85,600	2.4	6	85,600	2.2	12	178,329	3.5
10,000+	9	465,600	12.7	10	500,800	12.9	15	648,935	12.7

a = decrease.

NOTE.—The eight cities are Oporto, Braga, Funchal, Coimbra, Setubal, Evora, Angra, Elvas, being the large cities of 1800. As regards the sources, the data for 1890 are from the *Statesman's Year Book*, 1897; for 1878, from *Censo No. 1 de Janeiro*, 1878, *Populacao*, Lisbon, 1881; for 1801 and 1857 the population of Portugal is given in Block, *Bevölkerung Spaniens und Portugals* (1861), p. 53, while the population of the cities in 1800 is from Hassel, 1809, and other early hand-books; in 1857, from Kolb, 1860, etc. Additional references are Balbi, *Essai Statistique sur le Royaume de Portugal*, 2 vols., Paris, 1822; Minutoli, *Portugal und seine Colonien im Jahre* 1854, 2 vols., Stuttgart, 1855. The earlier figures are regarded as very inaccurate.

TABLE LXXXIII. GREECE.

	1852. Pop.	% of total	1879. No.	Pop.	%	1889. No.	Pop.	%
Greece	1,002,112	..	..	1,979,147	..	..	2,187,208	..
Athens	31,125	3.1	1	63,374	3.2	1	107,251	4.9
Other cities of 20,000+	......	..	3	67,794	3.4	3	89,960	4.1
Other cities of 10,000–20,000.	......	..	4	55,991	2.8	8	109,128	5.0
Total 10,000+	......	..	8	187,159	9.5	12	306,339	14.0

SOURCES—For 1879, *Almanach de Gotha*, 1885; the figures include parts of Thessaly annexed in 1881. For 1889, Supan. For 1852, Kolb, 1860.

TABLE LXXXIV. TURKEY IN EUROPE.

		1885.	
	No.	Population.	Per cent. of total.
Turkey	..	4,786,645	100.
Constantinople.........................	..	873,565	18.3
Salonica	..	150,000	3.1
Cities 20,000–100,000	4	166,000	3.5
Cities 20,000+	6	1,189,600	24.9

SOURCES.—Census of 1885, in *Statesman's Year Book* for 1897, p. 1018. The territory of Turkey has been so frequently altered that not even the old estimates can be given for comparison. Constantinople is said to have had a population of 597,600 (Hassel, 1823) at the beginning of the century, and 700,000 at its middle (Kolb, 1860). It has apparently not gained in population in recent years, for so late as 1885 the *Almanach de Gotha* credited it with only 6–700,000.

TABLE LXXXV. BOSNIA AND HERZEGOWINA.

	Census, May 4, 1885.	
Entire country	1,336,091	
Sarajewo	26,268	1.90
Mostar	12,665	.95
Banjaluka	11,357	.95
Cities 10,000+ 3	50,290	3.8%

SOURCE.—Von Asböth, *Bosnia und Herzegowina*, Wien, 1888.

TABLE LXXXVI. SERVIA.

	1800–10.		1854.		1874.[1]			1890.	
	Pop.	%	Pop.	%	Pop.	%	No.	Pop.	%
Servia	960,000	100.	985,000	100.	1,353,890	100.	..	2,161,961	100.
Belgrade	30,000	3.1	16,723	1.7	27,605	2.0	1	54,249	2.5
Cities 2,000–20,000.							4	55,812	2.6
Total 10,000+ ..							5	110,061	5.1
" 2,000+ ..							104	286,466	13.25

SOURCE.—*Statistique du Royaume de Serbie*, Belgrade, 1892–3.

Servian communes are unusually large (38.2 sq. km. on the average), but in this table only the agglomerated population is counted. If the unit taken were the commune instead of the dwelling-center, the result would be considerably different (1890):

	No.	Pop.	Per cent.
Total 10,000+	7	131,534	6.1
" 2,000	277	787,492	36.5

The statistics of 1800–10, from Hassel, 1809, are little more than guesses, but, even when discounted, show a large city population.

TABLE LXXXVII. BULGARIA.[1]

	1850.	1888.	
Entire country	......	3,154,375	100.0
Philoppel	40,000	33,032	1.0
Sofia	30,000	30,428	1.0
Other cities 20,000+	......	4– 96,504	3.1
Cities 10,000–20,000	......	15–189,203	6.0
Total 10,000	......	21–349,167	11.1

[1] Including East Roumelia. The authority is *Résultats du Récensement de la Population*, 1888 (Sofia, 1888) and Supan (*Ortsstatistik*), p. 73–5; for 1850, Kolb 1860. According to estimates at the first of the century, Sofia, the capital, had a population of 46,000 (Hassel 1809). But recently Sofia has grown rapidly and at the census of 1893 had a population of 47,000 (*St. Yr. Bk.*, 1897, p. 1034).

TABLE LXXXVIII. ROUMANIA.

	1800-10.		1859-60.			1889-90.	
Roumania..........	1,370,500	..	4,424,961	..	..	5,038,342	..
Bucharest	42,000	3.1	100,000	2.4	..	220,000	4.4
20,000-100,000	......	..	....	..	8	316,152	6.3
10,000-20,000	......	..	....	..	13	174,385	3.5
Total 10,000+....	......	..	....	..	22	710,500	14.2
Total "urban" (legal definition)						885,700	17.6

AUTHORITIES.—For 1800-10, Hassel 1809; for 1859-60, *Almanach de Gotha;* for 1889-90,
Supan, except Bucharest, which was returned at 194,633. This inaccuracy shows that the
attempt in 1890 to repair the defects of 1889 were unsuccessful. The census of 1859-60 is also of
doubtful value. The earlier figures are, of course, only estimates. It should be added that the
unit of city population is the territorial subdivision.

XVI. ASIATIC COUNTRIES.

Statistics of Asiatic Russia have already been presented.
Additional statistics for this ancient grand division are not
worth much space on account of the untrustworthiness of
mere estimates.   The modern periodical census so familiar
in the Western world has scarcely been introduced in Asia.
Even progressive Japan has not thoroughly learned the art
of numbering the people.   Hence the only really valuable
data for present purposes are in the English census of India.

§ 1. *Asiatic Turkey* covers a vast extent of territory and
contains numerous cities.   But only the larger cities are
known to the statisticians, and these imperfectly.   The estimated population in 1885 :

TABLE LXXXIX.[1]

	Population.	Per cent.
Entire country	21,608,000	100.
Cities 100,000+ (4).......................	700,000	3.2
17 cities, 25,000-100,000	691,000	3.2
21 cities, 25,000+.......................	1,391,000	6.4

Asiatic Turkey includes Asia Minor, Armenia and Khur-
distan, Mesopotamia, Syria and Arabia.   The four great
cities are Smyrna (200,000), Damascus (200,000), Bagdad

[1] *Statesman's Year Book,* 1894.

(180,000), Aleppo (120,000).   No statistics of growth can
be given, beyond noting that in 1823 Hassel published
these estimates: Damascus, 130,000; Bagdad, 96,000.   The
Oriental cities are, it appears, not stationary in population.

§ 2. *Persia.*—The latest estimates of the population of
Persia are as follows: [1]

TABLE XC.

	Population.	Percentages.
Inhabitants of cities	1,963,800	25.6
Wandering tribes.............................	1,909,800	24.9
Villages and country districts..................	3,780,000	49.5
Total.................................	7,653,600	100.0
Teheran	210,000 }	5.1
Tabriz	180,000 }	
Cities 25,000–100,000 (11)	444,000	5.7

§ 3. *British India.*—The official statistics at the present time
can be compared in accuracy and trustworthiness with those
of the Western nations.   And they are especially instructive
as presenting the distribution of population in a country
which is as densely populated as Europe, and has therefore
emerged from the barbaric state and even attained a considerable degree of civilization.   But the industrial organization of India is totally different from the European.   Industry
in India is mainly carried on in local, autonomous and self-
sufficing communities.   Between these communities there is
little commerce, for each devotes nearly its entire population
to supplying its own wants.[2]   This is essentially true of the

---

[1] *St. Yr. Bk.*, 1897, 811.

[2] *The Census of 1891* (*General Report*, p. 94), shows that nine-tenths of the
population are engaged in local industries:

	Percentage:	
	Total pop.	Rural pop.
Engaged in primitive occupations	84.84	88.26
Engaged in supplementary (semi-rural)	5.47	0.
Engaged in other	9.69	11.74
	100	100

rural population, amounting to nearly nine-tenths of the whole; [1]

TABLE XCI.

| | Total pop. | Urban population. | | Percentage of urban pop. in towns of | | |
		Actual.	Per cent. of total pop.	50,000 +	10,000- 50,000.	Under 10,000.
Bengal	71,346,987	3,443,876	4.82	44	46	10
Bombay	18,901,123	3,502,678	18.51	43	35	22
Madras	35,630,440	3,406,105	9.56	29	46	25
N.-W. Provinces	46,905,085	5,314,328	11.33	..	..	..
Other Provinces	48,389,317	4,724,142	9.80	..	..	..
Total Provinces	221,172,952	20,391,139	9.22	..	..	..
Feudatory States	66,050,479	6,860,047	10.38	..	..	..
Total India	287,223,431	27,251,176	9.48	35	36	29

The definition of a town in this table is not a statistical one, as there are many towns included whose population is under 2,000, and some villages excluded whose population exceeds 20,000. The census regards as "towns" all places "established as municipalities or brought under similar regulations for police and sanitary purposes," and secondly, all places wherein at least one-half of the population is non-agricultural; in the latter case the numerical standard of 5,000 was prescribed.[2] As regards the aggregate results, the two "tests" of urban population are tantamount to a statistical limit of 5,000, as will appear later. (Table XCII.)

While, then, nine-tenths of the people of British India are rural, and dwell in village communities, it might be expected that the introduction of railways would have developed a considerable migratory movement. But it is said that at least four-fifths of the people in the villages belong to the classes that composed the original village community;[3] and the new-comers occupy an inferior position. India's economic organization is therefore of an antiquated character, such as prevailed in Europe two or more centuries ago, and the distribution of the population bears about the same antiquated relation to that of the present Western world, as will appear from Table XCII:

[1] *Op. cit.*, p. 43, and appendix, p. xv.　　[2] *Op. cit.*, p. 42.　　[3] *Op. cit.*, p. 48.

TABLE XCII.

Places of	Towns and cities.		Villages.		Total.		Per cent of population of British India.
	Number.	Population.	Number.	Population.	Number.	Population.	
100,000+	30	6,173,123	0	....	30	6,173,123	2.1
20,000–100,000	197	7,747,288	17	314,181	214	8,061,469	2.8
10,000–20,000	407	5,487,983	109	1,455,214	516	6,943,197	2.4
Total 10,000+	634	19,408,394	126	1,769,395	760	21,177,789	7.3
3,000–10,000	1,197	7,369,667	....	16,738,260	....	24,107,927	8.4
Under 3,000	204	437,259	....	241,306,680	....	241,743,939	84.2
Unclassed	....	35,856	....	20,478	....	56,334	0.0
Not registered	....	.....	....	137,442	....	137,442	0.1
British India	2,035	27,251,176	713,924	259,972,225	715,959	287,223,431	100.
Total 5,000+	....	.....	....	.....	....	31,226,627	9.0
" 2,000+	....	.....	....	.....	....	64,399,332	22.4

NOTE.—Compiled from Tables in the 1891 *Census*, p. 49, and Appendix, iv.   On the former page, the total of villages 20,000+ is erroneously printed 314,481.

It would be interesting to know whether a tendency toward concentration of population in India has yet manifested itself. The following statistics indicate the rate of increase between 1881 and 1891, and answer the question in the affirmative:

TABLE XCIII.[1]

CLASSES OF CITIES.		PRINCIPAL CITIES.	
100,000+	10.58	Bombay	6.28
75,000—	6.54	Calcutta	8.25
50,000—	13.60	Madras	11.50
35,000—	9.48	Haidrabad	16.92
20,000—	11.58	Lucknow	4.49
10,000—	10.66	Benares	2 19
5,000—	7.54	Delhi	11.06
3,000—	1.54		
Under 3,000	.86		
Total	9.40		

The larger cities are evidently growing considerably more rapidly than the smaller places. The variations among the groups of large cities is undoubtedly due to the character of the towns,—whether commercial and manufacturing, or military or religious centres. This is shown in the second column where the half dozen principal cities are named. Benares is purely a religious centre of ancient renown, and is nearly stationary in population. Lucknow and Haidrabad are capitals of native states, but the latter has a large increase. The slow growth of Bombay and Calcutta, the great commercial centres, is explained by an overflow to the suburbs as in the case of London. As a general rule the largest increase is shown[2] to have taken place in the case of the industrial cities, *e. g.*, Hubli, 43.4; Karachi, 43.01; Ajmer, 41.26. The only military station or capital to approach such a rate is Rawal Pindi, 39.30. Many of the feudatory state capitals show an actual decrease, and nearly all of them are on the wane.

[1] *Op. cit.*, 79, 81.   [2] *Op. cit.*, p. 81.

An attempt has been made to discover the relative rates of increase of the population in the larger provinces and their chief cities, but no valuable results have been obtained. It is difficult to get any data earlier than 1871-2, the date of the first general census in India, and the frequent annexation of new territory, together with the prevalence of local famines or diseases, has broken in upon any uniformity that might otherwise have been discovered. The results obtained follow:

TABLE XCIV.[1]

PERCENTAGE OF INCREASE (+) OR DECREASE (—).

	1850-71.	1871-81.	1881-91.
Bombay	19.	18.	14.
Four chief cities [2]	—1.	25.	8.8
Northwest Provinces	29.	6.2	4.6
Six chief cities [3]	8.6	24.3	10.3
Bengal		—.165	+6.7
Calcutta,[4] Patna		—.826	+8.
Madras		—1.5	15.
Madras city		3.0	12.
Punjab		7.	10.7
Three chief cities [5]		24.	5.
Oude		1.3	11.
Lucknow		—8.2	4.5

In almost every instance there is one period in which the province had the larger increase and another period in which the cities grew more rapidly. During the last decade, the cities fell behind in Madras, Bombay, Punjab, and Oude, while they surpassed the general rate of growth in the Northwest Provinces, Bengal, and the feudatory state,

---

[1] The authorities are the *Census of 1891*, the *Census of England*, 1871, iv, 294, and, for 1850, Kolb, 1860, and *Harper's Gazetteer*, 1855.

[2] Bombay, Puna, Ahmadabád, Surat.

[3] Benares, Cawnpore, Allahabád, Agra, Bareli, Meerut.

[4] Calcutta, inclusive of Howrah and suburbs.

[5] Delhi, Lahore, Amritsar.

Haidrabad. It is therefore by no means certain that there is a tendency toward concentration in India, except such as results from the passing of cities from a lower to a higher group. The increase per cent. of the 26 "great cities" of 1891, whose population is given in 1881,[1] is 10, while all India increased by 11 per cent., even without reckoning the annexations.

This is due to the decay of many of the great religious centres or native capitals. Madras, for example, was reported to have a population of 817,000 in 1823 (Hassel) and 720,000 in 1860 (Kolb), but the census of 1881 gave it 405,848; Benares reported 580,000 in 1823, 185,984 in 1860; Delhi, 400,000 in 1823, 152,406 in 1860; Calcutta, 900,000 in 1823, 794,193 in 1871; Surat, 450,000 in 1823, 109,844 in 1881. No doubt many of these early estimates egregiously exaggerated the population, but there has certainly been a decline in some of the cities almost sufficient to balance the gain in others; so that the cities seem to be just about maintaining the same proportion in the general population.

§ 4. Of the other Asiatic countries, the only one whose statistics are worth attention is Japan. The Philippine Islands, indeed, are reported in the Spanish census of 1887, but, as in Spain, the local statistics are based on the township, a territorial subdivision, rather than upon the dwelling-centre, an agglomeration of people: [2]

		1887	
Philippine Islands	..	7,000,000	100.
Manila	1	154,062	2.2
Towns 20,000–100,000	21	526,152	7.5
Total 20,000+	22	680,214	9.7

[1] There were 28 cities in this class in 1891, counting Calcutta and three suburbs as one city; but Mandalay and Shringar were not given in 1881.

[2] Supan, 87.

§ 5. *China.*—The Chinese statistics are, of course, the crudest estimates, and do not claim even approximate accuracy. Still, some idea of the Chinaman's tendency towards agglomeration may be gathered from the statement that the aggregate population of the 52 cities in China which Supan estimates as above the 100,000 limit, is 88,336,000. This enormous " great-city " population forms 22 per cent. of the 402,680,000 persons accredited to China in the most recent estimates.[1]

§ 6. *Japan.*—Even the Japanese statistics are of doubtful value; thus, in the official statement of population of cities of 30,000+ which appears in the annual *Résumé Statistique* and the *Annuaire Statistique de l'Empire du Japon*, the population of the city of Sendai fluctuates in the following manner:[2]

January, 1884.. 55,321
December, 1886 91,709
December, 1887 71,517
December, 1889 90,231
December, 1890 66,310

The following table shows the distribution of the urban population 1887–90:[3]

TABLE XCV.

	No.	Pop.	Per cent.
Japan	..	40,453,461	100.
100,000+	6	2,353,807	5.84
20,000–100,000....................	49	1,829,601	4.53
10,000–20,000	80	1,099,389	2.72
Total 10,000+....................	135	5,282,797	13.09

[1] *Statesman's Yr. Bk.*, 1897.

[2] Cf. Supan, p. 83.

[3] The *Résumé Statistique de l' Empire du Japon*, 6th Year, 1892 (pp. 10, 16), gives the population of cities over 30,000 for Dec. 31, 1890; the smaller cities were found in Supan, the population being for 1887. The figures are all careful estimates (*Berechnungen*), not enumerations. In 1890 there were 141 towns of 10,000+.

There has naturally been a rapid urban growth in Japan in recent years. While a few cities, like Kanazawa, have lost in population, several of the commercial cities have had an astounding growth if the Japanese statistics may be believed. Thus Kobe had a population of 20,579 in 1881, and 136,968 in 1890; Yokahama, 63,048 in 1881, and 127,987 in 1890. Taking the six cities which severally contained 100,000 + in 1890, and the 11 cities of 50,000–100,000, and comparing their aggregates with 1881, the following percentages of increase are obtained: [1]

Japan 11.0
6 great cities... 51.0
11 other cities 16.0

There is, therefore, a strong tendency toward concentration in the great cities. In 1881 there dwelt in the "great cities" of Japan 4.4 in every hundred of the population, as compared with 5.84 in 1890.

XVII. AMERICAN COUNTRIES. [2]

§ 1. *Canada.*—The Dominion of Canada was established in 1867 and the statistics of urban population since then are as follows:

TABLE XCVI. [3]

	Total Pop.	Urban Pop.	Urban Percentage.
1871	3,635,024	680,019	18.8
1881	4,324,810	912,934	21.1
1891	4,833,239	1,390,910	28 7

The urban population is officially defined as the aggregate population of towns of 1,500 and upwards. This is a lower limit than elsewhere prevails, but as appears in Table

---

[1] For 1890 as above, for 1881 *Almanach de Gotha*, 1885.

[2] For the United States see Sec. I. of this chapter.

[3] *Statistical Year Book of Canada*, 1895, p. 167.

XCVIII, there is no great change in the percentage if the line be drawn at towns of 2,000.

The census of 1891 shows an exceedingly large urban increase; in fact, four-fifths of the entire increase in Canada in the last decade was in the towns. The official statisticians, in explanation, say that the phenomenon is "caused to a considerable extent by the growth of a number of places which had not attained a population of 1,500 in 1881."[1] But as there were only 29 such places, it is hardly possible that this element could have contributed more than 45,000, or less than one-tenth of the entire urban increase. The comparative rates of increase of large and small towns are herewith shown:

TABLE XCVII.[2]

	1851–71.	1871–81.	1881–91.
Canada	30.	18.97	11.76
11 small cities	..	71.	62.
7 middle-sized cities	..	33.	21.
2 great cities	85.	54.	58.
20 cities	..	46.	43.

Thus even with a fixed number of cities, the urban population is increasing three times as rapidly as the general population. The large percentages for the small cities is partly due to the fact that in 1851 only eight of the 11 existed as separate municipalities whose population could be ascertained; in 1871, one of the 11 is still unrepresented. Making allowance for these, it is probable that the rate would be lower than that of the middle-sized cities.

The tendency toward concentration is more adequately shown in the following table:

[1] *Statistical Year Book of Canada*, 1895, p. 167.

[2] The classification follows that in Table XCVIII., where the population of each group is given for 1891 and of Canada for 1851.

TABLE XCVIII.

	1851.			1891.		
	No.	Pop.	Per cent.	No.	Pop.	Per cent.
Canada..................	..	2,375,597	100.	..	4,833,239	100.
Cities 100,000+	0	....	..	..	2,397,870	8.2
" 20–100,000	5	175,287	7.4	7	291,578	6.0
" 10–20,000	2	25,697	1.1	11	139,938	2.9
Total 10,000+	7	200,894	8.5	20	829,386	17.1
" 2,000+	..	....	..	..	1,319,060	27.3

SOURCES.—For 1891, summarized from *Census of Canada*, 1891, iv, 400; for 1851, *The Census of 1851* for Upper and Lower Canada (Ontario and Quebec , supplemented by *Statistical Year Book of Canada*, 1896, p. 7, and *Harper's Gazetteer*, 1855. The population of Prince Edward Island (62,678 included in the total of 1851 is for 1848.

It is interesting to note the provinces that have contributed most to the urban increase. The proportion of urban (towns 1,500+) to total population:

TABLE XCIX.[1]

	1871.	1881.	1891.
Ontario	19.4	22.8	33.2
Quebec	19.5	22.8	29.2
Nova Scotia	14.0	13.6	21.2
New Brunswick	24.3	22.3	19.4
Manitoba...........................	1.2	12.1	22.5
British Columbia	8.9	11.9	42.5
Prince Edward Island..............	11.5	14.1	13.0
The Territories....................	..	..	5.6

That Ontario and Quebec should contain increasing proportions of town populations is natural, but it is surprising to find a relative decrease in New Brunswick,[2] and a wonderful increase in British Columbia and Manitoba.

§ 2. *Mexico.*—The Mexican statistics of city populations are too untrustworthy to demand serious study. In 1895, indeed, a fairly accurate census was taken, but the earlier

---

[1] *Census of 1891*, iv, 401.

[2] The New Brunswick towns have been losing in population, while the province itself is stationary.

data are absurdly inaccurate, as a few comparisons will indicate :

		Veracruz.	Guanajuato.	Puebla.
Almanach de Gotha	1880	......	56,112	75,000
Supan	1889	24,000	52,000	110,000
St. Year Book (Census)	1895	88,993	39,337	91,917

The best available statistics are the following :

TABLE C.[1]

	1889.				1895.		
	No.	Pop.	Per cent.		No.	Pop.	Per cent.
Mexico.............	..	11,632,924	100.		..	12,570,195	100.
Mexico City........	1	329,535	2.8		..	344,377	2.74
Cities 20–100,000 ...	20	730,261	6.3		18	892,052	7.
Cities 10–20,000 ...	30	400,156	3.4				
Cities 10,000+ ...	51	1,459,952	12.5				

The Mexican cities seem to be growing no faster than the rest of the country. A few commercial cities like Veracruz are indeed developing rapidly, but to counterbalance this is the slow growth or even decline of many ancient capitals :

	1850.[2]			1880.[3]	
Mexico	..	7,661,919		..	9,787,629
Capitals of provinces......	25	703,186 = 9.2%		29	946,886 = 9.7%

§ 3. *Brazil.*—At the middle of the century Brazil had about the same population as Mexico, but now has about twenty-five per cent. more, the census of 1890 giving a total of 16,330,216. The only available urban statistics are the official estimates of 1888 :

---

[1] For 1889, *Bureau of American Republics: Bulletin No. 50*, p. 166; for 1895, *St. Yr. Bk.*, 1897, p. 739. It is probable that the population of cities in 1889 is here underestimated; Supan's figures for the same year give a total of 795,200 for cities 20–100,000, or 6.8%.

[2] Harper, 1855.   [3] *Almanach de Gotha*, 1885.

TABLE CI.[1]

	No.	Population.	Percentages.
Brazil		14,002,335	100.
Rio de Janeiro.............		515,559	3.7
Bahia		162,065	1.1
Pernambuco		130,000	.9
Cities 100,000 +..............	3	807,600	5.7
" 20,000–100,000	11	420,000	3.0
" 10,000–20,000	17	206,000	1.5
Cities 10,000+	31	1,433,600	10.2

According to the census of 1856, Rio de Janeiro contained 300,000 inhabitants in a total population of 7,677,800 [2]—a percentage of 3 9. Apparently the metropolis has not grown as rapidly as the rest of the country, but there is a large suburban population not counted in the figures of 1888. It is stated that the city with suburbs now (1898) has a population of about 1,000,000.

§ 4. *Argentina.*—The noteworthy thing about this progressive republic is the remarkable concentration of population in one large city, the metropolis, Buenos Ayres. In 1869, at the time of the first authentic census, it had a population of 177,787, or 9.8 per cent. of a total population in Argentina of 1,812,490.[3] In 1887, suburbs containing 28,000 inhabitants were annexed to a population of 404,000. At the end of 1896 its estimated population was 712,095.[4] The results of the enumeration of 1895 are not entirely obtainable, and in the table below, the official estimates of 1890 are also given.[5]

[1] *Amer. Repub., Bul. No. 50,* p. 64.

[2] Kolb, 1860, p. 369.

[3] *Almanach de Gotha,* 1885.

[4] *Annuaire statistique de ia Ville de Buenos Ayres,* 1896.

[5] According to Kolb, 1860, Buenos Ayres and suburbs had a population in 1856 of 130.000, which is 8.7 per cent. of the estimated population of Argentina (1,500,000). Harper's (1855) gave the city in 1852 120,000, and the Republic 829,400 (excluding aborigines); *i. e.,* 14.5 per cent.

TABLE CII.

	No.	1890.[1] Population.	Per cent.	No.	1895.[2] Population.	Per cent.
Argentina............	..	3,456,000	100.	..	3,952,990	100.
Buenos Ayres	1	561,160	16.2	..	677,786	17.1
Cities 20,000–100,000	5	227,000	6.6	7	289,043	7.3
" 10,000–20,000 .	13	173,000	5.0			
Total 10,000+	19	961,800	27.8			

§ 5. *Chile.*—In Chile there apparently exists a tendency toward concentration, although the statistics are untrustworthy; for example, the fifth census (1875) warns its readers that an addition of 207,597 should be made for omissions, thus recognizing an error of 10 per cent.

TABLE CIII.

	1850. Pop.	Per cent.	1875. Pop.	Per cent.	No.	1885. Pop.	Per cent.
Chile	1,600,000	...	2,075,971	100.	..	2,527,320	100.
Rural pop.......	....	...	1,350,481	65.3	..	1,464,776	58.
Urban "	....	...	725,490	34.7	..	1,062,544	42.
Santiago	65,000 } 5.9		....	...	.. {	189,332	
Valparaiso	30,000 }					104,952	
Cities 100,000+ ..	....	...	....	...	2	294,284	11.6
20,000–100,000 ..	....	...	....	...	3	69,000	2.7
10,000–20,000 ...	....	...	....	...	5	69,000	2.7
Total 10,000+ .	....	...	....	...	10	432,300	17.1

SOURCES—For 1850, *Harper's Gazetteer*, 1855; for 1875, *Almanach de Gotha*, 1885; for 1885, *St. Yr. Bk.*, 1897, and Supan. The list of cities in *Bur. Am. Repub. Bul.*, 50, is evidently based on a territorial unit, as there are 46 "cities" of 20,000–100,000 with an aggregate population of 2,035,000!

The Chilean definition of urban population is unknown to the writer, but it obviously includes very small towns or else is based on a large territorial subdivision as the unit.

§ 6. The remaining American states are too unimportant to detain us long. They are either small and thinly populated or else their population consists largely of uncivilized Indians and half breeds. They are grouped in Table CIV:

[1] Supan, pp. 118–119. The list of cities in the *Bul. of Amer. Repub.*, does not seem to be complete for cities 10,000–20,000, but its figures for the population of Buenos Ayres and Argentina are here adopted.

[2] *St. Yr. Bk.*, 1897, pp. 322–3.

TABLE CIV.

NUMBER AND POPULATION OF CITIES AND PERCENTAGE IN TOTAL POPULATION.

	Authority.	Date.	Population of Country Specified.	Cities 100,000 +.			20,000–100,000.			10,000–20,000.			10,000 +.		
1. Colombia...........	estimates	1886–95	4,000,000	1	110,000	2.75	6	160,000	4.0	10	120,000	3.0	17	390,000	9.75
2. Peru	census	1876	2,621,844	1	103,956	3.96	4	100,500	3.84	8	104,000	3.96	12	308,500	11.76
3. Venezuela	"	1891	2,323,527				4	188,000	8.0	13	156,000	6.7	17	344,000	14.7
4. Bolivia	estimates	1882–6	2,000,000				2	76,800	3.9	4	51,200	2.5	6	128,000	6.4
5. Ecuador	"	1889	1,271,861				3	155,000	12.2	4	42,000	3.3	7	197,000	15.5
6. Uruguay	official estimates	1890	706,524	1	215,000	30.4							1	215,000	30.4
7. Paraguay	estimates	1890	600,000				1	24,000	4.1	3	37,000	6.5	4	64,000	10.6
8. Guatemala........	official estimates	1892	1,471,025				3	115,000	7.8	7	103,000	7.0	10	218,000	14.8
9. Salvador.........	"	1891	777,895				4	40,000	5.0	7	10,000	1.2	11	50,000	6.2
10. Honduras........		1889	431,917							2	22,600	5.2	2	22,600	5.2
11. Nicaragua.......	estimates	1889	312,845				1	25,000	8.0	5	55,000	17.7	6	80,000	25.8
12. Costa Rica......	census	1892	243,205				1	30,000	12.3	3	39,000	16.0	4	69,000	28.4
8–12. Central America .			3,237,200				7	210,000	6.5	18	229,600	7.1	25	439,600	13.6
13. Cuba...........	census	1887	1,631,687	1	200,000	12.3	7	265,000	16.2				1	200,000	12.3
14. Jamaica	"	1891	639,491				1	40,000	6.2				1	40,000	6.3
15. British Guiana ..	estimates	1892	288,328				1	47,207	16.4				1	47,207	16.4
16. Newfoundland	census	1891	202,043				1	29,000	14.4				1	29,000	14.4

SOURCES.—1. Colombia. *Bur. Amer. Repub. Bul., No. 50.* The population includes 220,000 uncivilized Indians and 80,000 more in attached territories. In 1850 Bogota contained an estimated population of 45,000, or 2 per cent. of the total population (2,243,054) (Harper, 1855).

2. Peru. *Ibid.* No census has been taken since 1876, but the population is generally supposed to be stationary. It is estimated that 57 per cent. are aborigines and 27 half-castes. In 1876–91 Lima gained only 3,800. Harper, 1855, gives Lima 70,000 and Peru 2,127,662 (3 3 per cent.).

3. Venezuela. *Ibid.* There are 326,000 native Indians, of whom 240,000 are civilized.

4. Bolivia. Supan, 116. The population now consists of about 1,000,000 aborigines, 700,000 mixed and 600,000 creoles according to *Bur. Am. Rep. Bul., No. 50,* p. 54.

5. Ecuador. *St. Yr. Bk,* 1897. The population comprises 870,000 Indians, 300,000 half-castes and 100,000 whites.

6. Uruguay. *B. A. Repub.,* 50. The authorities note that six per cent. should be added for omissions. The figures for Montevideo refer to the city and department of that name.

7. Paraguay. *Ibid.* 150,000 Indians included.

8–12. Central America. *Ibid.* Indians are included.

13. Cuba. Supan. The figures are for territorial subdivisions rather than for agglomerations, and are misleading; those under 20,000 are, therefore, omitted.

14. Jamaica. *B. Am. Rep. Bul., 50,* p. 297.
15. British Guiana. *Ibid.,* p. 285.
16. Newfoundland. *St. Yr. Bk.*

XVIII. AFRICAN COUNTRIES.

But a small proportion of the inhabitants of Africa have been enumerated. The most ancient country of African civilization, Egypt, has the largest population and the greatest cities. The census of 1882 yields the following results:

TABLE CV.[1]

		Population.	Per cent.
Egypt	..	6,817,265	100.
Cairo	..	374,838	......
Alexandria	..	213,010	......
Cities 100,000+	2	587,848	8.6
" 20,000–100,000	6	179,756	2.6
" 10,000–20,000	22	303,295	4.5
" 10,000+	30	1,070,899	15.7

At the middle of the century, Cairo and Alexandria contained respectively 250,000 and 60,000 inhabitants,[2] or 6.9 per cent. of the entire population. Their growth since has been at a more rapid rate than the population of Egypt in its entirety.

The other countries are summarized in Table CVI. Orange Free State, as well as Abyssinia, is noteworthy as having scarcely any towns of more than 5,000 population, and none reaching 10,000; but Bornu, a native state, has one large city and several smaller ones.

TABLE CVI.

	Source.	Date.	Population.	Cities 20,000–100,000		10,000–20,000		10,000+	
1. Algiers......Census		1891	4,124,732	5 248,690	6.0	6 94,401	2.3	11 343,091	8.3
2. Cape Colony "		1891	1,529,224	3 103,235	6.8	2 20,976	1.4	5 124,211	8.2
3. Natal .... "		1891	543,913	0	..	2 30,237	5.6	2 30,237	5.6
4. Orange Free State ...... "		1890	207,503	0	0	0	..	0	0
5. Transvaal ...off. est.		1896	790,000	(Johannesburg, the sole city,)		= 1 102,714			12.9
6. Abyssinia.... est.		1896	3,500,000	0	0	0	..	0	
7. Bornu (Soudan)........ "		1896	5,000,000	1 55,000	11.0	1			

AUTHORITIES.

Supan for 1, 2, 3, 4. *St. Yr. Bk.*, 1897, for 5, 6, 7   It is to be noted that the population of Johannesburg includes the district within a three miles radius.

[1] Supan, pp. 90–91.

[2] Harper, 1855. The population of Egypt at the census of 1846 was 4,463,244 (*St. Yr. Bk.*, 1897.)

XIX. AUSTRALASIA.

The most remarkable concentration, or rather centralization, of population occurs in that newest product of civilization, Australia, where nearly one-third of the entire population is settled in and about capital cities. The following
table gives the absolute numbers and ratios for 1891 and the
ratios for 1881 :

TABLE CVII.[1]

Colony.	Capital.	1891 Pop. of Colony.	Pop. of Capital.	Ratio of capital to colony.	Ratio 1881.
New South Wales	Sydney	1,132,234	383,386	34.27	28.79
Victoria	Melbourne	1,140,405	490,902	43.09	32.14
Queensland	Brisbane	393,718	101,564	25.80	13.70
South Australia	Adelaide	320,431	133,252	41.58	36.27
Western Australia	Perth	49,782	8,447	16 97	19.36
Tasmania	Hobart	146,667	33,450	22.81	17.75
New Zealand	Wellington	626,658	33,224	5.3	4.10
		3,809,895	1,184,225	31.1	25.10

The population of the capital city formed a larger percentage of the entire population in 1891 than in 1881 in all of
the colonies except Western Australia. Melbourne and
Adelaide contain over two-fifths of the whole population of
Victoria and South Australia. When it is remembered that
there are only seven States in the American Union in which
all the cities of 8,000 inhabitants and upward contain two-
fifths of the population, the condition in Australia can be
better understood. There are several countries in the world
that contain a larger proportion of urban population, but in
none of them is it so massed in a few centres.[2] The rate at

---

[1] T. A. Coghlan (Government statistician of New South Wales), *A Statistical Account of the Seven Colonies of Australia*, Sydney, 1892, pp. 335, 352.

[2] Except in individual States of the American Union, *e. g*, New York City contains fully 50 per cent. of the inhabitants of the State, and metropolitan Boston
40.17 per cent. of Massachusett's population.

which this centralization has been going on appears in the following figures:

TABLE CVIII.[1]

TOTAL POPULATION OF THE

	Seven colonies.	Their capitals.	Percentage of total population living in the capitals.
1801................	6,508		
1821 c	35,610		
1831................	79,306		
1841................	211,095	43,761	20.7
1851................	430,596	84,503	19.6
1861 c	1,252,994	276,960	22.1
1871 c	1,924,770	431,533	22.4
1881 c	2,742,550	689,634	25.1
1891 c	3,809,895	{ 1,184,225	31.1 [2]
		835,888	21.9 [2]

Up to 1871 the cities did not grow very much more rapidly than the rest of the population, but in the last two decades the difference has been marked.

On the whole, these figures may be fairly taken as representing Australia's urban population, but in one way they exaggerate the concentration, or congestion of population, inasmuch as they include large suburban districts. Thus, Sydney includes 35 suburbs, and its area is larger than any city in the United States except Chicago, being 150 square miles, or 96,000 acres. Chicago has 103,000 acres, Philadelphia, 83,000, and London, 75,000; the other great cities are smaller, Paris having an area of 19,000 acres, New York (before 1898) 25,000, and Berlin only 16,000.[3] Melbourne's acreage, 163,942, is still greater than Sydney's. If now the Australian suburbs be counted in with the great cities only when they form industrial parts thereof,[4] and

---

[1] Coghlan, *op. cit.*, 334, 352. "C" indicates census years.

[2] With and without the suburbs, respectively.

[3] *11th Cen., Soc. Stat. of Cities*, 13.

[4] The writer here follows Supan.

otherwise classed as separate municipalities, we shall have the following figures:

TABLE CIX.

CITIES OF 10,000+ IN 1891.

	No.	Population.	% of colony.	Per cent. in 1851.
New South Wales	10	381,444	33.6	28.2
Victoria	7	525,632	46.1	30.
Queensland..................	2	64,455	16.3	0.
South Australia	2	90,786	28.3	28. ca
Western Australia	0	....	0.	0.
Tasmania	2	46,487	32.0	
New Zealand	4	150,479	24.0	0.
Total....................	27	1,264,283	33.2	

There are now 27 cities that exceed the limit 10,000, whereas, if the official statistics of population be accepted many of these cities, together with smaller towns, would be assigned to Sydney and Melbourne, which would indeed reduce the number of cities, but increase their population. Following the official grouping, this classification will result thus:

TABLE CX.

NUMBER AND POPULATION OF CITIES IN 1881.

	100,000+.		20,000–100,000.		10,000–20,000.		Total 10,000+.		
							No.	Pop.	%.
New South Wales	1	383,386	1	51,561	4	52,596	6	487,543	43.1
Victoria..............	1	490,902	3	107,481	0	......	4	598,383	52.4
Queensland..........	1	101,564	0	......	1	13,380	2	114,944	29.2
South Australia	1	133,252	0	......	1	15,976	2	149,228	46.7
Western Australia	0	....	0	......	0	......	0	....	
Tasmania	0	....	1	33,450	1	17,208	2	50,658	34.5
New Zealand	0	....	4	178,062	0	......	4	178,062	28.5
Total	4	1,109,104	9	370,554	7	99,160	20	1,578,818	41.4
Percentage of Australasian population ...		29.1		9.7		2.6		41.4	

The historical development of urban population may be best studied in New South Wales,[2] the original colony from

[1] Coghlan, op. cit., 353.

[2] Census of 1891, Statistician's Report, p. 120.

which the other colonies of the mainland have been separated. The censuses proper begin with 1861, but before that year Sydney virtually represented the urban population, as New Castle (the next largest city) only reached 7,810 population in 1861. In 1790, at the time of the first " muster," all of the 591 European inhabitants of the colony lived at Sydney; in 1799 half of the 5,088 inhabitants lived there; in 1811, 4,895 out of 10,025 or 48.8 per cent.; in 1821, 13,401 out of 29,652, or 45.2 per cent.; in 1831, 16,232 out of 60,794, or 26.7 per cent.; in 1841, 29,973 out of 116,631, or 25.7 per cent. This was the smallest percentage ever reached for the city. In 1851 Sydney contained 53,924 out of 191,099 inhabitants, or 28.2 per cent. The movement toward the occupation of lands has stopped, and the population flocks to the great city. In 1861–71, as appears from the following table,[1] the outside districts gained two new settlers to one gained by Sydney; but in 1881–91, the condition was more than reversed, Sydney having an increase of 160,000 to 67,000 increase for the rural districts:

TABLE CXI.

		1861.		1871.		1881.		1891.
Sydney	1	95,789	1	137,776	1	224,939	1	383,283
Other cities 5,000+ .	3	19,081	4	32,987	6	58 481	8	120,753
Towns 2,–5,000	4	14,623	7	20,564	20	54,608	41	117,587
Total urban........	8	129,493	12	191,327	27	338,028	50	621,623
Villages	29	30,341	44	43,486	85	88,910	108	108,396
Rural	..	189,116	..	266,766	..	321,303	...	388,231
Total	..	348,950	..	501,579	..	748,241	...	1,118,250
Shipping, etc.	..	1,910	..	2,402	..	3,227	...	5,704
Aborigines.........	..	....	..	....	..	....	...	8,280
Grand total	..	350,860	..	503,981	..	751,468	...	1,132,234

PERCENTAGES.

Sydney............	27.45	27.47	30.06	34.27
Other towns	9.65	10.67	15.10	21.32
Villages	8.70	8.67	11.90	9.69
Rural	54.20	53.19	42.94	34.72
Total	100.	1CO.	100.	100.

[1] *Census of 1891, Statistician's Report*, p. 126.

In this classification "village" includes all municipalities with a population under 2,000; as will be seen, they average about 1,000 each. The purely rural or agricultural population has declined relatively from 54.20 per cent. in 1861 to 34.72 in 1891. The villages have done little more than hold their own, while Sydney and the other cities have grown rapidly.

XX. SUMMARY AND CONCLUSIONS.

In order to bring statistics of urban population in different countries into comparison, the author has aimed to secure, as the town unit, an actual agglomeration of people, and not a territorial unit or political subdivision. The distinction between the two modes of procedure has been discussed in Chapter I; here it is necessary only to call attention to the exceptions necessarily made in a table of comparisons. Where the local unit is not a territorial subdivision (*i. e.*, where it is the village, town or city, in the United States; the urban sanitary district in England; the *Centri* in Italy; and the German *Gemeinde*, virtually coinciding with the *Ort* or *Wohnplatz* in Saxony), it is unnecessary to pay any attention to the area; elsewhere the size of the territorial unit may appreciably affect urban percentages, because it will often contain a scattered or rural, as well as an agglomerated, population. The average size of the territorial unit in square kilometers is as follows:

Massachusetts, town or city	61.4
Spain, Ayuntamiento	54.
Netherlands, Gemeënte	28.7
Hungary, Gemeinde	22.
France, commune	14.62
Switzerland, commune	12.6
Belgium, commune	11.4
Austria, Gemeinde	10.6
Germany "	7.
Prussia "	6.34

It will be perceived that the danger of reckoning isolated residents among urban dwellers is at the minimum in the small *Gemeinde* of Germany, which, in extent, fairly conforms with the incorporated village in America. In France the *commune* is not much larger, and in ascertaining the urban population only those communes are included which contain an agglomerated population of 2,000 and upwards, although to all such the scattered population is then added. In the Netherlands, the territorial unit is still larger, and it affects the percentage of urban population considerably, as the note to the table shows. The Spanish *Ayuntamiento* (also in Cuba and the Philippines) is so large as to render the comparison worthless for the smaller towns, and these have therefore been enclosed in brackets. The New England township, again, must obviously include a rural population; but in the more careful computations of urban population there, it is customary to treat the incorporated cities (approximately those towns of 12,000+ agglomerated population) separately as constituting the urban population.

With the reservations here made, Table CXII is presented as a summary of results obtained in the statistical investigations of the present chapter.

In Table CXII the countries are arranged in the order of percentage of urban population (*i. e.*, population in towns of 10,000 or more inhabitants). In some cases where this population could not be ascertained, positions have been assigned after comparing the other percentages, and at the same time keeping in mind the different conditions. China's position, however, is an arbitrary one, as only one percentage is given, and that is of slight value. In this table, the official statistics of Australia, regarding the territorial extent of the great cities, have been followed; had the limits been drawn with Supan, at the actual municipality, the percentage for the seven colonies (10,000+) would be 33.2 instead of

TABLE CXII.

PERCENTAGE OF TOTAL POPULATION DWELT IN CITIES OF—

Countries.	1800.				1850.				1890.						Reference Table.
	Year.	100,000+	20,000+	10,000+	Year.	100,000+	20,000+	10,000+	Year.	100,000+	20,000–100,000	20,000+	10,000+	2,000+	
1. England and Wales	1801	9.73	16.94	21.30	1851	22.58	35.0	39.45	1891	31.82	21.76	53.58	61.73	72.05	XVII-XIX
2. Scotland	1801	0.	13.9	17.0	1851	16.9	27.7	32.2	1891	29.8	12.6	42.4	49.9	65.4	XXIV
3. Australia (7 colonies)	1800-10								1891	29.1	9.7	38.8	41.4		CX
4. Belgium	1846	0.	8.7	13.5	1846	6.8	16.6	20.8	1890	17.4	8.7	26.1	34.8		LXXVI
5. Saxony	1815	0.	7.7	8.9	1849	0.	9.9	13.6	1890	22.6	7.4	30.0	34.7	64.5	XLIX
6. Netherlands *	1795	11.5	24.5	29.5	1849	7.3	21.7	29.0	1889	16.6	12.7	29.3	33.5		LXXXIV
7. Turkey in Europe									1885	21.4	3.5	24.9			LXXXIV
8. China									1896	22.0					Par. XVI, §5
9. Uruguay	1816	1.8	6.0	7.25	1849	3.1	7.8	10.63	1890	30.4		30.4	30.4	48.5	CIV
10. Prussia									1890	12.9	10.1	23.0	30.		XLVIII
11. Germany									1890	12.1	9.8	21.9		48.5	XLVI
12. Argentina	1800	0.	3.8	3.8					1890	16.2	6.6	22.8	27.8	47.0	CII
13. United States					1850	6.0	9.8	12.0	1890	15.5	8.3	23.8	27.6	37.7	XVI
14. Cuba									1887	12.3	16.2	28.5			CIV
15. France	1801	2.8	6.7	9.5	1851	4.6	10.6	14.4	1891	12.0	9.1	21.1	25.9	37.4	XXXV
16. Denmark	1801	10.9	10.9	10.9	1840	9.6	9.6	0.6	1890	17.3	2.9	20.2	23.6	32.4	LXXXII
17. Spain	1810 ca.	1.45	9.75	[14.0]	1857	4.4	9.6	[16.2]	1887	6.8	11.2	18.0	[29.6]		LXXXII
18. Italy	1800 ca.	4.4			1848	6.0	6.0		1881	6.9	6.4	13.3	20.6	[13.4]	LXXX
19. Bavaria	1800 ca.	0.	3.7	7.8	1849	2.4	6.12		1890	8.8	7.0	15.8	20.5	31.9	L
20. Ireland	1800 ca.	3.1	6.6		1851	3.9	8.7	10.1	1891	10.6	4.7	15.3	18.0	26.4	XXXII
21. Canada					1851	0.	7.4	8.5	1891	8.2	6.0	14.2	17.1	27.3	XCVIII
22. Chile									1885	11.6	2.7	14.3	17.1		CIII
23. Norway	1801	0.	0.	3.3	1845	0.	4.2	5.3	1890	7.6	6.2	13.8	16.7	22.2	LXVIII
24. Switzerland	1822	0.	1.3	4.3	1850	0.	5.2	7.3	1888	0.	13.2	13.2	16.5		LXXVII
25. British Guiana									1892	0.	16.4	16.4	16.4		CIV
26. Persia									1896	5.1	[7.0]	[12.]			XC
27. Austria	1800 ca.	2.63	3.56	4.37	1843	2.8	4.2	5.8	1890	8.	4.	12.	15.8	32.5	LIV
28. Hungary †	1800 ca.	0.	2.31	5.35	1850	1.35	4.55	9.1	1890	3.23	8.03	11.26	[17.6]		LIX

* The figures for 1890 refer to the agglomerated population; for comparison with 1795 and 1849, the basis should be the territorial unit (Gemeïnte), giving the percentages 17, 14.3, 31.3 and 43.0.

† Cf. Sec. VI of the present chapter, where the urban population in 1890 is fixed at 16.1 per cent.

TABLE CXII.—*Concluded.*

Countries.	1800 Year	1800 100,000 +	1800 20,000 +	1800 10,000 +	1850 Year	1850 100,000 +	1850 20,000 +	1850 10,000 +	1890 Year	1890 100,000 +	1890 20,000–100,000	1890 20,000 +	1890 10,000 +	1890 2,000 +	Reference Table.
29. Egypt									1882	8.6	2.6	11.2	15.7		CV
30. Ecuador									1889	0.	12.2	12.2	15.5		CIV
31. Venezuela									1891	0.	8.	8.	14.7		CIV
32. Newfoundland									1891	0.	14.4	14.4	14.4		CIV
33. Roumania									1889–90	4.4	6.3	10.7	14.2		LXXXVIII
34. Greece									1889	4.9	4.1	9.0	14.0		LXXV
35. Sweden	1805	0.	3.	3.9	1850	0.	3.4	4.7	1890	7.34	3.5	10.84	13.74	18.0	CIV
36. Central America									1889–92	5.84	6.5	6.5	13.6		XCV
37. Japan									1890		4.53	10.37	13.1		LXXXIX
38. Turkey in Asia									1885		[7.0]	[10.2]	[13.0]		C
39. Mexico									1895	2.7	7.0	9.7	12.9		Par. XVI, §4
40. Philippines									1887	2.2	7.5	9.7	12.7		CVI
41. Transvaal									1896	12.9	0.	12.9	11.8		LXXXII
42. Bornu (Soudan)				12.7	1857	7.2	10.7	12.9	1896	11.0	11.0	11.0	11.2		CIV
43. Portugal	1801	9.5	10.3	12.7	1857	7.2	10.7	12.9	1890	8.8	0.4	9.2	10.6		LXXXVII
44. Peru									1876	4.0	3.8	7.8	10.2		CIV
45. Bulgaria									1888	0.	5.2	5.2	9.7		CI
46. Paraguay									1890	0.	4.1	4.1	9.3		CIV
47. Brazil									1888	5.7	3.	8.7	8.3		LXIII
48. Colombia	1820	1.4	2.4	3.7	1856	1.6	3.5	5.3	1886–95	2.7	4.	6.7	8.2	12.3	CVI
49. Russia									1885	3.2	4.	7.2	7.3		CVI
50. Algiers									1891	0.	6.0	6.0	6.4		CVI
51. Cape Colony									1891	0.	6.8	6.8	6.3		XCII
52. British India									1880–6	2.1	2.8	4.9	5.6		CIV
53. Bolivia									1891	0.	3.9	3.9	5.1		CVI
54. Jamaica									1891	0.	6.3	6.3	3.8		CIV
55. Natal									1890	0.	2.5	2.5	0.		CVI
56. Servia									1890	0.	1.9	1.9	0.		LXXXVI
57. Bosnia-Herzegowina									1885	0.	0.	0.	0.		LXXXV
58. Orange Free State									1890	0.	0.	0.	0.		CVI
59. Abyssinia									1896	0.	0.	0.	0.		CVI

41.4. But that would still leave Australia near the head of the list.

One is impressed with the extent of the variations in the percentage of urban population in the different countries of the world. On the one hand, England with 62 per cent. of its population city-dwellers; on the other hand, several Balkan states with only five city people out of every hundred, and the Orange Free State with no real urbanites at all.

Of the causes of such extensive variations, that which most readily suggests itself is density of population. Given two countries of equal area, it would naturally be expected that the more populous country would contain the larger number of cities. Thus it would seem impossible that people could be crowded together as they are in Belgium or England, without living in such close proximity as to constitute agglomerations. But such is the case. Bengal, for example, has as many inhabitants as the United States in a territory scarcely larger than Great Britain and Ireland; and the density of population in Bengal is exceeded only slightly by that of Belgium and England. Nevertheless, the percentage of urban population in Bengal is only 4.8 as compared with 47.7 in Belgium.[1] In order to compare the relation of density of population to its concentration, the following table showing the number of inhabitants to each square kilometer of territory has been compiled:[2]

---

[1] In both cases urban population = towns of 5,000+.

[2] *Statistik des Deutschen Reiches, Neue Folge, Bd.* 68, p. 6*. A few countries have been added from *Almanach de Gotha*, and are enclosed in parenthesis marks. The data refer to the censuses of 1889–91.

TABLE CXIII.

Saxony	234.	Servia	44.5
Belgium	206.	North Atlantic States	41.5
England and Wales	192.	Roumania	38.5
Bengal	181.8	Spain (1887)	34.8
North-West Provinces	168.5	Greece	34.
Netherlands	138.7	(Chinese Empire)	32.
Italy (1893)	107.	Bulgaria	31.8
Japan	106.5	Bosnia and Herzogowina	26.
Madras	97.4	(European Russia. 1897)	19.
Germany	91.5	(Cuba)	13.7
(China-proper)	87.	Sweden	10.8
Prussia	86.	United States	8.2
Austria	79.6	(Mexico)	6.4
Bavaria	74.	Norway	6.2
Switzerland	73.3	(Russia, 1897)	5.8
Punjab	72.8	Victoria, Australia	5.
France	72.5	(Colombia)	4.8
British India	71.1	(Chile)	3.8
Bombay	58.3	(Peru)	2.8
Ireland	57.6	(Cape Colony)	2.7
Denmark	55.1	(Brazil)	1.7
Hungary	54.2	New South Wales	1.4
Scotland	52.2	(Argentina)	1.2
Portugal (1881)	51.	Canada	0.6

India, Italy and Japan are densely populated countries; but they have relatively small urban populations. On the other hand, the United States and Australia are thinly populated and still have relatively large urban populations. Scotland and Argentina do not occupy parallel positions. Evidently there are other factors in producing agglomerations than mere populousness.

A more probable explanation of large urban populations is the organization of industry on a modern scale. It appears, indeed, that nearly all of the more advanced industrial nations are included among the first fifteen countries in Table CXII, while none of the countries in the second half of the list, with the exception perhaps of Japan, can be said to be in the forefront of modern industry.

It cannot be said that manufacturing or machine industry alone causes the concentration of population. Ranking the leading nations by the amount of steam power per 100 inhabitants, for example, does not yield the same order as that in Table CXII. Thus, the countries that utilize steam to the extent of at least 20 horse-power per 100 inhabitants are the United States, England and Scotland; more than 10 and less than 20—Belgium, Germany, France; more than 7 and less than 10—Netherlands, Denmark, Scandinavia, Ireland; more than 3 and less than 7—Russia, Austria, Hungary, Switzerland, Italy, Spain; less than 3—Portugal and the Balkan States, including Greece and Turkey.[1]

The United States should follow England and Scotland if manufactures alone determined the percentage of urban dwellers; while the Netherlands, Turkey, etc., would occupy positions much lower in the list. But Holland is a great commercial country, carrying on a larger commerce per capita than any other nation in the world; its large urban population is chiefly to be attributed to that fact. The same applies, to a less degree, to Turkey. Constantinople contains by far the larger portion of Turkey's urban population, its percentage being 18.3, while for all cities of 20,000+ it is only 24. In this case some influence may be attributed to politics as a cause of concentration; but it still remains true that it is Constantinople's commercial advantages which have made the city the seat of government.

It is of course true that back of density of population and industrial organization are the physical features of a country and its comparative natural advantages for different industries. Nature has perhaps determined that in Uruguay a very large percentage of the population shall be centered in the city and department of Montevideo. Nature has also

[1] Hobson, *Evolution of Capitalism*, 85-6.

favored the building of a great commercial city at Buenos Ayres and discouraged the dispersion of the population by providing better advantages for grazing than for cultivation of the soil. Such is emphatically the case in Australia, while in India a rich soil entices to an extensive cultivation, and supports a large agricultural population, which in the very nature of things cannot be brought together in great agglomerations. But after all, Nature has been subjected to man's commands, and if the English people and the East Indians were to exchange places, it is altogether likely that India would become a land of great cities and England an agricultural country with a scattered population. Hence in Australia, it is not a sufficient explanation to say that the physical features of the country (few harbors, few rivers, vast plains suitable for grazing) are the determining factor. It is rather the alertness with which the progressive Australian democracy has adjusted itself to the requirements of the modern industrial organization with its international and local division of labor. Australia has no anciently established manufactures like those of old England, nor even the vigorous " infant industries " of New England. On the contrary, Australia has vast tracts of unoccupied lands tempting men to agriculture. The main reasons why the Australians prefer to remain in the seaboard cities rather than settle the interior is that nineteenth-century industry requires few workers on the land. In European countries the process of agglomeration proceeds more slowly because the superfluous agriculturists have been brought up on the farm, and have to overcome the inertia of their position in order to find their true place in the industrial organism; it requires a distressful agricultural depression like the one that has prevailed since 1893 to bring home to the agriculturist the conviction that his labor is not wanted on the farm. But in Australia the mass of the population has been in the seaboard cities, where the emigrants land, and consequently has no such inertia to overcome. Australia is therefore the representative of the new order of things, toward which the modern world is advancing.

It is thus in the dynamic rather than the static aspect that the true significance of the agglomeration of population manifests itself. The reasons why the distribution of population in England is so different from that in India are clearly seen when one studies the causes of the movement which has made the England of to-day so different, as regards the distribution of population, from the England of 1800. Then it will appear that the physical features of, say, England and India, count for less as a factor in the problem than the qualities of the race and its progress in material civilization. It is not to be denied that even the material civilization of a country depends upon its natural advantages to a certain extent, but the principal consideration after all is the use to which such advantages are put by their possessors. China is known to be rich in coal and iron—the fundamental elements of machine industry—but China has not become a great industrial nation like England. While, therefore, the topography and the resources of the country and also the density of its population do sometimes influence the distribution of the population (notably Australia, Turkey, Uruguay, Argentina), in the majority of cases it is economic organization that constitutes the decisive influence.

If now the percentages of urban population in the different countries given in Table CXII, be compared for the years 1800, 1850, and 1890, as in the accompanying diagram, it will be found that the urban growth has very generally taken place since 1850. The exceptions are England and Scotland, the United States, and in a smaller degree, Belgium, Saxony and France. In the two former, the process of concentration wrought greater changes in 1800–50 than in

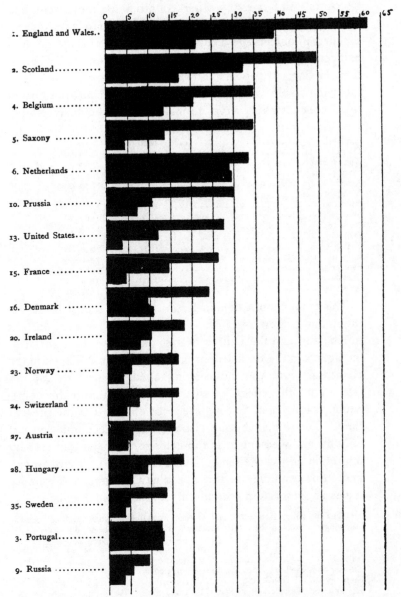

DIAGRAM showing the percentage of population, in the countries named, which dwelt in cities of 10,000 and upwards at the beginning of the present century, in 1850 and in 1890, or the nearest census years. (Based on Table CXII.)

NOTE.—Saxony's first percentage should be 8.9 for 1815, instead of 4.5 for 1800; that of France 95 instead of 4.5.

1850–90. But in many other countries the movement had scarcely begun in 1850. In Denmark and Holland, indeed, the urban percentage actually diminished during the first half century. In Portugal there has been a continual diminution, lasting, it appears, down to the present time. The following table showing roughly the principal periods of rapid concentration serves to make clearer the analysis:

TABLE CXIV.

England	1820–30,	1840–50	
Prussia	1871–80,	1880–90	
United States	1840–50,	1860–70,	1880–90
France	1850–60,	1860–70	
Austria	1846–57,	1880–90	
Hungary	1850 57,	1880–90	
Russia	1870–97,		
Sweden	1880–90,	1860–70	
Norway	1875 91,	1865–75	
Denmark	1870–90,		
Netherlands	1880–90,	1870–80	
Belgium	1866–80,	1880–90	
Switzerland	1850–60,	1880–88	
Canada	1881–91,	1871–81	
Australia	1881–91,	1871–81	

This amounts to a demonstration that the Industrial Revolution and the era of railways, both of which opened earliest in England and the United States, have been the transforming agents in the re-distribution of population. They are the elementary forces in the bringing about of Modern Capitalism. And the effects of their introduction into the continental countries of Europe are to be observed at the present time. The re-distribution of population is accomplished not only by a movement from the fields to the cities, but also by migration across the seas. This is a factor of prime importance, for example, in the Scandinavian countries, whence issues an emigration second only to that from Ireland.[1]

---

[1] Thus the emigration in the last 70 years from the countries specified bore the following relations to the total population of those countries in 1890–91:

From	Immigrants to the United States.	Total pop. in 1890–91 in millions.	Ratio.
Ireland	3,481,074	4,7	74.
Norway and Sweden	925,031	6,8	13.5
Germany	4,504,128	49,	9.2
England and Wales	1,637,065	29,	8.6
(*11th Cen., Pop.*, i, p. lxxxi.)			

In conclusion, it may prove of interest to place in comparison with the European countries of large urban populations, some of the American commonwealths. Of the four great Western nations, Great Britain very considerably outranks the others, which are very close together. France comes fourth, while Germany (Prussia) and the United States are very nearly equal. But the German urban statistics, as have been shown, are based on the *Gemeinde* (township) which gives it an advantage, and it is to be noted that if the comparison be restricted to cities of 20,000+ or 100,000+, the United States clearly ranks above both Germany and France. The only considerable portion of Germany that has a larger urban population than the United States is Saxony, a country somewhat more than half as large as Massachusetts,[1] which has an urban percentage of 66 to Saxony's 35.

TABLE CXV.[2]

PERCENTAGE OF POPULATION IN TOWNS OF 10,000+.

Massachusetts	65.9	Uruguay	30.4
Eng. and Wales	61.7	Ohio	30.2
Rhode Island	57.9	Prussia	30.0
New York	57.7	Utah	28.7
New Jersey	50.9	Washington	28.3
Scotland	49.9	Argentina	27.8
Maryland	43.9	Minnesota	27.7
Connecticut	41.9	UNITED STATES	27.6
(Australia	41.4)[3]	France	25.9
California	41.0	Missouri	25.6
Pennsylvania	39.1	New Hampshire	24.8
Illinois	38.1	Michigan	23.9
Colorado	37.1	Louisiana	23.7
Delaware	36.5	Denmark	23.6
Belgium	34.8	Wisconsin	22.5
Saxony	34.7	Nebraska	22.2
Netherlands	33.5	Italy	20.6
(Australia	32.2)[3]	Bavaria	20.5

[1] Area of Saxony, 5,787 sq. miles; Massachusetts, 8,315.

[2] Based on Tables XI and CXII.

[3] Varies with the inclusion or exclusion of suburbs of Sydney, etc.

This table shows that while the United States as a whole has a smaller urban percentage than several other countries, it contains States as large as those foreign countries, with larger urban percentages.   Scotland, Belgium, Saxony, Holland and Uruguay are all small countries as compared even with American commonwealths.   Even England and Wales embrace an area of only 57,766 square miles, which is almost precisely equal to the combined territory of New York, Massachusetts and Rhode Island.   And 60 per cent. of the aggregate population of these commonwealths live in cities of 10,000+, while in Massachusetts alone the percentage rises to 65.9.   Nor is this large percentage due to the large territorial extent of the Massachusetts town, for in 1895 the aggregate population of the State living under city government formed 65.43 per cent. of the total; and the smallest of the cities (Beverly) had a population of 11,806.[1]   Twelve American commonwealths rank above Prussia in urban population and contain 26 million people to Prussia's 30 million. These facts should be remembered when it comes to comparing the continental United States with the small countries of Europe.

[1] *Census of Mass., 1895,* i, 48–49.

CHAPTER III.

CAUSES OF THE CONCENTRATION OF POPULATION.

I. INTRODUCTORY.

IN seeking the causes of the remarkable concentration of population that has taken place in most of the civilized countries of the globe during the last fifty or one hundred years, careful discrimination must be made between this phenomenon and the growth of cities as a mere accompaniment to the general increase of population. The real checks upon the growth of population in previous centuries were war, famine, pestilence, and unsanitary cities involving particularly high infantile mortality. Hence, as soon as the progress of medical and sanitary science, transportation methods, industrialism and the other factors of modern civilization had mitigated the " scourges of mankind," there followed a period of unprecedented increase of population in all Western countries. In this general increase, the cities have naturally participated—and have even outrun smaller communities and scattered populations. For it was in crowded centres that modern science was most needed to render the conditions of life healthful. Throughout the middle ages and the earlier centuries of modern times, the cities of Europe depended almost entirely upon the influx of country people for their growth; the mortality was so high that the deaths annually equaled or exceeded in number the births. London was no worse off than other European cities, Paris and one or two other places possibly excepted; and yet London's birth-rate never exceeded its death-rate, for any considerable period, until the very beginning of the nineteenth century. It is a patent fact that the rapid growth of London in the present century has been in part due to its ability to confine the mortality within reasonable bounds and thus secure a natural increase (an excess of births over deaths); the natural increase has of course steadily augmented with the constant improvements in municipal administration and the application of the discoveries of medical science.

Nevertheless, the transformation of a deficiency into an excess of births is not the essential reason of city-growth, which must rather be sought in economic conditions. Comparing, for example, the demographical statistics of the French cities for the decade 1881–1891 it will be found that Lyons, Marseilles and Bordeaux had fewer births than deaths; and yet they surpassed the other large cities of France (Roubaix and Lille alone excepted) in their rate of growth.[1]

The "mushroom" growth of American cities, which has been the subject of considerable comment, should occasion no surprise, since it is mainly due to the settlement of uncultivated territory. It is only when the growth of a city has proceeded more rapidly than the development of its contributory territory, that one needs to study other underlying causes. For then one is face to face with the problem

---

[1] *Cf. Statistisches Jahrbuch der Stadt Berlin*, xix (1892), pp. 94–5:

	Natural increase or decrease.	Total increase.
Paris	+2.36	8.54
Lyons	—1.23	10.73
Marseilles	—2.56	12.34
Lille	+7.08	17.86
Bordeaux	—0.85	14.19
Roubaix	+13.38	24.40

The Italian statistics show even more striking instances, but owing to the absence of a regular census since 1881, they cannot be trusted.

of the concentration of population,—an increasing *proportion* of the population collected in cities.

While, then, it is generally true that the unprecedented increase of population during the present century has been a condition of the rapid growth of cities, it has not necessarily been a positive cause of their *relatively* rapid growth as compared with the remainder of the population—a cause, that is, of the phenomenon of concentration. Positive forces may exist to drive a larger proportion of people into the rural districts notwithstanding an all-round increase in population. Such has been the actual result in Portugal, where, if statistics are not at fault, a smaller percentage of the inhabitants is living in cities to-day than in the middle of the century.[1] On the other hand, the cities of France have been enjoying a rapid growth all the time that the population of the country has as a whole has been virtually at a standstill, and those of Ireland have likewise grown while the population in general has declined.

It is now clear that the growth of cities must be studied as a part of the question of distribution of population, which is always dependent upon the economic organization of society—upon the constant striving to maintain as many people as possible upon a given area. The ever-present problem is so to distribute and organize the masses of men that they can render such services as favor the maintenance of the nation and thereby accomplish their own preservation. Population follows the line of least resistance in its distribution, and will consequently be affected by changes in the methods of production. When the industrial organization demands the presence of laborers in particular localities in order to increase its efficiency, laborers will be found there; the means of attraction will have been " better living "—in other words, an appeal to the motive of self-interest. Econ-

[1] *Cf.* Table LXXXII.

omic forces are therefore the principal cause of concentration of population in cities; but there are other motives exhibited in the "Drift to the Cities," and these will also receive consideration.

What, now, are the economic forces that have caused the massing of people in large communities? The business man's answer would probably be short and trenchant, "Steam." Literary critics and *dilettantes* in political economy pronounce the present era of great cities a result of the "centripetal tendencies of steam," and congratulate their readers upon the dawning of a new era wherein the "centrifugal powers of electricity" will disperse the population of crowded tenements.

Steam and machinery have certainly been among the most important influences tending toward the concentration of population; but neither steam nor machinery was used by the ancient Egyptians, Medes, Phœnicians, Greeks, or Romans, who nevertheless built great cities. The fact is that no one human instrument can be held accountable for such an important social phenomenon, and one cannot make clear to oneself the true causes in their true relation without viewing the social body in its entirety. That is to say, a successful investigation of the causes of the city growth set forth in the preceding chapter must begin with a study of social, or more strictly speaking, economic evolution.

According to Herbert Spencer, evolution consists of two distinct processes—a differentiation and an integration.[1] By differentiation, he means increase of heterogeneity out of originally homogeneous conditions. By integration, he

[1] "Evolution is an integration of matter and concomitant dissipation of motion, during which the matter passes from an indefinite, incoherent homogeneity to a definite, coherent heterogeneity; and during which the retained motion undergoes a parallel transformation."—Spencer, *First Principles*, Sec. 145.

means a growing inter-relation and inter-dependence of parts. A simple biological analogy will serve to make clear the process. The lowest type of organism is simply an agglomeration of like cells; the creature is all stomach, all mouth, all hands and feet, so to speak. It has no special organs; one part of the body is just like the other parts. The first rude differentiation is into two layers, which develop later into a sustaining and a regulating system. A third stage is found in the formation of organs—the heart, stomach, eye, ear, etc. —each of which assumes a single function and performs it for the entire body. But in order to effect this distribution or specialization of functions, in which each organ relieves all the others of its special work, a system of complete and intimate communication between the parts must first be developed. That is to say, with differentiation, specialization, or division of labor, as we choose to call it, there must always go integration or combination.

Now, without stretching the analogy, we may liken industrial society of to-day—embracing all countries within the circle of exchange of products—to a great organism composed of heterogeneous parts. This organism, however, is the product of ages of slow growth. Originally, in place of the one all-embracing social organism, there were myriads of small social units, each complete in itself and independent of the others, if not positively hostile to them. The history of civilization is simply the narrative description of the breaking down of the barriers that separated the primitive social units —the original family group, clan, patriarchal family, the enlarged village community or the manorial group. And the most conspicuous and influential role in the process was played by the trader, working upon men's desires for what they did not possess or produce. Neither war (conquest) nor religion has been of so vital and far-reaching influence in the integration and amalgamation of isolated social groups as trade and commerce.

When, therefore, it is pointed out that towns owe their origin to trade, that the commercial metropolis of to-day is the successor of the primitive market-place established beside the boundary stone between hostile but avaricious tribal groups, that the extension of the market means the enlargement of the market-centre—then one will readily perceive the connection of the growth of industrial society to its present world-wide dimensions with our problem of the concentration of population. The relations of transportation systems and means of communication to commerce and commercial centres will therefore form one of the subjects of discussion.

The other side of the process, differentiation, involves, as we have seen, extensive changes in the units themselves. The results of territorial specialization, or the geographical division of labor, upon manufacturing and other industries will therefore require consideration. Special attention should also be given to the internal structure of industry, or the form of business organization in the various stages of evolution, as bearing directly upon the problem of concentration.

But first it is necessary to consider the negative side of the subject—that is, how the forces making for the dispersion of population have steadily lost ground in the evolution of society. The diminishing importance of agriculture will therefore constitute the first topic of discussion.

II.   THE DIVORCE OF MEN FROM THE SOIL.

If men were like other animals and had no further wants than bodily appetites and passions, there would be no large aggregations of people; for in order to produce food, men must live either in scattered habitations like American farmers, or in hamlets like the ancient family or tribal group, the village community, the Russian *mir*, and the modern agricultural village of Continental Europe. Even with a comparatively high grade of wants, men may live in these small groups, each of which is economically autonomous and self-sufficing, producing for itself and buying and selling little if anything. It is the period of the *Naturalwirthschaft*, in which all payments are in kind. The principle of division of labor finally led to the disruption of the village community, but its triumph was long delayed. The principle was of course grasped only imperfectly by primitive man. At first the only division of labor was that based on sex, age, muscular power, or relation to the governing head of the group; in other respects there was no assignment of special tasks to particular individuals. Very gradually men discovered among themselves differences of natural aptitude. The members of a community at length realized that it was more economical to have their flour made in a village mill by one member who should give all his time to that particular work, than to have it made by bits in a score of individual mills. One by one other industries have followed the mill—have departed from the separate households and taken up their abode in a central establishment. Clothing ceased to be made at home; there arose a village weaver and a village shoemaker. To this process of development there is almost no conceivable end. Only a few years ago the American farmer not only raised his own food, but furnished his own fuel and sometimes made his own clothing. Now, however, he is a specialist, and thinks nothing of going to the market even for table supplies. Formerly, the farmer made his own tools; now he buys implements made in factories. But yesterday, and the men who reaped the fields of ripe grain were bound to the soil and compelled to dwell in isolated homes or small communities; to-day these men live in cities and make machinery to reap the grain.

Thus, it appears that agriculture, the industry that disperses men, has ever narrowed its scope. Formerly, when men's wants were few and simple, agriculture was the all-embracing occupation. The agriculturist produced the necessary sustenance, and in his idle moments made whatever else he needed. But human wants have greatly multiplied and can no longer be satiated with food-products alone. Moreover, the business of providing for the new wants has been separated from agriculture. The total result is that the proportion of people who must devote themselves to the satisfaction of the elementary wants of society has vastly diminished and is still diminishing.

And this result is attained not only by the diminishing importance of bread and butter in the realm of human wants, but also by the increased per-capita product which a specialized body of workers can win from the soil. By the use of fertilizers, by highly scientific methods of cultivation, by labor-saving machinery, and by the construction of transportation systems to open up distant and virgin fields, the present century has immensely reduced the relative number of workers who must remain attached to the soil to provide society's food-supply.

These facts are of fundamental importance in seeking the causes of urban growth. For cities are made up of persons who do not cultivate the soil; their existence presupposes a surplus food-supply, which in turn promises either great fertility of the soil or an advanced stage of the agricultural arts, and in either case convenient means of transportation. All three conditions were present in the river valleys of the Nile and Euphrates when the first great cities of history arose—Thebes, Memphis, Babylon, and Nineveh. No accurate estimates of the number of their inhabitants exist; but as the Greeks, who had cities of their own with at least 100,-000 inhabitants, regarded the ancient cities with wonder, it may safely be said that they were great cities. Similar conditions were present during the period of Roman city civilization. The high perfection to which the arts of agriculture had been brought (only recently approached, perhaps, in the modern era), permitted the existence of a large number of Oriental cities with a population of 100,000 or more in the first century before Christ. Two cities, Rome and Alexandria, probably attained a population of half a million souls each—a number reached by no other cities until the end of the seventeenth century (London and Paris).[1]

The Italian peninsula could not furnish sufficient bread-stuffs for the growing population of Rome, and had to import them from other Mediterranean countries. The difficulties of transportation, while doubtless great,[2] were not to be compared with the difficulties of acquiring the grain by the method of legal appropriation. No very large portion of the supply was ever bought and paid for with the products of industry, for Rome was never an industrial city. The grain was regarded as one of the fruits of conquest, and was seized by the governors of the Provinces as legitimate tribute. Had Rome contained a manufacturing population, able to pay for its own food-supply, it is more than likely that the difficulties of transportation would have been overcome. It is only in this sense, if at all, that there is any truth in the contention of those writers who maintain that the fall of Rome was due to lack of means of communication with the provinces.

---

[1] On the population of ancient cities, see Beloch, *Die Bevölkerung der griechisch-römischen Welt.* The same writer gave an excellent survey of the development of the great cities of Europe from the earliest times, in an address before the eighth International Congress of Hygiene and Demography at Budapest in 1894; cf. the *Report of the Proceedings*, vii, 55-61. See also his article " Zur Bevölkerungsgeschichte des Altertums " in *Jahrbücher für National-ökonomie und Statistik* (1897), 68: 371 *seq.*

[2] Augustus is said once to have been on the verge of suicide out of fear lest his overdue corn-ships should not arrive.—Hume, *Essay on the Populousness of Ancient Nations.*

Within the last century the difficulties of transportation that troubled Rome so much have been solved by England, which likewise had to look to foreign countries for its food-supply. Not only that, but science has become so useful a handmaid of agriculture that the farmer by using a little more capital, secures a larger product without adding to his labor force. The net result of progress in these two directions is the removal of a surplus rural population to the manufacturing and commercial districts (cities), for " when the rural population has once become sufficiently numerous to carry on cultivation in the most profitable way, all further growth becomes disadvantageous; whereas the materials with which the varied manufactures deal are practically unlimited in amount and there is no other check to possible growth to such industries than the difficulty of finding markets for their products."

The improvements that have taken place in agricultural methods within the last one hundred and fifty years have been almost unprecedented; but they have been so over-shadowed in the minds of economists and statisticians by the revolutionary changes in manufactures and transportation that they have hardly received their due share of attention. We hear often enough of the Industrial Revolution in England in the second half of the eighteenth century, but we seldom hear of the Agrarian Revolution that took place at about the same time.

English agriculture had been progressing throughout the eighteenth century; while population had doubled itself, the number of persons engaged in agriculture had decreased not only relatively, but down to 1770, actually.[1] But the revolution in English agriculture, whereby unscientific methods were replaced with scientific methods, is connected with the

[1] Prothero, *The Pioneers and Progress of English Farming*, p. 38.

enclosure of the common lands, which began to be carried out on a large scale in the reign of George III, beginning in 1760.[1] The results of the enclosures were the extension of arable cultivation to inferior and waste lands, the destruction of the antiquated common-field system, whereby one-third of the land lay fallow each year, the consolidation of small farms into large and the consequent introduction of the principle of rotation of crops, of roots and artificial grasses, and other improved methods.[2] The common-field system, according to Arthur Young, yielded 17–18 bushels of wheat per acre, the new system of large farms 26; the fleece of sheep pastured on common fields weighed only 3½ pounds as compared with 9 pounds on enclosures.[3] Bakewell (1725–1794), whom a French writer pronounces " un homme de génie qui a fait autant pour la richesse de son pays que ses contemporains Arkwright et Watt," [4] began scientific stock-breeding; as a result of his efforts and the enclosure of the common pasture land, " during whose existence the cattle were stunted if not starved," the average size of cattle was greatly increased with scarcely any increase in expenditure.[5] At the Smithfield Market the average weight of animals was

In	Beeves.	Calves.	Sheep.	Lambs.
1710......................	370 lbs.	50	28	18
1795......................	800 "	148	80	50

The consequence of all these improvements was to set free a vast number of men who found employment in the new manufacturing industries which were supplying the markets

---

[1] *Cf.* the table in Prothero, *op., cit.,* p. 257.

[2] Prothero; *cf.* also Toynbee, *The Industrial Revolution,* 88–9 (Humboldt ed.).

[3] Gibbins, *Industrial History of England,* 117.

[4] Prothero, *op. cit.,* 49.

[5] *Ibid.,* 53.

of the world. "The enclosures drove the laborers off the land because it became impossible for them to exist without their rights of pasturage for sheep and geese on common lands."[1] At the same time the consolidation of farms reduced the number of farmers.[2] Thus, while the acreage under production and the aggregate product have greatly increased since 1750, the agricultural population has declined relatively to the industrial population. In 1770, Arthur Young estimated the total population of England at eight and one-half millions, of which three and one-half millions were agricultural and three millions manufacturing. Although the total numbers are too large, the proportions may be accepted as approximately correct.[3] Comparing these proportions with the results of census returns in the present century, we have the following table:[4]

	Proportion of agr. pop. to entire pop.
1770	42 per cent.
1811	34 "
1821	32 "
1831	28 "
1841	22 "

The figures since 1841 may be omitted, inasmuch as a decline in the aggregate production of cereals then began,[5]

[1] Toynbee, *op. cit.*, 89.

[2] Cobbett, writing in 1826, mentioned a single farmer who held "the lands that the now living remember to have formed fourteen farms, bringing up in a respectable way fourteen families." (Quoted by Toynbee, *op. cit.*, 89.) This, however, cannot be considered a typical case. Arthur Young found in 1801 that of thirty-seven enclosed parishes in Norfolk, the population had increased in twenty-four, diminished in eight, and remained stationary in five. (Prothero, *op. cit.*, 72.) There could have been no such extensive rural depopulation as took place in the period of the sixteenth-century enclosures, because now the object of the change was not more pasturage, but increased tillage.

[3] Gibbins, *Ind. Hist. of Eng.*, p. 152.

[4] Prothero, *op. cit.*, 111.

[5] Following upon the repeal of the corn laws in 1846.

and there would naturally be a decrease in the agricultural population. But up to the middle of the century England had grown the bulk of her own wheat, and the importations were mostly confined to the years of poor crops. The table therefore shows that while in 1770 42 per cent. of the population was attached to the soil in order to produce the nation's food-supply, in 1841 but 22 per cent. of the population was required for this purpose, thus leaving 78 per cent. to settle wherever other industries determined.

The increase in agricultural production might be followed out in other countries, but it would be unprofitable, inasmuch as England's progress is typical. A distinguished French authority wrote about the middle of this century that the total produce of French agriculture had doubled since the Revolution.[1] But it is very improbable that the agricultural population of France increased by more than 20 per cent. in that period.

In the United States, where machinery has been so extensively applied to agriculture, there is no lack of evidence as to the increased production per cultivator. Consider the application to agriculture of some of the most ingenious machinery invented by a nation of especial mechanical talent. Consider also the results of farming on a large scale by capitalistic methods. We hear of immense farms in the West like that of Dr. Glinn in California, who has 45,000 acres under wheat; and Mulhall estimates that one farmer like Dr. Glinn, with a field of wheat covering a hundred square miles, can raise as much grain with 400 farm servants as can 5,000 peasant proprietors in France.[2] It is no easy matter to estimate the saving in labor force which American methods have accomplished on the farm, but Mr. Mulhall may not be altogether out of the way. The special agent of

[1] L. de Lavergne, *Économie rurale de la France depuis 1789*, 2d ed., p. 59.
[2] *Progress of the World* (1880), p. 499.

the Tenth Census, who reported on Interchangeable Mechanism, made a somewhat more conservative estimate. Mr. Fitch said: " It is estimated by careful men, thoroughly conversant with the changes that have taken place, that in the improvement made in agricultural tools, the average farmer can, with sufficient horse-power, do with three men the work of fifteen men forty years ago, and do it better." [1] Nor is this all of America's contribution; her improvements in the raising of grain and production of meats have been matched by her improvements in the handling and marketing of the same supplies; by cutting down the wastes of distribution, such improvements reduce the amount of agricultural labor.needed.   The importance of transportation in bringing new lands into the area of cultivation for the world market has already been mentioned.   But transportation, in connection with the other modern mechanics of exchange, economizes the amount of agricultural labor by diminishing the need of over-production, and thus equalizing the supply in space and time.   The auxiliaries of transportation are characteristically American methods of centralization.[2]   Instead of the multitude of small buyers who conduct the grain business in Europe, America has concentrated the trade in the hands of a smaller number of large firms who have built the great grain-elevators and developed the system of handling grain in bulk, which, as much as anything else, has enabled American grain to enter the markets of the world.   In no other field have American business ability and capacity for organization produced greater economies; for along with the improvement in the technical means of handling grain, there has been developed a more efficient system of credit, of buying and selling (produce exchanges!), etc.[3]   The grand

---

[1] *10th Cen. Mfs.* (Section on Agricultural Implements), p. 76.

[2] See Sering, *Die Landwirthschaftliche Konkurrenz Nordamerikas*, 491 *seq.*

[3] For example, the grading of wheat whereby it is bought and sold without the use of samples.

result is an equal distribution of the food supply to all countries within the area of exchange. Local surpluses are abolished. Local scarcities are also abolished and therewith the fear of famine, which necessitated the maintenance of stores of grain. Both the surpluses and the stores denoted over-production, or the occupation of more laborers in tilling the soil than society really needed. They are now free to settle where they choose.

III. THE GROWTH OF COMMERCIAL CENTRES.

[AUTHORITIES.—Easily the best survey of economic evolution is Professor Karl Bücher's essay on *Die Entstehung der Volkswirthschaft* (Tübingen, 1893), a brilliant piece of work which ought long since to have been translated into English. Professor Schmoller's interpretation of economic history differs little from Professor Bücher's, and one of his studies of "Die Wirthschaftspolitik Friedrichs des Grossen," which contains his views, has been published in English as one of Professor Ashley's "Economic Classics" under the title of *The Mercantile System*. With this should be read Herbert Spencer's treatment of "Industrial Institutions" in the third volume of his *Principles of Sociology*.

The general features of economic organization are described in such works as Cunningham's *Growth of English Industry and Commerce* (2 vols., Cambridge, 1890-1), and Ashley's *Introduction to English Economic History* (2 vols., New York, 1888-93). The town economy will be understood by readers of Mrs. J. R. Green's *Town Life in the Fifteenth Century* (2 vols., New York, 1894). The patriarchal family is familiar to Americans from the works of Sir Henry Maine (*Ancient Law and Village Communities*) Hearn (*The Aryan Household*), de Coulanges (*The Ancient City*), and W. W. Fowler (*The City State of the Greeks and Romans*). For the abundant literature on the mark and the manor, the reader is referred to the bibliographies in Ashley.

The origin and location of towns is treated in a philosophic manner by Roscher in the introductory chapter of his work on commerce and industry; *System der Volkswirthschaft*, dritter Band, *Die Nationalökonomik des Handels und Gewerbefleisses*, "Einleitung—Aus der Naturlehre des Städtewesens im Allgemeinen." Roscher further develops the theory of the location of cities in an essay "Ueber die geographische Lage der grossen Städte," published in his *Ansichten der Volkswirthschaft*, vol. 1. Cf. the work by J. C. Kohl, *Die geographische Lage der Hauptstädten Europas*, and the latter's standard work, *Der Verkehr und die Ansiedelungen der Menschen in ihrer Abhängigkeit von der Gestaltung der Erdoberfläche*, 1843. This was written before the era of railways, however, and is in some respects superseded by the later works: E. Sax, *Die Verkehrsmittel in Volks- und Staatswirthschaft*, Vienna, 1878; A. de Foville, *De la Transformation des Moyens de Transport et ses Conséquences économiques et sociales*, Paris, 1880; the most recent treatment is by a young American, Dr. C. H. Cooley, whose book (*The Theory of Transportation*, in publications of the American Economic Association) will interest the general reader as well as the trained economist; it is by far the best study of the subject in English, buf, like the others, is written from the standpoint of transportation. Sir James Stewart devotes a chapter of his *Inquiry into the Principles of Political Economy* to this subject ("What are the Principles which regulate the Distribution of Inhabitants into Farms, Villages, Hamlets, Towns and Cities") chap. ix in vol. i of the *Works of Stewart*, edited by Gen. Sir J. Stewart, London, 1805. More recently the subject has been approached from the side of geography, *e. g.*, Ratzel's *Anthropo-geographie*, vol. ii, §§ 12-14, in which connection may also be mentioned a paper by Prof. W. Z. Ripley on "Geography and Sociology" (with bibliography) in the *Pol. Sc. Quar.*, x, 636-55.]

In point of time, the earliest economic force working for the concentration of the released agricultural population was trade. Without trade and commerce, indeed, no towns or cities could come into existence; for they presuppose a non-agricultural population which buys its food-supply. When a portion of the tillers of the soil abandon agriculture and obtain their food-supplies by the exchange of other products of industry, the foundation of trade is laid; the specialization of functions, or the division of labor in its broad sense, has then begun its course, which tends to an ever-widening circle of exchange and enlargement of the commercial centres. The economic historians, in tracing the development of industrial society, are accustomed to distinguish three or four periods, in which the predominating types of organization were, respectively, (1) the household or village economy, (2) the town economy, (3) the national economy, (4) the international economy, toward which we are approaching as the ultimate goal. The first period—represented by such diverse human groups as the patriarchal family, the village community, mark or *mir*—is much the longest, and endured in Europe to about 1000 A. D.[1] The characteristics of the village economy are generally familiar since the time of Sir Henry Maine. "The village is an economic and commercial system complete in itself and closed against the outside world." Salt, iron, and in the later stages, tar and millstones, were the only commodities brought into the village from the outside.[2]

[1] That is, in the advanced countries. It lasted until quite recently in Russia. *Cf.* Hourwich, *Economics of the Russian Village* (Columbia Studies).

[2] *The Mercantile System*, 5, 6. "It is hardly possible for [a villager] to come into closer intercourse with outsiders; for to remove any of the products, whether they may be derived directly or indirectly from the common land, is forbidden." And Prof. Thorold Rogers says: "The trader did not exist in the villages. In most villages he hardly existed at the beginning of the present century. In my native village the first shop was opened, for general trade, about 60 years ago." (*Six Centuries of Work and Wages*, p. 147.)

Trade was in fact impossible so long as villages were hostile to one another; but even then, as Cunningham notes,[1] its advantages were so clearly felt that the boundary place between two or more townships came to be recognized as a neutral territory, where men might occasionally meet for mutual benefit. The boundary-stone was the predecessor of the market-cross and the neutral area around it of the market-place. Trade was also promoted by religious assemblies. From very early times, says Cunningham,[2] men have gathered to celebrate the memory of some hero by funeral games, and this has given the occasion for meeting and trading; so that fairs were held annually at places of burial. Mediæval towns grew up around shrines and monasteries built at the graves of early martyrs.[3] Other towns grew up around forts or the castles of feudal lords. It is remarked that many of the earliest English towns (leaving out of account the cities of the Roman period), were founded by the Danes, who were noted traders.[4] During the invasion of the Northmen, the garrisons of both Danes and English became nuclei of towns. But the most common origin of American and English towns is the primitive agricultural village, or a coalescence of several villages. Thus the latter origin is attested in numerous cities by the survival of several agricultural functionaries like haywards, pinders, molecatchers, etc.[5] And since facilities for trade were the primary cause of the development of village communities into towns, it follows that those villages which were situated at fording places, in the midst of a fertile plain, or on good trade routes, would be favored

---

[1] Vol. i, p. 76.

[2] Ibid., i, 90.

[3] On the origin of ancient towns, see E. Kuhn, *Ueber die Entstehung der Städte der Alten*, Leipzig, 1878.

[4] Cunningham, *op. cit.*, i, 88.   [5] *Ibid.*, i, 23.

in growth. We are not especially concerned in this essay with the principles of city-location, and it will suffice merely to indicate the fundamental theory. It may, then, be stated with some confidence that while certain cities derived their location in former ages from proximity to a fort or a religious establishment; while many modern cities have had their location determined by political reasons (*e.g.*, Washington and many of our State capitals) ; while numerous cities in all periods have arisen in the vicinity of mines or other riches of the earth which furnished natural advantages for production—yet, nevertheless, the prevailing influences in determining the location of cities are facilities for transportation. The greatness of an inland city will depend on the size of the plain for which it is the natural centre of distribution, and in a second degree on the fertility of soil, which determines the number of inhabitants in the plain.[1] The factor of chief importance in the location of cities is a *break in transportation.* A mere transfer of goods will require considerable machinery ; and so we find commercial centres at the confluence of rivers, head of navigation, fords, meeting-point of hill and plain, and other places where the

---

[1] Paris became the metropolis of France because it was the center of a great plain including more than one-half of France; modern transportation has perpetuated its natural advantages. In new countries, however, transportation tends to emancipate cities from this condition of dependence. Bötzow ("Bodenbeschaffenheit und Bevölkerung in Preussen," *Zeitschrift des preussischen statistischen Bureaus*, xxi, 287–91), aims to show that density of population is largely determined by the fertility of soil, even in the industrial stage. The number of inhabitants to each 100 square kilometers of territory (excluding water surface) for the rich and the poor soils was :

	Good soils.				Poor soils.			
			Increase per 100 inhabitants.				Increase per 100 inhabitants.	
	1819.	1849.	1819–49.	1849–75.	1819.	1849.	1819–49.	1849–75.
Urban	1,259	1,891	150	170	170	260	153	145
Rural	4,313	6,184	143	125	2,723	3,961	145	115
Prussia	5,572	8,076	145	135	2,891	4,221	146	117

physical configuration requires a change of vehicle. But the greatest centres will be those where the physical transfer of goods is accompanied with a change of ownership; there is then added to the mechanical apparatus of temporary storage and transfer, the complex mechanism of commercial exchange. Importers and exporters, merchants and money-changers accumulate vast wealth and require the presence of other classes to satisfy their wants, and population will grow rapidly. It is therefore easy to understand why so many of the large cities of the world are commercial centres, if not actual seaports. Every *great* city owes its eminence to commerce, and even in the United States, where the railways are popularly supposed to be the real city-makers, all but two of the cities of 100,000 or more inhabitants are situated upon navigable waters;[1] the most rapidly growing cities of their class in the country are the lake ports, Chicago, Buffalo, Cleveland, Detroit, Milwaukee, etc.[2] One would expect that, in a country where cities have been located since the advent of railways, the matter of water communication would be of minor importance. That this is not the case shows the one-sidedness of the reasoning that steam alone is the fundamental cause of the concentration of population.[3] In Europe,

---

[1] The exceptions are Indianapolis and Denver. In its early days, however, Indianapolis was the seat of a considerable river trade. Denver, which is situated on the south fork of the small Platte river, is a great railway and distributing centre, reaching both the mining regions of the mountains and the agricultural districts of the plains. It is at once interesting and instructive to study a topographical map showing, along with the physical features of the country, the location of the principal cities. (Such maps may be found in the *Statistical Atlas of the United States*, the *Census Reports on Transportation*, and *Cram's Universal Atlas*, 1897, p. 33.)

[2] In his suggestive study of the "Density and Distribution of Population in the United States at the Eleventh Census" (*Economic Studies* of the American Economic Assn., ii, 448), Prof. Willcox emphasizes the fact that the most rapidly growing cities are the commercial centers, and especially the lake ports.

[3] There are a number of cities in central New York—Rochester, Utica, Syra-

too, the traveler is struck with the frequency with which
the blue strips of water appear on the street maps of cities in
his guide books.   That not all the large cities of Europe are
situated on navigable rivers, lakes or seas, is due not to their
recent foundation as railway centres, but to their original
foundation for political or military reasons.   New York's
primacy depends upon her location at the junction of land
and water transportation; in New York occurs the change
of ownership and transfer of goods in the commerce between Europe and the United States.   If the water route
could be extended inland to Chicago by means of a ship
canal, Chicago would become the terminus of European
commerce, and in the course of time would with scarcely
any doubt take from New York the rank of commercial and
financial centre of the New World, and prospectively, of the
globe.

But, to return to the history of the growth of commerce,
the primitive trading-point at a fort, monastery, ford, castle
or harbor, might long have remained a mere market-place or
fair-ground, if the trading class had not attracted to it other
industries, thus bringing about the division of labor.   The
earliest realization of this principle was in ancient times when
the *paterfamilias* abandoned his farm and a portion of his
dependents, and betook himself with another portion of his

cuse, etc.—that owe their early growth to the Erie canal; the steam engine has
but perpetuated them. And indeed the influence of steam on transportation
methods is frequently exaggerated. Ocean commerce expanded rapidly before
the application of steam to freight carriers. It is only two decades back that the
marine engine was perfected; prior to 1~75 the ocean steamship had not been a
formidable competitor of the sailing vessel. Even to-day sailing vessels constitute
a large part of the shipping of the United States, especially in the coastwise trade.
According to the Eleventh Census, 41 million tons of freight were carried in
steamers along the Atlantic coast and Gulf of Mexico in 1889, and 40 million tons
in sailing vessels. (*Compendium*, iii, 905.) Finally, it should not be forgotten
that the Roman world witnessed the foundation of great cities without the aid of
steam, thus testifying to the possibilities of water transportation routes.

slaves or dependents to the city. The Athenian lived upon
food sent to him from his own Attic estate outside the city
walls, and had almost everything else made for him by his
own slaves. In the later Roman times the division of labor
had been so far developed that some 150 different occupations were carried on by the slaves of a single family.[1] In
more recent times, when the original social unit was the village community of freemen, it was the artisan who abandoned
the soil and went to live in the town. It is hardly necessary
in this place to trace the process by which the members of
the village group became differentiated into farmers and
artisans. One member of the household after another, possessing some particular gift of skill or strength, found it more
advantageous to devote his whole time to one kind of work
than to take his turn at the various tasks of the household.
One man perhaps would begin by making all the shoes for
the household; having by long practice acquired more than
the usual skill at shoemaking, he would offer his service to
other households, traveling about like a modern umbrella-
mender or the village dress-maker. At length, instead of
carrying a few tools about with him he would learn that he
could do better by settling down in one place and augment-

---

[1] Prof. Bücher (*op. cit.*, 25) quotes a Dutch work of the seventeenth century as
enumerating 146 different occupations, and adds that modern scholarship has resulted in additions. The progress made in the separation of employment since
then may be seen in the following figures giving the number of trades practiced
at Frankfort, Germany, in the Middle Ages, compared with some ancient and
modern figures in other lands:

Rome	10–20
Greece, 337 A. D.	35
Frankfort, 1387	148
" 1440	191
" 1500	300
China, 1890	350
Germany, 1882	4,785

(Schmoller, " Die Thatsachen der Arbeitsteilung," *Jahrbuch für Gesetzgebung,
Verwaltung und Volkswirtschaft*, xiii, 1045.)

ing the number of his tools. And thus the shoemaker, the smith, the weaver, the dyer, the brewer, the bricklayer, the carpenter, accumulated capital and settled in the town. Such is the process of development of the free handicraftsman of the middle ages.

The differentiation between town and country is an important event in economic history, for it marks the separation of industry from agriculture.[1] Adam Smith could say that "the great commerce of every civilized society is that carried on between the inhabitants of the town and those of the country."[1] But while the towns thus carry on trade with the surrounding agriculturists, each town is as tightly closed against other similar groups as was the original household or village. This self-sufficing character of the mediæval town is not easily realized by the American of to-day, unless he has traveled in some backward country of Europe where the towns close their gates at nightfall and levy *octroi* duties on incoming merchandise. Perhaps Prof. Schmoller's description of town policy will aid in the realization of the separateness of mediæval communities: "Except during a fair, the foreigner was excluded from all retail trade, allowed to remain only a certain time, and prohibited from lending money to or entering into partnership with a burgess. He was burdened with heavier dues or fees for setting up a stall, for having his goods weighed, and for the services of brokers and exchangers. . . . In short, the town market formed a complete system of currency, credit, trade, tolls and finance, shut up in itself, and managed as a united whole and on a settled plan ; a system which found its center of gravity exclusively in its local interests, which carried on the struggle

---

[1] Karl Marx says that "the foundation of every division of labor that is well developed and brought about by the exchange of commodities is the separation between town and country." *Capital*, p. 212 (Humboldt edition). So also Adam Smith, Bk. iii, ch. i.

for economic advantages with its collective forces, and which prospered in proportion as the reins were firmly held in the council by prudent and energetic merchants and patricians able to grasp the whole situation."[1]

Nor was the solicitude of the mediæval town devoted to its market alone; it was equally concerned in preventing the contributory territory from trading with other towns. The cattle and dairy products must be sent to the town-market in order to keep down the cost of living of the townspeople; it would not do to have *their* produce go to other towns. Not only must the farmers not buy goods from any other town, but they must not make them for themselves; just as in the 18th century the colonial system expressed the policy of the mother country to do all the manufacturing and to confine the colonists to the production of raw materials, so the town economy of the middle ages aimed to take away from the country every competing industry that it possibly could. In Germany, when the towns were not curbed by a royal hand, they forbade the countrymen to brew beer, etc.

Now it is sufficiently obvious that, in an age when commerce was chiefly confined to the trade between a town and the surrounding country, the commercial centers would not attain large dimensions; and such was the character of the commerce that existed down to *circa* 1500 A. D., a fact apt to be forgotten when one thinks of the glory of Venice and the other Italian cities, which rested in the main upon foreign commerce. Nevertheless, this foreign commerce was concerned with draperies, silks, spices, gems, and other luxuries, and was really small in comparison with the annual commerce between the towns and the surrounding country.

The transition from the town economy to the national economy is often lost sight of in contemplation of the con-

---

[1] *The Mercantile System.* p. 11.   Cf. Ashley, *Introd. to Eng. Econ. Hist.*, vol. ii, bk. ii, ch. i, on the " Supremacy of the Towns."

temporaneous political changes, and it is forgotten that the central monarchy was but the outward expression in the political sphere of the triumph of new economic forces. The towns had been acquiring wealth with considerable rapidity before the Crusades began, but during the Crusades they absorbed a large share of the riches of feudalism, as a result of the willingness of the nobles to part with their estates and furniture in exchange for ready money with which to pay the expenses of their trips to the Holy Land. The cities then bought charters of freedom, and finally, through their alliance with the king, gave the death-stroke to feudalism. This happened in France in the reign of Louis XI. (1461–1483), and in England at the conclusion of the Wars of the Roses and the accession of Henry Tudor in 1485.

Industrial progress in the towns was preparing the way for that national unity which began to be realized with the disappearance of feudal sovereignty, and attained its object under the Mercantile system of Cromwell, Colbert and Frederick the Great. As far as England was concerned, a national economy might have existed in the fourteenth century. A national Parliament arose under Edward I. and soon accomplished national legislation that broke down local privileges; but there was no real national economic development until the end of the fifteenth century, and until then industry did not need a wider organization than the town community.[1] The growth of business enterprise and mercantile wealth conditioned the progress of the arts of production. But the entrepreneur, undertaker, adventurer, had made his appearance in English agriculture before the end of the fourteenth century, after the Black Plague (1348) had abolished serfdom and substituted money payments. The same spirit made its appearance in commerce. The Crusades not only transferred vast wealth from the nobility, who

[1] Ashley, *op. cit.*, ii, 89.

seldom used it productively, to the burgess of the towns, with whom it became capital, but stimulated commerce by the creation of new wants and tastes for Oriental luxuries. The annual visit of the Venetian fleet, laden with Oriental tapestries, jewels and spices, was a great event for England and the other nations of Western Europe. These commodities of foreign commerce were, to be sure, mainly luxuries. The arts of transportation at that time were adequate only for articles that were at once light, durable, valuable, and, therefore, purchasable by the few alone. But with the growth of commercial enterprise and wealth, trade began to embrace other goods, until it no longer remained true that the commodities used by the mass of the people were produced near the spot where they were consumed.[1] Already in the fourteenth century geographical specialization took place in wool; for, after the Black Plague, England became more and more devoted to sheep-raising, and sent her wool to Flanders to be made into cloth.[2] Not only did Flanders thus early become noted for its woollen fabrics, but Strassburg and other Alsatian towns in the same period drove the clothmakers out of Basel and other neighboring cities by their competition.[3] Between 1450 and 1550 the cloth manufacture of Germany was concentrated in places peculiarly fitted for it.[4] Gradually the weekly town market, in which the wares sold were almost entirely local products, gave way to the great annual fairs, which brought together the products of many cities and countries.[5]

[1] Cf. Schmoller's essay, " Der moderne Verkehr im Verhältniss zum wirthschaftlichen, socialen und sittlichen Fortschritt" (1870), in *Zur Social- und Gewerbepolitik der Gegenwart.*

[2] Gibbins, *Industrial History of England*, 48.

[3] Schmoller, " Die Thatsachen der Arbeitsteilung," in his *Jahrbuch*, 13: 1066.

[4] Schmoller, *The Mercantile System*, 32.

[5] The weekly local market began to give place to the fair in Germany about 1506 (Schmoller's *Jahrbuch*, 13: 1066), and the culminating point of the great

But as the towns thus came into closer connection, their rivalries led to innumerable petty conflicts which could be reconciled only by a superior authority. Town leagues were tried, and after their failure, the current set strongly toward nationalism.[1] Mercantilism is simply the attitude of this movement toward foreigners; the great Mercantilists were also engaged in sweeping away the internal barriers to nationalization. Colbert, whose name is so prominently identified with the mercantile policy that Colbertism has become a synonym of Mercantilism, built roads and canals, promoted technical and artistic education, and worked for a uniform customs system by reforming the river tolls, etc., within France, his aim all the while being to break down municipal and provincial autarchy and make of the French people a united nation.[2]

Frankfort fair was reached later in the same century (Bücher, *Entstehung der Volkswirthschaft*, 72). Until the era of these interstate or international fairs, the mediæval town, instead of importing goods from rival towns, had pursued the policy of importing skilled workmen, who thus became, according to Prof. Bücher, greater migrants than the artisans of these days of railways. (Essay on " Die inneren Wanderungen und das Städtewesen in ihrer entwicklungsgeschichtlichen Bedeutung," *op. cit.*, 302 ff. Cf. also Schmoller, *op. cit.*, xiii, 1066.)

[1] " With the transformation and enlargement of commerce, the growth of the spirit of union and the consciousness of interests common to whole districts; with the augmented difficulties in the way of a proper organization of economic life on the basis merely of town and village interests, and the increasing hopelessness of victory over the anarchy of endless petty conflicts, efforts and tendencies everywhere made their appearance toward some larger grouping of economic forces." Schmoller, *The Mercantile System*, 13.

[2] Cf. Schmoller, *op. cit.*, 54-5 : " The great laws of Colbert . . . . more important than the tariffs of 1664 and 1667 . . . . founded the legal as well as economic unity of France." Prof. Schmoller was one of the first investigators to seize upon the nation-building movement as the essence of Mercantilism; see his " Studien über die wirthschaftliche Politik Friedrichs des Grossen," in his *Jahrbuch*, 1884–8. Prof. Cunningham's great work, *Growth of English Industry and Commerce*, takes a similar view of the mercantile policy, as does also that brilliant historical essay of the late Prof. Seeley, *The Expansion of England*. Cf. also Bücher's *Entstehung der Volkswirthschaft*, 70 ff.

The nation, however, did not remain a self-sufficing industrial society. Mercantilism fulfilled its mission as soon as it unified the nation and gave national production a good start. When once it had produced a sufficient diversification of industries, it was permitted to lapse, and the nation gave itself to the production of those commodities for which it was particularly suited. Protectionism, the child of Mercantilism, has had a strong influence upon the industry of the United States; but no American statesmen have entertained the ambition of making the country absolutely self-sufficing. While protecting the infant manufactures of the United States against the competition of the established industries of Europe, they have kept the door wide open to the admission of tropical products. It may therefore be stated as a general truth that the whole world forms to-day a single industrial society.

The effect of this gradual enlargement of the economic society upon the growth of cities must be clear to every student. How different is London, a local market for the agriculturists of Essex and Middlesex, from London, the world's financial and commercial center! Or take the Dutch as a representative commercial nation, and compare their cities with those of their neighbors, the Belgians. Belgium is a great manufacturing country, consuming more coal and and iron per capita than any other European country except Great Britain. Holland has few manufactures, but carries on an extensive commerce.[1] It is also less densely populated

---

[1] Of the Belgians, 57 per cent. are engaged in manufacturing industry, the percentage in England being at the same date (1881) only 55 (Schmoller, " Die Thatsachen der Arbeitsteilung," in his *Jahrbuch*, 13: 1073). But statistics of occupation are difficult to compare, and for the Netherlands none comparable are at hand. The estimated annual value of manufactures in Belgium is 102 millions sterling, in Holland 35, being a ratio of 3:1, while the population of the two countries stands at the ratio of 4:3. (Hobson, *op. cit.*, 87.) On the other hand the Netherlands have the largest foreign trade in proportion to population of any

than Belgium.[1] Those who maintain that cities are the product of manufactures would expect to find a much larger urban population in Belgium than in the Netherlands. The actual percentages are as follows:

	Netherlands.	Belgium.
Townships of 2,000+	ca 85.	ca 75.
" " 10,000+	43.	34.8
" " 20,000+	31.3	26.1

The disparity of the percentages in favor of Holland might in the case of the townships having only 2,000 inhabitants, be due to the larger size of the Dutch township, which would thus include more of the scattered population, not really urban.[2] But in the case of the larger cities, the scattered population is too small to be a factor of any influence. The plain inference from the comparison is that commerce is one of the main causes of the concentration of population in large cities. The analysis of the growth of English cities after the opening-up of railways also confirms the hypothesis. It has been shown above (pp. 54–56), that nearly all of the cities which attained their maximum rate of increase in 1841–51, the decade of railway building, were seaports; the manufacturing centres having reached their highest rate of growth at the time when steam was applied to stationary machinery.

country in the world, averaging in the eighties over $200 per annum for each inhabitant, while the Belgian average is about $90. (Neuman-Spallart, *Uebersichten der Weltwirthschaft*, 1883-4, p. 549.) Hobson (*op. cit.*, 116) gives a map of the foreign trade of European nations; Holland is in a class by itself, while Great Britain, Belgium and Switzerland fall in the second class.

[1] The average size of the Dutch Gemeënte is 28.7 square kilometers, of the Belgian commune, 11.4 square kilometers. (P. 142.)

	Population.	Area.	Population to 1 sq. km.
[2] Belgium (1890)	6,069,321	29,456 sq. km.	206.
Holland (1889)	4,511,415	32,538 "	138.7

—*Statistik des Deutschen Reiches*, Neue Folge, Bd. 68, p. 6*.

As has been said, the growth of commerce is an accompaniment of the specialization of functions, or territorial division of labor. Recurrence to the biological analogy will serve to make clear this process.

Primitive society consists of the houseould group, which may be likened to the lowest type of organism; each is a composite of like cells. The differentiation of the organism into an inner and outer layer is paralleled by the first differentiation of society into town and country. Finally, there comes the formation of special organs and a distributive system—in other words, the agglomeration of population in centres of collection and distribution, and a system of transportation. To a highly developed society such centres of mass and force are as necessary as are its organs to any organism of the higher type. Economy of force, which is always the aim of specialization, is impossible of attainment without concentration. In the economic organism, transportation is the distributive system; differentiation is therefore impossible without improvements in this system. The better the transportation, the higher the specialization and the greater the concentration.

The close connection between transportation facilities and the territorial division of labor had led some writers to regard transportation as the sole agent in determining the distribution of population, its concentration in cities and the location of cities.[1] The truth doubtless is that transportation is one of the conditions, one of the external causes. The development of transportation proceeds *pari passu* with the evolution of the social body; as the differentiation progresses, transportation, like the distributive system in an organism, must be able to assume increased burdens. The growth of

---

[1] "The whole matter of the distribution of population, wealth and industries over the face of the earth is, in one of its aspects, a matter of transportation." Cooley, *Theory of Transportation*, 73. Cf. also Ratzel, *Anthro-geographie.*

commerce in the eighteenth century, due in large part to the growth of the American market, opened unlimited opportunities to the English manufacturer and brought out inventions that revolutionized the textile industry. The new machinery required for its highest efficiency a more regular power than that afforded by mill streams, and Watt invented the steam engine. Production therefore increased hundred-fold, and laid upon the canals and turnpikes impossible tasks; it called for improved means of transportation, and the railway came into being. As Hobson justly remarks, the history of the textile inventions does a good deal to dispel the "heroic" theory of invention—that of an idea flashing suddenly from the brain of a single genius and effecting a rapid revolution in trade. It should rather be said that inventions result from the inner " pressure of industrial circumstances which direct the intelligence of many minds toward the comprehension of some single central point of difficulty." [1]

IV. THE GROWTH OF INDUSTRIAL CENTERS.

[AUTHORITIES.—On the evolution of industry, Bücher is again the foremost authority, and no serious student of economics can afford to neglect his essay on " Die gewerblichen Betriebssysteme in ihrer geschichtli..hen Entwicklung" in *Enstehung der Volkswirthschaft*, Tübingen, 1893), and the article " Gewerbe," in Conrad's *Handwörterbuch*. Cf. also Held, *Zwei Bücher zur sozialen Geschichte Englands*, 541 and Erster Anhang entitled "Handwork und Grossindustrie"), and Schmoller's *Kleingewerbe;* while the Domestic System is portrayed in *Report from the (H. C.) Committee on the Woollen Manufacture of England*, 1806, pp. 3, 6, 8, 9, 10. The evolution of industries and towns in the United States may be studied in Weeden's *Economic and Social History of New England*, 2 vols., Boston and New York, 1891, esp., pp. 72, 271, 304, 305. (The development of Lynn as a typical factory town may be followed on pp. 308, 682, 735, etc.) The Factory System and Centralized Industry, or production on a large scale, are treated in the standard works on political economy; see especially, Mill, *Principles of Political Economy*, Bk. I, chs. 8, 9: Marshall, *Principles of Economics;* Walker's *Political Economy;* Hadley's *Economics;* the two American writers giving particular prominence to the undertaker or entrepreneur. The historical side is treated by Carroll D. Wright in his essay on the Factory System in *Rep. on the Mfs. of the U. S. at the Tenth Census*, and also in his little book entitled *The Industrial Evolution of the United States;* Levasseur, *L'Ouvrier Américain*, 2 vols., Paris, 1898; Stieda, Art. " Fabrik " in Conrad's *Handwörterbuch;* Marx, *Capital*; Hobson, *The Evolution of Modern Capitalism;* Schulze-Gävernitz, *Grossbetrieb* or *The Cotton Trade;* Wells, *Recent Economic Changes;* Atkinson, *The Distribution of Product ;* Schönhof, *The Economy of High Wages*, and *The Industrial Situation;* Mataja, *Grossmagazin und Kleinhandel;* Schmoller, "*Wesen und Verfassung der grossen Unternehmungen,*" in *Zur*

[1] *Evolution of Capitalism*, 57. Cf. Spencer, *Social Statics* (1893), p. 72; Schulze-Gävernitz, *Social Peace*, 15.

Social- und Gewerbepolitik der Gegenwart: also " Die Entwicklung des Grossbetriebs und die sociale Klassenbildung," in *Preussische Jahrbücher*, LXIX (1892), Heft 1; Sinzheimer, *Die Grenzen der Weiterbildung des fabrikmässigen Grossbetriebs*, a monograph in Brentano's *Münchener Volkswirthschaftliche Studien:* an interesting popular exposition of the management of large industries was given in a series of articles on " The Conduct of Great Businesses," in *Scribner's Magazine*, 1897.

The most luminous treatment of the principle of the division of labor is Bücher's " Arbeitsteilung and Sociale Klassenbildung," one of the essays appearing in *Die Entstehung der Volkswirthschaft;* Prof. Schmoller has also made noteworthy contributions to the subject, the most important being two articles in his journal (*Jahrbuch für Gesetzgebung, Verwaltung und Volkswirthschaft*, vols. XIII and XIV), entitled respectively " Die Thatsachen der Arbeitsteilung," and " Das Wesen der Arbeitsteilung; " see also Häckel, *Arbeitsteilung in Menschen und Thierleben;* Spencer, *Principles of Sociology*, esp. Part VIII, ch. II; Bagehot, *Physics and Politics;* Schäffle, *Bau und Leben des Socialen Körpers*, as well as his text-book of political economy, *Das gesellschaftliche Syst. m der menschlichen Wirthschaft;* Simmel, *Ueber sociale Differencirung;* Durkheim, *La Division du Travail;* Losch, *Nationale Production und nationale Berufsgliederung;* and the leading text-books—Mill, Walker, etc.]

In the foregoing section it was shown how economic development, or the integration of isolated social and economic groups, demands the concentration of a portion of the population in commercial cities. Similarly, it may be shown how the enlargement of the market, which is one aspect of the process of growth of industrial society from the village economy to the world economy, has brought about centralization in the manufacturing industries and enforced the concentration of another portion of the population in industrial, or perchance commercial, cities. A brief review of industrial evolution will suffice to show the importance of the size of the market with regard to the business organization or internal structure of industry.

In the evolution of industry, four principal stages may be clearly distinguished: (1) the household or family system, (2) the guild or handicraft system, (3) the domestic or cottage system, (4) the factory system or centralized industry. Under the household regime, each family manufactures its own supplies, and there is no buying and selling. The village community and manorial group are but enlarged families, and we have already pointed out their industrial autonomy. The advent of the trader and the introduction of money caused the disintegration of the village by differentiating its

members.   The family shoemaker, instead of helping on the
farm and making shoes for the other members of the family
at odd moments, began to travel about working for other
families like the itinerant village dressmaker still to be met
with in many parts of the country.   At length he would have
accumulated sufficient capital to buy his own materials, and
would then set up a shop and make shoes to order.   In
locating his shop he would naturally choose the most central site, and would therefore in all likelihood become a
neighbor of the trader in the town or a large village.   Thus
the handicraft system of industry and the town economy are
different aspects of one stage of economic evolution.   Both
lasted to about the middle of the fifteenth century.

In the course of time the primitive shoemaker's business
would have increased so much by reason of the growth of
population and the extension of the market, that he would
feel himself impelled to employ assistants or apprentices.
But before enlarging the capacity of his own shop, which
would probably require considerably more capital than he
could command in those early times, he would be more
likely to place orders with some of his fellow-craftsmen who
lacked his business talent and enterprise in attracting customers or in accumulating capital.   This new division of labor,
involving the differentiation of employing or wage-earning
classes (the capitalists, undertakers, business men on the
one hand, and the laborers or "hands" on the other), is the
beginning of modern Capitalism.   Logically, it is only a short
step hence to the factory system, wherein the employer
brings together the workers under one roof.   But it required
immense improvements in means of communication to
replace the local market, in which the handicraftsmen made
the vast majority of things to order, with a wider market
wherein the master (eventually the capitalist) sold his ready-
made products to whatever buyers appeared.   Historically

it required nearly three centuries to make a modern capitalistic employer out of the mediæval master handicraftsman employing one or two journeymen and apprentices. The first middleman in manufactures was the mediæval clothier, who owned no buildings, but bought the raw materials, distributed them among the weavers, and sold the cloth in the market.

The factory system was made possible by the gradual enlargement of the market;[1] its triumph was assured by the invention of power-machinery in the eighteenth century and the development of the modern systems of transportation and communication in the nineteenth century. The countries most energetic in introducing the new improvements in means of communication are the countries that have carried the factory system to its highest development. The tendency toward production on a large scale is too familiar a fact to the American to demand statistical proof; it is sufficiently illustrated in the statement that the average number of employees to an establishment in the textile industries has increased as follows:[2]

1850	48
1860	64
1870	58
1880	95
1890	124

In the surrender of the small producer to the corporation and trust lies, of course, the explanation of the decay of village or local industries carried on under the antiquated

---

[1] "Communication is the outer vehicle, commerce the inner soul which gave the impetus to centralized industry." Schmoller, in *Preussische Jahrbücher*, vol. lxix, pt. 4.

[2] *11th Cen. Mfs.*, Part III, p. 3. Cf. *ibid.*, Part I, p. 4. While in 1850 the average amount of capital to each manufacturing establishment reported was $4,300; in 1860 it was $7,100; in 1880, $11,000; in 1890, $19,000. The average number of employees rose from 8 in 1850 to 14 in 1890.

handicraft regime. The story of the decline of the villages in the United States has been told by Mr. H. F. Fletcher in an article entitled "The Doom of the Small Town," and published in the *Forum*, April, 1895. The number of village saw-mills, flour and grist-mills, establishments devoted to furniture and cabinet-making, and the manufacture of agricultural implements, brick and tile, etc., has perceptibly declined. Mr. Fletcher also investigated the statistics of population of the villages along the Chicago, Rock Island and Pacific and the Michigan Central railways from Des Moines to Detroit, a line of 500 miles, running through a flourishing agricultural region. The only villages along these two lines of railway that showed a gain of population at the last census were those immediately adjacent to Chicago; all the other small communities have steadily lost population. Mr. Fletcher attributes the decline to discriminating railway rates, favoring the great cities; but the more general cause is the substitution of production on a large scale for local industries.

The transformation of industry in Germany has been going on at a very rapid rate in the last decade, and the industrial census of 1895 showed that the old *Handwerker*, or master artisans, are disappearing before the advance of the factory system, thus:

	Percentage increase or decrease, 1882–1895.[1]
Persons working on their own account	— 5.3
" " in establishments of 5 or fewer workmen......	+23.0
" " " " " 6–50 "	+76.3
" " " " " more than 50 "	+88.7

Similar statistics may be given of village industries in England.[2] Thus, in the agricultural county of Huntingdon

---

[1] Cf. summary *Jahrbücher für N. O. und Statistik*, lxx, 665. The question is discussed by Sinzheimer, *op. cit.*

[2] Ogle, "The Alleged Depopulation of the Rural Districts," in *Jour. of Stat. Soc.*, liii (1889), pp. 219, 226, 228, 230. The subject is treated at some length by Graham, *The Rural Exodus*, chapter iv.

the number of handicraftsmen, tradesmen and other classes
was as follows:

	1851.	1861.	1871.	1881.
Building trades	1,140	1,050	1,092	997
Milliners and seamstresses	741	889	815	830
Lace makers	1,022	708	678	389
Shoemakers	700	669	499	364
Paper-makers	160	230	264	305
Total of 11 trades	4,932	4,611	4,307	3,704
Shopkeepers	1,338	1,370	1,513	1,444
Drink trade	319	324	415	268
Professional classes, teachers	332	369	408	421
do clerical, medical, etc	246	255	243	234
Personal services	2,308	3,165	3,638	3,293
Agriculture	12,256	12,173	11,819	10,161

In England the decline of agriculture is a cause of the
decay of villages which can scarcely be said to exist in the
case of the Western villages embraced in Mr. Fletcher's
investigation. But agricultural depression evidently cannot
account for the remarkable decrease in the number of shoe-
makers and lacemakers, the cause of which is indisputably
the centralization of industry.

The foregoing figures of Dr. Ogle's suggest other consequences of the modern transformation. Thus the decreasing
number of persons engaged in the drink trade results from
the decline of travel on the highways since the era of railways.[1] The professional classes, omitting teachers, are declining in number as a natural result of the modern tendency
toward specialization, and the ability of the rich cities to
attract to themselves the leading specialists. The village
doctor cannot compete against the specialists and hospitals
—both city institutions. The small decrease in the number
of shopkeepers is worthy of comment. The storekeeper

[1] But the bicycle era, upon which we have already entered, promises to re-
habilitate the country inn.

would naturally be among the last of the villagers to feel the competition of centralized industry. At first, indeed, the railway benefited the village tradesmen, for it enabled him to supply his customers with the most approved goods from the centres of fashion. Thus the village storekeeper prospered long after the downfall of the village manufacturer; but in these later days he is fast succumbing to city competition. The mail order system perfected by the city department stores has drawn much of the village trade to the city, and the cheapening of both passenger fares and express rates enables ever-increasing numbers of villagers to do their shopping in the city and have their purchases delivered free.

The department store, or Universal Provider, now found in every large American city, affords one of the best illustrations of the development of centralized industry, although it belongs properly to the topic of commerce. The evolution of retail trade may be presented in three stages: (1) A single store meets the demands of the entire community; its stock consists of nearly everything wanted, from a needle to an anchor. This is the old-time "village store" which still exists in small communities. But its inefficient organization prevents it from keeping pace with the growing demands of a rising community, and so (2) specialized or exclusive stores spring up, each of which in its own line outdoes the general store. But after a time the growth of capital and of business ability, and the expansion of the market, enable some sagacious man to unite several of the specialized businesses under one roof and management in (3) the department store, which is like the village general store in outward form, but very different in internal organization,[1] for it adheres to the specialization devoted in the second stage. Its large capital enables it to offer greater variety in each line of goods than the village store and lower prices than the specialized store.

[1] Each department has its own head.

Manufacturing industry has not yet reached the third stage, represented in retail trade by the department store. The tendency has been toward greater specialization of the processes; in the woolen industry, for example, the highest development (Bradford, England) has resulted in separate establishments for scouring, carding and combing, spinning, weaving, dyeing and finishing, packing. Some experts regard this as the final development.[1] But there is already one establishment in Germany (Krupp's gun works) which not only carries on all the purely manufacturing processes, but also works up its own materials. In the United States the tendency seems to be to distinctly toward the consolidation of the various processes; thus the great steel "barons" are acquiring control of iron mines and transportation lines, and the Standard Oil Company, which began as refiners, have become carriers and are now buying up the control of the crude oil product.[2] Similarly, there exists a tendency toward the consolidation of allied manufactures, the successful bicycle maker applying his capital and business methods to the production of a general line of sporting goods, and finding his market already secured by the advertising he gave to his original product. The advantage of conducting manufacturing on such a "department store" plan lies, of course, in the greater steadiness of the business. Competition in any one line can be met by a reduction of prices there, to be made up by the profits on other lines, and at a time of depression in one trade the idle workmen may be set to work in other departments.

The effect of centralized industry—production for the world market—upon the distribution of population has already been noticed, but it is an interesting question to con-

---

[1] Col. North in *11th Cen. Mfs.*, Part iii, 18.

[2] It is related that one of the great New York hotels grows its own celery and raises its own poultry on Pennsylvania farms.

sider future prospects. No one can expect that future development will be in the direction of production on a small scale and for the local market. But while the unit of capital will in all probability increase as time goes on, may it not be dispersed in several small establishments, rather than concentrated in a single large establishment? One of the most characteristic achievements of the modern corporation is the conduct of such a business as that of a London bread company with large capital, almost entire control of the market, and a highly centralized management, but with branch stores scattered all over the great city. Something of the same phenomenon is to be observed in the United States, where manufacturing establishments scattered from east to west and north to south, unite in syndicates and trusts with large capital and central control. Why may not this process of centralization and decentralization go on indefinitely and even extend itself to separate establishments as soon as the perfection of small electric motors permits the diffusion of motive power in small shops and the homes of workingmen? In other words, what is to prevent a return to the cottage system, or domestic industries, with the discovery of cheap methods of distributing water power, as foreshadowed already by the harnessing of Niagara Falls?

In the first place, it is to be observed that factories came into existence long before the age of steam. Even England, whose writers are prone to assume the origin of the factory system in the inventions of Watt and Arkwright, possessed large enterprises in the sixteenth century. Tradition tells of "the famous and worthy clothier of England, Jack of Newbury," or John Winchcombe, who kept a hundred looms at work in his own house, and marched to Flodden Field at the head of one hundred of his journeymen.[1] The "Weavers' Act" of 1555 suggests a movement toward factories, and the

[1] Cf. Ashley, ii, 229.

tendency reappeared in the seventeenth and eighteenth centuries before the introduction of power-machinery. The large manufacturer had the advantage of a greater division of labor and greater rapidity of production. We need not, therefore, be surprised at Professor Ashley's concluding " it is certain that in the sixteenth century it was not at all impossible that the large manufactory might become an important—if not dominant—feature in the woollen trade of England. The prevention of such a development was due primarily to legislative action."[1] On the continent of Europe there was a more considerable development of factory methods antecedent to the invention of the steam engine.[2]

The chief reason why the mediæval clothier concentrated his workers in a factory instead of allowing them to continue working at home was economic in its character and accorded with a fundamental tendency of evolution ; it was the division and combination of labor. That this was the main advantage of concentration will appear upon summarizing the advantages of production on a large scale, giving rise to the

[1] That is, by limiting the number of journeymen that a master might employ, and the numerous guild restrictions.

[2] In the second half of the sixteenth century, a great Basel merchant, Ryff, visited Geneva, and was astonished to see " gigantic six-story houses " in which spinning was done on a collossal scale (Stieda, art. " Fabrik " in Conrad's *Handwörterbuch*). He found similar enterprises in Venice engaged in making sail-cloth. In France mention is made of a woollen mill at Abbéville, opened in 1669 with 500 Dutch workmen. And so it was in other countries. The most convincing proof that steam favors the factory system only because it promotes the division of labor, is found in the existence of centralized industry in the ancient cities. Alexandria was the great industrial city of the Roman world, and " here we meet centralized-industry magnates of the most modern pattern like Firma, who, in the reign of Aurelian, even stretched out his hand toward the crown, a baron of industry who made such profits from his paper mills alone that he boasted of his ability to maintain an army on papyrus." (Pöhlmann, *Die Uebervölkerung der antiken Grosstädte*, p. 31. For the factory system in Rome, see Blümner, *Die gewerbliche Thätigkeit der Völker des classischen Alterthums*, 112 ff.)

law of increasing returns in manufactures: (1) Economy in motive power and in the erection and maintenance of the plant. One large mill costs much less than two small ones. (2) Economy in machinery. Modern industry is essentially machine production, and machinery is constantly becoming more complicated and expensive. Improvements and new inventions are so frequent that only the concerns with large capital can keep abreast of the times and survive fierce competion. (3) Saving in wages, by securing the most extensive division of labor,[1] and employing the most highly specialized ability. It is only the "big concern" that can afford to employ a superintendent of the highest ability; a small establishment would not have work enough to engage his utmost energy and talent. So, too, only the large establishment can maintain its own staff of inventors and experts to experiment and investigate suggestions. (4) Economy in the utilization of by-products, which become profitable to handle only in large quantities. The four advantages already mentioned may be regarded as belonging to production proper; a fifth class of economies belongs to the commer-

---

[1] A great deal has been added to the theory of the division of labor since Adam Smith's first attempt, which was very inadequate. Smith suggested three advantages: (a) Increased dexterity, because "practice makes perfect." (b) Close attention to a single process encourages the invention of machinery to take over automatic operations. (c) Saving of time in going from one operation to another—of very minor importance, since the time lost by the all-round artisan is fully compensated by the stimulus of variety and change. (d) The most important advantage of all was overlooked by Smith—the gradation of labor. The separation of a process into its simplest elements permits the use of cheap labor for the heavy, mechanical work, and the concentration of the skilled and expensive labor exclusively upon the finer tasks. In the French silk industry of the middle ages each artisan understood every one of the 100 operations in his trade (Schmoller, "Die Thatsachen der Arbeitsteilung," in his *Jahrbuch*, 13: 1047.) To-day such an all-round education is worse than useless, because many of the operations can be performed by the ordinary street gamin with the shortest possible training. (e) Saving in capital, because the several workmen no longer require full outfits.

cial side of the business, and consists of (5) special facilities for buying, selling, shipping and advertising. The enterprise backed by large capital can buy its raw materials in the cheapest market and at the most favorable time, and store them until needed; it can also hold its finished product until the most favorable opportunity for sale arrives. It secures discounts by buying in large quantities, and low freight rates by shipping in large quantities. It can maintain its own "drummers," or commercial travellers, and in other ways advertise on a large scale. In short, the motto, "Large sales and small profits" explains why the "big concern" is the fittest to survive in the economic world.

Of all these advantages of the "big concern," the most important without doubt are those of the fifth class, which are connected simply with large aggregations of capital. But next to those in importance are the economies connected with machinery and the division of labor. Machinery on the whole tends to become more complicated, uniting more operations and requiring the co-operation of more laborers in tending each machine. Its rapid evolution has almost always and everywhere favored the growth of the large establishment. Similarly, the efficient division of labor makes for centralization, on account of saving in wages of superintendence. As Marx says, "Laborers as a general rule cannot co-operate without being brought together."

An additional influence favoring the substitution of the factory system for cottage industries in those trades like that of ready-made clothing, where the division of labor is not particularly advantageous, is the necessity of public inspection of industries. From purely selfish motives, society cannot afford to permit the sale of garments made in rooms

---

[1] A New York department store finds it profitable to expend $300,000 a year for advertising. The immense expenditures of bicycle-makers and manufacturers of proprietary articles for the same purpose are well-known facts.

poisoned with disease, and it has all but decided to abolish the " sweat-shop" on account of the difficulty of supervision.

While, then, cottage industries have revived in some parts of the world (notably in Ireland) we must not be sanguine of any general revival, even should transmission of power become an established fact. Motive power is but one factor in the triumph of the factory system, as history shows, and those who look for fundamental changes in the structure of industry, as soon as electric motors shall have superseded steam engines, are doomed to disappointment.[1] We may be sure that the factory system has come to stay. But how does it affect the distribution of population ? First, by destroying family industry prosecuted in the farm houses, it diminishes the number of agriculturists, as pointed out in Section II; secondly, by destroying industries in the handicraft stage (village shoemaking, milling, etc.), it removes population from the villages. The entire effect on the distribution of population is therefore centralizing. But it remains a question whether it favors the growth of large cities, as commerce does, or of small cities and towns. It is a question of the advantageous location of the large factory. If local facilities for transportation preponderate among the natural advantages, then the factory will go to the great city; while, if local facilities for production determine the site, the factory is likely to go to the small city. Let us consider the problem.[2]

[1] The German professors, in their anxiety to disprove Marx's thesis regarding the concentration of capital, are unduly hopeful of such changes as those mentioned above. The writer recalls the statement of a Berlin professor, lecturing on *Unternehmungsformen*, that the baker's trade among others could never be centralized, since the area that could be served by one shop is so small. The possibilities of telephone and delivery service escaped him, but even on his assumption that each block must have its own bakery, there is nothing to prevent all these small shops from becoming branches in a large concern, as is actually the case in London.

[2] In addition to the literature given in the preceding section, the following ar-

In the first place, it may be observed that where the division of labor is undeveloped, industry is carried on in proximity to consumers, and with reference to the advantages of consumption alone. Such is the case in the household economy, and for the most part in the town economy. Natural advantages for production are ignored, and it is in fact the very purpose of utilizing these that gives rise to the division of labor. This leads to the improvement of ways of communication, which in time alters the conditions of production. With regard to agriculture, mining, and the cruder manufactures, such improvement emphasized and intensified every natural advantage possessed by one locality over another; without easy transportation the fertile land of North Dakota would not compete with the rocky soil of Massachusetts in raising food for the industrial population of the eastern commonwealths. It is cheap transportation that has transferred the Irish and German peasants to the western plains of America, and that, by making profitable the working of iron mines lying at a distance from coal fields, has scattered the Cornish miners all over the world. By making available every natural advantage, transportation disperses the agricultural and mining population.

But what is true of agriculture and mining does not necessarily hold of manufacturing, which is far less dependent upon special qualities of the soil. In manufacturing, the raw material that comes from the soil is but a single factor in production; other factors are capital, labor, rent, taxes, market for the sale, and facilities for the shipment, of the manufactured products. Now the effect of improved transportation

ticles may be referred to: Ross, " Location of Industries," in *Quarterly Journal of Economics*, vol. x (1895–96); E. Laspeyres, " Standort der Gewerbe " (in the United States), *Berlin Vierteljahrschrift für Volkswirthschaft*, 1870, Nos. II and III, 1871, p. 1; Roscher, "Studien über die Naturgesetze die den zweckmässigsten Standort der Industriezweige bestimmen," in *Ansichten der Volkswirthschaft*, 3d ed., vol. II.

is to cheapen the raw materials, and as a consequence diminish their relative importance as a factor of production. The very fact therefore that railways have so cheapened transportation as to permit the shipment of bulky and heavy commodities (*i. e.*, raw materials) has diminished the impor tance of local *natural* advantages and increased the importance of the non-natural or artificial advantages for production. The crude manufactures (*e. g.*, lumber mills, tanneries) are still located near the source of supply of raw materials, but not the finer manufactures, and the question arises, is their location determined by other conditions of production, or by the conditions of consumption, *i. e.*, facilities for marketing, and cheap shipment to consumers? If nearness to consumers is the most important advantage in a manufacturing site, then it might be expected that the great commercial centers would also be the manufacturing centres, for they not only contain a rich and numerous body of consumers, but apparently afford superior facilities for distributing goods to the remaining consuming population. The tendency in manufacturing would then be toward centralization, and the great cities would grow at an enormous rate.[1] Such, indeed, has

---

[1] This is the argument and conclusion of Dr. Cooley in his authoritative work on *The Theory of Transportation.* He says (p. 88): "Natural facilities for transportation in many, if not most cases, determine the seats of manufacturing industries and of the population associated. Convenience of transportation becomes itself, in all advanced conditions of industry, the most important of local facilities for production; only cruder processes (sawing lumber, smelting ore, etc,), need take place near the source of raw material. Those of a finer sort, in which the cost of moving the raw materials is relatively less important, tend to seek the large centers of the collection, distribution and exchange of products. The vicinity of cities, wherever they may be located, will always be the chief seat of the finer manufactures, on account of the convenience that cities offer for selling and shipping goods."

The important influence that transportation facilities have upon the location of industries appears from the following facts, which also illustrate the intricacies of railway tariffs. It is said on good authority that the principal reason that potteries thrive in Staffordshire is because the Liverpool ships, carrying iron from the

been the actual tendency.   In former times, the manufacturer located his plant chiefly with regard to two advantages, water power and nearness to raw materials.   Steam applied to stationary engines has made him independent of water power; applied to engines of locomotion it has made him all but independent of the source of his raw materials.   Cheap transportation may put the great city on a level with the small town adjacent to the raw materials, *i. e.*, one tendency of modern improvements is to make the commercial centre also a manufacturing centre.

The centralizing influence of railways is particularly strong in countries where competition has had full sway; the competitive points, enjoying lower rates than rival towns on a single line, absorb all the growth of a region.   This fact has been a matter of every-day observation in many parts of the United States, and it is confirmed by all railway authorities.[1] It is asserted that " the entire net increase of the population from 1870 to 1890 in Illinois, Wisconsin, Iowa and Minnesota, except in the new sections, was in cities and towns possessing competitive rates, while those having non-competitive rates decreased in population;"[2] and in Iowa it is the

adjacent counties, want some bulky but light goods to fill up the cargoes.   Pittsburg in times past received a low rate on rough goods from Cleveland because they could be transported in the empty cars that had taken coal to Cleveland.   A slight decrease in the railway rates on wheat, or increase on flour, from the West to the East, would probably transfer the milling industry from Minneapolis to eastern cities.

[1] See the *Second Annual Report of the Interstate Commerce Commission*, p. 30; also the *Ninth Annual Report*, p. 16: " The effect of these disproportionate charges aids the building up of large cities and the concentration of great numbers of people at a few central places."   The Massachusetts Board of Railway Commissioners reported (1884) that the short-haul law " has helped to save small industries and small places from being crushed out of existence; it has checked the tendency toward consolidation which would build up one place or a few places at the cost of local enterprise."   (Quoted in *Pol. Sc. Quar.*, v, 426.)

[2] Stickney, *The Railway Problem*, 62.

general belief that the absence of large cities is due to the earlier policy of the railways in giving Chicago discriminating rates.[1]

If in the United States excessive competition among the railways has concentrated population in a few competitive points, the absence of competition in France has produced a similar effect. The French government supervised the construction of railways very closely and never permitted the waste involved in building more than one line between the same two points; each road therefore had a monopoly in its own district, and as it could earn a higher rate of profit on through business than on the local traffic, it neglected the latter.[2] Local branches remained unbuilt until subsidies were forthcoming from the central government and local authorities (1865). Ten years later an attempt was made to divert the local roads from their true purpose, and by building connecting links bring them into competition with the old roads for the through traffic; general insolvency of the local roads resulted, which was followed by a new monopoly. The state's guarantee of dividends (1883) undoubtedly prevents the French railways from building many new lines to develop new business; but in America this has been overdone, and it is probable that the smaller places are better served in France than they are in the United States—at least in the West.

In Germany, too, there was a tendency for manufacturers to settle in the cities upon the opening up of railway communication. A careful statistical study of the effect of railways upon the growth of places of different size was made several years ago by Dr. Schwabe, of the Berlin Statistical Bureau. He calculated the rates of growth of 125 cities for a certain

---

[1] Dixon, *State Railroad Control*, pp. 204, 151.

[2] Hadley, *Railroad Transportation*, 192–9.

period (ranging from six to twenty-one years) before and after the formation of railway connections.[1] The result was as follows: (A) Of 80 cities having less than 10,000 inhabitants each, the increase in population was greater in 23 and less in 57 after the opening of the railway. (B) Of 37 cities with populations 10,000–50,000, 18 showed an increased rate of growth, 19 a decreased rate. (C) Of 8 cities of more than 50,000 inhabitants, all but one (Cologne) grew more rapidly after the introduction of railways than before. It thus appears that the railways stopped the increase of population in the smaller cities, except those of an industrial character, and hastened the growth of the large cities. The railways concentrate transportation in a few channels, and the termini get the benefit. Investigations similar to those of Dr. Schwabe have since been undertaken by the imperial German statistical office, and while the conclusions are less positive they tend to confirm his results regarding large cities.[2]

The statistics of manufactures furnished by the United States government are not altogether trustworthy, but they at least show that in the period 1860–90 the movement was a centralizing one, toward the larger cities. In 1860 the annual production of manufactures per capita was $60 for the United States as a whole, $193.50 for ten cities having a population of 50,000 or more, $424 for ten cities under 50,000, and $44 for the rural districts.[3] Thus the per capita production was

---

[1] " Statistik des preussischen Städtewesens," in (Hildebrand's) *Jahrbücher für Nationalökonomie und Statistik*, vii (1866), pp. 1–32.

[2] " The railways do *not* hasten the growth of the smaller cities; their absence does *not* hinder the development of small places in comparison with those of the same size that are provided with railway connections." October Heft of *Monatshefte zur Statistik des Deutschen Reiches für das Jahr* 1878, or *Statistik des Deutschen Reiches*, xxx, Theil II, p. 14. A second study appeared in the *Monatshefte* of 1884 (Mai), V. 9.

[3] E. Laspeyres, " Die Gruppirung der Industrie innerhalb der Nordamerikanischen Union," in *Vierteljahrschrift für Volkswirthschaft und Kulturgeschichte* xxxiv, 17.

at that time largest in the smaller cities. In 1890, however, the per capita product of manufactures was $455 in the 28 great cities, $355 in the 137 cities of 20,000–100,000 population, and $58 for the remainder of the country.[1] The superiority of the smaller cities in 1860 had in 1890 given way to that of the great cities.

But it is probably safe to affirm that the centralization of manufacturing industry has reached its limit. A reaction toward decentralization began when manufactures located their mills in the suburbs of large cities in order to escape the high city rents and still avail themselves of the city's superior shipping facilities. Suburban enterprises have in the last decade become increasingly familiar phenomena, not only in the United States, but also in England and Germany, and have brought hope to social philanthropists disheartened with the poverty and misery of congested cities. The statistics of manufactures do not portray the tendency, because it is comparatively recent; but the Twelfth Census, to be taken next year, will show how rapidly manufacturing industries are leaving the larger cities. To give one example: the writer was informed by William A. Perrine, of the Ironmoulders' Conference Board of New York, that of some 65 iron foundries in New York City fourteen years ago, only fifteen now remain. Some have gone out of existence; but most of the remaining establishments have removed to Brooklyn, or suburban towns on the Hudson or in New Jersey.

In recent years the decentralizing movement has taken a still more favorable turn, largely as a result of continued improvements in transportation methods and a more enlight-

---

[1] Computations based on the return of the *11th Census*. The statistics refer to gross values, and present some incongruities when individual cities are compared. When, for example, the raw materials constitute so large a proportion of the gross value of the product as do the cattle and hogs of the Kansas City and Chicago stockyards, a small establishment will be credited with a large gross product. But such differences vanish in general averages of a whole class of cities.

ened policy on the part of railway managers, who have learned that the factor of distance is of minor importance in the expense account as compared with the additions to the revenue that result from a judicious encouragement of industries in small cities along their lines. To-day, practically every shipping point in New England enjoys precisely the same freight rates to points south and west of New York city as does the metropolis itself.[1] This is in effect the zone tariff system, which has been fully developed in Hungary; it gives one and the same rate to all points within each zone. Many influences favor the adoption of a single, uniform rate, as in the postal system, for territories of moderate extent. A uniform rate for the whole United States is of course impracticable; so large a country would have to be divided into zones. But in a country like Belgium the distances are so short that a single rate seems feasible. Students of railway tariff are familiar with the financial basis of the cheap "long-haul" rate. The English railways, for example, have found it profitable to carry fish to London as cheaply from Scotland as from English ports halfway to Scotland; it is business that more than covers the actual cost of movement, thus contributing something to the permanent, fixed charges, and at the same time it is business that could be secured in no other way. The railways entering New York have carried

---

[1] Although the writer has not the tariffs of the English railways at hand, it is evident that they are pursuing somewhat of the same policy as the American roads, from the fact that decentralization has set in among the cotton factories of Lancashire. The new factories are established neither in the great city nor in its suburbs, but in small localities outside. Both Manchester and its environs are being abandoned as manufacturing seats. (Schulze Gävernitz, *The Cotton Trade,* 74.) Professor Marshall notes that although "Manchester, Leeds, Lyons are still the chief centers of the trade in cotton, woollen and silk stuffs, they do not produce any great part of the goods to which they owe their chief fame." (*Op. cit.,* 354.) The decentralizing movement is also in progress in German Manufactures; cf.. Jannasch, *Europäische Baumwollindustrie,* 11, 12, "Auswanderung der Industrie nach dem flache Lande."

milk to the metropolis at a single rate from all points within a radius of 100 miles at first, and now nearly 400 miles. George R. Blanchard, of the Joint Traffic Association, testified before the Interstate Commerce Commission that the single rate could profitably be extended to distances up to 1,000 miles, and the counsel of the Delaware, Lackawanna and Western railway favored the extension to any distance within which it is possible to transport milk without injury. Distances, except they be transcontinental, are in fact losing much of their importance for the modern railway, inasmuch as the cost of service in no wise corresponds to the length of haul. The following diagram, taken from the work of a practical railway manager,[1] will show how slight a factor is distance in the rates between New York and Chicago:

RATES ON SUGAR, PER CWT., IN CAR-LOAD LOTS.

From New York to	Distance in miles.	Cents.	Graphic comparison.
Harrisburg, Pa.	200	15	——— —
Altoona, Pa.	326	15	——— —
Pittsburg	444	15	——— —
Bucyrus, Ohio	640	21	——— ——
Hamlet, Ind.	840	25	——— ———
Chicago	942	25	——— ———

The effect of a single, uniform railway rate, if it is ever realized (and we have seen that it is, to a certain extent, already a reality for New England manufacturers), would be to eliminate the factor of transportation facilities from the advantages or disadvantages of particular localities for production. The great city would then distribute its products no more cheaply than the small city.

Of the remaining facilities for production, there is no preponderance on the side of the great commercial centers. The important functions of buying and selling, and the securing of capital and credit, which formerly determined the

[1] E. P. Alexander, *Railway Practice,* p. 16.

location of many enterprises in the commercial centers, can now all be accomplished by means of a city office; there is not the slightest need of bringing the factory itself to the city. On the other hand, the small town has the great advantage of much lower rents and taxes, which in most cases will be decisive, especially if the town offers freedom from taxation and sufficient land for a building site as an inducement, a policy that has been the making of many a small city in Michigan, New Jersey and other commonwealths.[2] As regards the supply of labor, the relative advantages of city and country differ according to the kind of occupations. As a rule, the wages of skilled workmen are higher in the city than in the village, largely because of the greater efficiency of labor organizations. Even where wages rule the same, many employers have abandoned the great city to escape other exactions of the labor unions. The typographers have one of the strongest of trade unions, and their aggressiveness has already caused the removal to suburbs or small cities of the printing houses of several New York and Boston publishers. It is difficult to say how far this movement will extend; it is opposed now with all the strength of the trade unions in the city, and on the other hand, improved means of communication may in the course of time permit the formation of labor organizations in the country that will be as strong and efficient as those in the city, where large numbers who can meet together on short notice render a powerful association easier of formation. When that time arrives, the small town loses one of its attractions for the manufacturer.

With regard to unskilled labor, the case is somewhat different. The great city contains a large population that is

---

[1] On the other hand, it often happens that a firm of manufacturers build a factory in the open country, and start a land speculation of their own. The result in either case is a small manufacturing town.

uneducated, unskilled and poverty-stricken. Incapable of organization, it sells its energies to the bidder at starvation wages. Its standard of living is that of the "submerged tenth" of London, or the slum population of New York and Chicago. Although rent and the necessaries of life are higher in the great city than in the rural districts, the middleman who runs the "sweat-shop" finds cheap city labor more submissive and profitable. In England such industries as glovemaking, hand-made lace, etc., are pursued successfully in the rural districts, where female labor is to be secured cheaply. The disadvantage of such labor, however, is its irregularity, which has prevented its employment in this country.

On the whole, the great city seems now to be at a disadvantage in manufacturing, except in the case of cheap and unskilled labor, such as that engaged in the clothing trade.[1]

The existence of other manufacturing enterprises in the metropolis may probably be set down to one of the following causes: (1) Certain old establishments started on the outskirts of the city in an earlier period, and now loath to remove, when the city's growth has enclosed them. (2) Certain industries requiring either traditionally skilled labor, which is not yet to be found outside the original seat, or a high development of technique and art. (3) Many industries whose product is chiefly for local consumption. The number of these is large, since the cities contain so large a proportion of scientific and mechanical contrivances of the age. New York and Chicago together probably possess a larger number of the modern web-perfecting printing presses than all the rest of the United States. Putting together all the paraphernalia of a great commercial city, vehicles of all kinds, vaults and safes, elevated railway apparatus, etc., one will see the necessity of the existence in the great city of a large num-

---

[1] The clothing manufacture is the principal industry of New York City.

ber of mechanical industries. To these must be added the enterprises that cater to the wants of the rich consumers of a commercial city—furniture, table-ware, carriages, etc. Some of the articles might, indeed, be made outside the city, but there is considerable advantage in "being on the ground." (4) Certain industries whose raw materials come equally by land and water routes. In this case the point of intersection —a commercial center—will be the most economical place of assemblage. An instance in point is the iron and steel industry of Chicago.

That local comsumption, unlimited supply of cheap labor, and other considerations just mentioned, rather than natural advantages, determine the location of manufacturing industries in the great city, plainly appears in the *Census Statistics of Manufactures* (Part III, p. xxxvii) which shows that the six leading industries of New York according to *net* value of product in 1890, were—

1. Men's clothing—factory product.
2. Newspapers and periodicals.
3. Women's clothing—factory product.
4. Tobacco, cigars and cigarettes.
5. Malt liquors.
6. Book and job printing and publishing.

With all the advantages for manufacturing industry possessed by the village or small city, it may look as if the country were destined to be covered with industrial villages built up around one or two immense factories. But there are many forces to oppose the tendency. In the first place, one large modern factory alone gives employment to hundreds of operatives and tends to attract other industries, for it is a well understood fact that place-specialization is extended not to a single trade but to a group of allied trades.[1] Hence, when the benefits of specialization cause a manu-

---

[1] Marshall, *Principles of Economics*, 353.

facturer to confine himself to a single process in any industry, say weaving in the textile trade, it is natural for other firms carrying on the processes of carding, dyeing, etc., to locate their establishments in the vicinity. Auxiliary trades and repair shops also attach themselves to the group. Further, there are by-products to be utilized; thus it happened that the erection of a large tannery in a western New York village was shortly followed by that of a glue-factory. Finally, in a factory town where the labor of one sex is exclusively employed, other industries will frequently spring up to utilize the labor of the opposite sex. Thus one of the earliest factories in the city of New Britain, Conn., was devoted to the manufacture of carpenters' rules and levels, and employed male labor alone; it was not long before a cotton factory, in which the cheap and abundant labor of women and children could be used to advantage, was planted in the town. A similar tendency[1] has caused the location of textile factories in mining, metal and machine towns in England.

These are some of the reasons why an industrial village soon becomes a large town. But the process does not stop there. New factories are apt to seek the neighborhood of old establishments in the same industry on account of the "initial difficulties" (familiar in the "infant industry" tariff argument) which attend the upbuilding of an industry in an entirely new atmosphere. The advantages of inherited skill and traditions favorable to the genesis of improvements, created by friction among the followers of the same skilled trade in one place, have been well described by Professor Marshall: "The mysteries of the trade become no mysteries; but are as it were in the air, and children learn of them unconsciously. Good work is rightly appreciated, inventions and improvements in machinery, in processes,

---

[1] Marshall, *Principles of Economics*, 353.

and the general organization of the business have their merits promptly discussed; if one man starts a new idea, it is taken up by others and combined with suggestions of their own; and thus it becomes the source of new ideas. And presently subsidiary trades grow up in the neighborhood, supplying it with implements and materials, organizing its traffic and in many ways conducing to the economy of its materials." [1] In former periods the cost of transportation afforded some protection to " infant industries," but the scaling down of these costs allow the established business in a distant city to compete with the local industry on equal terms in the local market. As we have seen, discriminating or differential rates in favor of competitive points are alleged as the reason for the decay of Western villages.

V. SECONDARY OR INDIVIDUAL CAUSES.

At bottom the question of the distribution of population is a question of economic organization, of the play of economic forces which we have been studying in the preceding sections. These economic forces, however, act upon men in various ways to produce the necessary shifting of population ; they play upon their motives to draw them where their productive power will be greatest. Legislation is a necessary part of the movement; sometimes legislators aid the action of economic forces blindly, at other times consciously and deliberately. In many cases the political and social movement seems to be independent of, and even antecedent to, the economic movement.

There is no doubt that what was at first an effort of economic causes, has in its turn become a cause. The tenement-house classes, for instance, came to the city in order to better their condition—that was an economic cause. But once settled in the city their love of society becomes so great

---

[1] *Op. cit.*, 352. See also Schulze-Gävernitz, *The Cotton Trade*, 82.

that they will not leave the city for the country even when they might thereby greatly improve their material condition. The effect has now become cause: these working classes furnish the manufacturer with an abundant labor supply and induce new industries to settle in the city. There is thus to be seen a continued interaction of cause and effect; and although we hold the growth of cities to be a matter of economic organization, we must not neglect what may be called secondary, or in contradistinction to the general causes already discussed, individual causes of the movement. For convenience of discussion, these may be classed as economic, political and social.

§ 1. *Economic Causes.*—Obviously, if the efficient organization of the industrial powers of society requires a transference of productive power from agriculture to manufactures, the transfer will be obtained by elevating the condition of the men in the latter industry or depressing the condition of the agriculturists. Such is the significance of the general agricultural counties for twenty years. The introduction of machinery and the opening-up of virgin fields in Argentina and the American West have rendered unnecessary and unprofitable much of the agricultural labor in Germany, France, England,[1] and the Eastern States of America. Amid such circumstances a considerable rural emigration is to be expected, and it has everywhere taken place. Without going into European statistics,[2] we may measure the extent of the

---

[1] " Of 1,995 ex-metropolitan sub-districts in England and Wales dealt with in the census report, 945 show a decline of population; and, roughly speaking, these localities constitute the farm land of the country." Graham, *Rural Exodus,* 11. Additional statistics will be found elsewhere in this essay.

[2] The subject of rural depopulation has given rise to considerable literature. In England, where the agricultural depression has been most severely felt, Parliamentary commissions have accumulated an enormous amount of evidence. The final report of the Royal Agricultural Commission of 1897 brings a long inquiry to an

movement in the United States from the data in the Eleventh Census. A glance at the "map showing gain or loss of rural population between 1880 and 1890" will give a good idea of the extent of the movement.[1] The area in which the rural population[2] declined includes most of Maine, New Hampshire, Vermont, New York, Ohio, Illinois and a large part of Indiana and Iowa. The States in which this area of declining rural population embraced more than half of the total area are the following:

	Per cent.			Per cent.
1 Nevada	90.50		6 New Hampshire	63.10
2 New York	82.66		7 Ohio	61.39
3 Vermont	77.20		8 Connecticut	60.85
4 Illinois	65.73		9 Maryland	54.11
5 Maine	64.96			

end. A popular treatment of the subject is given in two volumes of Methuen's Social Science series: *The Rural Exodus*, by P. A. Graham and *Back to the Land*, by H. E. Moore, and in Dr. Longstaff's article on "Depopulation," in Palgrave's *Dictionary of Political Economy;* while the statistics for England appear in Dr. Ogle's article on "The Alleged Rural Depopulation," *J. of St. Soc.*, 1889, vol. lii. Dr. Longstaff presented additional statistics for England and other countries in the same *Journal* in 1893, vol. lvi.

Agricultural conditions in Germany were thoroughly investigated in 1892–3 by the Verein für Socialpolitik (*cf.* the Verein's publications, vols. liii–lvi, *Verhältnisse der Landarbeiter;* an excellent summary of which is given by Drage in the British Royal Commission on Labor's series of *Foreign Reports*, 1893). See further the essay by A. Wirminghaus, "Stadt und Land" in *Jahrbücher für Nationalökonomie und Statistik*, vol. lxiv; and one by Vicomte de Beaumaire in *J. of St. Soc.*, xlix, 450.

For France the subject was thoroughly treated some twenty-five years ago by Legoyt, *Du Progrès des Agglomérations urbaines et de l' Émigration rurale*, and has since been continuously discussed in periodical literature, to which reference will be found in Lavasseur, *La Population Française.*

The causes of "Agricultural Discontent" are analyzed by Dr. Emerick in the *Pol. Science Quar.*, xi, while the whole subject is systematically and scientifically discussed in Buchenberger's *Agrarpolitik.*

[1] *11th Cen. Pop.*, pt. i, p. lxx, map 4; also in the *Statistical Atlas of the United States.*

[2] The method employed in these calculations is as follows: "From the total population of each county in 1890 has been subtracted the population of all cities

The actual net loss in the States whose rural population decreased in the decade 1880–1890 is as follows:

1 New York	163,176	7 Nevada	11,085
2 Illinois	66,741	8 Connecticut	11,964
3 Maine	24,391	9 New Hampshire	8,575
4 Vermont	18,944	10 Massachusetts	6,522
5 Maryland	17,220	11 Rhode Island	508
6 Ohio	13,274		

In many other States the rural population increased so slightly as to be virtually stationary; thus the gain in Delaware was but 40, in Indiana 8,073. The States mainly affected are the New England States, New York, Ohio, Indiana and Illinois, whose agriculture has been languishing under the competition of Western farms. Nevada's decrease may be ascribed to other causes.[1]

The rural emigrants from Europe and the Eastern States of America do not all settle upon the farming lands of the West. On the contrary, many of them go to the nearest city or town. Such internal migration we know to be on the increase in Europe, while the extraordinarily rapid growth of

or other compact bodies of population which number 1000 or more. From the population of the same counties in 1880 has been subtracted the population of the same places at that time, and the remainders, which are assumed to be the rural population are compared for increase or decrease."—*Op. cit.*, p. lxix.

[1] Rural depopulation in five great agricultural States is strikingly brought out in the following table:

	Number of towns which were			
	Stationary	Gained	Lost	
		in population 1880-90.		Total.
Ohio	32	529	755	1,316
Indiana	16	496	482	994
Illinois	45	579	800	1,424
Iowa	29	893	691	1,613
Michigan	22	506	416	944
Total	144	3,003	3,144	6,291

—Fletcher, "The Doom of the Small Town," *Forum*, xix, 215.

American cities indicates the existence of a similar condition here; and it has been statistically proved that interstate migration is declining in the United States.[1] From all but three[2] of the eleven States given in the list above, emigration decreased in the last census decade.

What motives induce the farmer's boy and the village lad to go to the city? At bottom it is undoubtedly the economic motive, although it may seldom resolve itself into a matter of dollars and cents, of higher wages pure and simple. Agricultural laborers in England are leaving the farms whether they have low wages, as in Wiltshire, or high wages, as in Northumberland.[3] The skilled mechanic, indeed, often moves from the town to the city in order to obtain better wages; but with the mass of the young men who go to the city, the magnet is the superior field for ambition which modern industrial organization has rendered the city. In former times a larger proportion of the prizes of life could be attained by the villager or countryman; to-day his only chance for leadership is in politics. In the trades and professions the great prizes must now be sought in centers of wealth, while in business there are no rewards at all for first-class ability outside the cities. Every young man is optimistic as regards his prospective achievements in life, and longs to compete for leadership; to enter the fray, to rise in the world, to make his mark, he must go to one of the great cities, which " afford such extraordinary facilities for the division and for the combination of labor, for the exercise of the arts and for the practice of all the professions."

§ 2. *Political Causes.*—As a political influence in favor of city growth must be reckoned all the measures of the state

---

[1] Willcox, " The Decrease of Interstate Migration " in *Political Science Quarterly*, vol. x (1895).

[2] Illinois, Maine, Nevada.

[3] Graham, *Rural Exodus*, 9.

that promote commerce and manufactures. The political unit and economic unit were identical for so many centuries that political growth meant the enlargement of the economic territory and vice versa. When the village economy and the town economy gave way to a national economy, Mercantilism was one of the causes. To-day, Protectionism discriminates in favor of manufacturing industry; at the same time, other forms of taxation (by the commonwealths) discriminate against the farmer, so that there is some ground for saying that legislation is one of the causes of agricultural depression.

It would be tedious to enumerate the various legislative acts which have influenced the distribution of population; they may be summarized under a few heads as follows:

(1) Legislation promoting freedom of trade. This acts in the same way as improved means of communication, by enlarging the market. As regards internal commerce, perfect freedom is now virtually realized by measures adopted in many of the European countries only in the present century. America, however, has not had any important restrictions on the internal movement of goods since 1789.

(2) Legislation promoting freedom of migration. This policy also favors the growth of cities by giving them greater opportunities for securing laborers from the superfluous rural population. Mediæval restrictions had to be swept away to secure freedom of migration and of domicile. It was only in 1795 that England modified the infamous law of settlement, which permitted the local authorities to drive any newcomer out of the parish under the pretence that he might become chargeable to the local poor rates. It was now enacted that a person should not be removed on the ground that he was likely to become chargeable to the parish, but only when he had " become actually chargeable." [1] In Germany, freedom

[1] Aschrott and Preston-Thomas, *The English Poor-Law System*, 18.

of movement (*Freizügigkeit*) has been more recently secured. The right to leave a community was of course first recognized in Prussia with the abolition of serfdom in 1808; the right to take up residence in another community than that of birth was long denied from fear of the responsibility of poor relief, and it was not till 1842 that the Prussia law of settlement followed the English act of 1795. The mobility of labor is now an accomplished fact in all civilized countries, as it has always been in the United States.

(3) Centralized Administration. The tendency toward administrative centralization is undeniable both in the United States and in England.[1] It exists not only in the transference of various duties from the local to the central authorities, but also in the consolidation of municipalities like New York and London. The transference of governmental machinery from the country to the city affects directly and indirectly considerable numbers of the population.[2] Especially is this true of military states like France and Germany. Formerly garrisons were much more scattered than they are now, when strategical reasons (railways!) require concentration. The young recruits from the country, after a compulsory residence of three years in the great city, yield to its fascinations and remain there under almost any conditions of life.

(4) Land Tenure. Exaggerated importance has often been attached to the form of land tenure as a cause of the

---

[1] The development of central administrative control in England is admirably set forth in Dr. M. R. Maltbie's *English Local Government of To-Day* (Columbia University Studies).

[2] Indirectly by contributing to the dullness of country life. The removal of local business to the State or national capital restricts by so much the range of local ambition and endeavor. The movement has proceeded further in England than in this country, but recent legislation in New York (excise, State insane asylums, etc.) manifests the tendency toward centralization. Cf. H. C. Stephens, *Parochial Self-Government in Rural Districts* (London, 1893), Part i, ch. v, "The Parish and Rural Depopulation."

migration from the country to the city.[1] And yet it has been shown that the rural emigration is as great from the districts of small holdings in southern and western Germany as from the north-eastern districts of large holdings;[2] from rural France with its peasant proprietors as from rural England, with its *latifundia*. Peasant proprietorship in England does not stop the drift to the cities.[3] " The movement is confined to no one locality, but is to be observed in every district that lies remote from towns."[4] The existence of communal lands, the *Allmende*, in Switzerland, has been thought by some to have had a decentralizing influence.[5] But our statistics (Table LXXVII) show that the concentration of population has been going on in Switzerland at an extremely rapid rate. If the system of land tenure has anywhere had a real

---

[1] Agrarian agitators who repudiate Henry George's policy of land nationalization, still hold to the necessity of *Allmenden* (commons) in each village, which will enable the agricultural laborer and smaller cultivators to pasture their cattle or sheep, if the drift to the cities is to be stopped. Cf. H. Sohnrey, *Der Zug vom Lande und die Sociale Revolution;* von der Goltz, *Die ländlichen Arbeiterclassen und die Stadt.*

[2] Cf. books cited in foot-note, p. 211, especially Sering, *Die innere Kolonisation im östlichen Deutschland* (vol. lvi of the publications of Verein für Socialpolitik). In Mecklenburg, the system of small holdings has been established, and "the conditions of labor are especially favorable;" but the children are not willing to follow the life of the agriculturist, and the emigration from Mecklenburg is exceeded in volume by no other province of Prussia except East Prussia, which in 1885–90 lost more inhabitants through emigration than it gained through the excess of births over deaths, and hence actually declined in population (*op. cit.*, p. 6). The statistical tables in vols. lvi and lviii (p. 55) of the Verein's publications clearly show that agriculturists prosper in Germany in proportion to their nearness to industrial cities, rather than in consequence of any particular form of land tenure.

[3] In 1890 Lincolnshire had 1,000 more small holdings (under 50 acres) than any other county in Great Britain; yet " the people are scurrying out of Lincolnshire faster than out of any rural district in Great Britain."—Graham, *Rural Exodus*, 137.

[4] Graham, *op. cit.*, 9.

[5] Laveleye, *Primitive Property*, 80.

influence upon the distribution of population, it is in Australia, where the squatter system of free land-grabbing has concentrated land ownership in a few hands and kept the people from the soil; but geographical and climatic conditions have also had a most important influence, by making sheep-raising (which requires few laborers) more profitable than agriculture.[1] In Victoria they have been pursuing a policy favorable to the taking-up of land;[2] a progressive land tax since 1877 has discouraged large estates; the Act of 1884 contains stringent regulations against owners who are not *bonà fide* cultivators, and there has been an import duty on cereals. Notwithstanding these endeavors and the fact that agricultural production has increased in a larger ratio than population,[3] the proportion of the population outside the cities has been steadily decreasing.[4] It is still too early to judge of the ultimate effects of the radical land legislation in New Zealand.

(5) Miscellaneous. Various special acts of the legislature have at different times contributed toward the concentration of population. Examples are the Enclosure Acts in England,[5] so numerous during the reign of George III, and the modern creation of deer forests.[6] The disbandment of the great Union armies at the close of the Civil War sent to the

---

[1] The 1891 census report of New South Wales (p. 128) says that the concentration of population in seaboard cities is the "only possible mode of development in Australia because there are no great rivers with leagues of navigable waterway stretching into the heart of the country, far remote from the seaports. Communication with the outer world has begun and ended with a good roadstead for shipping."

[2] Epps, *Land Systems of Australia*, 79–83.

[3] *Ibid.*, 80.

[4] From 45 per cent. in 1881 to 41 per cent. in 1891.

[5] Toynbee, *Industrial Revolution* (Humboldt ed.), p. 89.

[6] Longstaff, Art. "Depopulation" in Palgrave's *Dictionary of Political Economy*, vol. i.

cities many hundreds of men who found their places at home occupied; although the West absorbed perhaps even larger numbers. Considered as a secondary cause or reflector of economic causes, politics is a considerable factor in the distribution of population.

§ 3. *Social Causes.*—To enumerate the social advantages that the cities possess as compared with the country would demand too much space, but most of them will be found to be embraced in the following classification:

(1) Educational. The city alone must be the residence of those who study art, medicine, music, etc. Even in the matter of primary education, city advantages are superior to those of the rural districts, though not to those of the villages. Where, as in New York State, there are 3,000 school districts with an average daily attendance of fewer than ten pupils,[1] facilities are wanting for thorough instruction according to modern standards.

(2) Amusements. The opera, philharmonic concerts, art exhibits, etc., may be classed as educational advantages or mere amusements, but there are many other forms of recreation afforded by the city and not by the country, which come under the head of amusements alone.

(3) The standard of living. The desire for a higher standard of life, for purely material comforts and luxuries, brings many people to the city. Food is to be procured at prices almost as low as in the country, and in vastly

---

[1] Cf. *Report of Superintendent of Public Instruction*, 1896, vol. i, p. x; the exact figure is 2,983, while there were 7,529 districts in which the average attendance varied from one to twenty. Superintendent Skinner says that the cities have sucked the life out of the country schools; since 1860 the rural school population of the state having decreased 30 per cent. On the other hand it is to be remembered that the largest rural emigration in England is from the districts with the best educational advantages (*Census of 1891*, iv, 44). There are many objectors to popular education in England; but popular education is not so much at fault as the particular kind of instruction.

greater variety; while everything else is cheaper. The buyer enjoys a larger consumer's rent, as the economists say; that is, he can buy at prices much below those he would be willing to give if pressed, thus deriving a surplus of enjoyment. Then there are conveniences to be had in the city which in many cases could not be obtained in the country, on account of the small numbers to bear the heavy expenses. Such for example are establishments that bring light and fuel to one's door, furnish protection against fire (water works and fire departments), sewerage, rapid transit, etc. The field of municipal activity has been constantly widening, until now the city furnishes its residents not only parks and playgrounds, but museums, libraries and art galleries; [1] not only hospitals, but baths and washhouses, municipal lodging houses and model tenements. In order to guarantee the purity of food supplies the city has its abattoirs and market stalls, its public analysts and milk inspectors. [2] This movement is not transitory; it promises to continue all over the world, notwithstanding the cry of "Socialism." The advantages of collective action here appear at their best. But there will still be left a large field for private associations, whose activities have already added to the comforts of city life. Consider the conveniences at the disposal of the *fin de siècle* city housewife: a house with a good part of the old-fashioned portable furniture built into it, *e. g.*, china cabinets, refrigerators, ward-robes, sideboards, cheval glasses, bath tubs, etc.; electric lights, telephones and electric buttons in every room, automatic burglar alarms, etc.

---

[1] Melbourne employs a city organist, who gives free concerts on the fine organ in the city hall. Boston is experimenting in the same direction.

[2] Cf. Shaw, *Municipal Government in Great Britain*, ch. vii, "Social Activites of British Towns." An exhaustive study of municipal undertakings has been made by Dr. M. R. Maltbie in *Municipal Functions*, constituting the December, 1898, number of *Municipal Affairs*.

" The laundryman long ago joined the letter carrier, butcher, milkman, grocer and baker in their periodical visits to the basement door; and whenever madame shuts up her house —all barred and bolted and chained as it has been by the builders—she turns it over to a sort of care-taking or watchman's company. If she moves out of a house, there are companies to send packers who will bundle up her belongings with professional skill, and that will store them for her by carrying them in padded vans to fire-proof warehouses. Her rugs and carpets are now beaten by machinery, and she may hire her housecleaning done precisely as she gives out her washing. Before she rents a house she may order it inspected by a private company that will report upon the character of its construction and plumbing, and this company also offers to proceed at law against all nuisances in otherwise nice neighborhoods. Thus has vanished the necessity for drawing water, hewing wood, keeping a cow, churning, laundering clothes, cleaning house, beating carpets, and very much of the rest of the onerous duties of housekeeping, as our mothers knew it." [1]

(4) Intellectual Associations. The village is dull not only to the man pursuing light amusements, but to him who seeks cultivated associations, for in these days the cities are the centers of intellect as of wealth. Even the college town with its intellectual atmosphere is to many high-minded people less stimulating than the city, where intellectual ability is so much more varied.[2]

(5) Such are some of the advantages of city life; some

[1] Julian Ralph. Cf. also Salmon, *Domestic Service.*

[2] The decay of the small town caused by the emigration of the best minds to the city long ago gave rise to a religious problem which has been considerably discussed, namely, the religious destitution of villages. See the chapter on this subject in J. H. Crooker, *Problems in American Society*, which contains references to periodical literature. On the general subject of village deterioration, see Fletcher, "Decay of the Small Town," *Forum*, xix, 237.

of them are modern, and some are as old as civilization. Not the least important factor in city growth is gregariousness or the social instinct itself, which appears to be stronger than ever before in these days of restlessness. English investigators have noticed an increased objection among agricultural laborers to isolation.[1] "The isolation of the farm home; no provision for satisfying the cravings of the young people for having good social times" are reasons given for discontent with rural life by farmers of New York to a committee of the New York Association for Improving the Condition of the Poor.[2] Another thing to be reckoned with is the passion for "the crowd, the hum, the shock of men," among those who have once lived in the city. One of the trying difficulties of social workers in their efforts to improve the housing conditions of the tenement population is the strong desire of these poor people to be among their associates, and their absolute refusal to settle in more comfortable homes in the country or in the suburbs. The story is told of a kind lady who found a widow with a large family of children living in the depths of poverty and filth in the city. She moved them to a comfortable country home, where, with a moderate amount of exertion, they were sure of a living. Some six months later, her agent reported the disappearance of the family, and going back to their old haunts in the city tenement district, she found the family living there again. In great surprise she asked the widow how they could leave their comfortable home in the country for such squalid quarters in the city, and received the reply, "Folks is more company nor sthoomps, anyhow."[3]

[1] Cf. W. C. Little's report for the British Labor Commission, Fifth and Final Report.

[2] Cf. *Leaflet No. 1, An Inquiry into the Causes of Agricultural Depression in New York State*, p. 9.

[3] Kingsbury (President's Address at 1895 meeting of the American Social Science Association), "The Tendency of Men to Live in Cities," in *Journal of Social Science*, XXXIII, 8.

(6) Finally, we have to take into consideration the forces which in recent times have spread a knowledge of the advantages of city life among all classes of the community. Education has a great deal to do with it, especially the half education which prevails in the rural districts and gives the farmers' boys a glimpse of a more attractive life, without teaching them how to attain such a life at home.[1] Then the newspaper comes in to complete the enchantment, with its gibes against the " hàyseed " and " country bumpkin." Thus the spread of information, made possible by nineteenth-century improvements in communication, creates a distaste for country life, and more especially for rural life; while easier travel enables young men lightly to abandon the distasteful life.

VI.   CONCLUSIONS.

To what practical conclusions regarding the future distribution of population do the principles deduced in the present chapter lead? Are the rural districts and villages to continue pouring out streams of migration, which will flow toward the great cities? Or is the migratory movement from country to city but a temporary event, a transitional phenomenon?[2] The questions deserve at least an attempt to answer.

[1] Mr. Lecky seems to regard this, with an " increased restlessness of character and much stronger appetite for amusement and excitement," as the principal cause of agricultural depopulation. He affirms that national (popular) education produces " among the poor a disdain for mere manual labor and for the humbler forms of menial service." (*Democracy and Liberty*, ii, 477). But Mr. Lecky is not a Liberal in politics. Mr. Pearson has a much more pleasant way of expressing the same fact. He says that state education is raising the poorest classes to the level of the higher class with its taste and ambitions, and they are able to compete with it in commerce. " The cleverest boys of the village schools do not care to remain ploughboys." (*National Life and Character*, p. 145).

[2] This is the opinion of Prof. Karl Bücher, who says it is due to the transition from the town economy to the national economy. The features of the latter period, in his judgment, are similar to those of the movement toward the towns in the nineteenth century.—*Entstehung der Volkswirthschaft*, 303.

The industries of the human race may be conveniently grouped thus: (1) extractive, including agriculture, mining; (2) distributive, including commerce, wholesale and retail trade, transportation, communication, and all the media of exchange; (3) manufacturing; (4) services and free incomes, including domestic servants, government officials, professional men and women, students, etc.

The extractive industries generally require the dispersion of the persons engaged therein.[1] In particular, agriculture, the principal extractive industry, cannot be prosecuted by persons residing in large groups. It is conceivable that transportation methods might be so perfected as to permit the cultivator of the soil to reside in a city, but it is very unlikely. On the contrary, the improvements heretofore made in transportation have, as we have seen in Sec. II, only strengthened the dispersion of the agricultural population by permitting uninhabited parts of the earth's surface to be settled and brought into cultivation. This will probably be the development of the future as far as human eyes can see.

The distributive industries, on the other hand, are distinctly centralizing in their effects upon the distribution of the population engaged in them. As methods of distribution have been improved and the distributive area enlarged, the tendency toward concentration has increased. The consolidation of two railway lines transfers employees from the junction to the terminal city. Every improvement in the mechanism of exchange favors the commercial center. Of even greater importance is the fact that the production of

[1] In mining districts, it is true, the population is oftener than not quite dense. Nevertheless, it is seldom concentrated in great cities, the Transvaal being an exception to the general rule. At present about one-fourth of the total white population of the South African Republic is to be found in the Rand, (*i. e.* in the vicinity of Johannesburg), and Mr. Bryce (*Impressions of South Africa*, p. 467), thinks that ten years hence the Rand may contain 500,000 persons, or about one-half the total white population.

wealth is increasing at leaps and bounds; every year there is vastly greater wealth to distribute, and the process of distribution will require a growing percentage of all the workers for its efficient action. Hence, the more the social organism grows, and the higher its evolution, so much greater will the commercial centers become.

Manufacturing industries also tend toward the concentration of population, and up to recent years manufacturing centres were coincident with the commercial centres, *i. e.*, the great cities. Recently the equalization of transportation facilities and the excessive rents of great cities have caused the managers of a good many industries to abandon them as sites in favor of the suburb or small town. The reason that this movement does not make for complete decentralization is that production on a large scale is the goal toward which all industries are tending with enlarging and more regular markets, and more convenient means of communication; and production on a large scale requires, as a rule, the large factory and the grouping of allied trades. Other obstacles to decentralization are the presence in the large city of a supply of cheap, unskilled labor; of the best knowledge of art and technique; and especially of numerous industries whose products are intended for local consumption.

The remainder of the population will in the main follow where the preceding classes lead. Those engaged in the professions or the rendering of personal service must reside near the consumers of their products, that is, where people are numerous and money is plenty. Wealth is always concentrated in commercial centres, which therefore attract those employments that Adam Smith called "unproductive." To be sure, commercial cities do not always patronize music, painting and the other fine arts, but that is the general rule.

Thus it appears that the efficient industrial organization of a nation on modern lines requires the concentration of population in virtually all the industries except agriculture; and since this industry, for several decades, has been able to deliver its product by employing a continually smaller proportion of the total population,[1] it follows that the proportion in the centers of population has been increasing. This is the simple but philosophical explanation of the movement known by the popular phrase, " The Drift to the Cities."

Could it be known that the law of diminishing returns in agriculture would not come in force again, there would be some certainty in predicting a continuance of the movement toward concentration of the population; until it does reappear there will be no movement " back to the land." The reason why practical men deny the existence of the abstract law of diminishing returns—historically considered—depends upon the counteracting forces, which may be discussed in two groups. In the first place, science and invention have come to the aid of the farmers with the tender of fertilizers, improved processes, such as the rotation of crops, labor-saving machinery, etc., and have thus enabled them to increase their production without increasing the amount of labor. But the real counter-agent, without which the per-capita product must inevitably have declined in spite of this increased production, is the opening up of new territory. It is easy to see that twenty men will not be able to produce twenty times as much garden truck as one man, if their energies are confined to the piece of land that the one man has been using; but if his lot is surrounded with unoccupied land enough to give

[1] Mr. Hobson (in *Evolution of Modern Capitalism*) admits that the proportion of the population engaged in agriculture in England has decreased, but argues that somewhere on the globe there must have been a growth of the rural population to furnish means of subsistence for the large agglomeration in industrial states. Now the United States has usually had an annual surplus of breadstuffs sufficient to cover England's deficiency; the two countries together may therefore be regarded as a self-sufficing economy. Nevertheless, the rural population in each has been proportionally diminishing for a hundred years. And in the other countries which export breadstuffs, there is also an increasing concentration.

the twenty men full employment, the aggregate product may be multiplied twenty-fold or even more. This is essentially what has been happening in the world at large since the discovery of America: the per-capita product of the cultivators of the soil has been kept up and even increased by the occupation of virgin land as fast as the old farms became crowded.

But the amount of available and unoccupied land on the globe is not unlimited. The United States, east of the Mississippi, is now pretty densely settled, and it is improbable that additional labor force would augment the per capita agricultural product very considerably. The West is fast approaching the East in this respect, and the amount of arable land still unoccupied is so small that ten, or at most twenty years, will find it all brought under cultivation. Capital may aid the farmer in reclaiming barren lands, but sooner or later the time must come when capital will find more lucrative employment in manufacturing industries than in irrigation works on some desert plain in Arizona or New Mexico, or in fertilizers for Eastern farms. When capital thus ceases to replace labor in agriculture, the per capita product will diminish and, if population increases, there will result a movement " back to the land."

But there are two contingencies which may postpone the necessity. One is the importation of breadstuffs from the as yet unopened lands of Canada, Australia, Russia, South America and Africa. The amount of arable and unoccupied land in these countries is of course imperfectly known. Optimists think that the extent of this territory is large enough to last the rest indefinitely, but more careful statisticians, like Mr. Giffen, who have observed the rapid pace at which colonization is proceeding, are more conservative in their estimates.[1] In any event, the present generation is

---

[1] *Cf.* the luminous essay "The Utility of Common Statistics," in Giffen's *Essays in Finance*, 2d series.

not likely to see such a condition of "world crowding" as to draw a larger proportion of Americans into agricultural pursuits.[1]

A second means of postponing the return to the fields, even with stationary arts of agriculture, consists in changes of consumption, a theme so suggestively treated by Professor Patten. The diversification of consumption is a remedy which men have in their own hands. If those classes of people who marry early and have large families to support with incomes that barely suffice to buy bread and the other necessaries of life, would exercise more prudence and self-control and strive to attain a higher standard of life, they would probably consume a smaller quantity of the domestic staples and a larger quantity of luxuries. But a diversification of consumption even in the direction of economy would lessen the pressure toward diminishing returns; for example, should rye or corn come into use as food, a great deal of land unsuited to wheat-growing would be profitably cultivated.[2]

Finally, some mention should be made of the possibilities of the ocean as a food-producer, which President Andrews discussed a few years since in the *North American Review*.

Considering these possibilities and the more speculative possibilities of physical and chemical science in aiding agricultural production or even substituting chemical food-products, it does not seem irrational to regard the law of diminishing returns as a very remote contingency. But the

---

[1] The writer therefore disagrees with Sir William Crookes, President of the British Association for the Advancement of Science in 1898, Mr. C. Wood Davis, who writes for the *Forum*, and ex-Governor John W. Bookmaker, of Ohio, all of whom predict an early scarcity in the wheat supply, which will considerably raise the price of wheat; *ergo*, produce an exodus from the cities to the fields.

[2] It is unnecessary to pursue the subject further, as it has been so well developed in Prof. Patten's works. *Vide* especially the *Dynamics of Consumption*, and *The Premises of Political Economy*.

law of increasing returns, at present manifested in agriculture, would, if superseded, be followed first by the law of constant returns, which would require a permanently constant proportion of the population to be engaged in agriculture. When this happens, cities will cease to grow more rapidly than the rural districts. Only as population increases in density would its concentration take place; but this itself would disturb the equilibrium and would therefore cause a movement away from the cities. The occurrence of these conditions is too remote to be predicted.[1]

In the immediate future, we may expect to see a continuation of the centralizing movement. While many manufacturers are locating their factories in the small cities and towns, there are other industries that prosper most in the great cities. Commerce, moreover, emphatically favors the great centers, rather than the small or intermediate centers. And since, with ever-increasing production flowing from improved methods, commerce and trade are constantly expanding and absorbing an increasing proportion of the population, while manufacturing in a country where it has reached the stage of self-sufficiency employs a constant or even declining proportion of the population,[2] the prospect is

[1] Even should the law of diminishing returns require a larger proportion of the population to be engaged in raising food, there is no reason for pessimism regarding the per capita wealth and prosperity of society. If, for example, the present distribution of the population of the United States (two-fifths in agriculture, three-fifths in other industries) should be reversed a century hence, and three-fifths needed in agriculture, the remaining two-fifths, as a result of the law of increasing returns, would produce more and better form-utilities than do three-fifths at present. (Clark, *Philosophy of Wealth*, 101.)

[2] Occupation statistics are still very imperfect, but the inferences of the following English figures are confirmed by the French statistics extending back to 1851:

PERCENTAGES OF THE POPULATION.

	Agriculture and mining.	Mfs.	Trade and Transport.	Various.
1841	22.7	27.1	12.9	37.3
1851	24.9	32.7	15.1	27.3
1861	22.5	33.0	15.7	29.5
1871	18.7	31.6	18.7	31.0
1881	16.3	30.7	20.1	32.9

that the larger cities, including of course their suburbs, will continue to absorb the superfluous population of the rural districts and villages ; Greater London, New York, Paris, Berlin and Chicago show no signs of falling behind the smaller cities in rate of growth.

The occupations classed as "various" include building trades, civil service. army, navy, professions and non-working classes. These, together with the commercial industries, are increasing proportionally, and, as already pointed out, tend toward the larger cities. The progress of employments is discussed in chapter viii of Hobson's *Evolution of Modern Capitalism*, whence the foregoing statistics are derived (p. 230). The American statistics are incomplete for the earlier years, of the century, but since 1840, at least, the agricultural population has been decreasing in relative numbers, while, of course, the manufacturing population has increased even to the present time, although not to the same extent as commerce and transportation. In 1820, the percentage of the total population engaged in agriculture was 21.49; in 1840, 21.79; in 1870, 15.43; in 1890, 13.68, The similar percentages for manufacturers were 1820, 3.63; 1840, 4.64; 1870, 6.36; 1890, 8.13. (*Bulletin of the Department of Labor*, July, 1897, pp. 398-9.) The distribution of the "workers" (persons of 10 years old or over engaged in gainful occupations) at the last three censuses was as follows (*Ibid.*, 397):

	1870.	1880.	1890.
Agriculture, fishing, mining	49.11	46.03	39.65
Manufacturing and mechanical industries	19.61	19.63	22.39
Domestic and personal services	18.48	20.14	19.18
Trade and transportation	9.83	10.73	14.63
Professional services	2.97	3.47	4.15
	100.	100.	100.

CHAPTER IV.

URBAN GROWTH AND INTERNAL MIGRATION.

THE enormous and unprecedented growth of cities during the nineteenth century is often regarded as the result of a great migratory movement from the farm to the town ; the process appears in full light when one studies the growth of the Lancashire district in the thirties, or of Chicago with its vast throng of oversea immigrants. But before the recent growth of cities can be attributed solely to the factor of immigration from country districts at home or abroad, it must be shown that such immigration is of recent origin, coinciding with the recent concentration of population.

Such a demonstration will not be at once forthcoming. The fact is that migration cityward is not an economic phenomenon peculiar to the nineteenth century. The complaints of the Physiocrats, the first economists, about the scarcity of labor in the rural districts should be generally familiar. Quesnay, in his celebrated article *Fermiers* in *l'Encylopèdie*, noted that the most energetic and intelligent countrymen migrated to the cities, and attributed it to the expenditure of money in Paris and other large towns by the courtiers and nobles. The Physiocrats were in agreement as to the existence of a migration cityward, which they called depopulation of the rural districts, and declared was of long standing in France. It certainly dates back to the mercantilist and industrial policy of Colbert in the seventeenth century, and Legoyt quotes a writer of the fourteenth century, who complained of the increased difficulty of obtaining farm labor at remunerative rates, as confirmatory evidence of a rural emigration.[1] In France the official reports from the provinces to the *états généraux* recommended restrictive measures in order to keep a large supply of labor on the farms. But in England, where a similar migratory movement was at this time in evidence, the governmental point of view was the city instead of the country. Hence both Elizabeth and James I issued proclamations forbidding migration into London, whose population was swelling to portentous dimensions. In Germany, too, the evidence points to a large internal migration in the late middle ages, although it was in large part between the towns themselves.[2] Bücher, indeed, does not hesitate to compare the migratory movements of the fourteenth and fifteenth centuries with those of the nineteenth, the underlying cause in each case being the transition from one stage of industry to another.[3]

The most conclusive evidence of a large migration from the fields to the towns however, is afforded by the bills of mortality begun in several cities in the sixteenth and seventeenth centuries. These death reports formed the first material of the new science of demography or population statistics, at first known as "Political Arithmetic." Now these early bills of mortality almost uniformly showed more deaths than births each year ; the natural result of which would be the decadence of the city. But on the contrary,

---

[1] *Des Agglomérations Urbaines*, p. 7: Leopold Delile, (*Étude sur la classe agricole en Normandie au moyen-age*), raconte ques les chanoines de Mondaie, en Normandie, se plaignaient en 1388 que 'l'on ne peut trouver serviteur pour cultiver et labourer les terres qui ne veuille plus gaigner que six serviteurs ne faisent au commencement du siécle.' "

[2] Cf. Bücher, " Die inneren Wanderungen und das Städtewesen in ihrer entwicklungsgeschichtlichen Bedeutung," one of the brilliant essays in the collection entitled *Die Entstehung der Volkswirthschaft*.

[3] *Ibid.*, 285, 295, 303. In the middle ages the self-sufficing town was more likely to import artisans than merchandise.

the city grew ; its population even increased more rapidly than the rural population. The simple explanation of such a state of affairs was a large emigration from the rural districts to the cities. And this was the conclusion of Captain John Graunt, the founder of the new science.[1]   He estimated the annual immigration to London to be 6,000 persons.[2] While this number is purely conjectural, it raises a very strong presumption that migration to the metropolis was relatively greater 250 years ago than it is to-day. For, between 1871 and 1881, with a population nine or ten times as large as in 1650, London's net immigration amounted to less than 11,000 per annum.[3]

[1] *Natural and Political Observations made upon the Bills of Mortality*, 4th Impression, Oxford, 1665, pp. 81–84 (ch. vii) : " The next Observation is, That in the said Bills there are far more Burials than Christenings.   This is plain, depending only upon arithmetical computation, for in 40 years, from the year 1603 to the year 1644, exclusive of both years, there have been set down (as happening within the same ground, space or Parishes, although differently numbered and divided), 363,935 Burials and but 330,747 Christenings. . . . . From this single Observation it will follow, That London should have decreased in its people; the contrary whereof we see by its daily increase of Buildings upon new Foundations, and by the turning of great palacious Houses into small Tenements.   It is therefore certain that London is supplied with people from out of the country, whereby not only to supply the overplus or difference of Burials above-mentioned, but likewise to increase its Inhabitants, according to the said increase of housing."

London's growth might also be seen in the increasing number of christenings (p. 72 : " The Decrease and Increase of People is to be reckoned chiefly by Christenings, because few bear Children in London but Inhabitants, the others die there.")   Graunt's table of christenings in London (pp. 174–5) shows the following increase :

1604–11	52,190
1612–19	60,316
1620–27	62,124
1628–35	75,774
1636–43	80,443

London's population increased in the ratio from 2 to 5 in 54 years, while it took a typical rural district 200 years to double its population (p. 143).

[2] *Ibid.*, 131 ff.

[3] In 1580 there were said to be 5,060 foreigners resident in London, which then had a population of about 150,000—a larger proportion than now obtains of foreigners and colonials together.

The reason why the stream of emigration did not make the cities grow so rapidly in former centuries as in the nineteenth is the excessively high death-rate then prevalent. Not only did poor sanitation exact a heavy tribute from the infantile population year in and year out, but it also favored periodical visitation of the plague, which naturally wrought fearful havoc. Hence the difficulty of ascertaining a regular, uniform rate of death or migration. It appears that while migration to the cities was large, it did little more than fill the vacant places caused by death. And Captain Graunt was probably right in saying that no matter how great the number of deaths caused by the plague, the city would be quickly re-peopled; the influx of strangers would in the second year fill all the vacant places.[1]

But economy in the organization of industry has steadily demanded an increase in the number of city dwellers, and the cities have thus been able to absorb the migrants from the rural districts at the same time that they have found use for the net increases of their own populations, which have grown to large proportions as a result of the decline of death rates. Thus, statistics show that the migration into Berlin is now but slightly larger than it was in the first half of the century; but Berlin is now growing about twice as rapidly as it was then. That is because the excess of births over deaths is now large,[2] whereas in earlier times it was

---

[1] *Ibid.*, p. 75: "The next Observation we shall offer is the time wherein the City hath been Re-peopled after a great Plague; which we affirm to be by the second year. For in 1627, the Christenings (which are our standard in this case) were 8,408, which in 1624, next preceding the Plague-year 1625 (that had swept away above 54,000), were but 8,299; and the Christenings of 1626 (which were but 6,701) mounted in one year to the said 8,408. Now the Cause hereof, for-as-much as it cannot be a supply by Procreations; *Ergo* it must be by new Affluxes to London out of the Country."

[2] The following data were compiled by Kuczynski, *Zug nach der Stadt*, p. 252, and indicate the annual increase as percentage of the mean population:

very small or else vanished into an absolute deficiency of births.

It would make an interesting piece of investigation to trace the diminution of the city death rate from the sixteenth to the nineteenth centuries, as set forth in the works of Graunt's successors, Petty, Halley, Süssmilch, Déparcieux, and Wappäus. But it might be tedious for the reader, and is at any rate unnecessary for present purposes. A few examples will suffice to show the general tendency.

A German student who investigated the church record of baptisms and burials in several German cities came to the conclusion that on the average there were 80 or 90 births to 100 deaths in the period 1550–1750. In the last fifty years (1700–50) of this period the number of births fluctuated between 66 and 96;[1] but in 1877–82 the ratio of births to

	Excess of births.		Net Immigration.	Total Increase.
	Number.	Percentage.		
1711–1815	—31,310	—0.2	1.4	1.1
1816–37	23,505	0.5	1.3	1.8
1838–58	55,513	0.7	1.6	2.3
1858–75	95,460	0.8	3.2	4.0
1875–95	289,240	1.1	1.6	2.7

The period just previous to the Franco-Prussian war includes the heaviest migration to Berlin. (*Supra*, Table XLV.) This period was exceptional, and as appears from the foregoing percentages of net immigration, the present movement toward Berlin is not greatly in excess of that in the earlier periods of the century. And the statistics of *Fremdgeborenen* in Berlin do not indicate that the percentage of outsiders is now perceptibly larger than it was in 1875:

	Born outside Berlin, to each 1,000 inhabitants.
1864	520.9
1871	563.7
1875	586.6
1880	566.3
1885	576.0
1890	593.0

Kuczynski also shows (pp. 262–270) that the age-grouping of the Berlin population has not greatly changed since the beginning of the century, indicating that a large immigration then as now filled the middle age periods.

[1] J. Wernicke, *Das Verhältniss zwischen Geborenen und Gestorbenen in historischer Entwicklung* (Conrad's series of dissertations), pp. 57, 90.

deaths in 173 German cities was 147 to 100. Sir William Petty, writing in 1681, estimated the ratio of births to deaths in London at 5 : 8 or 62½ to 100, while in all England he said it was 125 : 100.[1]

Now the date at which the cities succeeded in turning the excess of deaths into an excess of births naturally varies according to country and circumstance. The very stream of immigration which was to maintain the population of a city was one circumstance ; for it brought strangers born outside the city to die in the city. Graunt noticed it but casually, saying that the 6,000 strangers who annually came to London added 200 to the burials every year. Edmund Halley was the first to emphasize the influence of immigration upon the death rate in the cities : " Both London and Dublin by reason of the great and casual accession of strangers who die therein (as appeared in both, by the great excess of the funerals above the births) rendered them incapable of being standards for this purpose, which requires if it were possible, that the people we treat of should not at all be changed, but die where they were born, without any adventitious increase from abroad or decay by migration elsewhere."[2] In Breslau, with its small migratory move- ment, Halley found a small surplus of births over deaths.

The disturbing effect of migration upon the relation between births and deaths, thus first emphasized by Halley, has been discussed by all subsequent writers without exhausting the subject. Dèparcieux demonstrated that while migration into the city might increase the number of deaths as compared with the number of births, it diminished the ratio of

---

[1] *Several Essays in Political Arithmetic*, 4th ed., London, 1755, p. 36: "Observations upon the Dublin Bills of Mortality," 1681.

[2] *Philosophical Transaction of the Royal Society*, vol. xvii, for the year 1693. No. 196: E. Halley, "An estimate of the degrees of mortality of mankind, drawn from curious tables of the births and funerals at the city of Breslau; with an attempt to ascertain the price of annuities upon lives."

deaths to the living, since the migrants were persons in the active, healthful years of life, with a death rate lower than the average.[1] Hence as respects France the death rate was found more favorable in Paris than in the small towns ; but one reason why Paris was the first great city to establish a clear preponderance of births over deaths was the French practice of sending infants to the country to be nursed. Their births were recorded in Paris ; their deaths in the country.

While Paris could show a small natural increase in the eighteenth century,[2] London did not succeed in doing so until the beginning of the nineteenth ; a result achieved more by the diminution of deaths than by the increase of births.[4] Berlin first attained a similar permanent status after 1810,[3]

[1] *Essai sur les probabilitiés de la durée de la vie humaine ; d'où l'on déduit la manière de déterminar les rentes viagérès tant simples qu'en tontines*, Paris, 1746,

[2] The annual average number of births in excess of deaths in Paris (according to Levasseur, ii, 395) was :

1750–59	323
1780–89	27
1799–1808	—668
1809–16	373
1817–30	3,177

[3] The data for London are as follows, the capital letter " P " designating the visitation of the plague or an epidemic (*Encycl. Brit.*, Art. " London ") :

Year.	Deaths.	Births.	Excess of deaths.
1593	17,844	4,021	13,823
1603	42,042 P	4,789	37,253
1625	54,265 P	6,783	47,482
1636	22,359	9,522	13,837
1665	97,306 P	9,967	87,339
(Annual average.)			
1700–1710	21,461	15,623	5,838
1740–1750	25,352	14,457	10,895
1790–1800	24,270	22,605	1,665

[4] The excess of deaths over births in Berlin fluctuated very considerably, and at times yielded to an excess of births (Kuczynski, 252; see also *supra*, foot-note p. 234) :

1709	+28	1770	—10,372
1720	+512	1780	—2,708
1730	—3,581	1790	+2,793
1747	—447	1800	—7,089
1755	—12,334	1810	+1,296
1763	+592		

while Leipzig reached that point in 1821–30, and Frankfort in 1840.[1] But the clearest picture of the whole movement is furnished by the statistics of Sweden,[2] where scientific carefulness and accuracy where early devoted by the government to the collection of population statistics:

TABLE CXVI.

Births per 1,000 population.

	1816-40.	1841-50.	1851-60.	1861-70.	1871-80.	1881-90.
Rural population	33 34	31 30	32.82	31.20	30.21	28.65
Urban population	30.95	29.29	32 53	32.95	32.13	31.07
Stockholm	33.03	32.59	35.49	34.56	31.75	32.39
Other cities	30.11	28.07	31.50	32.38	32.25	30.59

Deaths per 1,000 population:

Rural population	22 26	10.70	20.57	19.33	17.32	16.36
Urban population	34.44	28.73	31.20	26.17	24.05	19.74
Stockholm	45.09	38.11	41.51	32.25	30.28	22.60
Other cities	30.10	25.24	27.60	24.01	21.96	18.71

Natural increase per 1,000 population:

Rural population	11.08	11.60	12.25	11.87	12.89	12.29
Urban population	—3.49	0.56	1.33	6.78	8.08	11.33
Cities of less than 10,000	....	......	......	7.1	7.7	9.7
Cities over 10,000 pop	.....	......	......	6.7	8.2	11.9
Stockholm	—12.06	—5.52	—6.02	2.31	1.47	9.79
Other cities	.....	......	......	9 3	12 0	13.2
Cities without Stockholm	0.01	2.83	3.90	8.37	10.29	11.88

Gain or loss (—) by migration per 1,000 population:

Rural population	—1.45	—1.67	—3.22	—6 19	6.35	—12.03
Urban population	12.62	14.12	20.28	14.49	16.32	14.89
Cities under 10,000 pop	.....	......	......	6.7	13.7	7.1
Cities over 10,000	......	......	.....	17.9	17.4	17.9
Stockholm	17.70	15.61	25.49	15.99	19.66	26 95
Other cities	.....	......	......	19.2	16.1	12.6
Cities without Stockholm	10.55	13.56	18.45	12.95	15.21	10.55

Total increase per 1,000 population:

Rural population	9 63	9 93	9.03	5.68	8.54	0.26
Urban population	9 13	14.68	21.61	21.27	24.40	26.22
Cities under 10,000	......	......	......	13 8	21.4	16 8
Cities over 10,000	... ..	......	......	24.6	25.6	29.8
Stockholm	5.64	10.09	19.47	18 30	21.13	36.74
Other cities	......	......	......	28.5	28.1	25.8
Cities without Stockholm	10.56	16.39	22.35	22.32	25.50	22.43

[1] Bleicher, p. 239. It is worth noting that in Frankfort, a city of fairs, there was usually an excess of births in the citizen class:

	Aggregate excess of births (+) or deaths (—):		
	Frankfort.		Leipzig.
	Entire pop.	Resident class.	
1651-1700	— 1,056	+3,521	—5,638
1701-1750	—6,059	+ 1,259	—9,310
1751-1800	—11,975	—2,224	—19,687
1801-1840	—691	+ 1,513	—2,452
1841-1890	+29,266	......	+43,153

[2] Supplement to the census of 1890, *Befölkningsstatistik*, new series, xxxii, No. 1: *Bihang till Statistika, Centralbyraus Befölkningsstatistik för Ar 1890, Folksmängdens Förändringer Sverige Aren 1881-90, Jente Ofversigter för Aren 1816-90* (Stockholm, 1892), pp. ii-vii, etc.

The percentages of total increase show how the urban population has been growing ever faster and faster, while the rural growth falls off. The urban population is, moreover, tending to be absorbed in Stockholm. But the percentages of gain or loss through migration do not indicate that the more rapid growth of Swedish cities is due to immigration. Emigration from the rural districts has indeed increased, but much of it has been directed to foreign countries; the net immigration to the cities has diminished since 1851–60. Even in Stockholm the immigration for 1881–90 barely exceeds the percentage of 1851–60. The real explanation of city growth is therefore to be found in the percentages of natural increase. In the first period, 1816–40, the per *mille* of loss (*i. e.*, excess of deaths over births) was 3.49; in the succeeding decade this was turned into a positive gain of 0.56 per 1,000, which has steadily increased in the following periods until it reached 11.33 per *mille* in 1881–90, or almost as much as the rural natural increase. The tendency is even more marked in Stockholm, where a deficit of 12.06 per *mille* has finally been turned into an excess of 9.79.

Further analysis shows that the birth-rate is higher in the urban than in the rural communities; although the difference is not so great as in the case of the death-rates. But the difference between the urban and rural death-rates is now only 3.4 per *mille*, whereas in the period 1816–20 it averaged 12.2, and in the case of Stockholm nearly reached 23 per 1,000. Stockholm's death-rate of 45.1 per *mille* in 1816–40 was not an exceptional rate for cities in that period; and great alteration for the better is typical of modern cities. This is the real explanation of the *manner* of city growth.

The point of self-maintenance, which was reached in Paris before the close of the eighteenth century, in London in 1800, in the German cities in the first half of the present century, in Stockholm after 1860, has not yet been universally attained even in civilized Europe. In 1877 Dr. Dunant presented a paper [1] to the International Congress of Medical Science at Geneva in which he showed that of 30 great cities of Europe, 23 owed more than one-half their growth to immigration, and that seven [2] of these without it would have decreased. They were mostly Italian cities, but more recent statistics [3] show that six of twelve great cities of France are also subject to an excess of deaths. On the other hand, a considerable number of English cities are losing more by emigration than they gain by immigration; although as will appear hereafter the emigration is in large part directed toward the suburb. The following list of the larger European cities (*i. e.* those having a mean population of at least 200,000 in 1880–1890 or 1881–1891) shows the proportion which immigration (or emigration) bears to the total increase per 1,000 : [4]

Immigration.

Marseilles	1,183	Amsterdam		502
Lyons	1,115	Copenhagen		492
Bordeaux	1,060	Brussels		489
Rome	893	Vienna		410
Turin	881	Leeds		300
Buda-Pest	867	Birmingham		257
Milan	830	Naples		257
Munich	822	Edinburgh		94
Stockholm	734	Palermo		30
Paris	723			
Manchester	717	Emigration.		
Breslau	715	Sheffield		4
Prague	700	Dublin		120
Berlin	697	Bristol		785
Hamburg	690	London		1,289
Belfast	654	Liverpool (decrease)		2,481
Dresden	588			

[1] *Influence de l' Émigration de la Population des Campagnes dans les Villes;* published also in *Annales de Démographie Internationale*, vol. i. The important results are restated by Levasseur (ii, 386), and illustrated with a diagram.

[2] Milan, St. Petersburg, Venice, Odessa, Prague, Rome, Naples.

[3] Cf. *Statistiches Jahrbuch der Stadt Berlin* for 1892, xix, 94–5 : " Movement of population in 88 European cities for ten years."

[4] *Ibid.* The Italian figures are of slight value, because their population is estimated, no census having been taken since 1881.

According to these figures, immigration would seem to play the largest role in the growth of the French and Italian cities, then in the German, the Scandinavian, and finally the English cities. The explanation lies in the fact that the English cities have a lower death-rate than the Italian and a higher birth-rate than the French; in either case they have a larger excess of births over deaths, and derive a correspondingly smaller fraction of their growth from immigration. The following table covers several decades and takes into account annexations of territory as well as natural increase and net immigration :[1]

TABLE CXVII.

PERCENTAGE OF TOTAL INCREASE DUE TO

		Excess of births.	Net immigration.	Incorporation of suburbs.
London,	1852–91	84.03	15.97	
Copenhagen,	1801–90	42.98	57.02	
Cologne,	1821–90	34.10	27.48	37.42
Berlin,	1801–90	26.72		
Vienna,	1891–90	20.52	32.48	47.00
Leipzig,	1801–90	16.42	39.70	43.88
Paris,	1821–90	15.23	64.21	20.56
Breslau,	1821–90	15.16	79.21	5.63
Munich,	1811–90	10.59	72.26	17.15
St. Petersburg,	1801–90	—27.81 (deficit.)		

The fact that London's percentage of growth due to natural increase is so large arises partly from the fact that no changes of area are made, and partly from the fact that the data are comparatively recent; but after all, the real reason is London's precedence in the making of sanitary improvements.

From the data concerning 88 European cities which Professor Boeckh publishes in the Berlin municipal *Jahrbuch*, he draws the conclusion that migration is a wider movement

[1] Sedlaczek, " Die Bevölkerungszunahme der Grossstädte im XIX Jahrhundert und deren Ursachen," in *Proceedings of Eighth International Congress of Hygiene and Demography at Budapest* (1894), vii, 380.

than the natural movement of births and deaths; for in the former case the percentages range between +28.6 and —16, and in the latter case between +19.1 and —4.6.[1] As Table CXVII demonstrates, Professor Boeckh is entirely safe in concluding that fully one-half of the increase of population in the large cities is to be attributed to migration.[1] In the United States, accurate vital statistics are too scanty to permit wide generalizations. Moreover, frequent suburban annexations, which are not always mentioned in the census reports, complicate matters. But if Boston be regarded as a typical American city, investigation shows that about one-half of the increase in population between 1865 and 1890 was due to immigration, three-tenths to annexations and two-tenths to natural growth, which is thus seen to play a subordinate part in the increase of Boston's population.[2] Statistics are also available which allow a comparison to be made of the natural increase in urban and rural communities in Massachusetts; the urban population is here represented by the 28 incorporated cities, and the following data are averages for the five census years 1870, 1875, 1880, 1885, and 1890:[3]

	Birth-rate.	Death-rate.	Rate of natural increase.
Cities	28.4	21.4	7.0
Rural remainder	22.0	17.5	4.5

[1] *Op. cit.*, vii, 392 and 384: "Der Antheil der örtlichen Bewegung an der Zunahme der Bevölkerung der Grossstädte."

[2] Cf. Mass. *Census of 1895*, i, 220, and *Forty-ninth Registration Report* (1890), p. 156:

Population of Boston in 1865	192,318
" " Roxbury, Dorchester, Charlestown, West Roxbury, Brighton in 1865	76,288
Births minus deaths (245,958—194,890) in 1865–90	51,068
(Add for net immigration in 1865–90	128,803)
Population of Boston in 1890	448,477

[3] *Registration Report* as above, p. 372.

It is significant that the cities, instead of being the " destroyers of mankind," now produce a larger surplus of births than do the country districts. This result is due to a high city birth rate, as the urban death rate in Massachusetts still remains considerably above the rural death rate. Massachusetts may be taken as a typical state of the manufacturing East; in fact, entire New England is even more favorable than Massachusetts to the urban rate of natural increase.[1] Regarding the role of immigration in the growth of Massachusetts cities, it may be noted that the increase of population in the ten years 1885–95 on the territory of the present 32 incorporated cities was 38.05 per cent., or about 38 per 1,000 for one year;[2] but as was just indicated, the natural increase in the Massachusetts cities is only about 7 per 1,000 annually.

The value of these Massachusetts statistics is considerable, especially as they have been confined by computations showing the refined birth rates;[3] for Massachusetts is the

---

[1] *The Summary of Vital Statistics of the New England States,* for 1892 (p. 56), gives the following figures:

	Population 1892.	Birth-rate.	Death-rate.
Urban group (towns of 10,000+)	2,441,418 est.	29.68	21.01
Rural group (towns of 10,000—)	2,444,987 est.	20.00	18.72

The natural increase is thus 8.67 and 1.28 per *mille* for the urban and rural populations respectively.

[2] Mass. *Census of 1895,* i, 49.

[3] See Dr. Crum's article in the *Quar. Jour. of Econ.,* xii, 259, and one of his tables reprinted below (No. CXLV.). While his figures are based upon density of population, it will be shown that the grouping by density corresponds closely to grouping according to the populousness of cities. With Dr. Crum's figures may be compared the birth and death rates and rate of natural increase in Massachusetts towns in 1890 (*Registration Report,* as above, p. 374):

Number of towns	Population of the groups.	Birth rate.	Death rate.	Rate of natural increase.
95	Under 1,000	15.5	17.5	—2.0
84	1,000– 2,000	16.1	18.1	—2.0
48	2,000– 3,000	19.0	18.7	0.3
22	3,000– 4,000	21.6	17.1	4.5
30	4,000– 5,000	21.6	18.0	3.6
35	5,000–10,000	24.7	17.1	7.6
17	10,000–20,000	27.4	17.9	9.5
20	Over 20,000 { from	25.7	17.0	5.8
	{ to	34.4	22.5	12.2

leading industrial commonwealth of this country, and the type of that organization which seems destined to prevai more and more with the passage of years. It denotes the fact that the cities are no longer mere consumers of population produced in the rural districts, but will contribute their full share to the increase of population.

In Europe the urban population as a whole still has a smaller natural increase than the rural population, but the difference is not so great as in the case of the great cities. The Swedish statistics given in Table CXVI may be again referred to. It may be concluded that while the urban population has a lower death rate in Europe than in America, its birth rate is in comparison still lower. In England the natural increase in town and country is almost precisely the same;[1] hence the more rapid growth of the towns is due to migration. The relation which this immigration has borne to the natural increase may be seen in the following figures,[2] based on the assumption of a uniform natural increase throughout all categories of population, and showing the

---

[1] Cf. the following figures given by Charles Booth ("On Occupations of the People, 1801–81," in *Jour. of Stat. Soc.* 1889, p. 329):

	Birth-rate.	Death-rate.	Nat. increase.
London and 19 chief towns	37.21		
Fifty large towns	39.79		
Small towns	37.67		
Urban population	37.12	22.09	14.03
Rural population	33.13	19.00	14.13

Cf. also Longstaff, *Studies in Statistics*, p. 25, whence the natural increase for 1871–81 per 1,000 population in 1871 may be deduced as follows:

London	13.9
19 large cities	14.2
56 other cities	16.8
Total 76 cities	15.0
England and Wales	15.0

[2] Sir Rawson W. Rawson, in *Jour. of Stat. Soc.*, 1880, p. 501. Dr. Longstaff, *op. cit.*, p. 24, prints an interesting table which shows the daily increase, daily

percentage of gain or loss by migration in each decade, as
well as the proportion which the migration bears to the total
increase (or decrease);

TABLE CXVIII.

| | | Gain or loss (—) by migration. | | | Ratio of net immigration to total increase. | |
Decade.	London.	Other large towns.	Small towns.	Rural districts.	London.	Other large towns.
1801–11........	4.46	6.00	—1.20	—2.19	23.8	29.7
1811–21........	3.02	8.61	+0.94	—3.32	14.6	32.3
1821–31........	4.21	14.23	—0.83	—5.29	21.0	47.4
1831–41	3.25	12.00	—2.02	—4.79	18.3	45.3
1841–51.......	8.55	12.12	—2.18	—6.80	40.2	48.8
1851–61........	6.75	7.77	—4.64	—4.64	36.2	39.4
1861–71........	2.78	7.72	—2.11	—4.83	17.4	36.8

These figures apparently indicate that the influx into
London reached its height about 1850, as indeed did the
migratory movement cityward in general. Since then
London's gain by migration has diminished, and in 1881–91
turned into an actual loss, its natural increase being 12.71
per 1,000 and the actual total increase only 9.86. It is only
fair to remark, however, that part of the emigration from
London is simply into the suburbs.

In Germany, too, migration cityward can hardly be said

destination, and daily migrants per 1,000, in several categories of population in
England and Wales:

	Population in 1871.	Daily increase.	Daily destination.	Daily immigrants.
London........................	143	133	165	+32
19 large cities	142	135	156	+21
56 other cities	127	140	199	+59
Remainder of country..........	588	592	437	—155
Foreign countries..............	...	...	43	+43
	1,000	1,000	1,000	0

to be increasing, while the urban rate of natural increase on the whole approaches that for the entire country:[1]

TABLE CXIX.

| | Twenty-five great cities of Germany. | | | Prussia. |
	Natural increase.	Net immigration.	Total increase.	Natural increase.
1861–64	8.3	27.4	35.7	14.3
1864–67	4.3	17.7	22.0	10.9
1867–71	6.1	22.1	28.2	9.5
1871–75	10.4	21.7	32.1	12.3
1875–80	12.6	12.7	25.3	13.8
1880–85	9.9	14.3	24.2	12.0

In France the cities, considered in the aggregate, have virtually ceased to grow of themselves, but rely upon immigrants from the rural districts for recruiting their population, which, as we saw in the first chapter, is by no means at a stand-still. The following data relates to the urban population of France:[2]

TABLE CXX.

| | Aggregate numbers. | | | Percentages | |
	Total increase.	Excess of births.	Net immigration.	Natural increase.	Immigration.
1861–65	805,582	141,350	664,232	17.	83.
1872–76	742,497	117,667	624,830	16.	84.
1876–81	1,119,146	38,480	1,080,666	3.	97.
1881–86	669,966	43,665	626,301	6.	94.
1886–91	544,784	—1,129[3]	545,913	—0.2[4]	100.2
1872–91	3,076,393	198,812	2,877,710	6.	94.

It thus appears that in France the percentage of the growth of cities due to their natural increase has diminished since 1861 until in the last period there was an actual deficiency. Migration into the cities, although not increasing in absolute numbers, has assumed relatively greater prom-

[1] *Allg. Stat. Archiv.*, i, 167.

[2] *Résultats statistiques du dénombrement de 1891*, p. 72; and other census reports.

[3] Excess of deaths.   [4] Decrease.

inence. The statistics of 1876–81 may be further analyzed to show the movement of population in cities of different size. Without giving the actual numbers, the percentages may be reported as follows:[1]

	Natural increase.	Immigration.
Paris	8.3	91.7
47 cities (pop. of 30,000+)	2.5	97.5
All cities except Paris	1.8	98.2
Total urban	3.4	96.6

From this it appears that the deficit is due not so much to Paris and the larger cities, as to the smaller cities. But such statistics are not absolutely conclusive.

In Austria the natural movement of population in the cities contributes more largely to their growth than in France. Thus, of the total gain, in 1880–90, of 193,341 in the eight larger cities (50,000+), 79,395 or 41.1 per cent. came from the excess of births over deaths.[2]

In Hungary the natural increase constituted 32 per cent. of the total increase, 1880–90, both in the seven large cities (50,000+) and in the 25 free cities.[3]

The results thus show the greatest diversity. In France the cities do not sustain themselves, nor do many of the Italian cities. In Germany, Sweden, Austria, Hungary, etc., the cities furnish from one-fourth to one-half of their increase according to size. But in Great Britain immigration has so diminished that even the largest cities provide three-fourths and often more of their increase. In the United States, where the cities now show a larger natural increase than do the rural districts, there is still a vast immigration, four or five times as large as the natural increase.

[1] M. Loua, in *Journal de la Société Statistique de Paris* (March, 1885) xxvi, 124.

[2] Calculated from data in *Stat. Monat*, xviii, 234–46.

[3] Calculated from data in the Hungarian census of 1890, pp. 55–57*.

The method here used is liable to grave inaccuracies, since it assumes that the original population of a city is not going and coming, and that a resident population is alone responsible for the births and deaths. Now between any two points of time for which the natural increase is computed, the deaths registered may be affected by the emigration or immigration of particular classes, say of old people. If old people come to the city to spend their last days, it is evident that the number of deaths will be artificially increased, and vice versa when old people emigrate from the city. In the latter case we should have too few deaths, which would make the natural increase larger than it actually is and the immigration correspondingly smaller. Similarly, the number of births may be affected in two ways: (1) it may be increased by the registration of children born in the city and removed before the census has been taken, or (2) by the birth of children to women who have moved to the city within the period under consideration. In either case the result would be the same, the city would appear to grow by reason of surplus of births, whereas it might be supported entirely by immigration.[1] All these objections, however, are of theoretical rather than practical importance in any investigation of *tendencies*; they are not of sufficent force in reality to invalidate conclusions based on comprehensive data such as those presented in the present chapter.

Another method of approaching the question of city-growth is by means of statistics of birth-place. If, for example, 38.5 per cent. of the population of Boston were born there and 62.9 per cent. of London's population were native Londoners, it may be inferred that, other things being equal, Boston is receiving a proportionately larger

---

[1] This is substantially the argument of Ballod, *Die Lebensfähigkeit der städtischen und ländlichen Bevölkerung* (1897).

immigration than London.[1]   Hence for the study of internal
migration the statistics of birth-place have a real value and
will repay careful analysis.[2]

The vast dimensions of internal migration are often lost
sight of in the contemplation of the horde of emigrants who
go to foreign countries, though we in the United States, who
have seen these shiftings of the native American population,
are not so likely to fall into mistaken comparisons as are
European students, whose attention is attracted to the loss
of millions of their fellow citizens by trans-Atlantic migration.   In England, in 1891, 25 per cent. of the native-born
inhabitants were no longer residing in their native county,
amounting in round numbers to 7,000,000 souls; whereas
the number of Englishmen residing in the United States in
1890 was only 900,000.

The following table, based chiefly on the official sources,

[1] The assumption here made of " other things being equal " should be carefully
noted.   Circumstances may be conceived in which the conclusion would not follow.   Suppose, for instance, that cities A and B are of the same size (e. g., 1,000,-
000 inhabitants), and have the same annual increase, say 50,000, of which 25,000
represents the excess of immigration over emigration, and 25,000 the surplus of
births over deaths.   Now it might occur that city A had no emigration at all,
in which case 25,000 would represent the pure immigration, and the immigrants
would, in the first year, constitute 2.5 per cent. of the population of city A.   But
city B, we will say, sends out 100,000 of its population to other communities, and
receives an inflow of 125,000, the net immigration being as in town A, 25,000.
But in city B 12.5 per cent. of the population would now be outsiders.   Hence it
might be concluded that London's large percentage of native Londoners is due
not so much to a higher birth-rate and lower death-rate than Boston's, as to less
emigration.   Nor is it possible to ascertain the amount of emigration from the
city.   Though the English census may return the total number of the natives of
London within the British Empire, it does not give the number who are living in
France or America.

[2] In Germany they have a system of police registration of arrivals and depart-
ures, and these *Anmeldungen*, as the notices are called, are sometimes used to
study migration.   But it is obvious that these data can be of little value, inasmuch as they refer to cases of migration and not to the number of migrants.   Cf.
Brückner's article in *All. Stat. Archiv*, vol. i.

exhibits the range of migration in several of the leading countries:[1]

TABLE CXXI.

Country.	Date.	Township where enumerated.	Percentage of the population born in			
			Elsewhere in same county.[3]	County where enumerated.	Elsewhere in same country.	Foreign countries.[4]
Massachusetts,	1885	36.1	....	57.5	....	42.5
United States,	1890	....	....	66.86	18.37	14.77
Saxony.[2]	1885	50.07	19.03	69.1	20.82	10.08
Prussia,	1890	53.9	15.8	69.7	27.1	3.2
Eng. and Wales,	1891	....	....	71.6	24.5	3.9
Denmark,	1890	....	....	77.88	18.62	3.5
France,	1891	56.3	25.0	81.3	16.4	2.3
Switzerland,	1888	56.4	25.7	82.1	11.5	6.4
Austria,	1890	65.2	15.0	80.2	18.1	1.7
Belgium,	1890	65.2	....	....	....	2.8
Netherlands,	1889	65.4	21.6	87.0	11.2	1.8
Norway,	1875	73.05	14.15	87.2	10.7	2.1
Hungary,	1890	73.6	15.6	89.2	9.3	1.5
Sweden,	1880.	79.9	8.6	88.5	11.1	0.4

The table represents only the internal migration, not the migratory tendencies of the different peoples. The Swedes, from their position in the table, might be called a non-

[1] Cf. Wirminghaus, "Stadt und Land," in Conrad's *Jahrbücher für National-ökonomie und Statistik*, lxiv, 161, and Ravenstein, "Laws of Migration," in *Jour. of Stat. Soc.* (1889), lii, 241.

[2] In Saxony the birth place is given by towns or villages (*Orte*), since the township (*Gemeinde*) is virtually identical with the town.

[3] The "county" or district stands for the following political divisions: Saxony, Amtshauptmannschaft; United States, State or Territory; Prussia, Kreis; Denmark, Overovrighedskredsene; France, Department; Switzerland, Canton; Austria, Bezirk; Netherland, the Province; Hungary, Comität; Sweden and Norway, Län.

[4] The term "foreign countries" includes all States and federal commonwealths outside the State specified. Thus in the case of Massachusetts, it includes all other American States and Territories; similarly in the case of Saxony and Prussia, the other members of the German Empire. Of the 42.5 per cent. attributed to foreign countries in the case of Massachusetts, 15.3 per cent. were native Americans, and 27.2 foreigners in the usual sense of the word.

migratory people, while we know that proportionate to their numbers they send more migrants to the United States than any other country in Europe except Ireland.[1] There are some other considerations that prevent these figures being accepted as entirely trustworthy indications of the relative strength of migration. The size of the township often seriously affects the statistics of birth place; if the towns are territorially large, a short-distance migration might effect no change of residence, whereas, in case of townships of smaller area, even a half-mile journey might make the migrant a resident of some other town. A similar result would follow if the townships of one country were perfect squares or circles, while in another country they were very irregular in formation; or if some townships were bounded by natural barriers of mountains or water, rendering them more or less isolated. While these facts must make us realize the shortcomings of such statistics as are given in Table CXXI, they do not invalidate the table. While the fact that the Prussian township is very small in area compared with the others may partly account for its large inter-town migration; and while in Saxony the primary unit is not the township but the village or compact dwelling center, the fact remains that in Massachusetts, which has the largest inter-town migration of all, the township is several times larger than any of the European townships.[2] This is true even if we exclude the foreign-born element entirely; for the percentage of native Massachusetts people born in the township where enumerated is only 49.4. This brings out the fact of the superior mobility of Americans, which has long been familiar to us in a general way. Indeed, it appears from the table that Americans are more accustomed to migrate from State to State than are Europeans from county to county. The English are apparently the most mobile people of Europe, as regards internal

[1] *Supra*, p. 152.   [2] *Supra*, p. 142.

migration at least; and yet the percentage of native Englishmen living outside their county of birth was in 1871 almost exactly equal to the percentage of native Americans living outside the State in which they were born—the percentages being 25.66 and 26.2 (1870) respectively.

Within the last quarter of a century, however, internal migration in the United States has declined. Professor Willcox has shown that *interstate* migration in the United States reached its maximum in 1860–70; in only three States, indeed, (Maine, Indiana, Illinois,) has the maximum migration occured in a later period. The data for *intrastate* migration are less conclusive, but in the three States which afford such data the indications are all in the same direction.[1]

On the other hand conclusive evidence exists that internal migration is on the increase in Europe, though not necessarily the migration cityward. As the evidence in favor of this statement has never been presented in comprehensive form, to the writer's knowledge, the following percentages drawn from the official sources may be of interest; in

---

[1] Professor Willcox has computed the number of native New Yorkers living in the United States in three State census years with the following result:

Resident in	1855.	1865.	1875.
County of birth	56.0	55.3	57.8
Some other county of New York	19.9	17.8	16.0
Some other State	24.2	26.5	26.2

Thus the percentage of New Yorkers residing outside the county of birth was smaller in 1875 than in previous years. No later data are available in New York, the State census of 1892 having been a mere enumeration, but in Massachusetts there was a continued decline after 1875:

Natives of Massachusetts resident in	1875.	1885.
Town of birth	48 61	51.00
Some other town of Massachusetts	30.62	29.46
Some other State	20.77	19.54

In Rhode Island, also, the percentage of natives resident in town of birth increased more than the other categories.—"The Decrease of Interstate Migration," in *Pol. Science Quar.*, x, 603–614.

several of the countries the statistics of birth-place refer to a larger civil division than the township, such as the county or *Département:*

TABLE CXXII.

PERCENTAGES OF THE POPULATION RESIDING IN THE NATIVE

	Department in France.	County in England and Wales.[1]	Län in Sweden	District in Denmark.[1]
1860	....	....	92.8	
1866	88.4	....		
1870	....	....	90.8	
1871	....	74.04		
1876	85.7			
1880	....	....	88.4	83.15
1881	....	75.19		
1886	84.0			
1890	....	....	....	80.68
1891	83.2	74.86		

TABLE CXXIII.

PERCENTAGES OF THE POPULATION BORN IN THE TOWN WHERE ENUMERATED:

	Prussia.	Austria.[2]	Switzerland.[2]	Netherlands.	Belgium.
1846	....	....	....	....	70.2
1849	....	....	....	69.09	
1850	....	....	64.0		
1856	....	....	....	....	69.1
1859	....	....	....	68.90	
1860	....	....	58.7		
1866	....	....	....	....	69.4
1869	....	78.7	....	68.29	
1870	....	....	54.0		
1871	56.8				
1879	....	....	....	67.22	
1880	57.6	69.7	48.7	....	67.2
1885	54.3				
1888	....	....	45.9		
1889	....	....	....	65.4	
1890	53.4	63.9	....	....	65.2

In Ireland internal migration has on the whole increased,

[1] The percentages for England and Denmark are of the native, not of the total population.

[2] In Austria and Switzerland the figures express the percentage of population residing in the town of *legal settlement.*

although rather slowly. The following statistics of selected counties are given because they cover a longer period than do any of the more general British statistics :

PERCENTAGE OF POPULATION BORN AND STILL RESIDING, AT CENSUS, IN

	Dublin county.	Leitrim county.	Belfast county.
1841	73.8	95.6	84.9
1851	69.2	94.2	72.6
1861	68.9	92.7	75.2
1871	64.8	93.4	76.5
1881	62.6	93.5	77.3
1891	62.7	92.8	76.9

Of the larger countries named in the above tables, Prussia and Austria represent one extreme and England and France the other. In Austria internal migration has had a remarkable increase in the last twenty years. In Prussia the increase has been large since 1880; in the preceding decade mobility apparently decreased, but this was no doubt due in some measure to the displacement of population in 1871, the year of the war with France. Now Schumann has shown that interstate migration in Germany is chiefly in the direction of the centers of industry and commerce[1],—a fact which gives us the explanation of increasing mobility of the Germans, for no country in Europe has progressed so rapidly in manufacturing industry in the last quarter century as has Germany. In Austria, too, as Rauchberg has conclusively shown,[2] the current of migration is toward the cities, and the reason that it has increased so much is the transformation of Austria from an agricultural to a manufacturing and commercial country, which is now taking place. In England and France, on the other hand, this transformation took place long years since, and for that reason we see no marked tendency toward the increase of migration at present. Switzerland apparently has an increasingly mobile

[1] " Die inneren Wanderungen in Deutchland," in *Allg. Stat. Archiv.*, i, 518–9.

[2] In *Statistische Monatschrift*, xviii, 230 and 562.

population; but the figures given, which refer to the place of settlement, are dependent upon the laws of settlement and cannot therefore be accepted without reserve.[1] Owing to their peculiar situation and composition, the Swiss cantons are particularly liable to a large foreign immigration,[2] and do actually receive more immigrants than any other country in Europe.[3] Such immigration of course affects the figures of Swiss mobility. In Scandinavia, Holland and Belgium the internal migration has increased slightly more than it has in France. On the whole, it may be said that in the last quarter of a century the tendency to migrate has increased in a direct ratio with the distance east from the settled manufacturing and commercial countries of Western Europe. Great mobility in the latter countries was attained some decades ago, and now the other nations are rapidly approaching thereto. As we have seen in Table CXXI, England, Germany and France now lead the European nations as regards mobility, but the other countries of Western Europe are not far behind, while Northern and Eastern Europe are still bound to the old order of things with settled populations. It may be conjectured that at the present time the most rapid increase in migration would be found in Russia, which is now going over from the village economy to the national; but we are without statistics to support the supposition.

But while there are considerable differences among the countries as regards the inter-town migration, there is much less difference in the inter-county migration. In France, Switzerland, Netherlands, Norway and Hungary more than one-half of the migration is in fact within the *département* or

---

[1] Thus the percentage of native town inhabitants was 63.8 in 1860 and 56.4 in 1888, showing a smaller increase in migration.

[2] Switzerland is bounded by France, Germany, Austria and Italy, and her people are allied in race and language to all four nationalities.

[3] See Table CXXI.

province. Even in countries with a large migration over county lines, it is to be presumed that short-distance migration prevails. Thus, among the countries with the smallest percentage of the native county element is England, and even in England the larger portion of the internal migration is confined to neighboring counties.[1] Since migration is as active in England as in any settled country, we may regard as well established the proposition that internal migration is predominantly of the short-distance character.[2]

What, now, is the cause of this short-distance migration? And how is it connected with the growth of cities and the concentration of population? Both of these questions can be answered with a few statistics. Let us first look at the constitution of the native population of the German Empire in December, 1890, according to place of birth. The free city of Hamburg contained 294,174 Germans born in other States of the Empire, while only 47,674 Hamburgers were found residing outside their native city. Hamburg had therefore gained by the migration 246,500 or 686.5 per cent. of its native population. This was the largest gain made by any province of the Empire. The free city of Bremen was second with 400.7 per cent., then followed Brandenburg and Berlin 211.3 per cent., Alsace–Lorraine 93.7 per cent., Saxony 59.7 per cent., Westphalia 33.9 per cent., Rhine provinces 30.8 per cent., Schleswig-Holstein and Lübeck

---

[1] Of 1,000 migrants of English birth enumerated in the United Kingdom in 1881, 524 were found in border counties, 451 elsewhere in England and Wales, and 25 in Scotland and Ireland. Ravenstein, "The Laws of Migration," in *Jour. of Stat. Soc.*, 1885, p. 182.

[2] Dr. Schumann selected at random six rural townships in Oldenburg, and found that over four-fifths of the migrants moved no further than two (German) miles. The percentage of immigrants whose birth-place was within two miles of their town of residence was 95.6, 60.1, 83.5, 78.2, 88.1, 80.2. Similarly, of all the natives who had changed their place of residence without going outside the grand duchy, 83, 90, 86, 84, 68, 70 per cent. had not moved farther than two miles. —*Allg. Stat. Archiv.*, i, 509.

15.4 per cent. and Baden 8.8 per cent. All other divisions of the Empire lost in the exchange of population.[1] Now manufacturing industry in Germany is concentrated in the Rhine–Westphalian provinces, the kingdom of Saxony, the city of Berlin, and the acquired French territory of Alsace-Lorraine. It will be observed therefore that the districts which have gained through migration are distinctively the commercial and industrial centers of the Empire, with the single exception of Baden; Brandenburg and Schleswig-Holstein being in close dependence on Berlin and Hamburg-Altona respectively. Any one cause can explain internal migration in Germany, namely, the growth of the centers of commerce and industry, or in other words, of the great cities.

The figures just given cover migration for an entire generation; in the more recent years migration has concentrated itself upon still fewer districts. This may be ascertained by means of the births and deaths, as previously noticed. Thus in the five-year period 1885–90, all of the provinces of Germany had an excess of births over deaths, but most of them lost a part of this excess through migration, their total increase being less than their natural increase. The results of the movement are shown in

TABLE CXXIV.[2]

	Excess of births.	Increase in population.	Gain or loss by migration.	
			Total.	Ratio to excess of births.
Group I (East Prussia)	851,770	212,666	—639,104	—75.04
" II (West Prussia and middle German states)	611,538	531,089	—80,449	—13.15
Group III (South Ger. states).	500,787	347,520	—153,267	—30.61
" IV (Indust. centers)...	937,688	1,480,191	+542,503	+57.86
German Empire.....	2,901,783	2,571,446	—330,317	—11.38

Group IV comprehends Berlin with a percentage of 239.52, the district of Potsdam which encloses Berlin 140.54 per cent., the Hanseatic towns (Hamburg, Bremen, and

[1] *Vierteljahrshefte zur Statistik des Deutschen Reiches*, 1893, Heft, ii, p. 4.
[2] Cf. *Schriften des Vereins für Socialpolitik*, lvi, 6.

Lübeck) 214.82 per cent., the kingdom of Saxony 33.28 per cent., the Rhine provinces 14.65 and Westphalia 20.75 per cent. Nothing could more clearly and emphatically show the relation between migration and the centers of commerce and industry than these figures from Germany. If it were needful, similar figures could be adduced for the other industrial countries.[1]

Since, then, the current of migration is toward the cities and yet the bulk of migration is for short distances only, we can see the manner of the movement; it is a migration by stages having for its object the satisfaction of the demands for more labor in the cities. These demands are not met by the direct migration of superfluous labor from the fields to the cities, but by the flocking in of the inhabitants immediately surrounding the town; the gaps thus left in the rural populations are filled up by immigrants from more remote districts until the attractive force of a rapidly growing city makes its influence felt, step by step, to the most remote corner of the country.[2]

Thus, an analysis of London's provincial element shows that the emigration from the provinces decreases with the distance from London. In an essay on "Influx of Population," in Charles Booth's *Life and Labor of the People* (vol. iii, chaps. 2 and 3), Mr. H. Llewellyn Smith presents the following comparison for six concentric rings:[3]

Ring.	Average distance from London in miles.	No. persons per 1,000 of pop. of each ring, living in London, 1881.	Density of pop. per 1,000 acres.
1	23.8	166.0	800
2	52.5	121.4	488
3	90.9	61.2	540
4	126.0	32.0	516
5	175.7	16.2	800
6	236.9	24.9	406

[1] Ravenstein (*Jour. of Stat. Soc.*, 1885, p. 185, ff) established similar conclusions for England. The "counties of dispersion" are entirely agricultural, while the "counties of absorption" embrace the centers of manufacturing and commerce.

[2] Ravenstein, *ibid.*, 199.

[3] The average distance of a ring of counties is taken to be the result of multi-

This table clearly establishes the fact that London's provincial population was contributed by the outside counties in proportion to their distance from London. It fully confirms the opinion of Mr. Ravenstein that internal migration is of short-journey type. Distance is the controlling factor. The only exception to Ravenstein's rule is in the sixth ring, which includes the counties of Durham and Northumberland, Cornwall, Pembroke and Cardigan, and four others. It is to be noted that these are maritime counties with direct communication to London. It represents the current of migration, consisting of those who seek a distinct economic advantage; the bulk of migration, however, is a "drift" toward the great centers by successive stages. If emigrants do thus move by stages, settling at intermediate points for considerable periods in the interval, then we should expect to find the average ages of those coming from great distances to be greater than those whose birth-places are nearer the city. Mr. Smith has constructed the following table from the census returns of 1881, the last year for which figures were available:

Ring (as before].	Percentage of total migrants who were	
	Under 20 years of age.	Over 20 years.
1	22.4	77.6
2	18.1	81.9
3	16.8	83.2
4	15.4	84.6
5	19.1	80.9
6	15.9	84.1

In general, the proportion of adults increases with the distance from London until we reach the fifth ring, which includes the manufacturing districts of the North—Yorkshire, Lancashire, etc. Still too much weight should not be attributed to these figures, for it may be that the short-dis-

plying the population of each country by the distance of its center from London, adding the products and dividing by total population of the ring.

tance migration includes more families with children (which would reduce the average age) while the long-distance migration might be equally direct, although consisting more of single young men between the age of 20 and 30.

Again, with short-distance migration as the prevalent form, we should expect to find the native county element stronger in the great city than in the rural districts around it, while the border county element would be less strong in the city, having been, so to speak, deposited in the intervening rural parts of the county by the current toward the city. Ravenstein declares that this is the general rule in Great Britain. Forty-five out of 67 cities which he investigated recruit their population in the main from their own county, or in case of border towns, from two contiguous counties; they contained a smaller percentage of migrants from outside their own county than did the intervening rural parts.[1]

It is true, moreover, that with the development of railway communication the volume of direct and long-distance migration to the city has increased; men out of work will often migrate hundreds of miles in order to find work in their own trade, instead of remaining at or near home and changing their occupation.

This exception to the rule that internal migration is chiefly a short-distance movement brings us to the second law of migration, namely, that the distance traveled by migrants varies in the same ratio as the magnitude of the city which is their destination. The larger the town, the wider its circle of influence in attracting immigrants; the small city acts as a magnet for the neighboring counties, a large city (100,000+) attracts strangers from other parts or provinces, but only the great capitals exercise an international influence on

[1] But in cases where a large city is situated in a relatively small county, or where the city is growing much more rapidly than the rest of the county, it must needs have a larger feeder, and hence draws immigrants from beyond the county. —Ravenstein, *loc cit.*, pp. 200–218.

migration. This fact is clearly established in the following statistics from the Austrian census of 1890, which show the birth-place of every 1,000 persons enumerated in the class of towns specified in the first column:

TABLE CXXV.[1]

Dwelling-places. (*Ortschaften.*)	Town of residence.	Another town of same district.[2]	Another district of same province.	Another province of the kingdom.	Foreign country.	Total.
Under 500	657	215	100	22	7	1,000
500-2,000	735	149	85	23	8	1,000
2,000–5,000	699	132	119	36	14	1,000
5,000–10,000	556	142	210	67	25	1,000
10,000–20,000	464	122	310	77	27	1,000
Over 20,000	431	13	258	231	72	1,000
Austria	652	150	128	53	17	1,000

The table also illustrates a third law of migration, to which attention should be called, namely, that the percentage of immigrants increases in the same ratio as the magnitude of cities, but in inverse ratio with the magnitude of rural communities.[3] Thus, in Austria, 27 per cent. of the population of villages of 500–2,000 are outsiders and 73 per cent. are natives of their town of residence; but in the cities of 20,000+ the respective percentages are 57 and 43.

It seems somewhat singular that the native town element, which is weakest in the large cities and steadily increases in strength as the size of the town diminishes, should fall off so much in the very smallest towns, namely, those containing fewer than 500 inhabitants. Yet this is the fact to the best

---

[1] Rauchberg, in *Stat. Monatschrift*, xix, 129.

[2] The *Bezirk* or district, of which there are 359 in Austria, contains 323 square miles, and is thus less than half the size of a New York county (average 750 square miles).

[3] Georg von Mayr, who as chief of the Bavarian Bureau of Statistics, made the first thorough investigation in the field of internal migration in 1871, is the author of this law. Cf. *Heft XXXII der Beiträge zur Statistik des Königreichs Bayerns* (München, 1876): *Die bayrische Bevölkerung nach der Gebürtigkeit.*

of the writer's knowledge in all the investigations thus far made—the Bavarian census of 1871, the 1880 census of the duchy of Oldenburg,[1] and the Austrian census of 1890. One explanation of the fact may be that men living in the least populous places must oftener seek their wives in a neighboring community, the range of choice in their own village being so small. The Austrian statistics, however, show that this happens more frequently in the villages of from 500 to 1,000 inhabitants, where the native town element is strongest of all;[2] thus the number of women to 1,000 men was

Places.	In Austria.	Among those born In town of residence.	In another town of same district.
Under 500 pop	1,047	985	1,297
500–1,000 "	1,049	1,001	1,373

From which it follows that the large percentage of immigrants in the smallest places is not a result of marriages contracted by male residents with women of a neighboring place.

The more probable explanation is that the least populous communities are unable, with their own members, to carry out the division of labor to a sufficient extent, and are therefore obliged to recruit their force from neighboring places. But the conditions in Austria and Germany are peculiar to a fast disappearing civilization, in that the places with less

[1] The percentages of the native town element were as follows in the *rural* communes:

Under 500	45.02
500–1,000	62.65
1,000–1,500	58.30
1,500–2,000	59.57
2,000–3,000	71.31
3,000–4,000	77.18
4,000–5,000	79.42
5,000 +	70.60

—*Statistische Nachrichten über das Grossherzogtum Oldenburg*, Heft xix, p. 61.

[2] Rauchberg, as above, xix, 130.

than 500 population are usually manors. It is unfortunate that no data of this sort exist for countries without the manorial system.

Von Mayr's law as stated above has never been successfully disputed[1] and is confirmed by nearly all the statistics. Thus in Saxony the percentage constituted by the native element is as follows:

Rural townships:
Under 2,000 .... 52.4
Over 2,000 .... 49.7
Urban townships 48.0
Dresden 39.4
Leipzig 36.1

For other countries the facts may be summarized thus:

TABLE CXXVI.

PERCENTAGE OF POPULATION BORN IN TOWN OF RESIDENCE:

		Rural.	Urban.	Capital city.
1. Prussia,	1890	53.9	43.8	
2. Sweden,	1880	92.0	67.8	41.3
3. Denmark,	1890	86.77	75.16	55.92
4. Netherlands,	1889	68.34	64.54	
5. Belgium,	1890	70.4	59.4	57.0
6. Switzerland,	1888	60.7	34.7	24.3
7. France,	1891 .... ca 70.0	....	32.4	

[1] The rule that the native town element decreases in cities in inverse ratio to their population has been denied by Hansen in his noted work, *Die drei Bevölkerungstufen*, in which he prints a list of the 34 Bavarian cities (those with municipal institutions) arranged in order of size, and then points out irregularities. But it has never been claimed for the law that it applies to individual cities, but only to classes, and if the 34 cities mentioned be further divided into classes, the rule will be found to hold in most cases:

Per cent of native city element
in total population.

4 cities over 30,000 pop. 43
3 " 20–30,000 " 53
11 " 10–20,000 " 46
16 " under 10,000 " 54

Where the number of cases is so small, the liability to fluctuations is always present.

EXPLANATIONS.

1. The rural percentage is for all Prussia; the urban for cities of 20,000+.
2. The unit as regards birth-place is here not the town, but " Län " or province.
3. The unit is the district, or province.
4. The urban percentage is for cities of 20,000+; the rural for the remainder of the country.
5. Urban=communes of 5,000+. The percentage in the last column refers to cities of 100,000+.
6. Urban=communes of 10,000+.
7. In France we have the percentages of inhabitants who were born in the commune where they were enumerated. Taking the four departments that represent the largest and smallest percentages of urban population, we have the following figures for 1891:

Seine (99.13 per cent. urban) 32.4
Bouches de Rhone (83.5 per cent. urban) 54.7
Sauoie Haute (91.7 per cent. rural)... .... 73.
Côtes du Nord (90.0 per cent rural) .... 69.

These are the two extremes. There is not such a vast difference between the *département* of Bouches de Rhone (containing Marseilles, the second largest city of France) and Côtes du Nord, (a rural *département*) as regards the proportion of immigrants.

England's statistics do not admit of ready comparison between the urban and rural population in respect of immigration. Certain typical counties may be selected, however; thus, among the following counties the percentage of population born in the same county was:

Urban counties.		Rural counties.	
London	65.5	Rutland	63.8
Middlesex	32.9	Cardigan	87.6
Lancashire	75.9	Suffolk	82.3
		Hereford	70.0

It is certainly a striking fact that Lancashire, the typical manufacturing county of England, contains fewer residents of outside birth than do the rural counties of Hereford and Rutland. Even London has fewer immigrants than Rutlandshire. Middlesex, to be sure, has a large proportion of outsiders, but Middlesex should really be counted as part of one large metropolitan county including all London. Too much weight, however, should not be placed on these statistics, which are fragmentary at best and are in opposition to all others that we have on the subject.

The three laws of migration now laid down hold good in the United States, so far as can be judged from imperfect statistics; but the role of the foreigners is here a more important one:

TABLE CXXVII.

OF EACH 1,000 INHABITANTS THERE WERE BORN IN

		City named.	The same province or state	Another province, state or county.	A foreign country.
London,	(1881)	 629	732 [1]	204 [1]	63
Paris,[2]	(1891)	 324	398 [2]	541	61
Berlin,	(1890)	 407	599	394	17
Vienna,	(1890)	 349	470	420	110
Glasgow,	(1881)	 513	614 [1]	214	172
Boston,	(1885)	 385	492	167	341
"	(1890)	....	505	142	353
Amsterdam,	(1889)	 683	769	203	28
New York,	(1890)	....	489	99	422
Chicago,	(1890)	....	397	193	410

Among the seven cities in the foregoing table there appears a wide variation in the percentage of the native town element, which constitutes from one-third to two-thirds of the population. Very nearly as wide a range, however, may be found among the cities of a single country; among the 26 great cities of Germany, for example, it varies from 36 (Munich) to 62.4 per. cent. (Aachen), the average being 43.7 per cent. This percentage depends partly upon the individual city's industrial character; partly upon its area, and in a larger degree, perhaps, on the composition of the population of the surrounding country. Thus the number of foreigners in the general population will affect the city's composition, as it notably does in the United States. In Boston, the only large American city for which the necessary data were fully obtainable, the percentage of foreign born was 34.1, which is close to the average (31.8) of the 28 American cities of 100,000 and upwards. None of the European cities, of course, approaches the figure.

[1] For "province" read "county." "Foreign country" includes also Scotland and Ireland.

[2] Department of the Seine, nearly identical with Paris; the first column gives the percentage (32.4) of inhabitants of the department who were born in the commune of residence.

Even Glasgow's 17.2 per cent. consists almost entirely of English and Irish born (3.1 and 13.1 per cent., respectively). Vienna has the next largest percentage of foreigners, but these are in large part (77 of the 110 in a thousand) natives of the confederated country, Hungary.

But while foreign immigration contributes large numbers to the population of American cities, it is not true, as Mr. Ravenstein, for example, seems inclined to think, that " the migratory current from the country to the city is scarcely perceptible in the United States and other newly settled countries."[1] We have seen in a former chapter how villages have decayed and cities prospered even in the West, and the strong tendency of young men to abandon the farm in order to seek their fortunes in the city is a matter of familiar observation. The only statistics that we have on this point however, are those of Massachusetts. They show that 11 per cent. of Boston's population in 1885 had been born in other Massachusetts towns. Now it is possible, but hardly probable, that all these immigrants came from cities and none from the rural towns; but one thing is clear at least: Boston's growth is almost as much due to immigration of native Americans as to her own natural increase or to foreign immigration. Of Boston's total population in 1885, 38.47 per cent. were born in the city itself and 27.39 per cent. in the United States outside of Boston.[2] Now London contains only 30.7 per cent. of Englishmen born outside of London, Glasgow 31.5 per cent. of Scotchmen born outside of Glasgow, and Amsterdam 28.9 per cent. of Dutchmen born outside of the city itself. The French and German cities, it is true, have larger percentages, but in view of the comparison between Boston on the one side and London,

[1] *J. of St. Soc.*, 1889, p. 288.

[2] The remainder, born abroad, is 34.14 per cent. *Mass. Cens. of 1885*, vol. i, pt. i, p. lxviii.

Glasgow and Amsterdam on the other, it can hardly be said that "the migratory current of the rural population toward the cities is hardly perceptible in the United States." [1]

Except for the larger immigration from abroad, the migratory movement in the United States follows about the same direction that it does in Europe. In Massachusetts, for example, we have the following distribution of the population according to birth-place:

	Per cent. of total pop. 1885.[2]
Born in	
Town where enumerated...............................	36.1
Some other town in Mass.	20.8
Mass.—not specified	.6
Massachusetts..	57.5
Other New England States............................	11.2
"　North Atlantic States............................	2.7
South Atlantic States................................	.55
North Central States	.55
South　"　　"	.1
Western States and Territories	.1
United States—not specified	.2
United States.......................................	72.9
Foreign countries...................................	27.1
	100.

[1] The following table of comparisons may be found useful for reference:

TABLE CXXVIII.

PERCENTAGE OF POPULATION BORN IN

	Date.	City of residence.	Territory immediately surrounding.	Native country elsewhere.	Foreign country.
1. German cities (26) of 100,000 +	1890	43.7	30.7	23.5	2.1
2. Austrian cities (32) of 20,000 +	1890	43.1	26.6	23.1	7.2
3. Scotch cities (7)	1881	52.4	24.1	10.3	13.2
4. American cities (28) of 100,000+	1890	52.4		15.8	31.8
5. Boston	1885	38.5	12.9	14.5	34.1

AUTHORITIES.—The official German and Austrian censuses. The percentages for American cities are based on *11th Cen., Pop.*, i, p. cxxvi. For Scotland, Ravenstein, *op. cit.*, p. 195. The "immediately surrounding territory" comprises the *Gebietstheile* (provinces, etc.) in Germany; the *Land*, or province in Austria; the native county and border counties in Scotland; State or commonwealth in America. England and Wales are reckoned as "foreign countries" to Scotland.

[2] Based on the data given in *Mass. Census of 1885*, vol. i, part i, p. lxx. And if strength of migration be portrayed on county maps of any commonwealth by

It is unnecessary to go further in testing the hypotheses of von Mayr and Ravenstein. Detailed studies in several countries have been made, among which those of Dr. Rauchberg, of the Austrian statistical bureau, are pre-eminent; these are illustrated with maps which convey to the eye the meaning of internal migration under the attraction of centers of population. They confirm the conclusions stated in this paper.[1] They would also seem to meet the assertion sometimes made regarding the mode of internal migration, namely, that it proceeds *staffelweise*, from farm to village, from village to town, from town to city, from city to metropolis. If, for example, the migration into a great city proceeds in the main from the immediately surrounding territory, there can be scant opportunity for smaller cities to act as feeders. Berlin, in 1890, contained 936.143 persons born outside the city, or 59.3 per cent. of its total population. Brandenburg, the province in whose center Berlin is situated, contributed 287,540 of the immigrants, and the other 25 great cities (100,000+) of Germany contributed 53,856, or one-fifth as many. Nevertheless, the population of Brandenburg in 1890 was half a million less than that of the 25 great cities (4,600,000 and 4,120,577 respectively). Statistics prove that great cities receive a small part of their immigration from other large cities, although a relatively large percentage of emigrants from these cities go to other cities to live. In the

means of color or shading, it will usually be found that those counties which contain the largest percentage of natives of adjoining commonwealths are the border counties. Cf. maps showing interstate migration, in *Stat. Atlas of U. S.*

[1] " Die Gebürtigkeitsverhältnisse der Bevölkerung Oesterreichs nach den Ergebnissen der Volkszählung von 31 December, 1890," in *Statis. Monat.*, xvii (1892), 517-574, especially p. 556. Also " Der Zug nach der Stadt," *ibid.*, xix, 125-171. The student who is interested in the subject will find excellent studies of the internal migration in Germany by Brückner (" Die Entwicklung der grossstädtischen Bevölkerung Deutschlands ") and Schumann (" Die inneren Wanderungen ,") in the first volume of the *Allgemeines Statistisches Archiv.*

following table of the German cities, (a) denotes the percentage of persons born in other great cities among the immigrants of the specified city, (b) the percentage of those born in a great city and emigrating who go to another of the 26 cities:

	a.	b.		a.	b.
Berlin	5.8	13.3	Nuremberg	2.4	22.9
Hamburg	10.9	36.7	Stuttgart	2.4	13.3
Leipzig	6.5	25.9	Chemnitz	3.9	27.1
Munich	2.4	9.5	Elberfeld	14.6	41.3
Breslau	2.2	27.8	Bremen	4.9	22.8
Cologne	6.9	25.5	Strassburg	3.7	9.2
Dresden	6.1	20.0	Danzig	3.9	34.1
Magdeburg	5.0	34.7	Barmen	11.8	44.0
Frankfort	3.9	21.3	Stettin	3.9	41.7
Hanover	5.6	27.9	Crefeld	5.5	27.0
Königsberg	2.6	35.6	Aachen	5.6	28.1
Düsseldorf	9.3	31.9	Halle	6.2	30.5
Altona	14.6	67.5	Brunswick	5.0	32.7

Average (a) 5.9; (b) 26.6

The cities are arranged in order of size, and it will be observed at once that the percentages do not descend in the same order. Berlin, Munich, Breslau are all below the average. The cities that receive the largest proportion of their immigrants from other cities, are Hamburg, Altona, Elberfeld, Barmen; and a glance at the map shows the reason why. Hamburg and Altona are almost parts of one city and Elberfeld–Barmen also constitute a pair of "twin cities." Hence migration between them must be large. On the other hand, the cities with the smallest percentages, Munich, Breslau, Frankfort, Königsberg, Nuremberg, Stuttgart, Strassburg—are all isolated cities; size has therefore little if any influence on the origin of immigration. Location is the prime factor, because internal migration is for short distances.

Nor if one looks at migration from the opposite point of

view, does it appear that the largest city communicates primarily with other cities, and only secondarily with the rural districts or villages. While 67.5 out of every 100 persons born in Altona and no longer resident there, are in the other great cities of Germany, only 13.3 per cent. of emigrating Berliners are residents of other great cities. Practically the same rule holds as before; namely, it is distance rather than size of cities which determines the amount of immigration or emigration in connection with other places. Migration being predominantly short-distance, the character of immigration to any city will partake of the local surroundings. And as in most cases the surrounding country is filled with hamlets and villages, the immigrants will be of the rural class; but as the distance widens the urban communities will contribute more and more. This appears in the military rolls of Frankfort, 1890–2, containing the names of 2,293 young men not born in the city but living there and becoming subject to military duty in the years mentioned. The province or state of birth was given as follows:[1]

	Rural communes.	Towns.
Prussia :		
Hessen-Nassau	273	160
Rhine province	50	69
Rest of Prussia	134	188
Hessen	238	127
Bavaria	259	132
Baden	126	84
Wurtemburg	134	75
Saxony	30	48
Other German states	60	86
Total	1,304	969

All Prussia, except the province of Hessen-Nassau wherein Frankfort is situated, sends a majority of this par-

[1] Bleicher, p. 37; the distinction between town and country is the legal one.

ticular class of emigrants from the cities. From the four states of South Germany (being relatively near to Frankfort) the migration was primarily rural, but from Saxony and the rest of Germany it was predominantly urban. The classification of the 969 city men follows:

Towns under 5,000 inhabitants.. 369
  "   from 5,000–20,000 inhabitants.............................. 227
  "   "   20,000–100,000 inhabitants............................. 233
  "   100,000 +.. 140
                                                                    ———
                                                                    969

It cannot be said, however, that statistics of birth-place entirely disprove the hypothesis of migration by stages through village, town, city and metropolis, inasmuch as a man's previous place of residence does not always coincide with his birth-place. The migrant to London, who is credited to the rural county in which he was born, may have passed his earlier years in a neighboring city. The German municipal statisticians are now devoting some attention to the ascertainment of the immigrant's last place of residence as well as his birth-place, and these statistics, imperfect as yet, show that the cities figure more largely as feeders to other great cities than appeared in the statistics of birth-place. But as the percentages affected are those born in distant parts (who reach the city of their destination after residence in intermediate cities), the conclusions already stated need not be greatly modified. Dr. Bleicher, of the Frankfort municipal statistical bureau, has published a study of the migration for the year 1891. After eliminating travelers, visitors, and other persons whose sojourn was temporary, he had remaining 23,254 male, and 16,166 female immigrants, 11,440, or 70.8 per cent of the latter being domestic servants. Of the men, 8,656, or 37.2 per cent., were born in the town from which they moved to Frankfort; the other two-thirds had already left their place of birth. Of the women, excluding the servants, 43.9 per cent. came directly from the birth-place; or 58 per cent. if the servants be included. From these figures it is to be inferred that men are accustomed to migrate more frequently than women, although a larger number of women than men, as previously noted, participate in the migratory movement across township lines. A detailed analysis of the male immigrants to Frankfort in 1891 is presented in

TABLE CXXIX.[1]

Born in	Rural county of Frankfort.	Neighboring cities.	Male Immigrants from				Women.
			German cities of 100,000+.	Other places in Germany.	Foreign countries.	All places.	From all places.
Last place of residence.....	9.1	14.7	18.5	54.4	33.9	37.2	43.9
City of Frankfort	6.2	4.3	4.8	2.7	8.9	4.1	5.7
Rural county of Frankfort .	2.4	0.7	0.5	0.4	0.4	0.6	0.7
A neighboring city	6.4	4.0	2.3	1.9	2.8	2.6	3.6
A German city of 100,000+.	2.5	4.3	7.4	1.9	4.9	3.4	3.5
Some other German town..	72.2	67.3	57.0	57.2	20.0	47.0	34.9
A foreign country..........	1.2	4.7	9.5	1.5	29.0	5.0	7.7
	100.0	100.0	100.0	100.0	99.9	99.9	100.0

It appears from this table that the direct migration from birth-place to the great city is dependent upon distance. Of the immigrants from German cities of 100,000+ over eighteen per cent. were natives of the city from which they removed to Frankfort, showing that there is considerable mobility in great city populations; seven per cent. of these immigrants were natives of another great city, and 57 per cent. natives of a smaller city or village of Germany. It will be noted that the immigrants include a large number of born Frankforters returning to their native city; that, in fact, Frankfort contributed a larger percentage to the immigration than any other city.

The role played by people thus returning to their native town or former place of residence, is a considerable one. Dr.

[1] Bleicher, Heft II (1893), p. 46.

Bleicher found that of 4,541 emigrants from Frankfort in 1891, 2,082, or 45.85 per cent. returned to the place from which they had come to Frankfort.[1] Nor was this return current directed entirely to the small towns in the vicinity of Frankfort, as these figures will demonstrate:[2]

Original residence.	Immigrants.	Emigrants to former place of residence.
Places within 12 kilometers	144	43=29.9 per cent.
Cities of neighborhood	802	259=32.3 "
Great Cities	1,002	411=41.0 "
Other places in Germany	2,183	1,183=54.2 "
Foreign countries	410	186=45.4 "
Totals	4,541	2,082=45.85 "

The emigration to the great cities and to foreign countries consisted of those engaged in business and trade, while that to smaller places in Germany was made up chiefly of day laborers.

As between rural and urban communes in the vicinity of a large city, the latter will contribute more than proportionately to its immigration. Thus in the little German city of Oldenburg (pop. 20,575) in the enterprising duchy of the same name, it was found in 1880 that among 8,541 immigrants, 1,975 or 23 per cent. had been born in urban communities (places of 2,000+) and 77 per cent. in rural communities. But outside the capital the population is almost entirely rural, and it results that while the rural communes contributed 3.1 per cent. of their population to the capital, the towns contributed 8.3 per cent. of theirs.[3] There are other instances. Switzerland has not a very large urban population, and yet the city Basel in 1888 contained a body of persons, amounting to 14.5 per cent. of its population, who were born in other cities, 47.3 having been born in

[1] *Ibid.*, 53.   [2] *Ibid.*, 55.
[3] *Statistische Nachrichten Oldenburgs*, etc., xix, 212.

rural districts and 38.2 in Basel itself.[1] In Bavaria again the free (*unmittelbar*) cities, excluding Munich, contained 12.6 per cent. of the population in 1890; but they contributed 17.83 per cent. of Munich's Bavarian immigrants. In Saxony, where the urban population, excluding Leipzig, falls somewhat below the rural population, it nevertheless contributed to Leipzig's population of 1885, 32.40 per cent. while the rural communes contributed 31.67 and Leipzig itself 35.57.

The mobility of the great city populations may, however, be inferior to that of rural communities. Professor Karl Bücher, having in mind the factory operatives and sweat-shop victims of slum populations, affirms that poverty, as well as persistent clinging to familiar associations, prevents city populations from migrating as freely as country people. In support of his opinion he offers the following:[2]

TABLE CXXX.

PERCENTAGE OF (a) NEW CITIZENS COMING FROM

	Towns.	Villages and hamlets
Cologne, 1356–1479	37.4	62.6
Frankfort, 1311–1479	28.2	71.8
" 1401–1500	43.9	56.1
(b) JOURNEYMEN BOOK-BINDERS:		
Frankfort, 1712–50	97.5	2.5
" 1751–1800	94.3	5.7
" 1801–35	89.2	10.8
" 1835–50	86.0	14.0
" 1851–67	81.2	18.8

Such figures are inconclusive. It may be well that the increasing proportion of rural bookbinders in Frankfort is

[1] Bücher, *Die Bevölkerung des Cantons Basel-Stadt am I Dez., 1888.*

[2] *Enstehung der Volkswt.*, 62 ff. Llewellyn Smith shows that the twelve leading manufacturing counties of England had contributed only 2.4 per 1,000 of their population to the population of East London and Hackney in 1881, while the twelve leading agricultural counties had contributed 16 per mille. (Booth, *op. cit.*, iii, 71.)

due to the extension of the printing trade to small towns.
Formerly, this trade like all others not immediately connected with agriculture, was the virtual monopoly of the
cities.

Nevertheless, there is other evidence that the population
of a metropolitan city is less migratory than the average.
In 1881 of all the persons born in London and still living in
England and Wales, 80.4 per cent. were residents of London,
while in the general population of England and Wales only
75.23 per cent. were residents of the county where born.[1]
With regard to Vienna, 84.7 per cent. of the native Viennese
counted in Austria in 1890 were resident in Vienna; in the
entire population only 66.3 per cent. were residing in the
town where born:[2] that is, 153 out of 1000 born Viennese
remove to other parts of Austria, and 337 of 1000 people
on the average have left their town of birth.

Emigration from the great city follows the general laws
already formulated.   It is overwhelmingly short-distance
migration, since so much of it is directed into the suburbs.[3]
In the distribution of the natives of London in other parts
of England and Wales in 1881, the contiguous counties
(Middlesex, Surrey, Kent, Essex, Hertford) forming an
extra-metropolitan group received 53.73 per cent. of the
migrants.   Wales received only 1.36 per cent., but the
Northern groups (manufacturing counties) received a
slightly larger percentage than the midland group,[4] although
situated at a greater distance.   A better idea of London
emigration will perhaps be gained from the following table,

---

[1] Ravenstein, in *Jour. of St. Soc.*, xlviii (1885), 195, 171.

[2] Rauchberg, *St. Mon.*, xix, 152; xviii, 534.

[3] Economically this should not be regarded as migration since it does not
usually involve a change in the place of business.

[4] Ravenstein, *J. of St. Soc.*, xlviii, 206-7.

in which the counties of England and Wales are arranged in concentric rings about London:[1]

Ring.	Average distance from London in miles.	Natives of London living in each ring of counties, per 1,000 of the population of the ring in 1881.
1	23.8	142.3
2	52.5	42.5
3	90.9	17.7
4	126.0	9.8
5	175.7	8.5
6	236.9	6.5

Comparing this table with the one showing the influx into London from the same rings, it will be found that the first ring is more conspicuous here than in the inflowing movement, while the outside rings participate more largely in the inflow. This is what would naturally be expected; the great city's attraction extends to the remotest boundary, and the inflowing movement creates a counter current of emigration, which is, however, much less intense. On the other, the suburbs, receive more than they give. Remarking that the registration county of London includes parts of the historical counties of Middlesex, Surrey and Kent, we may note that in 1881 there were 76,771 natives of extra-metropolitan Middlesex in metropolitan Middlesex, and 80,271 natives of the city part of the county in the extra-city part,—a gain of 3,500 for the extra-metropolitan portion. These large figures represent migration in no real sense: they merely express part of the movement across an imaginary boundary line between registration London and Greater London.

But whither go the real emigrants and why do they leave London? Mr. Smith has followed up the native Londoners outside of London and the contiguous counties of Essex, Middlesex, Sussex and Surrey, and found 64,918 residing in

---

[1] H. L. Smith, in Booth, *op. cit.*, iii, 67, 126.

cities of 100,000 or more, this being equal to 17.4 per 1000 of their population, and representing their power of attraction upon London; 24,079 in cities of 50–100,000, or 14 per mile their population; and 196,415 in all places under 50,000, or 1.29 per mile of their population.[1] Outside the suburban movement therefore, it is the great cities that draw most heavily upon London. The movement toward the smaller places is partly non-economic, *i. e.*, non-workers seeking retirement in a small town amid inexpensive surroundings; the larger part of this outflow however is not represented in the figures given, for it consists of those returning to the county of birth. The outflow to the larger cities is without doubt on business lines and consists of artisans and business men of various kinds.[2]

The nature of the migratory movement having been considered at some length, it is now time to investigate the character of the migrants, and especially of the migrants to the cities. We have seen something of their character in studying the sources of the migration, but we may gain further light by considering the sex, age and social rank of the immigrants.

As to *sex*, it may be confidently declared that woman is a greater migrant than man,—only she travels shorter distances. In considering the sex of city population, we shall see that the excess of women among the immigrants is one of the causes of the general surplus of women in cities, which exceeds that of the rural districts.

---

[1] Smith, in Booth, *op. cit.*, iii, 126–7.

[2] In Germany, also, the larger portion of the emigration from the great cities is either to the surrounding province or to other great cities; in 1890, of the natives of the 26 great cities who were living in Germany outside the city of birth, 56.1 per cent, resided in the surrounding province, and 26.5 per cent. in the other great cities. (Calculated from statistics given in *Statistik des Deutschen Reiches.* N. F., vol. 68, p. 71* ff.) Cf. Table CXXIX, *supra*, and Bleicher, ii, 52.

Following was the number of women (all the females) to 100 men (all the males) in 1881,[1] among natives of

	England and Wales.	Scotland.	Ireland.
Residing in the county of birth................	104	108	104
" in another county of same country	112	114	116
" in another part of the United Kingdom.	81	91	92

The most marked predominance of the female sex is not among the "stay-at-homes," *i. e.*, among those residing in the county of birth, but among those who have moved to some other county. On the other hand however, the women predominate only among the short-distance migrants, for when it comes to emigrants to another of the three kingdoms, their proportion falls immensely. Other countries present similar statistics.[2] So do cities. Thus of all the persons born in London and living anywhere in the United Kingdom in 1881, there were 112 females to 100 males; but among those still residing in London, only 109.[3]

[1] *J. of St. Soc.*, 1885, p. 197.

[2] Some German statistics of 1890 present the facts clearly, the following figures being the number of females to 1,000 males:

Born.	Prussia.[1]	Austria.[2]
In township of residence............................	1,018	1,011
Elsewhere in same county [3]	1,254	1,311
" " the same province......................	1,064	1,023
" " " " country	820	889
In foreign countries	874	950
Total population	1,038	1,044

[1] *Preussische Statistik*, Heft cxxi.

[2] Rauchberg, *Stat. Mon.*, xix, 130.

[3] *Kreis* in Prussia, *Bezirk* in Austria.

Taking the average of towns in these countries, it appears that in the native town element the women are not so strong as they are in the general population; but the female newcomers are chiefly from the same county, their proportion among other immigrants falling below the general average. The farther the distance, the smaller the proportion of women. This rule apparently breaks down in the case of foreign countries; but as a matter of fact, international migration like that between Austria and Hungary is really short notice. Germany with its long boundaries is in about the same condition.

[3] Ravenstein, *J. of St. Soc.*, 48: 195.

The statistics show that while women move from town to town within the same county or province more readily than the men do, they are more loath to move to a distance. The reason is probably to be found in the marriages which take women into a neighboring town, as well as the demand for domestic servants,[1] while men go longer distances in search of the best labor market. The relative proportion in which the two sexes participate in the migratory movement appears with considerable distinctness in the following Austrian statistics:[2]

TABLE CXXXI.

FEMALES TO 1,000 MALES AMONG THOSE BORN

Places with a pop. of	In town of residence.	Elsewhere in same *Bezirk*.	Elsewhere in same province.	Another province of Austria.	Foreign countries.	Ratio in the whole pop.
Less than 500....	985	1,297	1,038	861	920	1,047
500–2,000	1,001	1,373	1,047	882	945	1,049
2,000–5,000	1,027	1,275	1,012	854	995	1,047
5,000–10,000	1,079	1,171	949	729	845	1,029
10,000–20,000	1,067	1,200	955	655	914	1,004
20,000+	1,100	1,099	1,039	951	968	1,039
Austria...............	1,011	1,311	1,023	889	950	1,044
Vienna	1,095	....	....	...	....	1,061
Graz	1,136	....	....	....	....	1,086

It will be observed that the number of women to 1000 men is the largest in the smaller places and steadily decreases until the class of cities having 20,000 inhabitants is reached, when it once more increases. In the very largest cities it exceeds any of the ratios, being 1,061 in Vienna, 1,086 in

[1] Thus, the distribution of the female immigrants in Frankfort (Cf. Bleicher, p. 15), as compared with the native Frankfort women was as follows:

	Born.		Foreign born to 100 natives.
	In Frankfort.	Outside.	
Children under 15.....................	18,876	4,237	22.4
Dependents (members of family, etc.)...	13,143	28,620	217.8
Domestic servants....................	383	16,242	4,240.7
Other occupations	3,881	9,211	237.3
Total	36,283	58,310	160.7

[2] Rauchberg, *Stat. Mon.*, xix, 130.

Graz and Triest,[1] etc.; here is where the influence of large numbers of domestic servants makes itself felt.

Considering the "stay-at-homes" alone, it will be noticed that women predominate the more conspiciously, the larger the town; that is, the males migrate in relatively greater numbers from larger cities than from small towns. But among the migrants the predominance of the females is especially marked, not in the cities, but in the smaller places. Both facts are explained by the fact already emphasized that the large places alone draw migrants from a distance; hence they attract a majority of men, since, as we just noted, women are short-distance migrants. Finally, the table shows that in the larger cities the female element predominates less strongly among the immigrants than among the natives, the contrary being the case in the smaller places. Thus immigration strengthens the native female element in small places, but weakens it in towns of 5,000 and upwards.

The distribution of the sexes in the United States has been thoroughly treated by Professor Willcox[2] who calls attention to two tendencies: while, in all the elements of the population, the females show a tendency toward concentration in the cities, the tendency is more marked among the negroes of the South and the immigrants of the North than among the native whites. In New York State, 50.46 per cent of the foreign born living in 118 cities and towns are females, and only 45 per cent in the rural districts,—a difference of 5.46. But among the native Americans the percentages are 51.32 and 49.74 respectively, or a difference of only 1.58. In Georgia 54.84 per cent of the negroes in the cities are females and 49.76 per cent in the rural districts,—a difference of 5.08. But among the whites the percentages are 50.33 and 49.88, or a difference of only .45. Professor Willcox does not think

---

[1] Rauchberg, *ibid.* xix, 153.

[2] *Am. Jour. of Sociology*, i, 725.

that this tendency toward dissociation and concentration among the female negroes and foreigners can be wholly accounted for by migration, but is in part due to the higher infant mortality among these classes in the cities.[1]

Age.—It is a matter of common observation that the migrants to the cities are chiefly young people; and in this case the results of common observation are confirmed by statistics. A good idea of the age classification of migrants to the cities is given in the following table in which the native and immigrant elements of the city of Frankfort are compared with the average of Germany[2] (1890 in each case):

TABLE CXXXII.

	Frankfort.				Germany.
	Born in Frankfort.		Born elsewhere.		
Age.	Male.	Female.	Male.	Female.	
0–5	227	204	17	14	130.1
6–10	182	163	26	23	111.9
11–15	169	154	41	36	109.5
16–20	111	112	110	117	93.2
21–30	105	130	299	316	161.9
31–40	67	75	218	209	127.6
41–50	57	62	158	143	103.8
51–60	41	48	82	81	78.3
61–71	27	33	33	40	52.0
71–80	12	15	12	17	23.6
81 +	2	4	1.6	3.2	4.2
Unknown	....	....	2.4	.8	
	1,000	1,000	1,000	1,000	1,000

Only 7 or 8 per cent of the migrants to a typical city are under the age of 15, while in a normal population the proportion of children of that age is about 33 per cent. And while normally about one-half of any population will be at the age of 16–50, the age of activity, the proportion among the immigrants to a city is fully three-fourths. *Over one-*

[1] Cf. *infra*, ch. v, Sec. I.

[2] Bleicher, p. 6; *Stat. des Deutschen Reiches*, N. F. xliv, 24* ff.

half the immigrants are of the age 20–40,—in many cases 20–30. Above the age of fifty, the percentages do not show any considerable variation.[1]

The effect of the migration of persons in the active period of life to the cities, is to wrest away from the city-born the real work of the city. When it is said that 58 per cent. of Berlin's population was born outside of Berlin, one is hardly prepared for the information that about 80 per cent. of its male workers of the age of 30–60 are outsiders. But the following table shows the number of immigrants per 1000 of each age group in Berlin in 1885:[2]

	Male.	Female.
0–15	166	163
Over 15–20	495	512
" 20–25	765	697
" 25–30	771	763
" 30–35	791	779
" 35–40	816	789
" 40–45	811	785
" 45–60	794	764
" 60	767	764
All ages	580	573

Of children under 15, the immigrants contribute only 17

[1] The foregoing statistics do not give the age at *the time of migration.* Such statistics would show that at least four-fifths of the migrants are young men and women. For example, of 295 migrants from English villages to London and other cities, 16 were under the age of 15; 235 (80 per cent.) were between 15 and 25, 27 were between 25 and 30, and only 17 were over 30. (Booth, *Life and Labor of the People*, iii, 139.)

Brückner, in his careful study of the German cities (*Allg. Stat. Ar.*, i, 650), has shown that the age-grouping depends chiefly upon the volume of immigration, and its duration. The greater the immigration, the larger the percentage of the higher age classes, and the smaller the percentage of children. The only exception occurs in the case of cities that have a strong current of emigration to the suburban districts, which embraces the young married people, and thus reduces the percentage in the higher age groups. Leipzig was, until the incorporation of the suburbs, a typical city of this kind.

[2] *Allg. Stat. Archiv*, i, 634.

per cent. in Berlin, but of adults at the age of 30-60, the immigrants from about 80 per cent. of the entire population at those ages. Such a vast number of outsiders in the important ages of life must necessarily have a deep influence on city life.[1]

The length of the residence of immigrants to the city is also of interest. The Berlin statistics may be considered fairly typical, although there is always variation between different times and places:[2]

	Male.	1885. Female.	Total.
Berlin born	420	427	424
Residence 0–1 year	94	67	80
" over 1–2 years	49	39	44
" " 2–5 "	94	92	93
" " 5–10 "	88	104	96
" " 10–15 "	96	100	99
" " 15 "	159	170	165
	1000	1000	1000

The immigrants who had been in Berlin less than 5 years in 1885 constituted one-fifth of the entire population, overbalancing those who had resided in the city more than 15 years. The proportion that had lived in the city over 5 years and less than 16 was also about one-fifth.

In these data, the age of persons has not been considered; but it has an important influence. Thus, most of the children are to be found in the class of Berlin-born, the recent emigrants are mainly young adults, and the immigrants of 10

---

[1] In this respect Berlin is not an exceptional city. In the same year (1885) the percentage of immigrants in the adult population (20 years+) was as follows:

	Male.	Female.
1. Hamburg	68.3	61.2
2. Berlin	78.7	76.0
3. Frankfort	79.4	76.6
4. Breslau	80.1	76.0
5. Leipzig	84.6	78.4

[2] Brückner, *ibid.,* i, 632.

years' residence, middle-aged and elderly people. But the following table shows the

LENGTH OF RESIDENCE IN BERLIN OF 1,000 ADULT IMMIGRANTS (OVER 25 YEARS) IN 1885:[1]

	Male.	Female.
0–1 year	71	51
Over 1–5 years	130	116
" 5–10 "	123	135
" 10–15 "	164	163
" 15 "	302	308
Berlin-born	208	227
	998	1000

It is somewhat reassuring to find that fifty per cent. of the city's adult population consists of native Berliners at least 25 years old and immigrants who have resided in the city at least fifteen years. But the other half of the adult population are such comparative strangers, that one can understand why municipal government resting upon manhood suffrage presents so many difficulties in these latter days.

To recapitulate: the *manner* in which the modern growth of cities has taken place is rather a larger natural increase in the city populations themselves (lower death rate!) than an increase in immigration from the rural districts; the current of migration cityward has been observed for several centuries, but it is only in the nineteenth century that any considerable number of cities have had a regular surplus of births over deaths.

Migration is predominantly a short-distance movement, but the centers of attraction are the great cities, toward which currents of migration set in from the remotest counties. The larger the city, the greater its power of attraction (*i. e.*, the larger its proportion of outsiders, and the more distant the counties or districts which contribute to it).

The mobility of great-city populations is below the average mobility.

[1] Brückner, *ibid.*, i, 639.

Women are greater migrants than men, but move only short distances; marriage and domestic service being the levers of their action.

Most migrants are young people, so that about 80 per cent. of the adult population of great cities is of outside birth.

Two-thirds of the immigrants have lived in the great city less than 15 years.

CHAPTER V.

THE STRUCTURE OF CITY POPULATIONS.

BEFORE any estimate can be made of the influence which the process of concentration of population exerts upon the industrial and social life of the nation, it will be necessary to study closely the structure and composition of the city populations themselves, and note the characteristic traits which distinguish them from the rest of the people. For after all that is said in derogation of the effects of mere association upon people's lives, it remains true that differences in the physical composition of any population do really explain many of its peculiarities. For the purpose of this analysis it will be best to study a few great cities, for they are the type of urban population that all masses of people dwelling in compact centers will tend to resemble as they approximate the great cities in populousness.

I. SEX.

The simplest distinction made between individuals is that of sex; it is important, because all social life is affected by the proportions of the sexes. Wherever there exists a considerable predominance of one sex over the other, in point of numbers, there is less prospect of a well-ordered social life. The determination of the numbers of the sexes is therefore preliminary to discussions of marriage ties and home life under the influence of agglomerated populations.

The important fact here to be recorded is that the cities contain a larger proportion of women than does the rest of the country; and as women outnumber the men throughout Europe and Eastern States of America, it follows that the preponderance of women is accentuated in the cities. As examples will serve the following statistics indicating the percentage of women in representative American cities and the commonwealths to which they belong:

New York City	50.66	State	50.37
Brooklyn	51.12	"	50.37
Philadelphia	51.18	"	49.29
St. Louis	49.51	"	48.30
Boston	51.44	"	51.42

Indeed, of the fifteen leading cities of the United States, all but three, (Chicago, Buffalo and Pittsburg), contained a larger proportion of women in 1890 than did the States in which they are situated.

In European countries, where the population is usually more homogeneous than it is in the United States, with its industrial East and its newly-settled, masculine West, the tendency of cities to produce a surplus of women is more conspicuous. The German figures, for instance, show that to every 1,000 males, there are the following numbers of females:

Germany (1890)	1,040
Small cities (5,000–20,000)	994
Middle-sized cities (20,000–100,000)	1,004
Great cities (100,000+)	1,057

Here one observes a regular increase in the proportion of women to men, as one ascends from the smaller to the larger cities.[1] Whether the same rule would hold in the case of villages does not appear; the Austrian statistics (Table CXXXI, last column) would indicate the reverse. But it is

[1] The garrisons, it appears, form a larger percentage in the populations of the middle-sized and small cities than in those of the great cities; but the difference is not great.—Kuczynski, 18.

capable of statistical demonstration that in the majority of
the older countries, the cities contain relatively more women
than do the smaller places. The following statistics, drawn
from the most recent censuses available, show that the only
exceptions are Bavaria (due to garrisons in the small towns
—Kuczynski, p. 27), European Russia, Servia and Australia:

	Females to 1,000 males.
England and Wales, 1891	1,064
1. London	1,116
2. Urban sanitary districts	1,090
3. Rural " "	1,010
Scotland (1881)	1,076
1. Rural districts	1,031
2. Villages	1,043
3. Towns	1,102
Sweden (1890)	1,065
1. Stockholm	1,204
2. Urban	1,191
3. Rural	1,038
Denmark (1890)	1,051
1. Copenhagen	1,179
2. Urban	1,133
3. Rural	1,011
Hungary (1890)	1,044
1. Buda-Pest	1,066
2. 27 other cities	1,084
3. Rural remainder	1,027
Netherlands (1889)	1,024
Urban (cities of 20,000+)	1,123
Rural	982
Spain (1887)	1,039
Urban (*capitales* and communes of 20,000+)	1,082
Rural remainder	1,029
Belgium (1890)	1,005
Urban	1,049
Rural	966
Servia (1890)	948
Urban	777
Rural	977
France (1891)	1,014
Paris (1886)	1,045

Females to 1,000 males.

Russia (1897) 999.7
   European Russia 1,028
     St. Petersburg........ 826
     Moscow 763
   Poland 986
     Warsaw 1,064

Percentage of males.

New South Wales (1891)...... .... 53.89
   Rural.. 58.07
   Urban 51.67
     Country towns 52.91
     Metropolis... 50.55

Professor Willcox was the first to give the data for the United States: [1]

	Males.	Females.	Per cent. of females.
Towns (2,500+ inhabitants).....	11,358,986	11,373,439	50.03 = 1001
Rural districts..................	20,708,894	19,180,931	48.08 = 926
	32,067,880	30,554,370	48.79 = 953

The causes of the peculiar distribution of the sexes are imperfectly understood. It is not an entirely new phenomenon, for many cities have long contained more women than men among their inhabitants. It existed in some German cities as far back as the fourteenth century.[2] In the Netherlands there was a large surplus of women in the cities sixty

---

[1] The difference is more marked if we exclude from the urban population the smaller towns. Thus, in New York State all but three of the cities of 25,000 and upwards have a preponderance of women, the average for this whole class of cities being 50.88 per cent., and only 49.80 for the remainder of the commonwealth. In Massachusetts the percentage of women in towns of 25,000+ is 52.70, in towns of less than 1,000 population, 49.63. Finally, in the aggregate population of the 28 American cities of 100,000+ the ratio is 999 as against 953 in the total population.—Cf. " Distribution of the Sexes in the United States," *Amer-Jour. oj Sociology* (May, 1896), i, 732.

[2] Bücher, *Die Bevölkerung von Frankfort am Main in XIV and XV Jahrhunderten,* i, 41 f.

years ago;[1] and the same held true in the northern countries generally.

In Paris the relative number of women has actually decreased, although it still exceeds that of the men, the percentage of women being in 1817, 53.4; in 1876, 52.6; in 1886, 51.1.[2] In Germany, on the other hand, the superiority of women in the cities is rather recent. Twenty-five years ago only a few of the great cities contained more women than men, but in 1890 there were only two of the great cities that had a surplus of men, Strassburg and Magdeburg, both being cities with large garrisons.

The question now is, where does this excess of females in the cities come from ? It has usually been held heretofore that it is due to the large number of domestic servants, who enter the cities from abroad or from the surrounding farms and villages. Thus in Boston in 1885 there was an excess of women of about 18,000, of whom 14,000 were born in foreign countries, Ireland alone contributing 10,000. The number of women to 1000 men in Boston was 1,024 among the native Bostonians, 1,025 among the natives of Massachusetts, 1,032 among the natives of the United States, 1,229 among the foreign-born, and 1,097 in the total population of Boston.[3] In this case the excess of women must be attributed mainly to immigration.

But it has been discovered that in many European and American cities, the excess of women is really among the

---

[1] The Dutch statistics show that to each 1,000 males there were the following numbers of females:

	1829.	1849.	1869.
Netherlands	1,045	1,040	1,029
Cities 20,000+	1,142	1,159	1,148
Rural districts.....................	1,005	1,002	990

[2] Levasseur, ii, 392.

[3] Cf. *Mass. Census of 1885*, vol. i, pt. i, p. 550.

city-born rather than the newcomers. This is notably true of the great German cities, as the following figures for 1890 demonstrate: [1]

	Native city element.	Immigrants.	Total pop.
Females	1,457,433	1,785,906	3,243,339
Males	1,303,927	1,756,175	3,060,102
Excess of females	153,506	29,731	183,327
Ratio, females to males....	1,118	1,017	1,060

Professor Karl Bücher, thus observing that the *Frauenüberschuss* of the cities was not the result of an immigration of females in excess of males, advanced a biological theory in explanation, saying that city population has of itself a tendency to produce an excess of women above the general average.[2] But he apparently overlooked the influence of emigration from the cities themselves. Unfortunately, no data are at hand for the ascertainment of the relative numbers of men and women born in the great cities of Germany who are no longer resident in the city of birth. But it is possible to compare the cities which are subject to the greatest amount of emigration with those subject to the smallest emigration and see what effect, if any, is exerted upon the proportion of women in the native population still remaining in the cities. The cities in which the percentage of those born in the specified city but now resident elsewhere in Germany was highest and lowest respectively, at the census of 1890, are given below, the second column denoting the number of females to 1,000 males in the native element remaining in the city: [3]

---

[1] Bleicher, p. 12.

[2] Cf. *Die Bevölkerung des Kantons Basel-Stadt am 1 Dez. 1888*, p. 19, and "Die Vertheilung der beiden Geschlechter auf der Erde," in *Allg. Stat. Archiv*, ii, 390.

[3] *Statistik des Deutschen Reiches*, N. F., vol. 68, p. 71*, and Bleicher, i, pt. 2, p. 12.

Stettin	38.78	1,182+
Königsberg	32.77	1,238+
Hanover	32.72	1,095—
Dresden	32.55	1,144+
Danzig	31.97	1,262+
Halle	31.55	1,118
Hamburg	13.92	1,130+
Cologne	17.90	1,093—
Crefeld	18.23	1,075—
Frankfort	18.47	1,109—
Berlin	18.70	1,098—
Aachen	18.83	1,076—
Average of the 26 cities	22.31	1,118

Now it appears that in the six cities having the largest emigration (within Germany) the excess of females is usually above the average (as denoted by the + sign), while in all but one of the six cities with the least emigration, the excess of females is below the average. This indicates that more males than females emigrate from the cities, producing a surplus of females which roughly corresponds to the amount of emigration.

More decisive are the statistics of Austrian cities. Taking all the people born in Vienna and enumerated within the Austrian empire in 1890, there were 1,082 women to 1,000 men; but in that portion of the native Viennese still resident in Vienna, the proportion of women was larger, namely 1,095,—thus showing that more men than women had migrated. And this leaves out of account the emigration to foreign countries [1] which drafted even more males from Vienna than did the local, or internal, migration, by virtue of the law that men are the long-distance migrants.[2]

[1] Sixty per cent of the emigrants to the United States are males.

[2] Cf. the following figures regarding the native Viennese:

Resident in Vienna	1,095	women to 1,000 men.			
" " neighboring districts	1,057	"	"	"	"
" " other districts of the same province	1,050	"	"	"	"
Resident in another province	972	"	"	"	"

—Rauchberg, *Stat. Mon.*, 19: 153.

But it remains true that taking in the city population as a whole and including that portion which had emigrated as well as the portion which was at home, the proportion of females is above the average. Thus, the number of women to 1,000 men was found to be as follows in the latest census of Austria:[1]

Austria, average	1,044
Towns of 500-2,000 (the maximum outside of the great cities)	1,049
All citizens of Austria born in Graz	1,066
" " " " " " Triest	1,040
" " " " " " Prague	1,130
" " " " " " Brünn	1,135
" " " " " " Lemberg	1,095
" " " " " " Cracow	1,190

Now unless it can be shown that the small towns lose fewer males by international emigration than the large cities do, it may be regarded as an established fact that the cities produce of themselves a larger preponderance of women than do the rural districts. This seems the more probable when it is considered that already among young children, among whom migration would affect both sexes alike, the ratio of females is higher in the city than in the country. In the entire United States[2] there are 960 girls to 1000 boys under the age of one year; in the 28 great cities there are 976. Again there are, in the United States, 965 girls to 1000 boys under the age of five years; in the great cities 982. In Maryland, the commonwealth surrounding Washington on three sides, there are only 981 girls to 1000 boys under the age of 15, and in the United States there are only 970; but in Washington there are 1,015, an excess which can scarcely be explained by the phenomenon of migration. The difference is even

---

[1] Rauchberg, *Stat. Mon.*, 19: 153.

[2] Cf. *11th Census, Vital Statistics of Cities*, p. 13, and *Report on Pop.*

more marked in the case of the colored children, for while
Maryland has 994 girls to 1000 boys, Washington has 1,061.

In Germany, too, the cities have relatively more girls than
boys as compared with the country at large. In 1890 the
number of females under the age of 15, to 1000 males of the
same age was 936 in cities having 5,000–20,000 inhabitants,
989 in cities of 20,000–100,000 population and 1,005 in cities
of 100,000 or over. As a further piece of evidence it is to
be noted that the immigrants to the cities form a larger percentage of the males than of the females under the age of 15;
thus, in 1885 the immigrants constituted the following percentages:[1]

	Boys.	Girls.
Breslau	19.1	18.0
Leipzig	25.9	25.1
Berlin	16.6	16.3
Frankfort	19.3	19.2
Hamburg	13.9	14.2

In Hamburg alone do the immigrants add a larger percentage of girls than of boys to the population under 15
years.[2]

These facts would indicate that some other force than
migration has been at work to cause the large excess of
women in cities. But how do cities of themselves produce
the *Frauenüberschuss?*

In the first place, it is to be noted that the proportion of

[1] Brückner, *Allg. Stat. Archiv*, i, 634.

[2] In Frankfort it is only in the age period of 16–20 that the females begin to
predominate among the immigrants; in 1890 the number of females to 1,000
males in each age-group was:

	City-born.	Immigrants.	Total.
0–5	997	918	988
6–10	993	976	990
11–15	1,004	955	994
16–20	1,122	1,178	1,157

—(Bleicher, pp. 5, 6.)

female births is larger in the city than in the country. This fact has long ago received statistical proof.[1] A good illustration is to be found in France. According to Levasseur,[2] the average number of male births to 100 female births during the period 1801–65 was 103 in the department of the Seine (which is nearly coincident with the city of Paris), 104.3 in the remainder of the urban population and 105.3 in the rural population. The difference is not due to the influence of illegitimate births, in which there are fewer boys than girls and which are especially prevalent in the cities; for, restricting ourselves entirely to the legitimate births the figures would be 103.6, 104.6, 105.7 in the order given above. In the city of Frankfort in Prussia the ratio has been remarkably steady for nearly two centuries, having been in the period 1701–50, 103.3; in 1751–1800, 103.4; in 1801–50, 103.3; in 1851–90, 103.7; the average in 1635–1890 being 103.8.[3] In Prussia itself the ratio has been higher, having fluctuated between 105 and 106 in 1874–91.[4] The causes of sex are still too imperfectly understood to permit an assignment of reasons for the great excess of male births in the country, but the most likely reason seems to be the inbreeding of a few family stocks, while in the city there is vastly more crossing. The fact

---

[1] The ratios for the middle of the century are given by Wappaeus and Legoyt, the latter's being as follows (p. 69):

	BIRTHS Boys to 100 girls.	
	City.	Country.
France	105.06	106.75
Prussia	105.31	105.95
Belgium	104.51	105.57
Holland	107.73	106.72
Denmark	105.73	106.19
Sweden	104.62	105.06

[2] *La Population Française*, ii, 20.

[3] Bleicher, p. 343.

[4] Conrad's *Hdwbh.*, Sup. i., 215.

that Jewish families have a notably large excess of boy births argues in favor of this hypothesis.[1]

Not only are relatively fewer boys than girls born in the city, as compared with the country, but more male children die in the earlier months of life. The science of demography recognizes the fact that infant mortality bears with more severity on boys than on girls, and as infant mortality is in most countries higher in the city than in the country,[2] it fol-

[1] Mayr, *Bevölkerungsstatistik*, 188, where a bibliography of the subject of sex at birth will be found; to it should be added the *Theory of Sex Development*, by Dr. Leopold Schenk, as well as the *Evolution of Sex*, by Geddes and Thompson (in Contemporary Science series), and Bertillon's monographs on *Natalité*. On the statistics, see especially Boeckh, in *Bulletin of the Intern. Institute of Statistics*, vol. v.

[2] In the urban population of Massachusetts, 1881–90, the infant mortality was 175, in the rural population, 129.5. (*Rep. of State Board of Health for 1896*, p. 753.) Some recent Prussian statistics may be cited in illustration of both the propositions in the text (Bleicher, p. 268):

TABLE CXXXIII.

NUMBER OF DEATHS OF CHILDREN UNDER ONE YEAR TO EACH 1,000 LIVING BIRTHS (1890–1) IN EACH CATEGORY.

	Male.	Female.	Total.	Legitimate.	Illegitimate.	Difference
	a.	b.	c.	d.	e.	a-b.
Prussia	220.9	188.7	205.2	192.7	357.3	32.2
Rural communes	210.8	180.1	195.8	185.7	333.1	30.8
Urban "	238.0	203.4	221.1	204.8	389.0	34.6
Cities under 20,000	225.3	190.7	208.5	194.4	378.3	34.6
Cities 20–100,000	230.5	197.8	214.5	199.8	389.9	32.7
" 100,000+	259.3	223.2	241.7	221.9	397.4	36.1
Berlin	269.2	230.8	250.5	227.6	412.7	38.4

Dr. F. S. Crum has recently shown (*Quarterly Journal of Economics*, 1897, xi, 259) that in Massachusetts infant mortality increases in direct ratio with density of population, or, in other words, with the numerical size of cities.

The subject of infant mortality is discussed in all hand-books of vital statistics or demography.— Newsholme, Farr, Bertillon, etc. The leading American authority is Dr. John S. Billings (*10th Census, vol. xi*, " Relation of Age to Deaths "). An excellent article on infant mortality is contributed by Dr. T. B. Curtis to *Buck's Hygiene and Public Health*, vol. ii, pp. 269-301. A comprehensive sociological study has been made by Seutemann, *Kindersterblichkeit sozialer Bevölkerungsgruppen*, which appears as vol. v of F. J. Neumann's *Beiträge zur Geschichte der Bevölkerung in Deutschland*. Cf. also Silbergleit, " Ueber den gegenwärtigen Stand der Kindersterblichkeit, ihre Erscheinungen und ihre Entwicklung in Europäischen Grossstädten," *Hygienische Rundschau*, 1895.

lows that the ranks of the males in the city are depleted by this natural cause.

The effect of infant mortality upon the numerical relation of the sexes is conspicuous in the case of the negro race. In New York city, for example, the number of deaths of children under the age of five years to 1000 living of the same age was 231.09 for the colored and 115.65 for the whites;[1] in the same city the ratio of females in the colored population was 1,029 as compared with 1,011 in the native population of native parentage.

Professor Willcox has observed that the six commonwealths in which the cities (towns of 2,500+ inhabitants) have a percentage of females above 52 are States with a large negro element (Mississippi, South Carolina, Louisiana, Georgia, District of Columbia, Maryland, North Carolina).[2] In the cities of these States the whites do not have a very large excess of females; it is rather among the negroes, thus:

PERCENTAGE OF FEMALES IN TOTAL POPULATION OF THE CITIES:

	Whites.	Colored.
Mississippi	50.55	56.00
North Carolina	51.12	53.33
District of Columbia	51.05	55.34
Georgia	50.33	54.84.

But it is not alone the high rate of infant mortality which depletes the ranks of males in the city; there are other dangers to the health of males which show their effects oftener in the city than in the country, and thus tend to accentuate the urban excess of females. City occupations are oftener subject to fatal accidents; and, in fact, violent deaths

[1] *11th Cen., Vital Statistics of Cities*, p. 44.

[2] *American Journal of Sociology*, vol. i.

of all kinds are more frequent in cities, as is expressed in the following Scotch statistics : [1]

	Proportion to entire pop., 1871.	Proportion of violent deaths, 1878.
Principal cities (25,000+ pop.)	31.80	39.98
Cities of 10,000–25,000	9.95	28.15
Towns of 2,000–10,000	23.10	11.83
Rural pop. (mainland)	31.22	11.94
" " (islands)	3.93	8.10
	100.	100.

Violent deaths, of course, affect principally men rather that women. On this point the statistics of the little duchy of Oldenburg once more afford invaluable evidence. On the average population of 1871–85, for each 10,000 living persons, there were the following number of deaths : [2]

TABLE CXXXIV.

Age-groups.	Urban (towns of 2,000+).			Rural.		
	Male.	Female.	Difference.	Male.	Female.	Difference.
0–5	654	573	81	534	471	63
5–10	97	87	10	87	86	1
10–15	51	62	—11	50	56	—6
15–20	77	73	4	65	58	7
20–30	125	96	29	95	84	11
30–40	158	138	20	103	126	—23
40–50	230	156	74	156	139	17
50–60	323	232	91	243	215	28
60–70	567	453	114	479	490	—11
70+	1,213	1,166	47	1,253	1,252	1
All ages	244	222	22	225	209	16

In the entire town population there is thus found a death rate of 24.4 for males and 22.2 for females, and in the country the difference is somewhat less, the rates being 22.5 and 20.9 respectively. In only two periods does the city,

[1] Walford, "On the Number of Deaths from Accident, Negligence, Violence and Misadventure," *J. of St. Soc.*, Sept., 1881, p. 28.

[2] *Statistische Nachrichten über das Grossherzogthum Oldenburg*, Heft xxii, p. 114.

as compared with the country, show more favor to man than
to woman; during the ages of 10–15 and 15–20, city females
die more rapidly than the men, as compared with the rural
rates.   In the ages 5–10 and 20–30, there is also little difference between city and country, as regards the comparative
death rates of males and females.   But that infant mortality
is higher in the city than in the country and is more severe
on boys than on girls, appears once more in the figures for
the age-period 0–5.   It is after the age of 30, however, that
city life appears to cause the greatest mortality of men as
compared with women.   In the years 60–70, the rural
death-rate is higher for women than for men, while the city
death-rate for men is far above that for women.

Why do so many more men, relatively, die in the city
than in the country?   All things considered, it must be explained on the ground that city occupations are more
dangerous to the health of males than are country occupations, while to females over the age of 5 years there is not a
great difference between city and country.   In other words,
it is not the city air and conditions of life, so much as the
peculiarity of city occupations, that cause higher mortality
in the city than outside.   The number of deaths among
adult males has apparently been increasing in the city faster
than in the other classes of population.   Thus in Frankfort
during four decades the number of female deaths to 100
males dying was as follows: [1]

	Total.	Married women.	Widows.	Girls.
1811–20	373	51	46	276
1821–30	326	47	47	232
1831–40	231	37	36	158
1841–50	189	33	32	124

[1] Bleicher, 244.   Cf. with the foregoing conclusions, the conclusions reached by
Dr. Kuczynski (p. 231) after a comprehensive statistical investigation: " While
it is true that on the whole the mortality of the male population in the great
cities of Prussia is somewhat more unfavorable than in the other parts of the
Prussian monarchy, the same cannot be affirmed of the female population."

Since, then, the cities have a high mortality among males, both infant and adult, and a relatively low percentage of male births, it follows that the cities would have an excess of females, even though they were entirely isolated and cut off from immigration or emigration. In the face of these facts, advanced students have abandoned the old belief that nature tended to equalize the number of the two sexes and that inequalities must be explained by migration, war, pestilence, etc.,[1] and Prof. Bücher has laid down the rule that the relative numbers of the two sexes are determined by the relation between the rates of natural increase of the two sexes and cannot stand permanently above or below this ratio, provided there be no migration. There will be an equilibrium, of course, when females become so numerous that even with a lower death-rate, the number of deaths among them would exceed the number of births.

To summarize: The excess of females in any population is usually ascribed, first, to the heavier mortality of male than of female infants, which within the first year usually effaces the superiority of male births. Then comes the great mortality of adult males due to the dangers of their occupations, as well as to vice, crime and excesses of various kinds which shorten life.[2] Now all these forces are accentuated in the cities, producing a greater excess of females there than elsewhere, even without the influence of emigration, which increases the surplus of women in cities. In the cities also, the

[1] Hence it was easy to explain the preponderance of females in Europe and of males in America as being the result of international migration. This is indeed the theory of the 11th Census (*vide Rep. on Pop.*, vol. i, p. lxxi). Unfortunately for the theory, however, there are some European countries, notably Italy, that are subject to heavy emigration, and yet have an excess of males, while in the United States the "native whites of native parents," a class obviously not affected by migration, also have a large excess of males (966 females to 1,000 males) instead of an equal number or slight excess of females, as the theory demands.

[2] Mayo-Smith, *Statistics and Sociology*, 41.

superiority of male births over female births is smaller than in the country.

II. AGE.

The age classification of any population is a record of biological facts second only to the distinction of sex. Not to mention the economic significance of the predominance of the productive classes, or of children and aged persons, one must recognize the influence of the age-distribution upon percentages that have wide-reaching social significance, such as the birth-rate or death-rate. As the standard text-books have pointed out, the curve of ages approximates to the form of a pyramid, the newly-born forming the base and the very aged the apex. The more rapid the increase, the broader the base. With a stationary population, on the other hand, the base narrows and the upper part of the curve, representing the middle and advanced ages, bulges out, so that the age curve becomes bell-shaped. Finally, when the normal age-classification is disturbed by migration, there result two typical forms of the curve: (a) in the case of immigration, the curve may be likened to a top, on account of the expansion of the middle age-periods; (b) in the case of emigration, the curve sinks in the middle and the figure becomes spindle-shaped. All but one of the forms are found in the United States, that of the stationary population, which France tends to approach.[1]

Now the age-curve of city populations inclines to the top-shape, apparently as a result of immigration. Compare, for example, the distribution by age-periods of the population of

---

[1] Levasseur (vol. ii, ch. 15) has a model chapter on age-groups, copiously illustrated with diagrams. Compare the summary in v. Mayr, *Bevölkerungsstatistik*, § 30; Mayo-Smith, *Statistics and Sociology*, ch. iv; and diagrams in *Statistical Atlas of the United States*.

the United States and that of its 28 great cities (those of 100,000+ inhabitants) : [1]

	U. S.	Cities.
Under 15	355.3	299.46
15–65	603.5	668.17
65+	38.6	29.43
Unknown	2.6	2.94
	1,000.	1,000.

Here, then, is a noticeable difference in age-grouping; the city population is markedly strong in people of the middle, active, productive ages, and has relatively few children and aged people. Similar contrasts are found in European countries. The Hungarian census for 1890 (p. 143*), for instance, compares the total population in the three classes, taking one class as a standard at 100:

Ages.	Budapest.	27 free cities.	Remaining population.
0–15	70	88	100
15–40	137	110	100
40–60	95	100	100
60+	78	111	100

The German statistics too, are, very informing:

TABLE CXXXV.

AGE DISTRIBUTION IN CITIES OF

	100,000 +.	20,000–100,000.	5,000–20,000.	Germany.
Under 15	292	321	345	351
15–40	474	450	417	387
40–60	177	169	170	182
60+	57	60	68	80
	1,000	1,000	1,000	1,000

FEMALES TO 1,000 MALES :

Under 15	1,005	989	986	995
15–40	1,010	916	909	1,027
40–60	1,136	1,142	1,109	1,094
60+	1,616	1,518	1,364	1,196
All ages	1,057	1,004	994	1,040

[1] Calculated from the *11th Census Reports on Pop.* and *Vital Statistics of Cities*, p. 16.

Starting with the percentages for all Germany, there is a steady decrease in the proportion of children and aged people, as one progresses through the small cities to the great cities, and on the other hand a steady increase in the number of persons at the active age of 15–40, while the proportion at the age 40–60 remains nearly constant.[1] The cause, as stated above in Chapter IV (p. 280) is in the main the migratory movement. The percentages there given to show the age-grouping among the native Frankforters and the newcomers would be more fully realized in a diagram,[2] wherein the curves should show the ages of native residents of Frankfort, and of immigrants. The former is bell-shaped, the latter top-shaped, as is the curve for the entire population, which is typical of all city populations. (Cf. the diagram representing the ages of men and women in *Stadt und Land* in Switzerland in the Census of 1888, *Schweizerische Statistik.*, Bd. 88.)

This difference of city and country as regards age grouping was remarked as early as 1872 by Georg von Mayr in taking the Bavarian census. And recent investigations show

[1] The Austrian statistics, even minuter, confirm the foregoing figures and deductions :

TABLE CXXXVI.

CLASSES OF TOWNS :

	Under 500.	500-2,000.	2,000-5,000.	5,000-10,000.	10,000-20,000.	20,000+.	Austria.
10 years and under.	268	278	269	243	226	193	260
11–20	194	195	197	199	202	193	195
21–30	144	150	159	183	201	214	160
31–40	124	125	130	132	134	151	129
41–50	107	106	104	103	100	113	107
51–60	84	79	76	73	72	73	79
61–70	54	47	45	45	44	44	48
70+	25	20	20	22	21	19	22

—Rauchberg, *Stat. Monats.*, xix, 133. For the elaborate statistics of France, see *Résultats statistiques du dénombrement de 1891*, p. 222.

[2] The usual form of diagram consists of two curves, one for each sex, thus making the figures already discussed.

that a difference has existed throughout the century in Germany. As preceding tables have indicated, the difference at present is about five per cent. in favor of the cities for the middle ages and of the county for childhood. In Prussia the same differences existed in 1816 and 1858:[1]

		MALES.			
		0–14.	14–60.	60+.	Total.
1816.	Urban	32.10	61.09	6.81	100.
	Rural	37.70	55.57	6.73	100.
1858.	Urban	31.92	63.03	5.03	99.98
	Rural	36.36	57.93	5.68	99.97

In Leipzig, the age-grouping in 1792–94 was about the same as it is now, and Dr. Kuczynski, to whose labors these results are due, concludes that at least in Berlin, Leipzig and Frankfort, the strong representation of the middle age classes and the small percentage of children are not phenomena of the most recent times, and that in fact the differentiation is not even a product of the present century.[2] Hence the conclusion that migration cityward began earlier than 1800.

Table CXXXV also illustrates the fact mentioned in the preceding section, that the preponderance of women in the great cities begins at an age when only biological forces could be at work, although its rapid increase in the later years shows that the high death-rate of males in middle life, and their emigration from the city, are also to be reckoned with. The preponderance of aged persons in the village and country districts, as contrasted with the city, is not to be explained by the existence of a " return current." In that case the excess of aged women would be greater in the country than in the city.[3]

As the result of the presence of a relatively large number

---

[1] Kuczynski, 262.   [2] *Ibid.*, 270.

[3] See further on the subject of a "return current of migration," Ogle, "Alleged Depopulation," etc., in *J. of St. Soc.*, 1889, 216.

of persons in the active period of life in urban populations, one would expect city life to be easier and more animated, the productive classes being large and having a smaller burden to bear in the support of the unproductive class. One would also expect to find more energy and enterprise in cities, more radicalism, less conservatism, more vice, crime and impulsiveness generally. Birth-rates should be high in cities and death-rates low, on account of age grouping.

III. RACE AND NATIONALITY.

A third natural difference among men is that of race, which may or may not be accompanied with a difference of nationality. The Italian and the German are racially differentiated, but men of both races are citizens of the Swiss republic. It will therefore be convenient to consider race and nationality together, although nationality is a political rather than a natural distinction.

In the chapter on migration it was shown that foreigners are found in largest numbers in cities. Table CXXV, indeed, shows that the larger the city, the greater the percentage of foreigners in its population. But while the foreign element is strong in European capitals compared with provincial cities, its numerical strength there is nothing compared with its position in American cities. The difference was brought out in Table CXXVII. The composition of the city populations of the United States is therefore of especial interest on account of their large contingent of European-born. Taking the 28 cities of 100,000 population and upwards in 1890, we find the following elements of population:

Born in		
State where resident	5,082,637	52 4
Some other American State	1,530,675	15.8
Foreign countries	3,084,648	31.8
	9,697,960	100.00

Somewhat over one-half the population of our cities was born either in the city itself or in the commonwealth to which it belongs, while a little less than one-third was born in foreign countries. In the entire country only 14.77 per cent. of the population is foreign-born. The cities therefore contain more than their due proportion of foreigners. Expressed in another form, the 28 great cities, while constituting in 1890 15.5 per cent. of the entire population of the United States, contained 12.4 per cent. of all the American-born, and 33.4 per cent of the foreign-born in the United States. There is therefore a decided tendency on the part of the foreigners to settle in our largest cities. The question is, Is this tendency recent and increasing, or is it a natural and permanent incident of the process of distributing the newcomers?

As to the process of distribution, it may be remarked at the outset that it is not entirely the task of the seaports; Chicago has had at nearly every census a larger percentage of foreigners than New York or San Francisco.

Table CXXXVII shows the proportion of the foreign-born in the population of the ten leading cities since 1860, compared with the proportion of the foreigners in the population of the commonwealths and the entire country. From this table may be deduced the rule that in the United States and in most of the commonwealths, the percentage of foreigners has uniformly and almost steadily increased since 1850, while on the other hand, it *has decreased in the cities.* The conclusion is the opposite of a very general belief,[1] which is probably founded on a comparison of the census figures of 1890 and 1880. The percentage of foreign-born in 1880 was almost

---

[1] "The tendency is to increased concentration of the foreign-born in large cities owing to the increased immigration of Latins and Slavs." Mayo-Smith, *op. cit*, p. 302. Cf. the arguments advanced in behalf of the Lodge bill restricting immigration.

uniformly lower, both in the city and in country, than at the preceding censuses. This was a result of the relatively small immigration in 1870–80 (2,800,000 as against 2,300,000 and

TABLE CXXXVII.

PERCENTAGE OF FOREIGN-BORN IN THE TOTAL POPULATION OF STATES AND CITIES NAMED:

	1850.	1860.	1870.	1880.	1890.
United States.............	9.68	13.16	14.44	13.32	14.77+
North Atlantic States (9)..	15.37	19.10	20.49	19.40	22.34+
Massachusetts..........	16.49	21.13	24.24	26.78	30.77+
1. Boston	...	35.87+	31.53	31.64	35.27
New York.............	21.18	25.80	25.97	23.83	26.19+
2. New York city	....	47.16+	44.49	39.68	42.23+
3. Brooklyn	....	....	36.54+	31.36	32.46
Pennsylvania	13.12	14.81	15.48	13.73	16.08+
4. Philadelphia	....	29.96+	27.24	24.12	25.74
South Atlantic States (9)..	2.24	3.03+	2.85	2.29	2.35
Maryland	8.78	11.28+	10.68	8.86	9.05
5. Baltimore	....	24.71+	21.09	16.89	15.88
District of Columbia	9.51	16.63+	12.34	9.64	8.15
North Central States (12) .	12.04	16.97	17.97	16.80	18.16+
Ohio	11.02	14.03+	13.98	12.35	12.51
6. Cincinnati	....	45.09+	36.81	28.09	24.05
Illinois................	13.14	18.96	20.28	18.96	22.01+
7. Chicago	....	49.99+	45.01	40.71	40.98
Missouri	11.23	13.58+	12.91	9.76	8.77
8. St. Louis	....	50.53+	36.11	29.96	25.43
South Central States (8) ..	3.18	3.99+	3.62	3.08	2.93
Louisiana	13.18+	11.44	8.51	5.76	4.45
9. New Orleans	....	38.31+	25.32	19.05	14.20
Western States and Territories (11)...........	15.11	28.92	31.64+	28.29	25.46
California	23.55	38.56+	37.95	33.87	30.32
10. San Francisco	....	....	49.32+	44.56	42.11

The sign (+) designates maxima. In most of the cities, the maximum occurs in 1860, while in the United States (and in many of the commonwealths, including most of the Northern States) the maximum was at the latest census, 1890. In connection with this table, the author desires to acknowledge his indebtedness to Dr. Delos S. Wilcox.

2,600,000 in the decades 1860–70, 1850–60). Unless the immigration constantly increases, the percentage of foreigners in the total population will diminish, as the children of the immigrants go to swell the number of natives. With the exception of 1880, therefore, the percentage of foreigners has constantly increased in the general population and as constantly decreased in the largest cities, signifying a slow but certain process of equalization. The cities, then, act as centers of dispersion for the immigrants, and the fact that in New York and most of the other great cities the percentage of foreigners was smaller in 1890 than in 1870 shows how rapidly dispersion takes place. The number of immigrants in 1880-90 was unprecedentedly large (5,200,000, or double the average of the three preceding decades), and without rapid distribution would have greatly increased the percentage of the foreigners in 1890 as compared with previous census years. Even as compared with 1880, the percentage of foreigners had increased less rapidly in the larger cities than in the rest of the country. Computations by Professor Willcox show that in the fifty most populous cities of the country in 1880, 29.9 per cent. of the population was of foreign birth, while in 1890 the percentage in the same cities had risen only to 30.8. Whereas the percentage of persons of foreign birth in the rest of the country (including substantially all places of less than 56,000 inhabitants in 1890) had increased from 10.0 per cent to 11.3 per cent.[1]

As to the inclination of the various nationalities to dwell in the large cities, the eleventh census gives us the following proportions of their total number who in 1890 were dwelling in the 124 cities of at least 25,000 inhabitants: [2]

---

[1] *The Federal Census*, Publications of the American Economic Association, New Series, No. 2, p. 24.

[2] *Rept. on Pop.*, vol. i, p. cl.

	Total number in United States.	Per cent. thereof in principal cities (25,000 +).
Italians.............................	182,580	58.79
Russians............................	182,644	57.90
Poles...............................	147,440	57.11
Irish	1,871,509	55.97
Austrians	123,271	48.33
Bohemians..........................	118,106	48.32
Germans............................	2,784,894	47.71
French	113,174	45.69
Hungarians	62,435	44.78
Scotch.............................	242,231	41.25
English [1]..........................	909,092	40.70
Chinese	106,688	40.19
Dutch	81,828	33.54
Swedes.............................	478,041	31.81
Canadians [2]	980,938	31.36
Swiss	104,069	31.15
Welsh	100,079	25.80
Danes	132,543	23.24
Norwegians	322,665	20.78
Mexicans	77,853	7.97
Other nationalities	127,467	39.22
Total........................	9,249,547	44.13

From this table it would appear that the least desirable class of immigrants—those from Southern Europe—are most prone to remain in the great cities. The fact is, however, that much, if not most of this immigration is very recent and there has hardly been time for the new arrivals to disperse. Comparing 1860 with 1880 it will be found that the percentage of those remaining in cities declined among the Italians, Poles and Hungarians, while only among the Russians did the increase considerably exceed the increase for the Germans and Irish. For the following data the author is indebted to Professor Willcox of Cornell:

[1] Includes Great Britain not specified.

[2] Includes Newfoundland.

PERCENTAGE IN CITIES [1] OF TOTAL IN U. S.

(Increase or decrease between 1880 and 1890 is denoted by + or —.)

	1880.	1890.
+Russians	24.2	53.8
—Italians	61.3	53.7
—Poles	53.5	51.7
+Bohemians	39.9	44.4
+Austrians	35.0	43.8
—Hungarians	58.6	39.4
+All six	44.0	49.4
—Other foreign-born	34.6	32.9
+Native	12.6	14.5
+Total	15.5	17.9
+Germans	39.4	42.0
+Irish	45.8	48.5
+English	30.7	33.0
+Canadians	21.9	22.4
+Swedes	17.0	25.1

While the immigrants from Southern Europe have been recent arrivals and have not widely dispersed, the Canadians, who have been coming across the boundary line for a long time without having to pass through a great city on their entrance, were widely scattered in 1890 and nearly as much so in 1880. The Mexicans, of all nationalities with a representation of over 50,000 in the United States, are the least concentrated in large cities; a fact which without doubt results from their manner of entrance and the size of the centers of population nearest their own country. With the decline of railway building and the complete occupation of public lands it may be expected that immigrants in the future will disperse less readily than in the past. As they belong almost entirely to the lower ranks of laborers they will be able to find employment only in the cities, whose large public works and manufactures demand muscular, unskilled labor.

[1] The cities referred to are the 50 principal cities of 1880.

It has been noted that while the foreign-born element constitutes 14.77 per cent. of the population of the United States, it forms 31.8 per cent. of the population of the great cities (100,000+ pop.). In the case of the negroes, the percentages are at present reversed, but since their emancipation they have been migrating to the cities to a considerable extent. Hoffman gives the following comparative rates of increase, 1860–90, in the Southern States and their sixteen principal cities (14 in 1860) for the whites and the negroes:[1]

	White.	Colored.
Cities	94.11	242.60
Remainder of population	45.52	41.23

This indicates a movement of the colored people cityward, causing a smaller rate of increase in the rural parts of the country and a much higher rate in the cities than obtained among the whites. The colored constituted the following percentages of the entire population of the

	1860.	1890.
Ten States	36.00	35.96
Cities specified	18.85	29.08

" In 1860, 11.67 per cent. of the white population lived in the large cities, increasing during 30 years to only 14.89 per cent.; in contrast with an increase from 4.82 per cent. of colored urban population in 1860 to 10.93 in 1890." [2] If present tendencies continue, the negroes will be more inclined to city life than the whites of the same State. Hoffman, indeed asserts that " during the last decade this migratory tendency of the colored population has been more pronounced than ever." [3] But a critic in the New York *Even-*

---

[1] *Race Traits and Tendencies of the American Negro* (*Pubs. of Amer. Econ. Assn.*, vol. xi, pp. 9, 10).

[2] *Ibid.,* 11.   [3] *Ibid.,* 12.

ing Post has pointed out that the changes noted by Mr. Hoffman as occurring in the period 1860–90 were for the most part effected in the era of emancipation (1860–70), when the negroes naturally felt themselves under a strong impulse to see something more of the world than could be viewed from the plantation. The percentage of negroes in the entire population of the selected cities increased as follows:

```
1860................................................   ..........  18.85
1870.........................................................  27.74
1880.........................................................  28.85
1890..  ...................................................  29.08
```

Mr. Hoffman also errs in his statistical tables designed to show that the negroes are increasing more rapidly than the whites in the large cities of the country. He includes in one table cities that contained more than 20,000 negroes in 1890, and in a second table those that contained between 10,000 and 20,000 negroes; but the sum total of all the cities in both classes contradicts his inference that the negroes are increasing in these cities more rapidly than the whites : [1]

	White population.			Colored population.		
	1880.	1890.	Increase %.	1880.	1890.	Increase %.
Group I ..	3,117,174	3,965,711	27.22	376,316	498,104	32.36
Group II ..	1,407,834	2,386,493	69.51	74,875	129,849	73.42
Total	4,525,008	6,352,204	40.00	451,191	627,953	39.00

Evidently Mr. Hoffman's methods are not beyond criticism. As a matter of fact, the percentage of negroes increased in very few of the great cities. Taking Mr. Hoffman's figures for a few of our largest cities that contained more than 10,000 persons of African descent in 1890, we find

[1] *Race Traits and Tendencies of the American Negro* (*Pubs. of Amer. Econ. Assn.*, vol. xi, pp. 12, 13.)

that they constituted the following percentages in the population of 1880 and 1890:

	1880.	1890.
New York	1.66	1.60
Chicago	1.30	1.31
Philadelphia	3.9	3.9
Brooklyn	1.45	1.29
St. Louis	6.8	6.3
Baltimore	19.3	18.3
Cincinnati	3.3	4.1
New Orleans	36.4	36.2
Washington	48.5	49.0

While there undoubtedly exists an important movement of the negroes to the north, directed in the main toward the cities,[1] negro mortality is here so high on account of climatic and other conditions, that in most of the great cities it prevents the negro race gaining upon the whites, or even holding its own. But in the smaller cities of the South it is otherwise, and trustworthy statistics clearly show that the movement cityward in the Southern States affects the negro more than it does the white population. Thus of the total white and negro populations in the States specified, the following percentages dwelt in towns of 4,000 and upwards in 1880 and 1890:[2]

TABLE CXXXVIII.

	Whites.			Negroes.		
	1880.	1890.	Difference.	1880.	1890.	Difference.
Alabama	4.44	7.79	3.35	4.82	8.68	3.86
Arkansas	1.29	4.63	2.34	2.14	7.25	5.11
Florida	10.02	14.39	4.37	7.96	14.89	6.93
Georgia	7.68	13.74	6.06	7.75	14.59	6.84
Kentucky	36.16	33.35	2.81[3]	13.79	13.96	.17
Mississippi	2.87	4.38	1.51	2.20	3.68	1.48

In five of the six commonwealths here represented, the

[1] Cf. F. J. Brown, *The Northward Movement of the Colored Population.*

[2] Lectures of Professor W. F. Willcox on Social Statistics.

[3] Decrease.

urban percentage increased more among the negroes than among the whites in the decade 1880–90; and Maryland is the only other Southern State that stands with Mississippi as an exception in this respect.

The consequences of this tendency of the negro race to move into the towns and cities are, in the opinion of the present writer, likely to be wholesome rather than the opposite, at least so long as the movement is toward the towns and smaller cities in the South, rather than toward the great cities of the North, where the conditions of life in the negro quarters are pitiable in the extreme.[1] To learn industry, thrift and self-reliance, the negro needs to be removed from the isolation, ignorance and shiftlessness of the farm or plantation and brought under white superintendence in the town. If the present experiments in the direction of employing negro labor in Southern cotton factories result successfully, there promises to be a period of real advance in the economic efficiency of the negro, and thus an eventual solution of the negro problem.

Mr. Hoffman pictures in lurid light the effects of the excessive mortality of the negro race (especially in the cities); its increase since emancipation; the impairment of the constitutional vigor of the race, as seen in the abnormal prevalence of consumption and other pulmonary troubles, and in the excessive infant mortality; the enormous economic waste involved in the death of many of the young and the survival of comparatively few to the productive ages; the hindrance that such a population offers to the development of our cities, etc.[2] It may be doubted, however, whether the negro race has not a considerable power of resistance to these forces of deterioration that Mr. Hoffman predicts will wipe

[1] See, for example, the letter of Mr. Paul Lawrence Dunbar to the New York *Sun*, Sept. 4, 1897, and for details, Hoffman, *op. cit. passim*, but especially ch. ii.

[2] Cf. the summary, *op. cit.*, pp. 145-8.

it out of existence after the manner of the Maories and Sandwich Islanders. For example, there is some evidence, not presented by Mr. Hoffman, to the effect that negro mortality is now diminishing rather than increasing in the Southern cities.[1] Whether or not an inroad has as yet been made upon the sexual immorality that is the bottom cause of race degeneration, there is this consolation: A band of intelligent, highly educated, self-sacrificing negroes has fully possessed itself of the perilous situation of the race and is struggling manfully and hopefully toward the true goal. So long as the race can produce leaders like Booker Washington and Paul Laurence Dunbar, there is no cause for despair.

Whatever tendency can be shown to make for the improvement of eight million Americans cannot fail to be of vital import to the nation as a whole. In the author's opinion, the nation can view with equanimity the movement of the negroes from the farm to the *smaller* cities. This is certainly preferable to a concentration of the race on farming lands in a " black belt."

IV. OCCUPATION.

The connection between occupation and place of habitation is as close as possible and requires few words of explanation in this place. The entire essay, as a matter of fact, is occupied with the theme in its broadest aspects,—how industrial organization conditions the dwelling-places of individuals.

---

[1] The *Bulletin of the U. S. Dept. of Labor*, May, 1897, presents the following statistics compiled from the official health reports of the several cities (pp. 270–283) :

DEATHS PER 1,000 OF NEGRO POPULATION :

	Atlanta.	Memphis.	Richmond.		Baltimore.	Charleston.
1882–85	37.96	43.01	40.34 [2]	1880–84......	36.15	44.08 [3]
1886–90	33.41	29.35	38.83	1885–89......	30.52	46.74
1891–95	32.76	21.11	34.91	1890–94......	31.47	41.43

[2] For 1881–85.   [3] For 1881–84.

The German census of occupations in 1882 affords the following comparison:

TABLE CXXXIX.

PERCENTAGE OF INHABITANTS BELONGING TO SPECIFIED OCCUPATION IN

	Cities 100,000 +.	Cities 20,000– 100,000.	Cities 5,000– 20,000.	Towns 2,000– 5,000.	Rural parts.	All Germany
Agriculture............	1.4	3.4	9.9	26.3	64.5	42.5
Mfs. and mining	47.3	52.8	53.6	49.0	24.4	35.5
Trade and commerce ...	26.6	19.5	15.6	11.6	4.9	10.0
Casual day labor	5.0	4.5	4.3	2.9	0.7	2.1
Liberal professions, etc. .	10.7	11.2	9.1	4.9	2.3	4.9
Free incomes; unknown.	8.9	8.6	7.6	5.4	3.7	5.0
	99.9	100.0	100.1	100.1	100.5	100.0

Agricultural pursuits naturally figure poorly in the great cities, and gain ground as one descends to the village and hamlet. Industry, it is worth noting, makes a smaller percentage in the great cities of Germany than in the smaller towns. While this is doubtless due in part to suburban development, and while the inclusion of mining in the rubric must also favor the smaller towns, it confirms the conclusion reached earlier in the essay that it is not so much manufacturing industry as commerce that builds up great cities. Casual labor is also affected by the degree of agglomeration; the statistics show that the process of concentration of population increases this unfortunate class. On the other hand, it also increases the strength of the liberal professions, which would usually be counted a blessing unless these ranks absorbed too many men in the effort to cure abuses in law, hygiene, medicine, religion and education. The sixth class is made up largely of people without occupation, inmates of institutions, and people living on their incomes. This class, too, is attracted to the cities.

It will be of interest to see what percentage of the population is engaged in gainful occupation in the various categories of towns, although, to be sure, such percentages depend in a measure on the proportion of children. This proportion being smallest in the great cities, one would expect to find there the largest working population. Such was the case according to the German occupation statistics of 1882:

	Percentage of inhabitants engaged.	Percentage of adult women. occupied.	in domestic service.
Cities 100,000+	40.3	24.1	14.4
" 20,000–100,000	38.1	21.1	12.6
" 5,000–20,000	37.4	20.9	10.7
Towns 2,000–5,000	37.3	23.9	8.2
Rural parts	39.7	31.2	6.2

The one exception to the rule stated above—that the percentage of workers in the population increases with the size of the town—exists in the case of the rural districts and is due to the common practice of women working in the fields, as appears in the second column of the table. Few women act as servants in the country, but the number steadily increases as one progresses towards the great cities.

A third question arises in this connection: What effect does agglomeration have upon the industrial *rank* of the individual? The following Austrian statistics would seem to indicate that agglomeration favors the upper ranks—employers, independent workers, and the higher employees—at the expense of the lower—the artisans and day laborers: [1]

PERCENTAGE OF PERSONS OCCUPIED IN

	Great cities.[2]	Other places of 2,000+.	Places of 2,000–.
Independent [3]	33.9	30.3	27.1
Salaried employees	15.8	8.6	1.3
Artisans	47.1	52.7	63.0
Day laborers	3.2	8.4	8.6
	100.0	100.0	100.0

[1] Rauchberg, *St. Mon.*, xx, 391.

[2] The seven principal cities; all but two, Brünn and Cracow, having more than 100,000 inhabitants.

[3] The German terms are Selbstsändige, Angestellte, Arbeiter, Taglöhner. "Angestellte" includes the superintendents, foremen, clerks, etc.—the higher personnel.

But this apparent advantage of the cities partly disappears on analysis into groups of industries, which shows that the high percentage of employers in cities is due to small undertakers in trade and commerce. In manufacturing industry, wherein the labor problem is more acute, the percentage of entrepreneurs is smallest in the cities, and of workmen largest, while the cities' advantage in case of the higher employees is minimized: [1]

TABLE CXL.

	Agriculture.			Industry.			Trade and Commerce.			Professions and Civil Service.		
	Large cities.	Urban.	Rural.	Large cities.	Urban.	Rural.	Large cities.	Urban.	Rural.	Large cities.	Urban.	Rural.
Independent.	275	262	233	187	211	213	409	380	329	707	715	871
Employees ..	29	4	2	25	16	7	220	106	65	211	207	104
Artisans	629	616	670	764	739	741	290	280	317	78	76	53
Laborers	67	118	95	24	34	39	81	234	289	4	2	2
	1,000	1,000	1,000	1,000	1,000	1,000	1,000	1,000	1,000	1,000	1,000	1,000

Thus it turns out that the growth of cities, like the growth of manufacturing, upon which it rests, favors the development of a body of artisans and factory workmen, as against the undertaker and employer. That the class of day laborers is relatively small in the cities is reason for rejoicing, though much may here depend on the methods of classification adopted by the census authorities.

[1] *Ibid.*, xx, 394.

CHAPTER VI.

THE NATURAL MOVEMENT OF POPULATION IN CITY AND IN COUNTRY.

IN the preceding paragraphs, an analysis of city populations at rest has been given—the static aspect; it is now proposed to analyze city populations in motion — the dynamic aspect; and the three great subjects to be discussed are marriages, births, and deaths. The following typical figures express the ratios to 1,000 of population, in Massachusetts, for the two years 1894 and 1895: [1]

TABLE CXLI.

	Persons marrying.	Births.	Deaths.
Boston	23.10	31.24	23.23
Cities 100,000–50,000	18.89	29.72	19.49
" 50,000–25,000	18.08	29.00	18.03
" 25,000–10,000	15.92	27.57	16.68
Total urban	19.47	29.67	19.85
" rural	13.77	21.76	17.38
" State	17.68	27.19	19.07

It is clear that such a regular progression must have accountable causes. Let us analyze them.

[1] *28th Annual Rept. of State Board of Health of Mass.* for 1896, p. 826. The *Summary of the Vital Statistics of the New England States* for 1892 (p. 56) shows the relation of the urban and rural groups by comparing their rates with the New England rate as a standard of 1,000:

	Marriages.	Births.	Deaths.
Urban pop.	1,114	1,195	1,058
Rural	886	805	943

I. MARRIAGES.

The law of population is the most difficult subject in social statistics, and statisticians are not even yet agreed upon a law or theory of population that has universal application. We may begin our researches in this field with the statistics of marriage, which naturally lead up to those of births.

In Massachusetts, the number of persons marrying to 1,000 of the total population is smallest in rural districts, and increasing with the magnitude of the dwelling-center, attains its maximum in Boston. Other countries, too, have their largest marriage-rates in the urban populations.[1] But does this crude rate indicate a stronger tendency toward marriage in the city? Considering that the cities contain a relatively larger number of persons of marriageable age, they naturally ought to have more marriages;[2] and when the marriages are compared with the adult and unmarried rather than with the total population, the superiority of the city tends to disappear.[3] Only in appearance, concludes Levasseur, is *nuptialité* greater in the city than in the country.[4] Thus, the Swedish statistics show an apparently higher mar-

---

[1] For England, cf. *J. of St. Society* (1890), 53 : 267. For France, Levasseur (ii, 77) gives the ratios of marriages, which are here doubled to show the ratios of persons married :

	1860.	1885.
Department of Seine	19.8	16.6
Urban population	16.4	14.8
Rural "	15.4	14.6
France	15.8	14.8

[2] Mayo-Smith, *Statistics and Sociology*, 98.

[3] Persons marrying (1886) to 1,000 of the adult unmarried population of each sex (Levasseur, ii, 397) :

	Men over 20 years.	Women over 15 years.
France	61.7	66.0
Paris	59.4	58.6

[4] *Op. cit.*, ii, 86.

riage rate for Stockholm and the urban population throughout the century: [1]

	1816-40.	1841-50.	1851-60.	1861-70.	1870-80.	1881-90.
Rural	15.70	14.56	15.00	12.88	13.20	11.94
Urban	15.72	14.44	16.98	14.64	16.20	15.34
Stockholm	16.34	14.62	18.44	15.48	18.14	17.72

But the city rate is increased by the relatively small number of children in urban populations; hence when the number of marriages in 1881-90 is compared with the adult population, the ratios are transformed:

	Sweden.	Stockholm.
Marriages per 1,000 men of 20-50 years	68.9	59.8
" " " women of 20-45 years	75.8	57.0

In England and America and perhaps other countries, however, the marriage rate remains higher in the cities even when based on the adult population; [2] and Dr. Ogle put forth the hypothesis that the marriage-rate varies with the amount of employment among young women. He noticed that the marriage-rate among single men between the age of 20 and 45 was highest in the rural county of Bedford, which is particularly distinguished for its straw-plaiting and lace industries, occupying many young women. His hypothesis that "men are more ready to marry girls or young women who are themselves earning money" is substantiated by the statistics showing the proportion of women 15-25 years old

[1] Swedish Census of 1890, Bihang, p. vii. (For title, see Table CXVI.)

[2] See Dr. F. S. Crum's essay, "The Marriage Rate in Massachusetts," *Publications of the American Statistical Association* (Dec., 1895), iv, 338. In the following, "adult" means a person over 15 years of age:

	PERSONS MARRYING, 1885.	
	The 28 cities.	Rural remainder.
Per 1,000 of total population	19.2	15.0
" " " adult "	27.0	20.8
" " " " marriageable population	110.1	97.04

industrially occupied.[1] And as a general rule this proportion is largest in the cities, with their factory operatives.

This hypothesis also seems to afford an explanation of the high (refined) marriage-rate in the industrial towns of Massachusetts, where conditions are nearly similar to those in England. The cities with the highest marriage rates in the years 1894 and 1895 were:[2]

Chicopee	27.3
Boston	23.1
Lawrence	22.1
New Bedford	21.9
Lowell	21.4
Chelsea	20.6
Lynn	20.4
Fall River	20.2
Fitchburg	19.7

Now it will be seen at a glance that this list includes the principal textile cities of Massachusetts, *i. e.*, those cities devoted to an industry that employs a large percentage of female labor. And in the list of textile cities appearing in the State census of 1895, there are only three other cities mentioned—North Adams, Pittsfield and Taunton, all of which have other and probably more important manufacturing interests. Boston, although not a textile city, offers a vast amount of employment to women; Lynn is devoted to the boot and shoe industry; but Chelsea, the only remaining city unaccounted for, is a Boston suburb, and no apparent reason exists for its abnormally high marriage-rate. At the opposite extreme are the cities and towns of Woburn, whose marriage-rate was 13.9; Medford, 13.2; Marlborough 13.1; Quincy, 12.8 and Peabody 22.8. Three of these

[1] " On Marriage-Rates and Marriage-Ages," *J. of St. Soc.* (1890), 53: 267.

[2] *28th Rep. of Mass. State Board of Health*, 826.

towns are devoted to the leather and boot and shoe industries, while Bedford and Quincy are suburbs of Boston.

The comparative statistics now presented show wide differences in the marriage-rate among countries and cities. As a rule, the tendency toward marriage appears stronger in the rural districts than in the cities; but industrial cities, and especially cities devoted to industries that employ female labor, are exceptions, marriage being there more frequent and at an earlier age than elsewhere.[1] When, however, we come to the question of family life, there is no doubt that the cities make the more unfavorable showing.

From the relatively small number of children, or non-marriageable persons in the urban population, one would expect that its percentage of *married* persons would be considerably larger than the average. On the contrary, the statistics show the cities have abnormally large percentages of the *unmarried*. This fact is illustrated in some very old (1830) Swedish statistics:[2]

	Urban.	Rural.
Children	275	360
Single	367	223
Married	267	355
Widowed	91	62
	1,000	1,000

It is thus found that the bachelors and spinsters as well as the widowed predominate in the cities, while the country has

---

[1] On the other hand, Parisians marry later than do other Frenchman. In 1885, the average age of marriage (Levasseur, ii, 81) was:

	Men.	Women.
Department of Seine	31 years, 9 months.	27 years, 5 months.
Urban population	29 " 7 "	25 " 8 "
Rural population	29 " 3 "	24 " 8 "

[2] Legoyt, p. 38, where other data are presented similar to these.

the larger percentage of children and the married. This is the relation which exists in the United States to-day; thus, the conjugal condition of the adult population (20 years and over) in 1890 was—[1]

	MALES.		FEMALES.	
	The 28 great cities.	United States.	The 28 great cities.	United States.
Single	362	309.5	263	199
Married...................	590	638.	588	664
Widowed	42	46.5	145	132
Divorced	2	3	3	4
Unknown	4	3	1	1
	1,000	1,000	1,000	1,000

The exclusion of children is necessary to statistical accuracy, as they are incapable of marriage. But it sometimes happens that the cities, notwithstanding the large proportion of adults residing in them, still have fewer married people than do the rural districts. Such is the case in Austria:[2]

TABLE CXLII.

Places of	Single.	Married.	Widowed, divorced or separated.	Total.
Less than 500	612	335	53	1,000
500–2,000	592	353	55	1,000
2,000–5,000	609	335	56	1,000
5,000–10,000	627	314	59	1,000
10,000–20,000	632	309	59	1,000
20,000+	629	305	66	1,000
Vienna	620	311	69	1,000
All places	608	336	56	1,000

In Europe generally, with the exception of England,

[1] *11th Cen., Pop.,* i, p. clxxxvi.

[2] Rauchberg, *St. Mon.,* xix, 135.

the percentage of married people in the cities is below the average :[1]

ENGLAND.

NUMBER OF PERSONS MARRIED IN 1,000 OF EACH SEX BETWEEN THE AGES OF 15 AND 45 YEARS. (CENSUS OF 1891.) :

		Male.	Female.
London Lancashire } urban counties		{ 464 460	456 475
Rutlandshire Herefordshire } rural counties		{ 388 402	427 422

In the main, the statistics of conjugal condition agree with the statistics of annual marriages; in both cases England's urban communities show a stronger tendency toward marriage and home life than do her rural communities, while on the continent the reverse is usually true. But in the United States, the singular result is reached of a relatively high urban marriage-rate and at the same time a relatively small proportion of married people in the cities. Inasmuch as the marriage-rate has been high in Massachusetts cities during a long period of time, one would naturally expect that the proportion of married people as revealed in the census would be large; but just as the 28 great cities of the country have fewer married people than the United States as a whole, so has Boston fewer than Massachusetts.[2]

[1] For France (Levasseur, ii, 390) :

POPULATION BETWEEN AGES OF 20 AND 60 YEARS.

	Male.		Female.	
	Paris.	France.	Paris.	France.
Single	385	348	314	270
Married	570	609.5	566	640
Widowed	43	42	117	89.5
Divorced	2	.5	3	.5
	1,000	1,000.0	1,000	1,000.0

[2] Of the population 20 years old and over in 1890, the following percentages were married (*11th Cen., Pop.*, i, 851, 888) :

	Males.	Females.
Massachusetts	61.1	55.8
Boston	55.3	50.5

Of the adult male population, 32.8 per cent. were single in Massachusetts, 38.1 per cent. in Boston.

A number of explanations may be offered for such an apparent contradiction. For one thing, rural emigration takes away most of the bachelors and maids, leaving in the country a population with a large proportion of married people; and at the same time that marriages are comparatively infrequent, social circumstances may be such as to impel rural couples to go to the cities for the performance of the marriage ceremony. Moreover, in many German cities it is found that city young people often remove to a suburb shortly after marriage in order to begin house-keeping in a cottage of their own; [1] the marriage is thus credited to the city, while the census counts the married couple in the suburb. The most probable explanation, however, is that city marriages take place at an earlier age than country marriages, where the city marriage rate is the higher of the two, and that they are dissolved sooner by the relatively high mortality to which males are subject in the city. This would account for the larger number of widows in urban populations. Divorce is also more frequent in the city. By the re-marriage of widowed and divorced persons, the city marriage rate is raised, without any real addition to the number of married people, as compared with the rural community where the first marriage would have continued longer. If the city of Copenhagen, for example, be compared with a Danish rural district (Fünen), it will be found that Copenhagen has the higher marriage rate. But it is due simply to early marriages, for by the time the age of 45 years is reached, Copenhagen has relatively fewer married people than has Fünen. The rural population marries later, but of all the males who reach the age of 45, and of all the females who reach the age of 35, more are married in the rural than in the urban population. [2] Now, whether people marry early

[1] Brückner, *Allg. Stat. Archiv*, i, 662.
[2] Rubin and Westergaard, *Statistik der Ehen.*

or marry late depends chiefly on their foresight and self-control; as a rule it is the higher social classes, the wealthier or at least the propertied classes, which possess these qualities. And in proportion as they predominate in a city, will the city's marriage-rate be low and its birth rate also. With this brief indication of the theory of population, it may be reserved for more careful discussion in connection with birth-rates and the fecundity of marriage.

The explanation advanced in the eleventh census for the relatively small number of married people in the urban population is its peculiar composition as regards the native and foreign elements.[1] Now as a matter of fact, the largest single element in the population of the 28 great cities considered, is the foreign element, which contains a larger proportion of married people than any other element, and so far as race enters into the question, it is the native white element in which the greatest difference between city and country is found. A similar difference, explained very likely by the number of domestic servants in the city, is found among the negroes, who, however, constitute a much smaller element of the aggregate population of the 28 cities. On the whole, it appears to be the postponement of marriage on the part of native Americans that tends to reduce the proportion of the married in the city below that in the country.

In Austria such a postponement of marriage in the cities is shown by an admirable compilation of statistics, which can be only partially reproduced here:

[1] *Pop.*, i, p. clxxxvi.   The facts:

	Males.	Twenty-eight Great Cities. Per cent. married.		United States. Per cent. married.	
		M.	F.	M.	F.
Foreign white	1,357,779	67.3	62.7	65.9	68.1
Native white, native parents..	780,947	57.1	58.0	66.1	67.9
Native white, foreign parents..	656,053	45.6	54.0	48.6	58.8
Negro.....................	128,145	59.5	51.9	69.0	65.0
Aggregate	2,952,238	59.0	58.8	63.8	66.3

TABLE CXLIII.[1]

NUMBER OF WOMEN MARRIED AMONG EACH 1,000 FEMALES OF THE AGE

Places with a pop. of	11-20.	21-30.	31-40.	41-50.	51-60.	61-70.	70+.	All ages.
Less than 500	28	482	757	738	611	425	221	330
500-2,000	47	566	798	748	598	405	207	347
2,000-5,000	45	532	744	694	552	378	197	328
5-10,000	32	465	696	655	531	353	176	311
10-20,000	23	431	686	643	513	333	164	305
20,000+	19	349	621	618	490	309	139	298
Austria	36	495	745	714	578	392	199	331

NUMBER OF BACHELORS AMONG EACH 1,000 MALES OF THE AGE

Places with a population of	0-10.	11-20.	21-30.	31-40.	41-50.	51-60.	61-70.	70+.	All ages.
Less than 500 .	1,000	1,000	677	238	149	129	128	121	627
500-2,000	1,000	999	602	164	101	89	86	91	611
2,000-5,000...	1,000	1,000	645	207	140	123	113	101	631
5,000-10,000..	1,000	1,000	734	257	172	135	127	108	656
10,000-20,000.	1,000	1,000	755	255	158	133	123	116	661
20,000+	1,000	1,000	799	310	173	134	117	113	657
Austria	1,000	1,000	677	219	135	114	110	107	628

It thus appears that among the women, the married *in every age group* become relatively fewer as the size of the dwelling-place increases; and the corresponding table, not here reproduced, shows the same thing for men, although in the advanced ages the differences between the various categories of towns are much less marked than they are in the lower age classes. The second table shows that in the higher age classes the cities have no more unmarried men than the small towns, a result not irreconcilable with the foregoing statement, as the widowed and divorced, not the married, absorb the difference. Rauchberg's conclusion for Austria is of wide application: "The marriage-rate, the age at marriage, the preponderance of unmarried among the migrants and the direction of migration (toward the cities) work together to raise the participation in married life, especially in the younger years, to a higher level in the villages and country places than in the middle-sized and large cities."[2]

[1] *St. Mon.,* xix, 136.   [2] *Ibid.,* 137.

The influence of migration upon marriage-rates is readily seen. Rural emigration, being predominantly of young unmarried persons, leaves a large married population in the country. But it is doubtful if it materially diminishes the percentage of married in the city. Frankfort statistics (1890) afford the following example: [1]

FEMALE POPULATION OVER 20 YEARS OF AGE

	Born Frankforters.	Born outside.
Single	35.2	40.9
Married	47.5	47.0
Widowed and divorced	17.3	12.1
	100.0	100.0

The young people who go from the village or farm to the city cannot, to be sure, marry at once, for they are obliged to obtain a position in the ranks of industry that will enable them to earn a living and support a family; but this requires only a few years. Hence, as years pass, the percentage of the unmarried in the city steadily diminishes and approaches the rural percentage, as already noted in Table CXLIII. That the two percentages do not coincide seems to be due, not to the immigrants to the city, but to the native citizens themselves, who are less inclined to marry than the immigrants, as appears in the following statistics from the Berlin census of 1885:

PER CENT. MARRIED OF ALL OVER [2]

	Male.		Female.	
	20 yrs.	30 yrs.	20 yrs.	30 yrs.
Berlin-born	55.6	77.6	49.6	57.8
Born elsewhere	58.8	79.5	53.8	62.6
Immigrants within preceding 5 years	30.7	66.9	37.0	51.9
Other immigrants	74.6	82.2	60.5	64.7

Comparing the city-born with those born outside, it will be seen that the proportion of married people among the

---

[1] Bleicher, p. 7.   [2] *Allg. St. Ar.*, i, 640.

latter is 3 or 4 per cent. higher than among the former, and this notwithstanding the large number of immigrants of youthful age, among whom the percentage of the married is necessarily low. As a result the proportion of the married among the older immigrants is extremely high (74.6 and 60.5) as compared with the Berlin-born.

Nor is the difference merely the results of difference in age classification, for closer analysis shows that only in the lower age groups (below the age of 30) is the percentage of the married greater among the Berlin-born than among the immigrants.[1] The latter, moreover, have a larger percentage of second marriages than the natives. The strong tendency of immigrants toward marriage is, perhaps, to be attributed to lack of prudence and foresight, as compared with the better-fed city people.

Mention has just been made of the heavy percentages of city marriages dissolved by divorce. This does not contradict the statement in the Eleventh Census that the "proportion of divorced persons in the cities is less than that in the country at large;"[2] for many persons who are divorced remarry and are then no longer counted among the divorced. The evidence is conclusive that in Europe the number of divorces is three or four times as great in the cities as in the rural parts.[3] In France the peasantry, constituting one-half

---

[1] Brückner, *ibid.*, i, 641, note 1.

[2] *Rep. on Pop.*, i, p. clxxxvii. As a matter of fact, the census enumeration of divorced persons is acknowledged to be extremely defective.

[3] Cf. Korösi's *Statistiques des grandes villes*, and J. Bertillon's *Étude démographique du divorce et de la séparation de corps* (p. 55), from which the following are taken:

DIVORCES PER 100 MARRIAGES IN

Brussels .	1871–73	12.4	Belgium	3.5
La Hague	1865–74	11.1	Netherlands	4.6
Munich,	1868–74	15.3	Bavaria	5.0
Stockholm	1864–73	28.1	Sweden	6.4
Copenhagen	1870–74	29.2	Denmark	12.6

the population, contributes only 7 per cent. of the divorces. The number of divorces (100,000 inhabitants) in France was as follows in 1885 : Department of the Seine (Paris), 47 ; urban population, 19 ; rural population, 3.5.[1] In the United States the evidence against the cities is less conclusive, but it justifies Hon. Carroll D. Wright in stating " that not only is the increase of divorce proportionately greater in the cities than in the country, but the ratio of married couples to each divorce is also greater."[2] Any marked divergence from this rule may partly be due, as Professor Wilcox suggests,[3] to the presence of a foreign-born Catholic population in the cities, and partly to the more approximate equality of the rural and urban populations in this country as regards the reception of new ideas than is the case in Europe with its rural population composed of peasants.

II. FECUNDITY.

The fruitfulness of marriage is commonly expressed in the ratio of annual births to each 1,000 of total population,— the birth-rate. In former times the cities had a considerably lower birth-rate than the country, which was explained by the statisticians as the result of late marriages and limitations on the size of the family. " More wants," says Süssmilch in 1760, " and increased splendor, with higher prices for the necessaries of life, keep men from marrying in the cities." [4]

---

[1] Levasseur, ii, 91.

[2] Report, as Commissioner of Labor, on *Marriage and Divorce in the United States, 1867-86*, p. 162. Cf. tables on pp. 159–161.

[3] *The Divorce Problem*, Columbia Studies, i, 33. Professor Willcox also notes that the divorce rate in the District of Columbia (an urban population) is nearly three times that of the adjacent commonwealths—a ratio which approaches European conditions. (*Ibid.*, 39.)

[4] *Die göttliche Ordnung* (2d. ed.), i, 257. Süssmilch's statistics of births in city and country are not very satisfactory; perhaps the rates (1 birth to 24 living) and 36 (1 : 28) for the rural and urban populations, respectively, would express his opinion, if reduced to figures. (Cf. i, 225.) He estimates the num-

In another epoch-making work on population statistics [1] a century later, a countryman of Süssmilch's could present statistics showing that, in most European countries, the urban birth-rate exceeded the rural. Only Sweden and Prussia were exceptions, and as indicated in Table CXVI, Sweden ceased to be an exception at the very time Wappäus was writing. At the present day the crude birth-rate is almost universally higher in city than in country,[2] and, indeed, as shown in the Massachusetts statistics given in the introductory treatment of the movement of population, the birth-rate increases with the populousness of cities.

The most obvious explanation of a high birth-rate would be a large proportion of women in the child-bearing period. The cities have a larger percentage of such persons; hence for this reason, and not because of greater fecundity of city women, do the cities often have a high birth-rate. The following table shows, in the ideal or normal rate, that the fecundity of women should be greatest in the cities on ac-

ber of children to a marriage at 3.5 in the city and 4 in the whole country (i, 175). The birth rate in large cities fluctuated enormously in previous centuries because of frequent epidemics.

[1] *Die allgemeine Bevölkerungsstatistik* by J. E. Wappäus (Leipzig, 1861), ii, 481.

[2] In Prussia there is still some difference between city and country: *

	Urban.	Rural.
1849-55	37.98	40.6
1856-61	38.1	40.9
1862-67	39.0	41.2
1867-86	39.3	40.4

	Prussia.	Germany.	25 great cities of Germany.
1861-64	40.8	....	36.9
1864-67	40.4	....	38.7
1867-71	38.5	....	38.3
1871-75	41.4	41.4	41.9
1875-80	40.9	40.8	42.1
1880-85	38.9	38.5	37.4

* Brückner, *Allg. Stat. Archiv*, i, 160-1.

count of the favorable age-distribution; following the crude, or uncorrected, birth-rate, is the true rate,—for both legitimate and illegitimate births (1890–91):[1]

TABLE CXLIV.

	Births to 1,000 inhabitants.		To 100 women aged 16–50.		
	Normal.	Actual.	All women: total births.	Married: legitimate births.	Single, widowed, etc.: illegitimate births.
16 great cities........	42.4	35.9	12.1	22.8	2.6
Cities 20–100,000.....	39.4	37.9	14.5	26.7	2.2
Cities under 20,000 ...	37.3	35.6	14.4	26.3	2.2
All cities	38.9	36.3	13.5	25.1	2.4
Rural...............	38.2	40.0	16.8	28.9	2.5
Prussia............	38.5	38.5	15.4	27.4	2.5

These figures plainly show that fecundity is greatest among the women of the rural districts of Prussia, and steadily decreases as the dwelling-center becomes more populous,—except that the middle-sized cities show no decrease over the smaller cities. Illegitimate births, it may be noticed incidentally, are relatively more numerous in the country than in the city, although the larger proportion of maidens and widows in the city would lead us to expect the contrary. In the great cities, indeed, the percentage of illegitimates increases, but here there is the additional factor of maternity hospitals and clinics which receive a great many women from outside,—the majority of such women, it is unnecessary to add, being unmarried.

The Prussian statistics hardly justify us in making the

[1] The computations for the ideal or normal rate were made by Dr. Bleicher of Frankfort, and will be found in his paper on "Die Eigenthümlichkeiten der städtischen Natalitäts und Mortalitätsverhältnisse," in the report of the proceeding of the 8th International Congress of Hygiene and Demography at Budapest (1894), vii, 468. The other statistics appear in his tables, and are also to be found in Bleicher, 267.

generalization that city marriages are less fruitful than country marriages. Indeed, the opposite is true in several countries, if the great cities be excepted. Thus, in Denmark the average annual number of births (1880–9) to 1,coo women, aged 16–50, married and unmarried, respectively, was: [1]

	Legitimate.	Illegitimate.
Copenhagen	234.1	48.5
Other towns	259.6	23.1
Rural communities	245.9	24.3
Denmark	246.3	28.6

Additional examples from European statistics might be given,[2] but the most pertinent one is found at home. Dr. F. S. Crum has shown that in Massachusetts the fecundity of marriage increases with the density of the population, and reaches its maximum in the largest city: [3]

---

[1] Rubin, " Population, Natalité et Mortalité du Royaume de Danemark," Int. Cong. of Hygiene, 1894, *Proceedings*, vii, 489.

[2] In Saxony the number of births to 100 women of child-bearing age (1879–83) in the five government districts is as follows (*Zeitschrift des K. Sächsischen Stat. Bureaus*, 1885):

		Legitimate.	Illegitimate.
Dresden	Rural	28.0	5.9
	Urban	28.2	4.2
	Dresden city	21.9	4.6
Leipzig	Rural	30.4	6.9
	Urban	31.9	8.2
	Leipzig city	28.3	3.6
Zittau	Rural	19.6	7.3
	Urban	20.8	5.0
Bautzen	Rural	22.5	6.7
	Urban	23.9	3.4
Chemnitz	Rural	32.8	9.4
	Urban	26.3	8.5
	Chemnitz city	26.0	4.8

[3] " The Birth-rate in Massachusetts," *Quar. Jour. of Economics*, xi, 259.

TABLE CXLV.

Pop. per sq. mile.	No. of towns.	Births per 1,000 married women.			Deaths of children aged 0-1 year. Per 1,000 total deaths.	No. of survivors at one year per 100 married women.	Percentage of increase (or decrease—) in pop., 1875-85.
		Total.	Native.	Foreign.		Per 1,000 living births.	
0-24	39	59.7	57.1	64.5	97.4	106.6	5.34	—13.9
25-49	64	62.9	58.2	89.1	103.7	121.5	5.53	—13.3
50-99	103	74.1	61.5	117.9	140.3	126.6	6.45	+2.2
100-199	44	83.0	67.2	119.0	148.9	122.5	7.28	+6.3
200-499	52	106.3	87.6	133.2	193.1	135.3	9.19	+15.9
500-999	22	106.0	84.1	146.3	194.3	136.3	9.13	+37.0
1,000-4,999 ...	19	120.0	86.0	153.0	249.7	175.3	9.91	+29.5
5,000+	4	124.0	99.0	139.0	229.9	185.8	10.10	+17.0

In the first place, it should be observed that the correspondence between density and populousness is close. The four cities in the densest group are Boston, and its three principal suburbs, Cambridge, Somerville, Chelsea; and all the thirteen cities which, in 1885, contained 25,000+ inhabitants are found in the last two groups of the table. Roughly speaking, the last group signifies Boston, the second densest group, the industrial cities.

In the second place, the table shows that the high birthrate of the large cities is not solely due to difference in race, as has often been asserted; for native women, as well as foreign, are more productive in the cities, the only irregularity in the progression being in the group of towns with a density of 200-500.

In the third place, it is to be remarked that the high birthrate of Massachusetts cities is not accounted for, as is sometimes urged,[1] by the fact that " in the cities there is a larger proportion of population between the ages of fourteen and fifty." Calculations by the present writer show that whereas the number of births to 1,000 women aged 18-45 years was about 110 in Massachusetts in 1894-5, it was about 125 in Boston.[2] True, the Boston women marry younger than do

[1] *Annals of American Acad.*, v. 87.

[2] It might be objected that the percentages given above do not distinguish the native and foreign mothers, and that the predominance of the latter gives Boston

the women of Massachusetts generally, and Boston consequently has a larger proportion of its married women in the
age-group 20–30 years, the most fertile period of woman's
life, than Massachusetts has; the percentages being 27 and
24.1 respectively.[1] But such a slight difference cannot alone
explain the relatively high birth-rate of Boston.
The evidence as to relative fecundity of city and country
women is therefore conflicting. Heretofore the European
statisticians have explained the relatively high birth-rate
(crude) in cities as a result either of favorable age distribution or of more illegitimacy. Wappäus, for example, showed
that the number of children to a marriage was almost invariably higher in country than in the city; but he found a
larger number of illegitimate children in the cities, which
fact, in connection with the more frequent marriages in the
city, gave the latter a higher birth-rate.[2] At the present

its high rate. The probabilities are against this; in Boston 70.5 per cent. of the
foreign and 73.7 per cent. of the native married women are under 45; in the rest
of Massachusetts the percentages are 66.0 and 64.6 respectively (*11th Cens., Pop.*,
i, 851, 888).

[1] Calculated from *11th Cens., Pop.*, i, pp. 851, 888. In Prussia the respective
percentages for cities of 20,000+ and rural districts are 23.82 and 20.35; in Bavaria,
for town and country, 21.94 and 15.49 (Cf. *Zeitschrift des Königl. Bayerischen
Statis. Bureaus*, 1892, p. 309.

[2] By deducting the number of deaths of infants under 5 years, Wappäus was able
to show a still larger fruitfulness of marriage among countrymen. A portion of
his table is reproduced herewith (Cf. *Allgemeine Bevölkerungsstatistik*, ii, 483-4) :

TABLE CXLVI.

	Children to a marriage.		Same at end of fifth year.		Percentage of illegitimate births in total.	
	City.	Country.	City.	Country.	City.	Country.
France	3.16	3.28	2.03	2.34	15.13	4.24
Netherlands	3.91	4.32	2.49	3.07	7.71	2.84
Belgium	3.80	4.17	...	...	14.49	5.88
Sweden	2.99	4.19	1.83	3.16	27.44	7.50
Denmark	3.04	3.34	2.14	2.58	16.05	10.06
Saxony	4.60	4.13	2.77	2.64	15.39	14.64
Prussia	4.00	4.44	2.56	3.13	9.80	6.60
(Saxony	4.30	4.22	2.59	2.81	15.34	11.58)

Saxony is the only exception to the general rule, and Wappäus accounts for it

day it is not so generally true that the larger families are found in the rural districts. In France, indeed, the proposition remains true, as the following comparison (from Levasseur ii, 398), indicates:

Families having (1886)	Dept. of Seine.	France.
0 child	323	200
1 child	276	244
2 children	201	218
3 "	105	145
4 "	53	90
5 or more children	12	103
	1,000	1,000

But in the United States, on the other hand, the average number of persons to a family (4.93) is smaller than it is in the 28 great cities of 1890 (4.99). The difference is really greater than appears, because the United States average is raised by the large families of negroes in the South, which contains only four of the 28 great cities.[1] Comparing the ten leading cities with the commonwealths to which they belong, it will be found that the difference is nearly always in favor of the city:[2]

by the fact that, in this industrial kingdom, manufacturing industries had spread from the towns into the open country and villages. If the population be divided into industrial and agricultural groups, instead of city and country, the result will agree with the other countries. (See the last line of the table.)

[1] Cf. the following:

North Atlantic States	4.69
North Central "	4.86
Western States	4.88
South Atlantic States	5.25
South Central "	5.30

[2] *11th Cens., Pop.*, vol. i, p. cxc *ff.* The census interpretation of the decline in the average size of a family is open to criticism.

	City.	State.
New York	4.84	4.59
Chicago	4.99	4.92
Philadelphia	5.10	4.95
Brooklyn	4.72	4.59
St. Louis	4.92	5.07
Boston	5.00	4.67
Baltimore	5.01	5.16
San Francisco	5.69	4.92
Cincinnati	4.67	4.68
Cleveland	4.93	4.68

The statistics of families, however, are not absolutely trust-worthy information regarding the fruitfulness of marriage. The census definition of family is necessarily loose, and includes the inmates of an hotel, an asylum, etc.; and many other factors have to be considered. A possible explanation is the presence of so many foreigners in the great cities, amounting to 32 per cent. of their total population as against 15 per cent. for the United States. That the foreigners have larger families than the Americans is well known, and is demonstrated anew by the Massachusetts statistics just referred to. But these latter statistics show that the native, as well as the foreign married women, have more children in the cities than in the country.

In fact, there seems to be no direct connection between agglomeration and fecundity. In Berlin, Leipzig and Munich, three of the four leading cities of Germany, the refined birth-rate is below the average of the twenty-six great cities, while in the smallest six cities of this class the birth-rate is above the average. And among the cities of equal size, even in the same country, notable differences in the birth-rate are familiar; factory towns generally having a high birth-rate without any advantage in the age distribution. The conditions affecting the fruitfulness of marriage are so numerous and complicated that statisticians and social philosophers are still in dispute as to their relative influence. The

theory which at present commands the largest body of ad-
herents is the one set forth in Professor Fetter's *Versuch zu
einer Bevölkerungslehre*, which, it is hoped, may be put by
the author into more easily accessible form for American
readers. Substantially the same theory, however, is pro-
pounded in Professor Hadley's new work. According to
this theory, the birth-rate (as the expression of fecundity) is
not dependent on the peculiarities of population groups, nor
even the general economic condition of the population; but
both the rate of increase and the economic condition depend
on a third factor,—the economic foresight and prudence of
the individual. "High comfort and low birth-rate are commonly associated, because comfort is made to depend upon
prudence. Let the comfort be made independent of prudence, as in the case of the pauper or criminal, and the birth-
rate tends to increase rather than diminish. . . It is not
that social ambition *in itself* constitutes a greater preventive
check to population than the need of subsistence; but that
the need of subsistence is felt by all men alike, emotional as
well as intellectual, while social ambition stamps the man or
the race that possesses it as having reached the level of intellectual morality. Ethical selection can therefore operate
on the latter class as it does not on the former. The intellectual man has possibilities of self-restraint which the emotional man has not." [1]

One of the statistical proofs that the birth-rate diminishes
with each advance in civilization was furnished by Miss J. L.
Brownell in a study of the American statistics in the *Tenth
Census*. Miss Brownell took as statistical indices of civilization the percentage of all deaths (from known causes) that
were due to nervous diseases, the density of population, the
intensity of the cultivation of the soil as indicated by the

[1] Hadley, *Economics*, pp. 48-9.

value of agricultural products per acre, and the value of manufactured products per capita. In comparing the forty-seven states and territories, Miss Brownell found that a low birth-rate generally accompanied high percentages of the other factors, and vice versa. Her table [1] may be summarized as follows:

	Deaths from nervous diseases.	Density.	Value of agricultural products per acre.	Value of mf. products per capita.
Coherences with birth-rate......	8	8	16	7
Opposition to birth-rate........	39	39	31	40
Total States and Territories.....	47	47	47	47

In order to ascertain the relation of the birth-rate to agglomeration of population, Miss Brownell's comparison has been extended by the writer. In the following list the plus or minus mark signifies that the rate or percentage for the State specified is above or below the average for the United States; the asterisk simply denotes coherences: [2]

TABLE CXLVII.

	Birth-rate.	Density of pop.	Percentages of pop. urban.
1. Alabama	+	—	—
2. Arizona	—	—*	—*
3. Arkansas	+	—	—
4. California	—	—*	+
5. Colorado	—	—*	+
6. Connecticut	—	+	+
7. Dakota	+	—	—
8. Delaware..................	—	+	+
9. Dist. of Col.	—	+	+
10. Florida	+	—	—
11. Georgia	+	—	—
12. Idaho....................	+	—	—
13. Illinois..................	+	+	+

[1] *Annals Amer. Acad.*, v. 74.

[2] The percentage of urban population for the United States in 1880 was 21.47, the line being drawn at towns of 10,000+. The authority is *11th Cen., Stat. of Cities*, p. 1.

	Birth-rate.	Density of pop.	Percentages of pop. urban.
14. Indiana	—	+	—*
15. Iowa	+	—	—
16. Kansas	+	—	—
17. Kentucky	+	+*	—
18. Louisiana	+	—	+*
19. Maine	—	+	—*
20. Maryland	—	+	+
21. Massachusetts	—	+	+
22. Michigan	—	+	—*
23. Minnesota	+	—	—
24. Mississippi	+	—	—
25. Missouri	+	—	—
26. Montana	+	—	—
27. Nebraska	+	—	—
28. Nevada	—	—*	—*
29. New Hampshire	—	+	—*
30. New Jersey	—	+	+
31. New Mexico	+	—	—
32. New York	—	+	+
33. North Carolina	+	—	—
34. Ohio	—	+	+
35. Oregon	+	—	—
36. Pennsylvania	—	+	+
37. Rhode Island	—	+	+
38. South Carolina	+	+*	—
39. Tennessee	+	+*	—*
40. Texas	+	—	—
41. Utah	+	—	—
42. Vermont	—	+	—
43. Virginia	+	+*	—
44. Washington	+	—	—
45. West Virginia	+	—	—
46. Wisconsin	+	—	—
47. Wyoming	+	—	—

In 39 out of 47 cases, a high birth-rate is opposed to the concentration of population; where a large proportion of the population is in cities, the birth-rate is low, and vice versa. The States in which there are coherences are Arizona, Indiana, Maine, Michigan, Nevada, New Hampshire, and Vermont, with both rates below the average of the United States ; and Louisiana, with both rates above the average.

The theory of population herein adopted is, in brief, that a declining birth-rate accompanies an advancing civilization.[1] In so far as cities represent the highest culture and comfort of a country, just so far will they have a low birth-rate and families below the average size. Now, in the past, the classes devoted to manufactures and to commerce have had radically different standards of living. Under the factory system a man marries early because, with female and child-labor in demand, his family soon becomes a help rather than a burden. We have but lately seen that in both England and the United States (Massachusetts), marriage is most frequent in towns where women can find employment.

Dr. Ernst Engel was probably the first statistician to advance statistical data in favor of the proposition that it is chiefly the occupation rather than the mere association of people in large or small dwelling centres which causes the difference in fertility of city and country women.[2] In a thorough analysis of births in various groups of the population of Saxony, for the decade 1840–49, he demonstrated that the birth-rate in towns 91 to 100 per cent. of whose

---

[1] Additional statistical proofs of this theory consist in compilations showing that the birth-rate in large cities diminishes as one goes from the poor to the rich quarters, and that the age at marriage increases, and size of family diminishes, as one passes from the classes low in the social scale to the responsible mercantile and professional classes. Cf. Fetter, *op. cit.;* Levasseur, ii, 398, and iii, 218; Charles Booth on the birth-rate in London districts, *Jour. of St. Soc.*, 1893; criticism by R. H. Hooker, *ibid.*, lx, 753; Brownell, " The Significance of a Decreasing Birth-Rate," in *Annals of the Amer. Acad. of Pol. and Soc. Sc.*, v (with references); Billings,· " The Diminishing Birth-Rate in the United States," *Forum*, June, 1893; Edson, " American Life and Physical Deterioration," in *North Amer. Review*, Oct., 1893. A very good summary is given by Prof. Marshall in the third edition of his *Principles of Economics*, p. 263 ff. And see especially Tallqvist, *La Tendance à une moindre Fécondité des Mariages*, and Rubin-Westergaard, *Statistik der Ehen*.

[2] Cf. Wappäus, *op. cit.*, ii, 481, and Table CXLVI, *supra*.

population was devoted to agricultural industry was 30 per
1000, and in towns where 91 to 100 per cent. of the population was engaged in manufacturing and commerce, 48.4 per
1000.[1] English statisticians, moreover, long since pointed
out the high birth-rate peculiar to mining and industrial
districts.[2] In Germany, the cities which indisputably have
the largest proportion of births to child-bearing women, are
the purely industrial cities of the Rhine-Westphalian district.[3] On the other hand, the commercial cities, with their
greater wealth, comfort and culture, have the lowest birth-
rate.

What effect has migration cityward exercised on the urban

[1] *Statis. Mitteilungen aus d. Königr. Sachsen*, herausgeg. vom Statis. Bureau
des Minist. des Innern, *Bewegung der Bevölkerung*, etc., *in d. Jahren, 1834–50*,
Dresden, 1852, Introd., pp. 20, 56. (Also privately published under the title *Die
Bewegung der Bevölkerung im Königr. Sachsen, etc.: ein Beitrag zur Physio-
logie der Bevölkerung*, vom E. Engel, Dresden, 1854.) . . . . Taking the entire
population, the standard birth-rate of Saxony was 41.0; of the towns which were
predominantly agricultural, 38.8; of the towns predominantly industrial and commercial, 42.2.

[2] Cf. Newsholme, *Vital Statistics*, 57.

[3] Brückner, *Allg. Stat. Archiv*, i, 162. Brückner's comparisons are based on
the crude birth-rate, but inasmuch as the Rhine cities have a small stream of immigration, it is fair to infer that the proportion of adult women is not unduly
large, as indeed proves to be the case. Brückner's study covers, for most of the
German *Grossstädte*, the period 1861–85, and his grouping of the cities according
to birth-rate is copied below. Those familiar with German industrial conditions
will recognize the identity of the first group with the factory industries, that of
the third with commerce:

High birth-rate.	Medium birth-rate.	Low birth-rate.
Chemnitz.	Danzig.	Strassburg.
Barmen.	Breslau.	Dresden.
Elberfeld.	Cologne.	Hanover.
Krefeld.	Halle.	Königsburg.
Altona.	Düsseldorf.	Bremen.
Aachen.	Stuttgart.	Stettin.
Magdeburg.	Nuremberg.	Leipzig.
Berlin.	Hamburg.	Frankfort.
Munich.		

birth-rate? In many countries the greater fecundity of women in industrial centres has been explained by the fact that, one or two generations back, the workmen came from rural districts, and naturally from the largest families, not all of whom could be provided for out of the family estate. In other words, the urban immigrants were children of productive women, and fecundity is an hereditary quality.[1] Capt. John Graunt's authority was cited in support of the theory; but when he speaks of "breeders" migrating to London he seems to be referring rather to women of marriageable age. In the United States, especially in New England, the high birth-rate of industrial centres is largely due to the fertility of the women of French Canadian and Irish stock; but aside from the element of race, the determining influence on the birth-rate is social and psychological, rather than physiological. Whatever their capabilities, the rural emigrants have small families when they have once attained a certain standard of life adherent to the higher social classes.

III. DEATH RATES.

The discussion of mortality is not so beset with statistical difficulties as are the subjects of births and marriages; for it is almost everywhere true that people die more rapidly in cities than in rural districts. The statistics of deaths already incidentally introduced do not, therefore, require augmentation, for they are typical of all countries. To render clearer the relations of population-centres to mortality, the following ratios have been computed from *The Vital Statistics of New England* (1892, p. 57), which are regarded as equal to the European statistics in accuracy:

---

[1] This is urged with force by Ziegler, *Die Naturwissenschaft und die social-demokratische Theorie*, 147.

RATIOS TO THE NEW ENGLAND RATE TAKEN AS 100:
Cities.

100,000+ 116
50,000–100,000 110
25,000–50,000 105
10,000–25,000 95

Total urban 106
   " rural 94

The death-rate is the lowest in the rural parts and steadily increases with the size of the city. Further, it is to be observed that these crude rates are too favorable to the cities in that they do not take into account the larger proportionate number of people of healthy ages residing in the cities, as set forth in a preceding paragraph on age classification.

The following is a comparison between the actual death-rates with the rates that would prevail in Prussia, if all groups of population had the *same mortality* at the same ages:

TABLE CXLVIII.

DEATHS PER 1,000 POPULATION.

	In 1890-91.[1]	With uniform mortality.
Prussia	23.5	23.5
Rural	23.4	26.7
Urban	23.6	24.4
Cities under 20,000	24.2	25.9
" of 20,000–100,000	23.5	23.5
" of 100,000+	22.8	22.6

That is to say, the age constitution of the rural population is such that if the same mortality prevailed at each age as prevails in the city, its death-rate would be much higher (26.7) than the urban rate (24.4); whereas, actually, the rural rate is the lower of the two (23.4 as against 23.6). The smaller cities make a good showing, but the large cities (100,000+) have a higher death-rate than they should have.

These statistics controvert the long-current dictum that mortality always increases in the same ratio with density of

[1] Bleicher, 268–9.

population, and the still more refined rule of Dr. Farr's that the mortality of a district is approximately equal to the sixth root of its density.[1] But the only satisfactory method of contrasting urban and rural mortality is to compare the mortality at different ages. In the United States such a comparison results as follows:[2]

[1] This hypothesis never gained general acknowledgment, and in recent reports of the Registrar General of England it is abandoned. But there still exists in the United States and France, as well as in England, a close connection between mortality and density. Thus the *Supplement to the 55th Annual Report of the Registrar-General* (Part i, p. xlvii), divides the population into 15 groups, increasing in density from 138 to 19,584 persons to the square mile, and in mortality from 14.75 to 30.70 (crude death-rates; the corrected rates being respectively 12.7 and 33.0).

The American Statistics (*11th Cens., Soc. Stat. of Cities*, p. 7):

Cities of	No. of cities.	Pop. per acre.	Persons to each dwelling.	Death-rate.
10–15,000	41	2.43	5.45	17.86
15–25,000	39	2.79	5.85	19.45
25–50,000	40	4.67	6.06	21.81
50–100,000	25	9.04	6.28	22.43
100,000+	28	15.15	7.64	23.28
Total	173	8.73	7.05	22.62

The French Statistics (*Statistique sanitaire des villes de France*, 1886–90):

Cities.	Deaths per 1,000.
Under 5,000...	20.91
5,000–10,000	21.58
10,000–20,000..	25.80
20,000–100,000..	25.75
100,000–400,000...	26.65
Paris	23.69
France..	22.21

[2] Exclusive of still-births. Source, *11th Cens., Rep. on Vital and Social Statistics*, Pt. i, pp. 17–19. The registration States are New Hampshire, Vermont, Massachusetts, Rhode Island, Connecticut, New York, New Jersey, Delaware and District of Columbia. Cities of 5,000+ population in these nine districts are classed as urban, the remainder of the population as rural. The statistics of the great cities (28 in number) are less trustworthy, as their registration systems are still often defective. The metropolitan district includes the counties of New York, Kings, Queens, Richmond, Westchester (in New York), Hudson and Essex (in New Jersey), and the cities of Paterson and Passaic (*op. cit.*, appendix).

TABLE CXLIX.

DEATHS PER 1,000 POPULATION AT SPECIFIED AGES:

	Registration States.		Cities of	Metropolitan
	Rural.	Urban.	100,000+.	District (N. Y.).
All ages	15.34	22.15	21.62	24.61
Under 1 year	121.21	243.32	236.81	264.35
Under 5 years	37.12	80.40	78.00	89.25
5–15 years	4.03	6.21	5.96	6.16
15–45 years	6.89	10.80	10.71	12.07
45–65 years	15.19	26.27	26.62	31.52
65 years+	67.83	88.60	89.76	96.62
Unknown	54.98	20.65	20.76	14.72

In the United States, therefore, the mortality is heavier in the city than in the country in every period of life; and as a rule it increases in severity in the same ratio as the magnitude of the city. Only in the age-period 5–15 years is the mortality less in the metropolitan district than in the registration cities, and nowhere does it approach the more favorable rate of the rural districts.

What significance has the heavy urban mortality to the average citizen? It means that whereas the average person born in Massachusetts may expect to live 41.49 years, the average person born in Boston may expect to live only 34.89 years;[1] that while 426 out of 1000 men born in Prussia survive to the age of 50 years, only 318 out of 1000 native Berliners reach the same age;[2] that while the mean age at death is 42 years 2 months in France, it is but 28 years and 19 days in Paris;[3] that while the average duration of life in the rural population of the Netherlands is 38.12 years, in the urban population it is only 30.31 years.[4] The contrast be-

---

[1] *Op. cit.*, 484–5.

[2] Levasseur, ii, 312.

[3] Turquan, "La vie moyenne en France," *Revue Scientifique*, 24 Dec., 1892, pp. 812, 817. Cf. Lagneau, *Essai de statistique anthropologique sur la population parisienne.*

[4] *Bevolkingstafeln*, etc., *voor het Konigr. der Nederlanden*, Staat A, pp. 388, 391.

tween what is and what might be the healthfulness of city people is strikingly shown by recent computations of the Registrar-General of England, who has grouped together the districts with low mortality (14–15 deaths per 1000 population) under the term of "selected healthy districts." They embrace about one sixth of the population of England and Wales, and are chiefly rural. Manchester township, on the other hand, is taken as a fair representative of the urban and industrial population. On the basis of mortality in 1880–90, it is figured that the expectation of life at birth is as follows:[1]

Selected healthy districts...................................... 51.48 years.
Manchester township.. 28.78 "
England and Wales.. 43.66 "

That is to say, a person born in one of the "selected healthy districts" of England may expect to live, on the average, nearly twice as many years as a person born in urban Manchester! To show the social waste involved in such heavy mortality, it is sufficient to point to the fact that 100,000 males born in Manchester would be reduced to 62,326, and 100,000 females to 66,325, in *five* years; while in the healthy districts it would take fifty and forty-eight years, respectively, to bring about the same reduction.[2] Clearly, the concentration of population produces an enormous drain on the vitality of a people.

[1] *Supplement to the 55th Annual Report*, Part ii, p. cvii.

[2] *Ibid.* Comparisons of the duration of life and expectation of life, based on life tables of urban and rural populations, are now becoming abundant. They may be said to have begun with the English Friendly Societies, which furnished statistics for rural, town and city districts. Cf. Radcliffe, *Observations on the Rate of Mortality and Sickness existing among Friendly Societies* (Manchester, 1850, Colchester, 1862, Sup. Rep., 1872); F. G. P. Neison, *Contributions to Vital Statistics* (1875). On the subject of longevity, compare Levasseur (vol. ii), von Mayr, *Bevölkerungsstatistik*, and Mayo-Smith, *Statistics and Sociology*.

But it does not follow that the case is hopeless for the cities and hence for society in general, which is destined to see an increasing number of its members concentrated in cities. There is no inherent and eternal reason why men should die faster in large communities than in small hamlets, provided they are not too ignorant, too stupid, or too selfishly individualistic to coöperate in the securing of common benefits. In some degree, doubtless, the mortality of city adults must exceed that of rural adults, on account of the dangerous nature of city occupations; much of this occupational mortality is irremediable, but it should no more be charged up against the city than the mortality in railway accidents should be charged against the country. In each case the mortality is the price paid for progress; we might secure relief by abandoning both railways and machinery, and returning to the economic system of previous centuries.

But leaving aside accidental causes, it may be affirmed that the excessive urban mortality is due to lack of pure air, water and sunlight, together with uncleanly habits of life induced thereby.[1] Part cause, part effect, poverty often accompanies uncleanliness : poverty, overcrowding, high rate of mortality, are usually found together in city tenements.[2] Even though indigence be not carried to the point of starvation, it has decided effect on the production of effluvial poisons as well as on the tendency to disease of every kind.

---

[1] As Dr. Farr once said (*Sup. to 25th Annual Rep. of Reg.-Gen.*, p. xxxiii–v), " there can be no doubt that mere proximity of the dwellings of people does not necessarily involve a high rate of mortality. When any zymotic matter, such as varioline, scarlatinine or typhine finds its way into a village or street, it is more likely to pass from house to house than it is when the people are brought less frequently into contact. The exhalations in the air are thicker. But if an adequate water supply, and sufficient arrangements for drainage and cleansing are secured, as they can be by combinations in towns, the evils which now make dense districts so fatal might be mitigated. Indeed, some of the dense districts of cities are at the present day comparatively salubrious."

[2] Cf. *Report of New York Tenement House Com.*, 1894, pp. 433-4.

Thus a report of the medical officer of health for the London County Council shows that mortality (a) increases in the same ratio as the proportion of population living more than two in a room in tenements of less than five rooms (b)—

a.	b.
17.51	under 15 per cent.
19.51	15–20 " "
20.27	20–25 " "
21.76	25–30 " "
23.96	30–35 " "
25.07	35–40 " "

Still more striking was the result of the Berlin inquiry of 1885:

a. 73,000 persons living in families in tenement of 1 room.
b. 382,000 " " " " " " " 2 rooms.
c. 432,000 " " " " " " " 3 "
d. 398,000 " " " " " " " 4 "

Class (a) supplied nearly one-half of the total deaths, although it constituted only six per cent. of the population. While government cannot cure poverty, it can remedy some of the results of poverty, and that is what the government of Berlin has done in the enactment of wise building laws, which have abolished the insanitary conditions that led to such frightful mortality.[1]

That cleanliness and healthfulness may co-exist with indigence is shown by the example of the tenth ward in New York city. For it is not only by far the most densely popu-

---

[1] The death-rate in the first ward of New York in tenements where there were front and rear houses on the same lot was 61.97, while it was 29.03 in houses, of the same ward, standing singly on a lot. (Report of *Ten. House Com. of 1894*, p. 33.) In an English city the death-rate was 37.3 in districts which contained 50 per cent. of the back-to-back houses, as against 26.1 in districts containing no such houses. In Glasgow the death-rate was 27.74 for families living in one and two rooms; 19.45 for those in three and four rooms, and 11.23 for those in five or more rooms. (Newsholme, *Vital Statistics*, 140, 155.)

lated ward in New York both as regards number of inhabitants to the acre and number of tenants to the house,[1] but it
also contained a large number of the rear tenements[2] so
scathingly denounced as death-traps by the Tenement House
Committee of 1894. Yet, notwithstanding these conditions,
the tenth ward had the extremely low death-rate of 17.14[3]
and was surpassed in healthfulness by only two wards (one a
business and the other a suburban district) out of the entire
twenty-four wards in the city.[4] This favorable death-rate was
not the result of superior economic conditions; on the contrary, the population of this ward consists almost entirely of
Russian and Polish Jews, who are among the poorest classes
of the city.   Nor was it the result of a favorable age constitution, for the tenth ward swarms with children. We may,
indeed, exclude the adults entirely, and we shall still find that
the death-rate in the tenth ward is more favorable than that
in all but three other wards of the city: the number of deaths
of children under five years of age to 1,000 living of that age
in the tenth ward was 58.32, a remarkable showing when the
rates in the other wards, running as high as 183, are taken
into consideration.[5] What, then, is the explanation of the
handsome record made by the tenth ward in the face of its
unfavorable conditions?   There is but one answer: its people are careful in the observance of sanitary laws. Being

---

[1] The density per acre was, by the census of 1890, 543; that of New York city,
59. (*Social Stat. of Cities*, 11.) The density of the tenement-house population
of New York was 103, that of the tenth ward, 622 (*Report of the Tenement
House Committee of 1894*, pp. 23-4). The average number of tenants to a house
was 57.2 in the tenth ward, 34 in the entire city (*Ibid.*, p. 25).

[2] Cf. Table A, p. 274 of the *Report*.

[3] The statistics all refer to the year 1893.

[4] *Ibid.*, p. 25.

[5] *Ibid.*, Table B, p. 278. The average rate for the whole city was 76.6. The
rate for London in 1891 was 66.4, in England, 59, and in the rural county of
Hereford, 39.2. (*Registrar-General's Report*, p. xliii.)

Hebrews, they observe the strict Mosaic laws regarding cleanliness, the cooking of food, habits of eating, drinking, etc.

This illustration is sufficient to show that the most difficult problem connected with the health of cities is not incapable of solution. Personal cleanliness in the home has become more and more a subject of legislation in the way of stringent building laws[1] and proceedings for the condemnation of old tenements. All the great cities now have laws regulating the proportion of the building-lot that must remain unbuilt (*i. e.* the amount of court space), the height of buildings, their construction, the size of rooms, height of ceilings, sanitary appliances and methods of artificial lighting. Where such regulations cannot be enforced on account of the age and situation of the buildings, the buildings have been condemned and demolished by public authority, as instance the British Housing of the Working Classes Act of 1890 (53 and 54 Victoria, ch. 70, sec. 21) which provided for the destruction of the fearfully unhealthy "back-to-back" houses, and the New York Law of 1895 (chapter 567, sec. 7) which provided for the condemnation of the equally insanitary rear tenements and other disease-breeding structures. The length to which sanitary legislation may go in order to prevent the city from becoming a "pest-house" is to be observed in the measures taken against overcrowding. Thus, the New York Law of 1895 (ch. 567, sec. 10) makes it mandatory upon the Board of Health of New York city to see that at least 400 cubic feet of air shall be afforded to each adult and 200 to each child occupying a room in tenement houses with insufficient ventilation. The recent movement toward

---

[1] According to the New York Tenement House Committee of 1894 (*Report*, p. 62), the New York building laws, as regards tenement-houses and dwellings for the poor, are "superior to any that prevail elsewhere." But they are not strictly enforced.

the building of model tenement houses, which has assumed large proportions in New York city, is another step in the direction of preventing overcrowding. The possibilities of progress toward healthfulness which are afforded by such improvements in the housing of the people, are demonstrated by the mortality statistics of the Peabody tenements in London. In these buildings population is very dense,—751 to the acre as compared with 58 for all London,—and the age distribution is less favorable to low mortality than is that of the city at large. But the death-rate in the Peabody buildings (1886–89) was 18.6 per 1000, as compared with 19.6 for London, 25.6 for the central districts, and 26.9 for the eastern districts of London.[1] Even more encouraging is the reduction in infant mortality (deaths of infants under one year to 1000 births) :

	1887.	1889.	1891.	1893.
Peabody buildings	141	127	134	126
London	188	141	154	164
Central districts	175	151	177	181
Eastern districts	172	146	161	175

While in other groups of population the infant mortality increased from 1889 on, it slightly diminished in the model tenements. The housing of the working classes is therefore one of the most urgent duties of cities to themselves.

It has often been objected to the policy of demolition and reconstruction that new slums are created as fast as the old ones are abolished. The Royal Commission on the Housing of the Working Classes in 1884 reported that "where the demolitions are so extensive that the people have to depart, then new slums are created." Since workmen must and will live near their work, the immediate effect of any considerable demolition of their dwellings is the overcrowding of the

[1] Newsholme, "The Vital Statistics of Artisan Block-Dwellings," in *Proceedings* of the 8th Inter. Cong. of Hygiene, Budapest, 1894, vii, 430.

neighboring houses; and it is only by the enforcement of stringent building and sanitary laws that the city can prevent the formation of new slums. The demolition of old buildings needs to be done with judgment, since it is often better policy to wait for the pressure of high rents to compel the factory to remove to the suburbs, taking the workmen with it. To the erection of model tenements in the suburbs no possible objection can be offered, and this is unquestionably the direction private philanthropy should take.[1]

There are other ways in which government may provide material remedies for personal and family uncleanliness engendered by the conditions of life in tenements; such as, for example, public baths, or still better, cheap water rates that will encourage house-owners to put bath-rooms in the tenements. Public baths is the European policy,[2] but the American policy tends rather toward cheap water rates, as is notably the case in Buffalo. As for the rest, education must be trusted to teach the city-poor proper sanitary habits. Education is no doubt a process both long and toilsome; but it is withal a hopeful process and forms the basis of modern democracy.

Outside of private dwellings of the people, the scope of private and municipal activity is less restricted. In the matter of securing light and air, it is now admitted that the provision of numerous small parks or recreation piers as

[1] The question of the housing of the working classes has given rise to an abundant literature, references to which may be found in the encyclopedias of political sciences (*e. g.*, Art. "Arbeiterwohnungen," in Schönberg's *Handbuch der Pol. Economie;* Art. "Wohnungsfrage," in Conrad's *Hdwbh.*). An excellent summary of the legislation together with a clear statement of the problem, is given in Bowmaker's little book, *The Housing of the Working Classes,* which also contains a bibliography: see also *The Housing of the Working People,* by Dr. E. R. L. Gould (8th Special Report of the U. S. Commissioner of Labor).

[2] Twenty-five parishes in London maintain 31 bathing establishments. Cf. Hartwell, in *Bul. of the Dept. of Labor,* July, 1897: "Public Baths in Europe."

breathing spaces is not a luxury, but a matter of absolute necessity to the city. Of equal or greater importance is the provision of children's play-grounds on an adequate scale. People having once realized that city life is to be the permanent lot of a majority of the inhabitants of civilized countries, it becomes the undoubted policy of their governments to make the city healthful. In line with this policy there has grown up a vast administrative system, unknown to our rural ancestors, which is charged with the inspection of workshops and the conditions under which clothing is manufactured; with the inspection of food and the prevention of adulteration, etc. Perhaps the most important single factor in the reduction of the death-rate in New York city has been the reduction of infant mortality brought about by a rigid inspection of the milk supply and the encouragement of the use of sterilized milk.[1] As will shortly appear, the widest divergence of rural and urban mortality occurs in infancy; hence all measures designed to affect infant mortality favorably are to be energetically promoted. The medical inspection of children in the public schools and the care taken to isolate contagious diseases are also factors in the reduction of the city death-rate.[2] Finally, the modern Babylons are endeavoring to secure health for their residents by improving methods of communication between their business centres and residential outskirts. The London County Council, as Dr. Albert Shaw has observed, is giving more attention, if possible, to efforts to induce the railroads to improve their suburban morning and evening train service for workingmen. and to develop all parts of London's underground, surface and suburban transit systems, than it is to dealing directly

---

[1] *Reports of the Board of Health of New York City, passim.*

[2] The decrease in the New York death-rate from contagious diseases for the first half of the year was 3.17 per cent. in 1894, 2.23 in 1895, 2.07 in 1896, and 1.49 in 1897.

with the housing question.[1]   This subject will engage discussion in a subsequent chapter.

Considering the effort devoted to improving the healthfulness of cities, one would naturally expect a diminution of their death-rates in recent years, and of course such a diminution is familiar to all. In a preceding chapter a table was given showing the progress made in the capital and other cities of Sweden. In England the gradual approximation of the urban to the rural death-rate is shown in the following percentages from the Registrar-General's *Reports* of 1891 (p. lvii) and 1893 :

	Urban sanitary districts.	Rural	Deaths in town to 100 in country.
1851-60	24.7	19.9	124
1861-70	24.8	19.7	126
1871-80	23.1	19.0	122
1881-90	20.3	17.3	117
1893	20.2	17.4	116

Like the Swedish rate, these are the crude death-rates, in the calculation of which age and sex are neglected ; but it is legitimate to use crude rates in comparison as regards time, since in any given place the age-distribution is not subject to great change. Compare these rates with those given by Süssmilch[2] more than a century ago, rates which continued until the middle of the present century :

Rural	25
Small towns	31
Large cities	36
Capital cities	40+

Within a period of twenty-five years, London reduced its death-rate from 50 to 25, thereby increasing the average

---

[1] Testimony before the N. Y. Tenement House Com. of 1894, in *Report*, p. 373.

[2] *Die göttl. Ordnung*, 1761, i, 79–91.

length of life from 25 to 37 years. New York city has also made some progress in the last 40 years:[1]

Deaths per 1,000.

1856–65	32.19
1866–75	29.77
1876–85	26.32
1886–95	25.18
1896	21.52

In the introduction of enlightened sanitary methods we should expect the largest cities to lead the way. How effectually they have met their obligations may be ascertained by a review of the mortality statistics of the Germanic countries. Within a century Vienna has reduced her death-rate from 60 in the 1000 to 23 (1886–90); the urban rate (50–53 cities), following Vienna's, was 24, while for the entire state the rate was 29.[2] Allowing for differences in age distribution, it remains true that the cities of Austria are more healthful than the rural districts. This is indicated by the relatively low infant morality in Vienna and the other cities; it being 208 per 1000 living births in Vienna, 227 in 53 cities and from 243 to 260 in the entire state.[3]

Still more instructive are the Prussian statistics. The following table covers the years 1890–91, but for the sake of comparison the mortality of each group of towns for 1880–81

---

[1] *Report of the Board of Health for year ending Dec. 31, 1896*, p. 14.

[2] Von Juraschek, "Die Sterblichkeit in den Oesterreichischen Städten," *Proceedings of the Eighth Inter. Cong. of Hygiene*, Budapest, 1894, vii, 491.

[3] *Loc. cit.*, p. 502. The urban mortality in Austria can hardly be called favorable; it is rather that the rural rate is so unfavorable. Still it demonstrates the fact that the cities in Austria can no longer be called "destroyers" of population, but are rather showing the rural districts the path toward helpfulness. In Hungary a similar condition exists, so far as we can judge from imperfect data. Dr. Thuroczy calculated the death-rates in 3,284 towns of various sizes, and found the highest rate (47) in the smallest places, and a steady decrease as the towns became larger, until a population of 40,000 was reached (27.9). After that, the rate increased slightly. (*Op. cit.*, vii, 222.)

has been added and for the 16 great cities the mortality in each age period :[1]

TABLE CL.

DEATHS PER 1000 IN EACH AGE GROUP

	16 large cities. 1880-1.	1890-1.	Cities 20,000 100,000.	Cities under 20,000.	Urban communes.	Rural communes.	Prussia.
0-15........	53.5	41.6	37.6	33.7	37.2	32.3	34.0
15-20...........	4.9	3.9	4.5	4.6	4.4	4.5	4.5
20-30...........	7.7	5.8	6.5	7.0	6.4	6.2	6.3
30-40...........	12.3	9.8	10.8	10.1	10.2	8.1	9.0
40-50........	17.2	15.2	16.2	14.5	15.2	11.4	12.9
50-60...........	26.3	24.4	26.3	23.7	24.5	20.8	22.1
60-70...........	46.9	46.8	50.2	48.7	48.5	46.7	47.3
70-80.....	99.4	99.1	107.3	103.7	103.3	105.7	104.9
80+............	210.5	221.8	229.3	227.1	226.2	230.9	229.2
All ages, 1890-91.		22.8	23.5	24.2	23.6	23.4	23.5
" 1880-81.	27.5	....	26.1	25 8	26.4	24.6	25 2

Observe, first, that the crude death-rate has decreased in the rural population only from 24.6 in 1880 to 23.4 in 1890, while the urban rate diminished in the same period from 26.4 to 23.6, and the rate of cities with population of 100,000 and upwards from 27.5 to 22.8. Obviously, it is the class of great cities that made the best showing. The inference is confirmed by an examination of the death-rate in the various age-groups, from which it appears that the great cities of Prussia have a lower death-rate than the smaller cities at every age-period except 0-15 and 40-60 years ; and lower than the rural population itself at the ages of 15-30 and 70+. In an extended comparison of mortality by age-classes in the several *Grossstädte* of Prussia and the provinces in which they are situated, it has been pointed out that among males at least one-half of the cities have as low a rate of mortality as the provinces, at the ages of 4 and 5 years, and nearly all in the period of 20-25 years; but in the later ages the cities are much more unhealthful. On the other hand, the female mortality is less in the majority of the cities

[1] Bleicher, 268-9.

at almost every age after the first three years of childhood. On the whole, the cities make the worst showing in the age-period 1–3 years, and the best in years 5–25.[1]

Somewhat similar results are yielded by the statistics of other countries. Thus, the only age-period in which the male mortality is less in the urban than in the rural population of Denmark is 10–15,[2] while Copenhagen stands above the urban population for the age-classes 5–25. As regards the mortality of females, on the other hand, the urban population leads the rural in the years 10–25, and Copenhagen has the advantage of both from 10 to 35 years, as well as in old age. In Bavaria, again, the cities make the better showing during the age-periods 10–15 and 21–30 among males, and 21–40 among females.[3] In England, the cities have the advantage of a lower rate of mortality than the rural districts during the ages 15–35 for females alone. Taking the national death-rate at each age as 100, the death-rates of selected localities will be expressed in the following figures: [4]

TABLE CLI.

I. RATIOS OF MALE DEATH-RATES.

	0–.	5–.	15–.	25–.	35–.	45–.	55–.	65–.
London............	111	103	92	106	113	115	113	106
Pleasure places	77	75	90	105	105	93	91	98
Seaside places	78	78	108	111	98	90	82	85
Manchester	139	141	124	136	152	157	153	144
Dockyard towns	104	104	111	111	109	109	96	95
Staffordshire potteries	134	101	98	101	125	148	144	132
Lancashire mfs	123	116	100	104	109	120	130	130
North collier districts.	109	128	118	89	87	91	101	106
Rural districts (450).	74	83	91	88	79	76	78	86

[1] Kuczynski, 231.

[2] And the oldest ages. See Rubin, vol. vii, p. 490, of the *Proceedings of the Eighth Inter. Cong. of Hygiene and Demography*, Budapest, 1894.

[3] Kuczynski, 214 ff.	[4] *Jour. of Stat. Soc.* (1897), 60: 65.

2. RATIOS OF FEMALE DEATH-RATES.

	0-.	5-.	15-.	25-.	35-.	45-.	55-.	65-.
London	113	100	78	89	102	108	104	101
Pleasure places	74	80	75	78	84	87	87	91
Seaside places	76	83	83	84	82	82	79	82
Manchester	141	137	111	126	143	158	159	145
Dockyard towns	105	106	100	99	100	102	93	97
Staffordshire potteries	131	94	111	119	118	118	128	129
Lancashire mf. dist	121	109	111	112	110	122	137	133
North collier districts	112	126	124	118	110	106	107	111
Rural districts (450)	72	87	105	96	86	80	82	88

These statistics will throw some light on the causes of the high rate of mortality in towns,—whether town-made, due to occupation, or brought about by the migratory movement. First, it is to be noted that the rural death-rate is below the average for England at every age for male and every age except 15–25 for female. But the urban rates (London, Manchester, Staffordshire and Lancashire) are almost invariably higher than the national rates, although in London the rates of female mortality are very little above the national average except during the first five years of age. The presence of so many domestic servants is sufficient to explain this, since the male mortality-rate is not so favorable in London, nor the female in manufacturing and mining districts. Generally speaking, the urban rate is most unfavorable in infancy, Manchester being an exception. But Manchester's excessively high rate of adult mortality is not representative even of the manufacturing cities of Northern England. There are many factors other than conditions of residence which cause the differences in mortality heretofore noted; such, for example, as the presence of many female servants in London. Hospitals and similar institutions also disturb the rates. Occupation of course exercises a very considerable influence, which may be seen in the high death-rates of Manchester and the Staffordshire potteries. According to Dr. Ogle's investigation, the lowest mortality was among the clergymen, and the highest among hotel servants, while coal miners had a lower mortality than commercial clerks, and the street hawkers, who lead a healthy outdoor life, had about the same mortality as the men engaged in the lung-destroying pottery manufacture.[1] It is obvious that statistics of occupation and mortality will aid us little. Dr. Arlidge, who has written the most authoritative book on the subject, virtually confesses that it is impossible to determine how far diseases are trade-made, and how far town-made.[2] Some influence on urban mortality is doubtless exercised by those trades in which men are subject to injuries arising from dust fumes, or from contact with poisonous substances, or from handling heavy tools and machinery. It is doubtful if indoor or sedentary labor, of itself, produces a high death-rate; social position and economic condition, on the other hand, seem to have more influence. That the high urban death-rate is not primarily due to the nature of the city trades may be inferred from the fact that the widest difference between urban and rural mortality exists among children under the age of five years. In other words, the high urban death-rate is primarily a result of high infant mortality. In the average com-

---

[1] Taking 100 as the standard, the comparative mortality in certain trades was as follows:

Clergymen	100	Printers	193
Farmers	114	Glassworkers	214
Paper-makers	129	Cutlers, scissors makers	229
Lawyers	152	File-makers	300
Coal miners	160	Costermongers, street sellers	308
Bakers	172	Earthenware makers	314
Commercial clerks	179	Hotel servants	397
Railway and road laborers	185		

Additional figures are given and discussed at some length by Professor Mayo Smith in *Statistics and Sociology*, pp. 165–7.

[2] *Hygiene, Diseases and Mortality of Occupations*, p. 33.

munity about one-fifth of all deaths are children under one year of age.[1]

Not only in England, but in Prussia (*cf.* Table CXXXIII, *ante*), France and the United States (Massachusetts, *cf.* Table CXLV), do the cities show a higher rate of infant mortality than the country. But the situation is not irremediable. Not all the evils are of a permanent nature; for example, the employment of married women in factories.[2] In addition to the lack of proper sanitation already described, the essential reason of excessive infant mortality in cities is poor nourishment. This was proved beyond question by the classical investigation of Boeckh in Berlin. A supply of pure milk, fed through non-rubber tubes, is absolutely necessary where wet-nurses are lacking; even with proper precautions the infant death-rate always increases in the summer-time when the mothers work out, and it is so much more difficult to obtain sterilized milk. That the cities

---

[1] Levasseur ii, 164. The fact will be made plainer than it has yet been made by the following figures showing how many persons out of 1,000 at the beginning of a quinquennial period will on the average survive to its end (1881–90) : [3]

	England. and Wales.	Manchester township.	Healthy districts.
0–5	751	623	827
5–	976	952	982
10–	990	970	989
15–	981	967	983
20–	974	951	977
25–	965	928	971
30–	956	903	966
35–	946	880	961
40–	933	854	954

After the age of 5 years is reached, Manchester remains for a time subject to only a slightly greater mortality than the healthy districts, although the difference increases again after the age of 35.

[2] Demonstrated by Miss Collet, " The Extent and Effects of Industrial Employment of Women," *Jour. of Stat. Soc.* (June, 1898), 61 : 219–60.

[3] *Sup. to 55th Annual Rep. of Registrar-General*, Part ii, p. cxi.

will ultimately learn how to deal with this problem, is indicated by the successful efforts of several European countries. As has already been pointed out, the Austrian cities have a lower rate of infant mortality than the rural districts; and the following statistics show that Austria does not stand alone:[1]

DEATHS OF INFANTS UNDER ONE YEAR TO 1,000 LIVING BIRTHS:

Countries.		Cities.	
Germany,	200	193 and 206 cities in 1889–92	237.0
Belgium,	166	70 cities in 1889–92	187.5
France,	166	Cities of 25,000+ in 1891–92	170.7
England,[2]	145	28 and 33 cities (80,000+) in 1891–92	163.4
Austria,	254	57 cities (12,000+) in 1889–92	238.6
Switzerland,	194	15 of the large cities in 1890–92	157.5
Netherlands,	203	12 large cities in 1891–92	195.0

In Bavaria, as was recently pointed out by Kuczynski,[3] the cities have been able to present a lower rate than the rural districts since 1882, with the exception of the years 1886 and 1893. The most favorable showing was in the provinces containing the largest cities, Munich being especially distinguished for a low rate. In Bavaria, too, the cities have a lower rate of infant mortality among the illegitimate children, than have the rural districts. Elsewhere the fact that the city illegitimate children form a larger proportion of the total number of children than is the case in the rural districts,[4] often accounts for the more unfavorable general rate of infant mortality; since illegitimate children are everywhere subject to a heavy mortality.

In Saxony the urban rate of infant mortality is elevated by a high rate in industrial Chemnitz; nevertheless, the large

[1] Silbergleit, " Kindersterblichkeit in Europ. Grossstädten," *Proceedings of Budapest Cong. of Demography*, vii, 445.

[2] In 1881–90 the rural rate was 128 as compared with an urban (78 cities) rate of 160.—*Suppl. to 55th Rep. of Registrar-General*, Pt. i, p. lxviii.

[3] P. 199.

[4] Not necessarily a larger number of illegitimates in proportion to the number of unmarried women.

cities make a more favorable showing than do the small cities.[1]

The reduction of the rates in Prussian cities in the last decade is noticeable:[2]

	1880-1.	1890-1.
Prussia	208.3	205.2
Rural	195.0	195.8
Urban	233.2	221.1
In 16 largest cities	267.0	241.7
In all cities 20,000–100,000	224.4	214.5
" " " 20,000	216.3	208.5

The infant mortality of illegitimate children increased slightly in the rural communes, while it diminished in all the cities, most of all in the great cities.

In discussing remedies for a high rate of infant mortality, it is well to bear in mind that the real excess in cities does not occur in the first week after birth or even in the first month. It really begins with the second month and reaches its maximum in the sixth month.[3] In Prussia, indeed, an in-

[1] *Zeitschrift des königl. Sächs. Statis. Bureaus,* xxxiv, 16; xl, 4, 11, 12:

TABLE CLII.

AVERAGE ANNUAL NUMBER OF DEATHS OF CHILDREN UNDER ONE YEAR TO 100 LIVING BIRTHS:

Cities of	1881–85.	1886–90.
100,000 + inhabitants	25.9	25.7
20,000–100,000	31.1	28.8
10,000–20,000	30.5	31.2
5,000–10,000	30.1	29.0
3,000–5,000	29.6	30.7
2,000–3,000	28.6	28.6
1,000–2,000	} 25.7	24.8
Under 1,000		26.1
All cities	28.55	28.05

[2] Bleicher, 267.

[3] English experience. The Registrar-General (*Sup. 55th Rep.,* Pt. ii, p. cix) makes a comparison between three cities (Preston, Leicester and Blackburn) which have a high rate of infant mortality, and three rural counties (Hereford-

fant born in the city has a better chance of living, during the first 15 or 30 days, than has a country child; of 100 children dying in first year after birth the following number died in the first 15 days:[1]

	Male.	Female.
Prussia	21.6	19.6
Rural	23.5	21.4
Urban	18.6	16.7
Cities under 20,000	20.1	18.0
" 20,000–100,000	18.3	16.6
" 100,000+	16.4	14.8

The geographical distribution of infant mortality in Prussia hardly confirms the current opinion that a high birth-rate must be accompanied by a high rate of infant mortality; the Rhine cities have the former without the latter. On the other hand, in Massachusetts, as we saw in Table CXLV, the rate of infant mortality moves hand in hand with the birth-rate. But the infant mortality is probably as much cause as

shire, Wiltshire, Dorsetshire) which have a low rate. Taking the latter's rates as 100, the following figures express the urban rates:

Age in days.	Ratio.	Age in months.	Ratio.
0	120	0	127
1	164	1	221
2	123	2	301
3	102	3	308
4	95	4	303
5	109	5	373
6	136	6	337
Weeks.		7	279
0	123	8	325
1	164	9	292
2	183	10	278
3	197	11	275

P. cx.—"In the first week of life the town rate exceeds the rural rate by 23 %; 2d wk., 64 %; 3d wk., 83 %; 4th wk., 97 %. First month, 27 %; 2d mo., 121 %; 6th mo., 273 % (max.).

[1] Bleicher, *Proceedings of Budapest Congress,* vii, 477.

effect; by shortening the period of suckling and diminishing the intervals of child-bearing, it leaves a vacancy to be filled by another birth.[1]

It has been affirmed that the decrease in the death-rate, so far as it comes from a reduction of infant mortality, is no economic benefit because it merely preserves unsound bodies and minds. The fallacy of such reasoning has frequently been pointed out[2] and need not be repeated here. The smaller the infant mortality, the heavier must be the mortality in the latter years; for men must die sooner or later. The crucial point is whether the lives saved will be extended to old age or will be lost in earlier adult years as the result of weak constitutions. Dr. Ogle maintained the latter, in which event the extension of life could hardly be regarded as an unmitigated blessing. But his statistics[3] are now superseded; in the last decade, 1881–90, the English death-rate decreased for both sexes at every age-period except 65–75, clearly indicating a greater length of life. And the Prussian statistics already presented point to the same conclusion: mortality diminished at every age except among those over 80 years old.

One question still remains,—What effect, if any, have migratory movements between city and country upon the death-rates of each? We found that as a rule the urban rates were most favorable at the age 15–35 and the rural rates then most unfavorable. Many people regard this simply as a result of migration. Mr. Thomas A. Welton in an article on "Local Death-Rates in England" (from which the statistics of Table CLI are derived) assumed at the outset that if the death-rates in the age-periods 5–45, and especially 15–35,

---

[1] Newsholme, *Vital Statistics*, 57.

[2] Mayo-Smith, *Statistics and Sociology*, 179–80. Cf. Bleicher, 274.

[3] According to Dr. Ogle, the death-rate for males over 35 and for females over 45 increased between 1838–54 and 1871–81. (Cf. Mayo-Smith, *op. cit.*, p. 178.)

were depressed in London and other places attracting workers, and simultaneously raised above the national proportion in the districts supplying the bulk of such workers, his case would be made out. It was easy to prove the facts, but the assumption cannot be granted. It is quite as likely that the low urban rate at the age-period 15–35 is due to superior nourishment as to the immigration of healthy persons from the country. Ammon has compiled statistics tending to show that city workers are better fed than country workers.[1] At any rate it is a reasonable hypothesis.

In Frankfort, Germany, an attempt was made (1890–1) to compare the mortality of citizens born in the country and those born in the city itself, with the following result:[2]

TABLE CLIII.

DEATH-RATE OF FRANKFORTERS BORN.

	In the city.	Outside.
0–5	72.3	68.5
5–10	10.2	11.8
10–15	3.8	5.2
15–20	4.3	3.5
20–30	6.5	5.7
30–40	8.4	9.8
40–50	13.5	16.3
50–60	22.4	27.0
60–70	43.8	53.2
70–80	109.5	105.3
80+	224.0	251.8
All ages	25.0	14.5
Excluding children under 5 years	13.0	13.7

Clearly the influx of countrymen does not reduce the city death-rate among adults; for the outsiders have a heavier mortality at every age except 0–5, 15–30, and 70–80.

[1] *Die Gesellschaftsordnung und ihre natürlichen Grundlagen*, p. 117; *Die natürliche Auslese beim Menschen*, 123, 170.

[2] Bleicher, II Heft, p. 24.

Whether they are stronger than the city-born or not, cannot be easily determined; but they certainly endure less pertinaciously the heavy draughts on vitality made by city-life, than do the city-born. What John Graunt wrote 200 years ago seems true to-day: "As for unhealthiness, it may well be supposed that although seasoned bodies may and do live near as long in London as elsewhere, yet newcomers and children do not."[1]

To recapitulate: The tendency to marry and the fruitfulness of marriage are but slightly affected by the concentration of population. The theory of population now accepted makes economic and social position the determining factors, rather than the degree of density of population. Hence marriage and birth rates differ in cities of the same magnitude according to the prevailing industry and occupation.

Death-rates, however, vary with the degree of agglomeration of population. But there is no inherent reason for the relatively high urban mortality except man's neglect and indifference. Recent tendencies show that the great cities are leading the way in making sanitary improvements, and in several countries, of which Bavaria is an excellent example, the large cities now make a more favorable showing as to mortality than do the other communities. This holds true even of infant mortality, which is one of the most decisive indices of a locality's healthfulness.

[1] *Bills of Mortality*, p. 90.

CHAPTER VII

THE PHYSICAL AND MORAL HEALTH OF CITY AND COUNTRY

THE field opened up in the study of death-rates is the most important and one of the most interesting yet encountered. That the townsman on the average is shorter-lived than the countryman is incontrovertibly established; and it is commonly believed that the city man is also less healthy, vigorous and capable, both physically and mentally, than the countryman. In short, cities are the site, and city life the cause, of the deterioration of the race.[1] The severest indictment is drawn by Nordau, the apostle of Degeneration: "The inhabitant of a large town, even the richest who is surrounded with the greatest luxury, is continually exposed to the unfavorable influences which diminish his vital powers far more than what is inevitable. He breathes an atmosphere charged with organic detritus; he eats stale, contaminated, adulterated food; he feels himself in a state of constant nervous excitement, and one can compare him without exaggeration to the inhabitant of a marshy district. The children of large towns who are not carried off at an early age suffer from the peculiar arrested development which Morel has ascertained in the population of fever districts. They develop more or less normally until they are 14 or 15 years of age, are up to that

---

[1] Such is the concurrence of opinion among all the writers of former generations. Says Rousseau (*Émile*, 1819, vi, 61) : " Les villes sont le gouffre de l'espèce humaine. Au bout de quelques générations, les races périssent ou dégénèrent." Similarly, Henry George (*Social Problems*, 317): "This life of the great cities is not the natural life of man. He must under such conditions deteriorate physically, mentally, morally."

time alert, sometimes brilliantly endowed, and give the highest promise. Then suddenly there is a standstill. The mind loses its facility of comprehension and the boy, who only yesterday was a model scholar, becomes an obtuse, clumsy dunce, who can only be steered with the greatest difficulty through his examinations. With these mental changes, bodily modifications go hand in hand." [1] And it is in the remarkable growth of great cities that Nordau finds the explanation of the equally striking increase in the number of degenerates in the last half century. [2]

Nordau, however, is an extremist, whose opinion many people regard as too pessimistic, not to say fanciful. Let us therefore quote the testimony of a sane, conservative English physician,—Dr. G. B. Longstaff, one of the best-known statisticians in England: "That the town life is not as healthy as the country is a proposition that cannot be contradicted. . . . The narrow chest, the pale face, the weak eyes, the bad teeth, of the town-bred child are but too often apparent. It is easy to take an exaggerated view either way, but the broad facts are evident enough; long life in towns is accompanied by more or less degeneration of race. The great military powers of the continent know this well enough, and it may be surmised that with them agricultural protection is but a device to keep up the supply of country-bred recruits." [3]

Finally, the theory of city degeneracy is met with in the proverb that one cannot find a London cockney whose father was born in the city, and in the oft-quoted assertion that no business houses can be found in the city whose members have resided in the same city more than one or two

---

[1] *Degeneration*, Trans. from 2d Ger. Ed. (N. Y., 1895), p. 35.

[2] *Ibid.*, p. 36.

[3] *Jour. of Stat. Society*, 1893, p. 416.

generations.[1] The belief that city families die out early is widespread, and is expressed in nearly all literatures. Its most impressive statement has been formulated by Dr. George Hansen in his oft-abused and oft-praised work, *Die Drei Bevölkerungsstufen,*[2] which is essentially an argument for the preservation of a peasantry or agricultural class, not only as a military measure, but as the fundamental condition of national vigor and well-being. Hansen's argument for the superiority of country-bred people embraces a considerable number of propositions that require critical examination, the principal ones being the following:

(1) The city-born reside in the poorest quarters of the city; the country-born in the wealthiest (p. 147).

(2) The city-born predominate in the lowest occupations and the lowest social classes (p. 150).

(3) The city-born contribute an unduly large proportion to the class of degenerates (criminals, lunatics, suicides, etc., pages 196–202).

(4) The cities have a low rate of natural increase, often indeed a deficit of births (p. 28).

(5) The city population always consists of at least as many country-born as city-born (p. 27).

(6) The typical city class, the middle class or *bourgeoisie,* is incapable of self-perpetuation (p. 27).

The fact that the poorest districts of great cities often

---

[1] Thus Cantlie, author of *Degeneration among Londoners,* "after prolonged and careful search could not find a single person whose ancestors, from their grandparents downwards, had been born and bred in London."—Strahan, *Marriage and Disease,* p. 31. Dr. Pratt, in a paper before the American Social Science Association in 1887, accepted the statement as authoritative. *Cf.* also Booth, *Life and Labor of the People,* iii, 65: "There is a strong conviction in the minds of many, incapable however of strict verification, that Londoners tend to die out after the second or, at least, the third generation "

[2] Ein Versuch, die Ursachen für das Blühen und Altern der Völker nachzuweisen, München, 1889.

contain the largest percentage of city-born has led other writers than Hansen into serious error. From this error even the great work of Charles Booth *(Life and Labor of the People of London)* is not free; thus, his investigators found that while 34.3 per cent. of the population of all London in 1881 were countrymen (*i. e.*, born in the United Kingdom outside of London), only 24.2 per cent. of East London's population were countrymen. For the other districts the percentages were as follows: North, 44.4, West, 37.3, South, 34.1, Central, 30.4. North and West London, it is needless to say, are the wealthy residential quarters, while East London is the home of the "submerged tenth." Bethnal Green in East London is one of the poorest quarters in the city, and it contained 12.5 per cent. of countrymen; while London City, the heart of the metropolitan business and commercial interests, contained 39.5 per cent.[1] But it is a mistake to infer off-hand, as do Mr. Booth's investigator and Hansen, that the countrymen constitute the wealthy class and the city-born the proletariat.

In the first place, a large portion of the countrymen residing in the wealthy districts are servants, janitors, etc., a class which, as will shortly appear, is recruited almost entirely from the country. Another large portion are clerks and other subordinate employees. But even were the rich themselves largely of outside birth, it remains to be shown that they are rural rather than urban-born. Take the newcomers in Friedrichstadt, the business centre of Berlin, for instance; they consist not only of provincials but also of foreigners, and the latter are more likely than not to be city-born, for as a previous chapter showed, long-distance migrants are more likely to be urban than rural. And in thickly settled countries, a large part of the short-distance migration originates

---

[1] Booth, *op. cit.*, iii, 121–3.

from the smaller cities and towns. The Leipzig census of 1885, for example (Theil, II, p. 7, ff), showed that fully one-half (50.6 per cent.) of the immigrants had been born in places of 2000+.

But the main reason, after all, why the city-born predominate in the poorest quarters of Berlin, London, New York, etc., is that the poorer classes of immigrants have so many children, who, of course, are classed as natives of the city. The slums of these cities were originally created by the flocking in of the most degraded peasant classes, who have married and propagated their kind until they now figure in the statistics as natives of the city, the product of urban conditions, the urban proletariat. The fact is amply demonstrated by the Vienna statistics, which show that the central and wealthy districts contain a larger percentage of immigrants than the outer districts when the children of the immigrants are credited to Vienna; but when the children are credited to the father's birthplace (*i. e.*, place of settlement), it appears that the immigrants predominate in the outer and poorer districts of the city.[1] In Frankfort, again, the heaviest immigration is not into the wealthier, but into the poorer districts.[1]

---

[1] Rauchberg, " Der Zug nach der Stadt," in *Stat. Mon.*, xix, 162. The percentage of immigrants was as follows according to place of—

	Birth.	Settlement.
Central districts	57.35	63.23
Outer districts	50.53	67.10

It is not always true, as Hansen assumes, that the center of a city is its richest and most prosperous part; in fact, the reverse holds true in most American cities, it being the well-to-do classes who can afford to live in the suburbs at a distance from their shops and offices. Even in some of the continental cities, where the storekeeper usually resides over his store, and the laborer near the factory, this relation is beginning to disappear. In Frankfort, for example, the inner city, where the business is transacted, receives the largest immigration, but this does not prove the truth of Hansen's theory that the immigrants step at once into the most important positions, for, as a matter of fact, the leading business men (judged by their wealth) dwell in the outer districts. The following table show-

Even more conclusive evidence that the wealthy classes are not to be identified with the country-born is furnished by the statistics of occupation and social rank, contrary to the interpretation imposed upon them by Hansen. The Berlin census of 1885 shows that the percentage of native Berliners was largest in manufacturing and trade, and smallest in personal service. But the class of casual laborers also contained a large proportion of the city-born, especially among females. The summary is as follows:

TABLE CLIV.

SHOWING THE REPRESENTATION OF NATIVE BERLINERS IN THE CITY'S INDUSTRIES, 1885.

			Born in Berlin.			Per cent.
		Per cent. of		Per cent of		of all
	Total.	census total.	Males.	all males.	Females.	females.
Population, 1885........	557,222	42.4	265,184	42.0	292.042	42.8
Dependents..........	391,819	60.6	157,781	82.5	234,038	51.4
In all occupations	165,407	24.74	107,403	24.31	58,004	25.57
(1-24) Industries	112,317	29.53	80,321	27.59	31,996	35.87
(25) Personal services...	7,683	8.78	1,653	10.68	6,030	8.72
(26) Casual laborers	20,428	26.51	11,791	22.37	8,637	35.5
(27-38) Liberal Professions *a*	10,993	16.01	8,809	14.33	2,184	30.75
(39) Free income	11,808	26.5	4,696	21.8	7,202	30.7
(40) Not given.........	2,088	20.4	133	18.5	1,955	20.6
a Professions, without military	10,011	20.9	7,827	19.3	2,184	30.75

ing the distribution of the male immigrants to the city in a single year (1891) will make this clear (Bleicher, II, p. 37, and I, pt. 2, table 35):

	Immigration.	Population.	Am't of income tax per taxpayer.
	1891.	1890.	Marks.
Old city	25.18	15.24	8.8
New city	25.92	19.69	12.1
Southwest	7.39	4.22	13.1
West end.....................	2.17	3.56	11.2
Northwest	3.59	6.78	16.4
North end....................	6.94	11.14	16.8
Northeast	8.55	12.19	12.8
East end	5.96	7.62	13.5
Bornheim	2.90	5.90	8.4
Sachsenhausen-Inner............	5.12	6.19	9.2
" " -Outer............	6.8	7.47	14.3
	100.0	100.0	12.0

The most wealth is in the Northwest district and North end, where immigration is proportionately the lowest.

EXPLANATIONS.

The source of all the Berlin statistics is the census of 1885: *Die Bevölkerungs-, Gewerbe-, und Wohnungsaufnahme vom 1 Dez. 1885 in der Stadt Berlin*, im Auftrage, etc., herausgegeben **von** Richard Boeckh, Berlin, 1890 *ff.* It is impracticable to refer to volume and page, as computations have been made from many different places. . . . The numbers in parenthesis refer to the official classification of occupations. The term "casual laborers" is a translation of "Arbeiter ohne nähere Angabe;" "free-income" of "Ohne Beruf," most of this class being *rentiers* and *pensionäre* or students (table CLV). The 40th group, "Ohne Berufangabe," contains about 1,000 persons in hospitals, prisons, etc. The other German expressions translated are as follows: Entrepreneurs or undertakers, "Selbsständige:" employees, "Abhängige." Each of the 40 classes of occupations contains several minor groups which ought to be mentioned. The entire classification is admirable.

TABLE CLV.

OCCUPATIONS OF BERLINERS, 1885.

		Males.		Females.	
		Total.	Percentage thereof Berlin-born.	Total.	Percentage thereof Berlin-born.
I. Industries (1-24):					
1.	Trade (19)	60,494	28.34+ [1]	13,531	29.55— [1]
2.	Clothing, etc. (15)	36,516	15.83—	65,005	35.88+
3.	Metal working (7)	32,122	37.62+	505	52.87+
4.	Wood working (13)	31,973	32.15+	664	48.78+
5.	Building trades (16)	27,978	16.53—	25	44.00+
6.	Food supplies (14)	18,562	18.92—	1,128	32.27+
7.	Transportation (22)	15,456	15.64—	210	29.52+
8.	Paper and leather (12)	13,324	41.03+	1,703	61.59+
9.	Machinery, tools, etc. (8)	12,050	36.93+	162	45.67+
10.	Hotels and restaurants (23)	11,586	13.38—	1,477	14.15—
11.	Printing (17)	9,178	55.15+	451	59.42+
12.	Textile (11)	7,405	42.63+	3,739	50.26+
13-15.	Clay and stone, chemical, heat and light (6, 9, 10)	6,753	31.9+	162	37.6+
16-20.	Agr., gardening, fishing, mining (1-5)	2,985	18.00—	208	30.0+
21.	Art industries (18)	2,715	60.11+	64	39.06+
22.	Insurance (20)	1,444	23.62—	1	0.—
23.	Peddling (21)	102	16.68—	62	12.90—
24.	Amusements (24)	513	31.35+	108	22.22—
	Total (1-24)	291,156	27.59	89,205	35.87
II. Liberal professions (27-38) total		61,516	14.33—	7,101	30.75+
1.	Army and navy (37)	20,607	4.79—	0	0.—
2.	Public adminis. (34, 35, 38)	13,124	14.00—	78	19.2—
3.	Rys., telegraphs, post (27, 28)	11,719	15.5—	103	22.3—
4.	Teachers (30)	3,802	17.26—	3,648	39.09+
5.	Arts (31)	3,628	41.46+	1,400	33.85+
6.	Legal prof. (36)	3,069	23.50+	0	0.—
7.	Literary prof. (32)	3,003	27.93+	78	25.64+
8.	Medical prof. (29)	2,035	18.08—	1,790	12.96—
9.	Clerical prof. (33)	529	17.20—	4	0.—
III. Rentiers (39)		10,938	24.0—	14,280	32.8+
	Students (39)	8,292	17.0—	1,117	24.08—

[1] The plus and minus signs in these columns indicate that the percentage is above or below the average in all occupations.

Table CLV presents in a clearer light the facts we are seeking. A few words will suffice to state the position of the 226,885 women engaged in gainful occupations in Berlin in 1885. As shown by the table 89,205 are found in the general industries, and the table also shows that the industries that absorb nine-tenths of these are the clothing-manufacture, trade (store-keeping or clerking), and the textile industries. Nearly as many (73,335) are found in personal service, and the remainder are chiefly classed as laborers (24,336) or as living on free income, the latter including *rentiers* and students. A few are also in the literary professions. The percentage of Berlin-born women in these eight groups is as follows:

Servants 8.72
Students 24.08
Trade.. 29.55
Liberal professions 30.75
Rentiers... 32.8
Laborers 35.5
Clothing manufactures 35.88
Textile industries 50.26

The largest percentage of native Berlin women is found in the lowest skilled, worst-paid industries. Even the domestic servants, who are chiefly immigrants, enjoy an economic condition superior to that of the poor sewing-women engaged in the ready-made clothing business; nor are they much poorer than the factory operatives in the textile industry. In trade, moreover, the native women are more often clerks than employers, their percentage in the two ranks being respectively 39.4 and 22.7.[1] Similarly, in the clothing manufacture: undertakers, 11,507 out of 36,682 or 30.4 per cent.; employees 11,783 out of 28,323 or 41.6 per cent.

[1] Of the 7,948 female undertakers, 6,146 are immigrants and 1,802 Berlin-born; of the 5,583 employees, 3,386 are immigrants and 2,197 Berlin-born.

Indeed, the social rank of the native Berlin women in the whole group of industries 1–24 is inferior to that of the immigrants (Table CLIV). Of the 89,205 women in these occupations nearly one-half are employees, and of these the Berlin-born constitute 42.5 per cent., although they form but 30 per cent. of the entrepreneurs and only 25.6 per cent. of all women actively engaged in work. Among the employees, again, there is little encouragement for the city woman; 5,940 of the employees are classed as salaried officers or superintendents, but as 4,726 of them are in mercantile businesses, it is plain that most of them are nothing but clerks. Nearly 25,000 are ordinary laborers, of whom the city-born constitute 35.5 per cent.—an ominous sign of a city proletariat.

Let us now confine our attention to the male population. If we add to Table CLV the domestic servants and casual laborers, and then arrange the percentages according to maxima and minima of the Berlin-born, we shall have these two groups:

TABLE CLVI.

Above the average (24-31).		Below the average.	
Art industries	60.11	Servants	10.68
Printing	55.15	Hotel and restaurant	13.38
Textile industries	42.63	Transportation	15.64
Arts	41.46	Clothing manufactures	15.83
Paper and leather	41.03	Building trades	16.53
Metal working	37.62	Peddling	16.68
Machinery, etc.	36.93	Students	17.01
Wood working	32.15	Teachers	17.26
Chemical industries, etc.	31.9	Agr., gardening, etc.	18.0
Amusements	31.35	Food supplies	18.92
Trade	28.34	Lib. professions (excluding military)	19.3
Literary professions	27.93	Casual laborers	22.37
		Legal professions	23.50
		Insurance	23.62
		Rentiers and pensionärs	24.00

The foregoing table would seem to be a sufficient answer to the pessimism of those who regard the London "submerged tenth" as a type of the city-dweller. The industries in which more than the average proportion of Berlin-born men are occupied are, almost without exception, the skilled trades; in fact, the very highest percentage is found in the art industry. On the other hand, the industries filled with immigrants are the low-skilled ones, or trades requiring muscular strength more than mental ability. To this general rule there is an exception in favor of the liberal professions, which in most cases contain an unusually large percentage of immigrants. This is to be expected; the cities are the centers of art and culture, and not only attract to themselves from the most distant quarters of the land students in search of artistic and professional training, but retain the best of them after the schooling has been completed.

Neither table makes the distinction between entrepreneur and employee for the men engaged in industry. The native Berliners apparently make a better showing among the employees than among independent workers. It should be remarked, however, that most of the latter, although entrepreneurs, are not employers, and under modern conditions may not be so well situated as employees—especially the employees of the higher class (designated as *angestellte Beamten*, or salaried officers, in the tables). The classification of entrepreneurs (males), according to number of men employed, results as follows:

	Total.	Per cent. thereof Berlin-born.
With no employees	56,046	21.2
" 1–5 "	22,424	23.9
" more than 5 employees	6,021	31.2
Total	84,491	22.7

This shows that in the higher ranks of entrepreneurs the

native Berliners are stronger than they are among the employees of all classes, except apprentices.   At the same time, it must be noted that this superior showing of the city-born among large employers is confined principally to store-keeping, inn-keeping and the clothing manufacture; it exists in a small degree, if at all, in the skilled trades.

It can hardly be said that the Berlin statistics favor Hansen's contention, and even his own manipulations of them have failed to put his cause in a good light.   The recent Austrian statistics[1] are even less useful to Hansen's theory:

TABLE CLVII.

BIRTH-PLACE.

	Males.	Vienna. Females.	Both sexes.	Elsewhere in Austria.	Foreign countries.	Total.	Percentage of females in the group.
Undertakers	27.5	42.3	34.4	49.2	16.4	100	46.8
Salaried employees.	35.7	44.5	36.7	47.8	15.5	100	8.5
Artisans	30.4	44.4	34.4	57.4	8.2	100	28.5
Unskilled laborers..	23.6	13.4	21.1	66.4	12.5	100	24.4
Servants	16.8	12.2	12.4	73.3	14.3	100	94.3
All occupations....	30.2	42.7	34.2	54.1	11.7	100	31.4
Dependents	83.8	54.1	63.3	30.1	6.6	100	68.9
Total population...	44.0	45.4	44.7	45.2	10.1	100	51.5

The term " undertakers " here designates all persons carrying on independent enterprises, whether they employ other labor or not.   The class of higher employees (Angestellte) includes approximately all persons on a salary, *i. e.*, not only public officials, but also the superintending *personnel* of commerce and industry.   The artisans (qualificierte Arbeiter) are the skilled laborers, the workmen of special training or of those engaged in a particular occupation.   The unskilled laborers (Taglöhner) include other workmen receiving wages, and the servants (Dienende für persönliche Zwecke) are those who render personal service.[2]   The dependents include all

[1] Rauchberg, *Stat. Mon.*, xix, 639, 625.   The military is excluded, except from the last line.

[2] *Ibid.*, 164.

persons not engaged in a gainful occupation. Inasmuch as this class is in large part composed of children, few of whom are immigrants, it contains a large percentage of native Viennese.

It must be admitted that hard-and-fast lines between social ranks cannot be drawn. Such will apply especially to the distinction between artisans and other laborers. But the Austrian statisticians are among the acutest in the world and may be trusted to have done their best. What the table shows conclusively is that the native Viennese are the leaders in industry. While they constitute 34.2 per cent. of all occupations, they form a larger percentage of the higher ranks, and only 21.1 per cent. of the unskilled laborers and 12.4 of the domestic servants. On the other hand, the immigrants from other parts of Austria average higher in the two lower ranks and do not hold their own in the two higher ranks. Their largest percentage is in the class of servants, of which they form nearly 75 per cent. The real foreigners, on the other hand, show a different grouping; while their percentage in the higher ranks exceeds their general average (11.71), the same is true, though in a less degree, of the two lower ranks, while a deficiency is shown in the ranks of artisans. The probability is that the lower ranks are filled with Hungarians, who have but a short distance to travel, while the contributions to the upper classes come from a long distance, which exercises a selective influence in favor of the highest talent. If Hansen's theory of urban degeneration were true, we should see the largest percentage of native Viennese in the ranks of day laborers and servants; instead of which, we find the largest percentage among the higher employees. It may be observed, however, that Vienna's showing is less favorable when we separate the sexes, for it appears that among the native men there is a greater proportion of unskilled laborers and servants than among the native women.

The male servants, however, form but six per cent. of all servants (*vide* the last column in table CLVII), and the females but a fourth of the unskilled laborers, so that the general total is not much altered; but the percentage of native men among independent workers (27.5) now falls below the general average (30.2). It is singular that the native Viennese women should have gained so much more ground than the men, so that they have a larger percentage in the higher ranks and a smaller percentage in the lower ranks than do the native men.

The distribution of the *Berufsthätigen*, shows the foregoing facts in another light: [1]

TABLE CLVIII.

BIRTH-PLACE.

	Vienna.	Elsewhere in Lower Austria.	Elsewhere in Austria.	Foreign countries.	Total.
Undertakers	311	277	240	386	285
Higher employees	109	60	87	126	95
Artisans	516	464	490	320	474
Unskilled laborers	17	30	31	27	26
Servants	47	169	152	141	120
	1,000	1,000	1,000	1,000	1,000

Of all the native Viennese engaged in gainful occupations, 52 per cent. are in the artisan class, while the general average is only 47.4. In the ranks of independent workers and higher employees, the percentage of native Viennese also exceeds the general average, which in turn is higher than that among the persons born elsewhere in Austria. The foreign countries, as might be expected, have the largest percentage in the two higher ranks. In the two lower ranks, the native Viennese have 6.4 per cent., the lower Austrians 19.9 per cent., those born in other parts of Austria 18.3 per cent. and the foreigners 16.8 per cent. The natives of Vienna

[1] Rauchberg, xix, 165.

contribute far less than the immigrants to the lower social classes.

Detailed statistics published by the city of Frankfort do but confirm the deductions already made. Frankfort's fame rests upon her great financial and commercial interests, and it is noteworthy that the percentage of outsiders among her merchants and bankers is exceedingly low.[1]

So much for the comparative industrial ability of the city-born and the immigrants. Such a comparison cannot give a complete answer to the allegation that the native city element is pushed to the wall by the country-born, for the men whom our statistics designate as "natives" may be the sons or grandsons of immigrants.[2] Nevertheless, it shows that the first generation of natives, at least, has not deteriorated; on the contrary, they hold their own against the newcomers in Vienna, Frankfort and Berlin. Finally, the lower ranks are not filled up with the city element, as Hansen's theory in any form would demand. The only approach to it is in the case

---

[1] Bleicher, p. 14. Taking the adult male population (over 15 years) of 1890, it is found that to every 100 born in Frankfort there were the following numbers born elsewhere:

Agriculture, gardening, fishing	66.3
Trade and communication	291.2
Industry	421.3
Personal service and unskilled labor	666.5
All others	417.3
Total	374.7

The largest proportion of the immigrants is found among the servants and day laborers, and the smallest among persons engaged in trade (excepting the unimportant agricultural group). In the higher branches of commerce the proportion of immigrants is still lower, being 240.3 among merchants generally, and 163 among bankers, commission agents, etc. In industry and manufactures, moreover, the higher grades are filled with native Frankforters.

[2] It is however by the use of similar statistics (Berlin!) that Hansen attempts to prove the truth of his contention that the country-born preponderate in the higher classes of city occupations and in the higher ranks of each occupation, while the city-born fill the lower ranks (cf. *Die drei Bevölkerungsstufen*, 150 ff).

of women in Berlin, and female labor is in so unsettled a condition in modern industry that too much weight should not be laid on this fact. It should also be mentioned that if the immigrants seem to obtain a relatively large number of the higher positions among the employed, they are helped toward this end by the immigration of able men from other cities. The best ability trends toward the capital,—and not all the best ability by any means comes from the rural districts. On the whole, it seems reasonable to deny the truth of the generalizations made by Mr. Smith on basis of inferences drawn from East London,—that the great city tends to create a "submerged tenth" of the industrially inefficient, pauper and criminal type. Mr. Smith's statistics are too fragmentary to have weight against the complete returns of the cities of Vienna, Berlin and Frankfort.[1]

There is in fact much to be said in favor of the opposite view, that the migration of countrymen to the city actually injures the city populations and threatens the existence of city civilization. This is especially true of American cities so far as regards a large class of European immigrants. But here as elsewhere discrimination is imperatively demanded. There are few who will affirm that the migration of American country youth to the cities is an evil, so far as the cities themselves are concerned. (Whether or not it works injury to the nation or the race will be considered later.) The youths of the farms and villages in America have not been brought up to an inferior standard of life, and while they may

---

[1] According to Mr. Smith, the native Londoners constituted only 30 per cent. of the policemen, who receive high wages and stand for the higher class of labor, while they amounted to 56 per cent. of the army recruits, who are said to come from the unemployed. Forming 46 per cent. of London's adult male population, they constituted 59 per cent. of her criminals (prisoners in 1888), 60 per cent. of her semi-paupers (those on the lists of the Charity Organization Society), and 70 per cent. among the casual dock laborers, the residuum of all occupations (Booth, *op. cit.*, III, 82–90, 142).

not have enjoyed all the material comforts that are the lot of the city-bred, they certainly find no difficulty in acquiring a taste for them, and are therefore quickly assimilated in the city population. With European peasants the question is different, and it may be surmised that their migration is causing some trouble in European as well as in American cities.

Closely related with the question of industrial efficiency is that of degeneracy. The fragmentary London statistics presented by Mr. Smith (*supra*, p. 382) indicate that Londoners contribute more than their share both to pauperism and to crime; but the continental statistics demonstrate that the countrymen contribute chiefly to the ranks of pauperism. Vienna, Leipzig, Frankfort, and Magdeburg have collected poor-relief statistics which have been carefully edited by eminent statisticians.[1] They all show that the proportion of paupers in these cities is relatively greater among those born outside than those born within the city. Even when one considers the difference in age classification, the inference holds. In Frankfort in 1885, the percentage of paupers to the total population in each age-group was largest among the immigrants, except for women of 55 to 65 years of age.[2] The number of paupers to 1,000 of each sex of all ages was as follows:

	Male.	Female.
Born in Frankfort	14.82	18.53
" elsewhere	43.78	35.04
Paupers in the population over 26 years of age:		
Born in Frankfort	46.58	51.70
" elsewhere	57.10	47.96

[1] For Vienna: v. Inama-Sternegg, *Die persönlichen Verhältnisse der Wiener Armen nach den Materialen des Vereins gegen Verarmung und Bettelei*, Vienna, 1892; for Leipzig, Heft xx of the *Mitteilungen des Statistischen Amtes der Stadt Leipzig*: A. Lehr, *Individualstatistik der öffentlichen Armenpflege in Leipzig*, 1886; for Frankfort, Bleicher, *op. cit.*, i, pt. 2, ch. 14; for Magdeburg, Silbergleit, *Armenstatistik*, a reprint from the *Verwaltungsberichte, 1892–3, der Stadt Magdeburg.*

[2] Bleicher, *op.cit.*, 213, and table 38.

While pauperism is apparently greater among the adult native women than among the immigrants, this simply results from the fact that among the immigrants those age-classes which are least subject to poverty are very much more strongly represented than the older groups where poverty makes its inroads. The evidence is decisive, notwithstanding the fact that the children of the poorer immigrants are classed with the native population.[1]

As regards crime, the statistics of birthplace are too imperfect to warrant any dogmatic conclusions. It is said[2] that of the arrests in New York and Paris in 1865, 68 and 70 per cent., respectively, were of persons born outside the city. The percentage of immigrants in the total adult population was probably about the same in New York, probably smaller in Paris.

In 1873, of 2,224 prostitutes counted in Berlin, 44.5 per cent. were natives of the city;[3] at the time, the proportion of Berlin-born women in the entire population of the same age was probably somewhat smaller. Notwithstanding these imperfect figures, representing but a fraction of Berlin prostitution, it is generally believed that prostitutes come principally from the country.

Hansen's point that the cities have a small natural increase or none at all is easily disproved. Dr. Kuczynski, whose *Zug nach der Stadt* is essentially a critique of the Hansen theory, shows that none of the larger cities in Germany has had a deficit of births for a five-year period in the last quarter century.[4] In several years the ratio of births to

---

[1] It need not be said that among the *permanent* paupers, the city-born predominate; for permanent aid is given only to such immigrants as have acquired settlement in the city.

[2] Von Oettingen, *Moralstatistik*, 3d ed., p. 525.

[3] Schwabe, *Berliner städtisches Jahrbuch für Volkswirthschaft und Statistik*, Erster Jahrgang, p. 60 ff.

[4] *Op. cit.*, p. 80.

deaths has been larger in the great cities than in the Empire as a whole,[1] and in recent years the two ratios have been about the same.[2]   In Bavaria the larger cities have for several years had the largest surplus of births of any class of towns ; thus the ratio of living births to deaths was : [3]

	Cities of 20,000 +.	Other cities.	Rural population.
1888	129	110	128
1889	132	118	137
1890	134	111	128
1891	142	120	133
1892	143	114	132
1893	141	120	135
1894	149	124	141
1895	146	121	144

But it is needless to pursue this subject farther, in view of its extended treatment in a previous chapter.   Nor is it neces- sary to tarry long in discussing Hansen's proposition that the native population of a city is completely replaced in two generations by the influx of outsiders, which is based on the premise that the population of the average large city always contains at least 50 per cent. of country born.   The propo- sition is not demonstrable by statistics even in the case of a stationary population ; and as city populations grow rapidly, it may well be that the natives increase in absolute members, although constituting a decreasing proportion of the entire population of the city.[4]

[1] For example, in 1890 the great cities had 148.2 births for every 100 deaths, the Empire, 146.7;   in 1894 the respective ratios were 163.4 and 160.9. (*Ibid.*, 80.)

[2] *Ibid.*, 83.   [3] *Ibid.*, 194.

[4] Dr. Kuczynski's discussion of this point (pp. 71-8) is not restricted to Han- sen, but includes also Ammon and others.   He mentions the fact that Berlin in 1840 contained 165,722 native Berliners;   50 years later (1890) there were 39,782 survivors.   Naturally some of them had descendants, even if Hansen re- fused to admit it.   Paris, on the other hand, is not self-sustaining, and Lagneau reckons that if left to itself, it would diminish 50 per cent. each generation, and in 18 generations or 5½ centuries would be effaced. (*Essai de statistique anthro- pologique sur la population parisienne.*)

Of rather more interest is Hansen's final point about the dying-out of the real city-makers,—the intellectual, mercantile, employing class.[1]   In order to clear the ground for his case, he first attempts to prove that the only cities which provide their own natural increase are the factory cities, which require only " hands," and are supplied with the progeny of the proletariat; while commercial cities, where the intellectual ability identified with the middle class is concentrated, are dependent for their growth upon immigration.[2]   A kernel of truth may doubtless be found in this proposition, as reference to Chapter VI on the natural movement of population will show.

But this is the only statistical proof Hansen advances in favor of his theory that the intellectual workers are incapable of self-continuation.   For the rest, he quotes proverbs about wealth not remaining in a family for more than three generations, about the disappearance of great-mercantile families,[3] etc., and instances the rise of new men into the ranks of the " captains of industry." etc.   The reasons he gives for the dying-out of the merchant princes and directors of industry are failure of intellect, causing them to sink into the proletariat, and late and infrequent marriages and consequent small families.   It is not a necessary consequence of the latter, however, that fewer children should be reared by the prosperous classes than are reared by the poorer classes with their larger families.   The Massachusetts statistics already presented do indeed indicate that the diminution in infant mortality in small and well-nurtured families is too slight to

[1] *Drei Bevölkerungsstufen*, Bk. iii, ch. 4, 5, esp. pages 174–180.

[2] *Op. cit.*, 27, 39, 208, 209.

[3] It may not be out of place here to observe that the export hand-book of Hamburg, the great German commercial center, contains a list of 62 firms who were in business in Hamburg in the eighteenth century.   Details of their careers, with old documents, etc., will be found in *Hamburgs Handel und Verkehr : Illustrirtes Export Handbuch der Börsen-Halle, 1897–99*, i, 438.

counterbalance the diminution in fecundity; as Dr. Crum remarks, "foresight and prudence seem to exercise a more powerful influence in restricting fecundity than in reducing infant mortality." But the careful study of marriage statistics according to social groups of the population which was made in Copenhagen by Rubin and Westergaard, leads to the conclusion that the upper classes, with a low birth-rate, often bring up as many children as do the lower classes, with a high birth-rate. Comparing the rates of the several classes or social groups with that of the fifth class (factory operatives, day laborers, sailors, etc.) as a standard (100), the following relations are found to exist:[1]

	Births.	Survivals.
Class 1	97	109
" 2	94	97
" 3	84	90
" 4	90	94
" 5	100	100

The subject of the preservation of an intellectual aristocracy which shall add to human knowledge and lead the human race in its progress, has been ably discussed,[2] and it must be admitted that the trend of opinion is against the conclusion reached by Rubin and Westergaard in their authoritative investigation of the marriage statistics of a single city.[3] Sir Francis Galton is inclined to the opinion

[1] *Statistik der Ehen*, p. 122. The first class consists of employers and professional men; the second of independent artisans, small tradesmen, superintendents, etc.; the third of teachers, public officials, etc.; the fourth of clerks, servants, etc.

[2] See the admirable discussion by Professor Marshall, *Principles of Economics*, 3d ed., pp. 283-5.

[3] But Dr. Engel, who investigated the marriage statistics of Saxony, reached a similar conclusion. He says: " We derive from this investigation the conviction that while indeed more children are born from a marriage in the industrial population than from one in the agricultural population, nevertheless the children of the latter have a greater vitality." (Cf. Wappäus, *Allg. Bevölkerungsstatistik*, ii, 487.)

that while the "upper" classes are capable of producing
large families, they either consciously refuse to do so, or else
marry heiresses who are of course hereditarily unproductive.
The Spencerian school takes the ground that the higher the
development of the individual, the smaller his capacity for
reproduction, etc. The salvation of society therefore depends
upon a mobility sufficient to permit or even encourage the
rise of individuals from the lower to the upper social ranks.
The process of recruiting the real aristocracy of ability and
character must be unimpeded. *And it is the concentration of
population in cities which best promotes the process of bringing
capable men to the front.* Here is the one kernel of truth in
Hansen's work,—the cities are the instruments of natural
selection. As such they may be destroyers of human vigor,
but not in the sense understood by Hansen. It is rather a
social service that they perform in weeding out the incapable
and inefficient, while advancing the more capable members of
society. Let us briefly consider Hansen's suggestive theory
of the *Bevölkerungsstrom*, which may help us in reaching a
right conclusion concerning the process of natural selection.

Society, according to the Hansen theory, consists of the
three classes,—(1) land-owners; (2) intellectual workers or
the middle class, including artisans, merchants, and professional men; (3) the unskilled laborers and factory operatives, or the city proletariat. The land-owning, agricultural
class is the great reservoir of vigor and life in any nation;
but it cannot hold itself together, for the reason that men
multiply more rapidly than land can be made. The land-
owning class is therefore continually throwing off a portion
of its recruits and these form the current of migration to the
cities. There they enter the middle class and struggle upward toward leadership; but no family can long sustain the
rigor of city competition, and eventually deteriorates whether
it has attained the highest position or not. Hence there is op-

posed to the upward current a downward current of degenerates. The upward current is composed almost wholly of the
country-bred (offspring of the land-owners), but the downward current is composed of the city-bred. The reservoir
which absorbs the survivors in the downward current is the
class of unskilled laborers or the city proletariat, who multiply abundantly but never rise in their position. The city thus
becomes an instrument of social degeneration. It takes the
crude vigor and vitality of the agricultural population,
develops and appropriates to itself their highest intellectual
abilities, and then casts them aside into the ever-increasing
number of non-efficients. It is obvious that if the cities keep
on growing at their nineteenth-century rate, they will dry up
the reservoirs of strength in the population and leave in their
place an immense proletariat, practically good for nothing.

Now is it true that cities would stagnate and decay, if the
stream of migration were stopped? Are they incapable of
producing the intellect and energy requisite for progress?
Is it "the result of the conditions of life in great towns that
muscular strength and energy get gradually used up; that
the second generation of city men is of lower physique and
has less power of persistent work than the first, and the third
generation (where it exists), is lower than the second?"[1]

All of our investigations in the course of the present
chapter point to the conclusion that the townsman is on the
average a more efficient industrial unit than the rural immigrant. The city proletariat, contrary to Hansen's theory,
appears to be recruited from the country-born rather than
from the real city dwellers. In fact, the countryman coming
to the city begins a slow ascent, rather than a descent; his
children, instead of being men of "lower physique with less
power of persistent work," advance to a higher rank on the
industrial and social ladder, while the third generation, in-

[1] H. L. Smith, in Booth, *op. cit.*, iii, 110.

stead of dying out, is still more capable and efficient. This is also the opinion of Ammon, Hansen's most famous disciple, whose researches in Carlsruhe may be summarized thus (without guaranteeing their value for generalizations): [1]

	Lower classes.	Middle classes.	" Studierten."	Total.
Immigrants	82	14	4	100
Their sons	41	49	10	100
" grandsons	40	35	25	100

As a class, the country immigrants do not at once assume the higher positions in the economic organism, but enter the unskilled occupations where muscular strength and vigor are in demand. Among the rural immigrants there are indeed some few skilled artisans, but there are very few cases of country laborers becoming artisans in the cities.[2] The im-

[1] *Gesellschaftsordnung*, 145.

[2] H. L. Smith who investigated the cases of 500 village emigrants (the great majority of whom moved to London), found only six such cases. His table showing the occupations of the 500 migrants before and after migration, confirms the conclusions in the text, which are based chiefly on the more precise data of Continental cities. The table may be condensed as follows:

PERCENTAGE OF MIGRANTS IN THE OCCUPATIONS NAMED:

	Before migration.	After
A. Outdoor labor.		
Laborer	64.0	16.9
Other	5.5	25.2
B. Service—personal and domestic	5.8	15.8
C. Public service—soldier, policeman, etc	..	14.5
D. Building trades	8.3	6.4
E. Other industries [3]	7.6	9.1
F. Retail dealers and innkeepers	7.8	9.7
G. Miscellaneous :		
Clerk	.7	1.5
Teacher, etc	.3	.9
	100.	100.

—Booth, *Life and Labour of the People*, iii, 140.

[3] In the original table this group as designated is " other skilled occupations," but, as Mr. Smith observed, the soap, chemical, gas-works, etc., here included probably employ many ordinary laborers.

migrants at first take up with such menial occupations as domestic and personal service, work in hotels and restaurants, postmen, cab-drivers and truckmen, and in some cases, with the building trades. It is only gradually that they work their way into the skilled industries, in which the city-born have a far larger representation. An illustration of this fact is given in the following figures from the Berlin census of 1885, showing the distribution, for both sexes, of the *erwerbsthätigen* native Berliners, immigrants, and immigrants within the five years just preceding the census : [1]

TABLE CLIX.

| | Berlin-born. | | | Total Immigrants. | | | Immigrants in 1881-5. | | |
	Male.	Female.	Total.	M.	F.	Total.	M.	F.	Total.
Industry, trade, transportation	748	551	679	631	339	533	580	228	453
Common laborers	110	149	123	122	93	113	94	59	81
Domestic servants	4	89	35	13	375	135	21	593	229
Other servants	11	15	12	24	23	24	26	12	21
Military	9	..	6	58	..	39	135	..	86
Public service	73	38	61	99	29	75	78	27	59
No profession	45	158	85	52	141	82	67	81	72
	1,000	1,000	1,000	1,000	1,000	1,000	1,000	1,000	1,000

And just as the newcomers work their way up from the unskilled into the skilled industries, so do they rise from the ranks of employees into those of undertakers and employers. The immigrants who had been in Berlin five years or less in 1885 formed 29.3 per cent. of the working population, but only 12 per cent. of the entrepreneurs, and only 5.5 per cent. of the entrepreneurs who employed more than five workmen. On the other hand the older immigrants, who had been in Berlin over 15 years, constituted 22.7 per cent. of those in gainful pursuits, 40.9 per cent. of the entrepreneurs, and 45 per cent. of the large employers:

[1] Brückner, *Allg. St. Archiv*, i, 645.

TABLE CLX.

Residence in Berlin.	Population. 1885.	All occupations. Females.	All occupations. Males.	Entrepreneurs (males), with number of employees. o.	Entrepreneurs (males), with number of employees. 1–5.	Entrepreneurs (males), with number of employees. Over 5.	Entrepreneurs (males), with number of employees. Total.
Less than 5 years	21.6	32.6	29.3	13.0	9.9	5.5	11.7
5–15 years	19.5	22.1	23.7	25.4	24.8	18.7	24.7
Over 15 years	16.5	19.7	22.7	40.4	41.4	44.6	40.9
Total immigrants	57.6	74.4	75.7	78.8	76.1	68.8	77.3
" Berlin-born	42.4	25.6	24.3	22.7	23.9	31.2	21.2
Total	100.0	100.0	100.0	100.0	100.0	100.0	100.0

Notwithstanding such facts, it is commonly held that city life produces dwarfed, stunted men and degenerates; fortunately, statistics of physical infirmities exist which dispel such fears about the effects of city life. It is now generally recognized that a connection exists between congenital blindness, congenital deaf-mutism and congenital imbecility or feeble-mindedness, *i. e.*, they are all results of impaired constitutional vigor. Now recent statistics show that these infirmities are rather more prevalent in rural districts and small towns than in the cities, while insanity, which is rather a nervous than a bodily failing, prevails chiefly in the cities. From the exceedingly valuable report by Dr. John S. Billings on the Insane, Feeble-minded, Deaf and Dumb, and Blind, in the United States at the Eleventh Census, the following figures are derived, showing the ratio of the specified classes to 100,000 of the population:

	United States.	Cities of 50,000 +.	Authority.
Insane	170.0	242.9	Tables 151,153
Feeble-minded	152.7	74.3	" 172,174
Deaf mutes	64.8	48.7	" 189,191
Blind	80.8	53.5	" 223,225

These results are confirmed by European statistics.[1]   And lest it be inferred that the difficulty or apportioning inmates

[1] Levasseur, *La population française*, i, 344; Rauchberg, *Die Bevölkerung Oesterreichs*, 232 ff.

of institutions to their real home, city or country, impairs the value of the statistics, it may be well to refer to the classical work of Dr. Mayr, in which these classes in Bavaria were distributed according to birth-places.[1] For the last three classes, Dr. Mayr found geographical differences, but for the insane the local variation was almost entirely due to the size of the town. His results may be summarized thus:

	Rural districts.	Cities.	Munich.
Insane	88.1	185.4	221.
Feeble-minded	153.3	136.5	130.
Deaf and dumb	91.1	73.3	59.
Blind	78.6	119.8	117.

It is clear then that while city life produces, or at least maintains fewer of the severer physical infirmities, like blindness, deaf-mutism and idiocy, than does the country, it does favor the increase of insanity.

The average height and girth of chest are significant criteria of physical vigor; and of the two, the latter is the more important, since it is indisputable that the strongest individuals and races are those that have the greatest chest capacity and lung power.

As regards stature, the preponderance of opinion in the past has been that city life exerts a depressing effect upon the individual.[2] The city of Hamburg is below the average for Germany, Geneva below the average for Switzerland, and Madrid has almost the shortest male population in all Spain. Ammon, the Carlsruhe anthropologist, holds the contrary

[1] *Die Verbreitung der Blindheit, der Taubstummheit, des Blödsinns und des Irrsinns in Bayern. XXXV Heft der Beiträge zur Statistik des Königr. Bayerns*, 1877, pp. 71-2, 304. Additional references are given in Mayr's *Bovölkerungsstatistik*, § 33.

[2] This is the conclusion of Professor Ripley, who surveys the evidence in an essay (" Racial Geography of Europe, xii, Urban Problems ") in the *Popular Science Monthly*, March, 1898. Most of the statements made above depend on the authorities cited by Dr. Ripley (*loc. cit.*, 52: 602).

opinion;[1] but his statistical methods are open to grave suspicion,[2] and his deductions from observations in Baden are not necessarily true of large populations. Dr. Beddoe, the leading British authority, declares that "it can be taken as *proved* that the stature of men in the large towns of Britain is lowered considerably below the standard of the nation, and as *probable* that such degeneration is hereditary and progressive."[3]

Ammon finds, moreover, that the townsman, who works in closed rooms and makes little muscular exertion, is considerably inferior in chest capacity to the countryman.[4] And the difference is not due to the migration cityward of countrymen below the general standard of the nation, for the countrymen residing in cities have a larger girth of chest than the city-born.

From Cato's time down, statesmen have declared that the bravest men and most daring soldiers have come from the land.[5] In 1856, Dr. Engel, the statistician, concluded that of 100 candidates examined from the country districts, 26.6

---

[1] *Die Gesellschaftsordnung* (1895), p. 117. Ammon affirms that townsmen grow taller and mature earlier than countrymen as a result of superior nourishment (*Die natürliche Auslese*, 123). It is undoubtedly true that a connection exists between stature and economic position; thus, it is found that the height of persons in Paris uniformly increases as one passes from the poorer to the wealthier wards. In Menilmontant (ward xx), where 80 per cent. of the funerals are at public expense, the average height was 1.637 metres; in the Opera (ix), with only 27 per cent. of public funerals, the average was 1.660 m.—Manouvrier, "Sur la Taille des Parisiens," *Bulletin de la Soc. d' Anthrop.* 3d ser., ix, 168.

[2] Cf. Kuczynski, 124–9.

[3] *On the Bulk and Stature of Man in Great Britain* (1867), p. 180.

[4] *Die natürliche Auslese*, 170.

[5] M. Porcius Cato, *de Rustica*, c. 1: *Fortissimi viri et milites strenuissimi ex agricolis gignuntur, minimeque male cogitantes.*

Plinius, *Hist. Nat., Lib.* 18, c. 5.

Mémoires de Maximilien de Béthune, Duc de Sully, etc. (Lond., 1747), T. ii, p. 289.

Engel, " Die physische Beschaffenheit der militär pflichtigen Bevölkerung im

were declared fit for service, as against 19.7 from 100 urban candidates.

Now it is to be observed that the believers in town degeneracy base their arguments on antiquated statistics. There can be no doubt that down to very recent times the health and vigor of urbanites compared unfavorably with that of men who worked in the open air, just as their death-rates did.[1] But in the last quarter century the evidence in both cases has changed. In 1874 a French authority[2] declared that fitness for army service depends less on density of population than on wealth, climate, daily life.[3] Health and vigor may always be preserved if men in cities will make proper provision for open-air exercise, cleanliness and a pure food supply. Professor Marshall, who is not afraid of looking the

Königr. Sachsen," in Zeit. des Stat. Bureaus des K. Sächs. Ministeriums des Innern, 1856, Nr. 4–7 (esp. pp. 111, 112).

E. Helwing: " Ueber die Abnahme der Kriegstüchtigkeit der angehobenen Mannschaften, namentlich in der Mark Brandenburg, Berlin, 1860.

[1] Exceptions, however, can be found in former centuries. A recent writer has called attention to the facts that the city-bred infantry of the Flemish towns was more than a match for the best troops French chivalry could bring against them in 1302, and that the citizen soldiers of southeastern and eastern England in the War of the Roses gave the victory to the Yorkists over the masses of peasants and huntsmen of the North and West.—Contemporary Review (Oct., 1891), 60: 554.

[2] Art. Récrutement, Dictionnaire encyclopédique des sciences médicales, 3d series, vol. ii.

[3] Taking the three densest departments of France and comparing them with the three least dense, it was found that the number of men who had to be examined to secure 1,000 soldiers was (Ibid., 644, 646) :

	Pop. per sq. kilometer.	Number examined.
Seine	64.5	1,790 (Paris)
Nord	3.5	1,815 (Lille, Roubaix, etc.)
Rhone	3.5	1,776 (Lyons)
Hautes Alpes	.5	2,580
Lazère	.3	2,050
Basses-Alpes	.3	2,190

evils of town life in the face, is right when he says that "it is not to be concluded that the race is degenerating physically, nor even that its nervous strength is, on the whole, decaying. On the contrary, the opposite is plainly true of those boys and girls who are able to enter fully into modern outdoor amusements, who frequently spend holidays in the country, and whose food, clothing and medical care are abundant and governed by the best knowledge." [1]

But after all, progress depends less on purely physical strength than on moral resolution or nervous strength. In the words of the writer just quoted, "the power of sustaining great muscular exertion depends on force of will and strength of character as well as on constitutional strength. This energy (strength of man, not of body) is moral rather than physical; but yet it depends on the physical conditions of the nervous strength. This strength of the man himself, this resolution, energy, and self-mastery, or in short this 'vigor' is the source of all progress: it shows itself in great deeds, in great thoughts, and in the capacity for true religious feeling." [2]

Now, it is precisely the high nervous organization of city-bred soldiers that has enabled them to last through long campaigns as well as or better than countrymen with their rude physical health. It made the students of Berlin University able to bear fatigue better than the average soldier in the war of 1870–1, and rendered the New England store-clerks equal to all the strain of Sherman's march to the sea in 1864. When to nervous strength is joined the muscular development to be found among the athletic middle-class youth in American and English suburban towns, one is justified in hailing them as world-conquerors. Seven years ago an English writer, referring to the young men of Wimbledon and Battersea, near London, had the foolhardiness to eulo-

[1] *Principles of Economics*, p. 281. [2] *Ibid.*, 275.

gize them as future victors of Marathons;[1] but yesterday, and he saw his prediction fulfilled as American city lads marched to victory on Cuban soil, side by side with the rough cowboys of the western plains.

Having dealt with the subject of physical health and vigor, it now remains to consider the influence of city life upon intelligence and morals.

Education.—As regards education, it must be obvious that the agglomeration of population is more favorable than its dispersion can be. In fact, one would naturally turn to the cities and towns for the best schools, since they alone can afford to provide the expensive advantages incident to the grading of pupils and the division of labor educationally. It is not surprising, therefore, that the urban schools of the United States have 190 class days per annum, and the rural schools only 115; and that the attendance in the city is 70 per cent. of the enrolment, while in the country it is 62 per cent. Moreover, the statistics of illiteracy in the United States are favorable to the cities, notwithstanding the reception by the cities of the bulk of illiterate foreigners. The following comparision embraces all of the 28 large cities (100,000+) of the United States and the commonwealths in which they are situated (Washington, which coincides with the District of Columbia, being ranged under Maryland):

PERCENTAGE OF ILLITERATES IN THE POPULATION, 10 YEARS OF AGE AND OVER, 1890:[2]

New York	5.53	Pennsylvania	6.78
New York	7.69	Philadelphia	4.97
Brooklyn	3.25	Pittsburg	6.93
Buffalo	5.38	Allegheny	3.77
Rochester	3.56	Missouri	9.09
Illinois	5.25	St. Louis	5.89
Chicago	4.63	Kansas City	5.78

[1] Low, "The Rise of the Suburbs," in *Contemp. Review*, 60: 555.

[2] *11th Cens., Comp.*, iii, 301, 317.

Massachusetts	6.22	New Jersey	6.50
Boston	5.69	Newark	4.81
Maryland	15.70	Jersey City	5.91
Baltimore	9.80	Minnesota	6.03
Washington	13.20	Minneapolis	2.39
California	7.67	St. Paul	4.54
San Francisco	5.35	Kentucky	21.65
Ohio	5.24	Louisville	10.69
Cincinnati	4.27	Nebraska	3.11
Cleveland	6.49	Omaha	2.86
Louisiana	45.83	Rhode Island	9.76
New Orleans	15.70	Providence	7.73
Wisconsin	6.73	Colorado	5.24
Milwaukee	5.34	Denver	2.83
Michigan	5.92	Indiana	6.32
Detroit	6.66	Indianapolis	6.12

With very few exceptions (New York City, Pittsburg, Cleveland, Detroit), the cities have a better educated population than the rest of the State in which they are situated. The difference in favor of the cities is in many instances very marked, although in the case of Baltimore, New Orleans and Louisville, it is explicable by the different proportions of negroes in the population. There can be no doubt about the superiority of the city schools, both primary and secondary. Educators in fact now recognize the inferiority of rural schools as one of their most pressing problems, and the National Educational Association is even now discussing the ample report on rural schools presented at its 1897 meeting by its Committee of Twelve.

But the education of the schools forms only a part of a man's education. Their discipline must be supplemented by outside reading and experience; alone it too often promotes superficiality. And this is the peculiar danger of urban habits of life. The city boy is taught to read, but not to think; the result is seen in the immense constituency of "yellow journalism." Country newspapers are trivial enough, but they do not descend to the depths of moral degradation of sensational metropolitan journals, manufactured for city readers.

Town education has been so well described by Mr. Hobson [1] that it would be a loss not to quote his words:

"That town life, as distinguished from town work, is educative of certain intellectual and moral qualities, is evident. Setting aside that picked intelligence which flows to the town to compete successfully for intellectual employment, there can be no question but that the townsman has a larger superficial knowledge of the world and human nature. He is shrewd, alert, versatile, quicker and more resourceful than the countryman. In thought, speech, action, this superiority shows itself. The townsman has a more developed consciousness, his intelligence is constantly stimulated in a thousand ways by larger and more varied society, and by a more diversified and complex economic environment. While there is reason to believe that town work is on the average less educative than country work, town life more than turns the scale. The social intercourse of the club, the trade society, the church, the home, the public house, the music-hall, the street, supply innumerable educative influences, to say nothing of the ampler opportunities of consciously organized intellectual education which are available in large towns. If, however, we examine a little deeper the character of town education and intelligence, certain tolerably definite limitations show themselves. School instruction, slightly more advanced than in the country, is commonly utilized to sharpen industrial competition and to feed that sensational interest in sport and crime which absorbs the attention of the masses in their non-working hours; it seldom forms the foundation of an intellectual life in which knowledge and taste are reckoned in themselves desirable. The power to read and write is employed by the great majority of all classes in ways which evoke a minimum of thought and wholesome feeling. Social, political and religious prejudices are made to do the work which should be done by careful thought and scientific investigation. Scattered and unrelated fragments of half-baked information form a stock of 'knowledge' with which the townsman's glib tongue enables him to present a showy intellectual shop-front. Business smartness pays better in the town, and the low intellectual qualities which are contained in it are educated by town life. The knowledge of human nature thus evoked is in no sense science; it is a mere rule-of-thumb affair, a thin mechanical empiricism. The capable business man who is said to understand the 'world' and his fellow-men, has commonly no knowledge of human nature in the larger sense, but merely knows from observation how the average man of a certain limited class is likely to act within a narrow prescribed sphere of self-seeking. Town life, then, strongly favors the education of certain shallow forms of intelligence"

Religion and Morality.—According to the special report of

[1] *The Evolution of Modern Capitalism*, pp. 338–9.

Dr. H. K. Carroll on *Statistics of Churches and Religious Denominations at the Eleventh Census*,[1] the cities contain a larger proportion of church members, or communicants, than do the smaller places; but on the other hand, the cities have by far fewer church buildings, as will be observed in the following statistics:

	Communicants (percentage of total population).	One church edifice to a pop. of
United States	32.85	440
All cities of 25,000+ (124)	37.90	1,439
Cities of 25,000–100,000 (96)	39.10	1,052
" " 100,000–500,000 (24)	38.90	1,468
" " 500,000+ (4)	35.60	2,147

Thus the population to a church building steadily increases with the size of the city, and it is a question whether the seating capacity of the buildings increases in the same ratio. It is also noticeable that while the cities have a larger proportion of communicants than the entire United States, yet this proportion steadily diminishes as we pass from the class of smaller cities to that of the larger. To put the facts in another light they may be thus summarized:

	Ratio to the U. S.
Population of 124 cities of 25,000+	22.5
Communicants of 124 cities of 25,000+	25.72
Number of church edifices in 124 cities of 25,000+	6.82
Value of church property in 124 cities of 25,000+	46.13

Of the leading denominations (numerically), the Roman Catholics are strongest in American cities, although the Hebrews tend to concentrate in cities even more than the Catholics. Of the total strength of the several denominations in the United States the following percentages were in the cities of 25,000+ in 1890:[2]

[1] Pp. xxvi and xxvii.

[2] *Op. cit.,* p. xxvii.

Jewish (orthodox).. .... 91.71
" (reformed).............. .... 84.57
German Evangelical Protestant 77.97
Roman Catholic... 48.26
Unitarians 48.08
Protestant Episcopal.. 48.03
German Evangelical Synod 38.56
Reformed in America 30.85
Presbyterian (North)... 29.85
Lutheran Synod, Conference 29.77
Lutheran General Council 25.75
Congregational... 25.57
Regular Baptist (North).. 25.06

And since only 22 per cent. of the total population of the
country is resident in these cities, the denominations above
mentioned are disproportionately strong in the cities.

The only statistical measure of morality, as distinguished
from religion, is negative, being in fact a measure of immorality,—the amount of vice and crime recorded by the police
authorities. But first, let us consider the phenomenon of
suicide. As is generally known, this phenomenon is more
frequent in the city than in the country.[1] In the United
States, as far as we can judge from the imperfect returns of
vital statistics in the Eleventh Census, the disparity is not so
great as it is elsewhere; the rate per 1,000,000 population
being 92.9 in the cities of registration States, and 80 in the
rural parts, while in the outside cities it was 126.5.[2] The
following table is from Morselli, Levasseur, von Mayr, etc.:

SUICIDES PER 1,000,000 POPULATION.

	Urban.	Rural.	Capitals.	
France (1883)..........	263	172	Dept. of Seine	472
Prussia (1869–72)	162	97	Berlin	191
Italy (1877).............	66	29	Rome, 111; Milan..........	199
Norway (1866–9)........	92	72		
Sweden (1871–5)........	167	67	Stockholm	440
Denmark (1869–75)	283	257	Copenhagen	350
Belgium (1858–60)	64	34		
Bavaria (1876)	118	104	Munich (1860–69)	190
Saxony (1859–63)	317	219		

[1] Morselli, *Suicide*, pp. 161–186, esp. 172; Levasseur, *La. pop. fran.*, ii, 133.

[2] *Vital and Social Statistics*, Part i, pages 463–4.

Without exception, the suicide-rate is higher in the urban than in the rural communities, and highest of all in the great cities. Both von Oettingen and Wagner have called attention to the excessive rate in the capitals:[1]

St. Petersburg	180	Russia	28
Vienna	290	Austria	13c
Leipzig	450	Saxony	394
London	85	England	69
New York	121-181	United States	32 (?)

In fact, there seems to be a regular progression in the suicide-rate from small centers to large centers, as may be seen in the following Prussian statistics:[2]

	Suicides to 1,000,000 inhabitants.
Prussia, 1881-90	202
"　　cities of 15,000+	256
"　　"　　" 20-100,000 (1892)	247
"　　"　　" 100,000+　　"	308
"　　Berlin	329

The fact that cities contribute more heavily to the number of suicides than do rural communities has been established. But it is not to be inferred that those countries which have the largest urban populations also have the largest relative number of suicides; in fact Morselli has shown by comprehensive statistics[3] that many of the countries in which population is most concentrated (*e. g.* England, Holland, Belgium), have a low suicide-rate. Race is the most important single factor in the production of suicides; hence in the Netherlands the highest suicide-rate is not in the

---

[1] Von Oettingen, *Die Moralstatistik* (1882), p. 765; Nagle, *Suicide in New York City;* Wagner, *Die Gesetzmässigkeit in den scheinbar willkürlichen menschlichen Handlungen vom Standpunkt der Statistik,* 2 Theil, i, *Vergleichende Selbstmordstatistik Europas,* etc., Hamburg, 1864.

[2] Von Mayr, Art. "Selbstmordstatistik" in Conrad's *Hdwbh.*, 1st Sup., p. 700.

[3] *Op. cit.,* 170, 157.

south-western provinces which contain the large cities but in the north-east, where the Germanic element is strong.[1]

The analysis of suicides by occupation shows that the phe nomenon is also connected with the predominant professions. Thus, in France the number of suicides per 1,000,000 of population, is 120 in agriculture, 130 in commerce, 190 in industry, 290 among domestic servants, 550 in the liberal professions and 2,350 among those of no profession or of unknown profession.[2] Suicide is really one of the penalties paid for progress. It is one of the processes of natural selection, resulting from failures in the "struggle for existence" and is therefore most prevalent where the competitive struggle is keenest. As cities are the centers of the severest competition, they naturally have the largest number of suicides.

It is to be observed, however, that suicide is not increasing in the large cities, or at least is increasing less rapidly than in the smaller places. Morselli reviews the evidence at length and regards it as establishing the "fact that the tide of suicides rises in all countries, and especially in the provinces, whilst it remains stationary or decreases in the great and most civilized capitals of Europe."[3]

Criminal statistics undoubtedly put the cities in a bad light. In England, for example, the cities have double or even quadruple the amount of crime that the rural communities have, as will be seen in the following table giving for the year 1894 the number of offenses per 100,000 population :[4]

[1] *Op. cit.*, 47.

[2] Levasseur, ii, 127.

[3] *Op. cit.*, 183. According to the latest English *Judicial Statistics* (for year 1894, published in the 1896 Parliamentary papers), the county of London ranked tenth among English counties, with a suicide-rate of 100.6 (p. 47).

[4] *Judicial Statistics*, in Parl. Papers, 1896, vol. xciv, p. 24.

TABLE CLXI.

Indictable crimes.

	Crimes; all indictable offenses. reported.	Offenses against property.	Offenses against persons.		Offenses tried summarily.		
			Crimes of violence.	Crime against morals.	Assaults.	Drunkenness.	Vagrancy Acts.
Metropolis..........	416.7	386.2	10.6	5 9	390.1	637.4	148.8
Mining countries....	234.3	214.3	8.3	8.1	286.8	1,136.7	280.3
Mf. towns	351.8	332.4	6.6	4.4	272.6	470.1	244.9
Seaports............	643.6	597.9	22.5	8.4	426.0	1,260 8	368.3
Pleasure towns......	265.7	250.4	4.3	4.1	180.5	289.3	82.9
Agr. counties:							
East "	128.2	119.1	3.7	3.6	120.3	109.9	55.4
S.-W. "	182.9	163.5	5.2	8.1	150.1	209.4	155.7
Home counties......	202.1	185.9	4.2	6.5	146.7	245.0	52.2
Eng. and Wales.....	296.7	275.9	7.2	6.1	252.2	616.3	191.1

The vast majority of crimes are against property, having numbered 53,621 in a total of 56,281, and these are largely larcenies. As regards the graver offenses against the person, London occupies a middle rank (murder) and a low rank in sexual crimes (rape).

But it does not appear that crime increasing disproportionately in the cities. The French statistics, for example, separate criminals according to their domicile or legal residence. In 1841–5, 38 per cent. of those charged with offenses were domiciled in the urban communes (2,000+ pop.), which then contained about 23 per cent. of the population, In 1866–70 the respective percentages were 44 and 31; in 1881–5, 46 and 35.[1] Crime has therefore increased less rapidly than population in the towns.[2]

Our statistics of vice are mainly restricted to the subject of illegitimacy. We have indeed just seen in Table CLXI that violations of the person are less frequent in the English

[1] Levasseur, op. cit., ii, 455.

[2] Porter (Progress of the Nation, p. 646) figured that between 1805 and 1841 crime increased by 1,277 per cent. in 20 agricultural counties of England and 1,252 in 20 industrial counties. But Leone Levi denies the validity of Porter's proceeding. (Jour. of St. Soc., 1880.)

cities than in the rural counties. Illegitimacy, on the other hand, appears to center in the cities. It is nearly a half-century since Wappäus showed that illegitimacy was about twice as great in the cities as in the rural parts of Europe; the average percentage of illegitimate births in all births being 14.7 in urban populations and 7.6 in the rural.[1] The difference between city and country is very marked in France, and illegitimacy culminates in Paris, where between one-fourth and one-third of all the births are illegitimate.[2] In 1879–83 there were the following numbers of illegitimates per 100 births:[3]

Department of the Siene (Paris) 24.1
Urban population 10.1
Rural   " 4.2

France 7.4

Judging from the foregoing statistics, the cities must be hot-beds of immorality. But their case is not so bad as it seems. It must be remembered that maternity hospitals are always located in cities, and many of the women who enter these are countrywomen who come to the city to conceal their shame. Levasseur is the authority for the statement that over one-fourth (4,405) of the illegitimate births in 1884 (16,137, or 26.7 per cent. of all births) were such cases. He says that nearly one-half were the fruits of *liaisons*, which in Paris are regarded as a form of marriage, leaving something over one-fourth the alleged number as the real product of Parisian immorality. With these deductions, the Paris rate

---

[1] *Supra*, Table CXLVI.

[2] Even Paris, however, ranks below some other European cities. In Munich, Vienna and Prague one-half the births were illegitimate a few years since, and Rome had a percentage of 44.5; Stockholm, 40; Moscow, 38.1; Budapest, 30.5; Paris at that time 28.6, and London 3.9.—Levasseur, ii, 400–1.

[3] Levasseur, ii, 34.

would be somewhat less than twice that of the rural populations.

But there is still another factor in the problem, namely, the larger proportion of young unmarried women in the cities. This factor, taken into consideration, will account for much of the city illegitimacy; in Germany, as we have seen (Table CXLIV), the number of illegitimate births to 1,000 unmarried women of child-bearing age is actually less in the cities than in the country, and the same fact has been observed in Scotland.[1] On the whole, it is to be doubted if the cities are much worse than the rural districts as regards illegitimacy; the question cannot be determined definitely until other countries furnish the refined rate. In this country, unfortunately, no distinction between rural and urban populations has been made in the matter of illegitimacy.

Infanticide, as the European criminal statistics have shown, is more prevalent in the country than in the city, while abortion seems to be less prevalent there.

Prostitution, regarded as a profession, is certainly a city institution, but many social workers doubt whether the sexual morality of the country is on a higher plane, from their knowledge of the large proportion of prostitutes who were first corrupted in country homes. The morals of " wicked Paris " have frequently been impeached, but sociologists who know the facts declare that a very large part of the Parisian vice is supported by travelers and foreign sojourners. If such is the case, it is wrong to regard the entire Parisian population as immoral. Similarly with other cities: they have a great deal of vice, to be sure, but it is the property of a distinct class of the population.

In the United States, the number of drinking saloons affords a rough index of a town's morality, and the New York State figures for 1897 show that while the cities on the whole

[1] Levasseur, ii, 206.

have a larger relative number of saloons than the rural parts, the largest cities do not take the lowest rank: [1]

	No. of saloons per 1,000 population.
New York State	3.6
Rural	2.8
Urban	4.5
Cities of first class [2]	4.3
" " second class [3]	4.0
" " third class [4]	4.5

The amount of viciousness and criminality in cities is probably exaggerated in popular estimation from the fact that the cities have long been under the blaze of an Argus-eyed press, so that the worst is known about them. They have hitherto overshadowed the evils in the moral life of villages, but several recent rural crimes of unwonted atrocity have awakened in the nation a truer realization of the actual facts.[5] Many sociologists have also realized that the rural center is not so "idyllic" as has been imagined.[6]

[1] *Second Annual Report of the State Commissioner of Excise,* for year ending Sept. 30, 1897, p. 105.

[2] New York, Brooklyn, Buffalo.

[3] Rochester, Albany, Syracuse, Troy.

[4] Thirty-four cities with population ranging (1892) between 8,000 and 50,000.

[5] Reference is here made particularly to the assault, robbery and murder of Mrs. McCloud of Shelburne Falls, Mass. Note the following specimen of newspaper comment on the crime (Hartford *Times*) : " There is a lesson for our New England communities in the career of Jack O'Neil, the Shelburne Falls hoodlum and ne'er-do-well. O'Neil was what the specialists would describe as a true degenerate. He was an idle, worthless, drunken, penniless fellow, hanging around the entrances to the village dramshops (of which Shelburne Falls plainly has too many), sponging his food and lodging out of his mother, a hard-working washerwoman, and as sure to develop into a criminal as darkness is to succeed daylight. . . . The evidence at the trial in Greenfield showed that O'Neil was only one of a gang of youthful ' bums ' and hoodlums who are tolerated in Shelburne Falls, and whose ill-gotten gains furnish considerable support for a lot of cheap and nasty dramshops which disgrace the place. How many other New England villages present the same conditions? A good many to our certain knowledge."

[6] *Vide* Prof. Blackmar's studies of the " Smoky Pilgrims " in the *American Journal of Sociology,* January, 1897.

But if there is actually a larger criminal and vicious class in the cities, as would be *a priori* expected from the fact that the cities are the foci of attraction, it does not follow that the danger of contamination is greater. The fact is that in the city the crime is *localized;* it is confined to particular classes and the remaining social classes are so much the cleaner. There are perhaps relatively more offenses committed in the city than in the village,[1] but not so many more offenders. And most people will admit that there is considerable difference between a society where the same man comes before a magistrate six times, and another society where six men come before the judge once.

The cities, moreover, have the benefit of an educated public opinion on moral questions which is often effective to suppress the beginnings of vice. The power of social opinion, supported by legislation, has been abundantly demonstrated in the transformation of factory labor. There was a time when factories were actual " men-consumers," producing a morally and physically dwarfed and stunted race. That time is forever past in America and England, while to-day the worst conditions are found in the home ("sweating") industries. The same strong social opinion that wiped out factory abuses by the Factory Acts must now be concentrated on the evils of city life.

Finally, the fact must not be overlooked that the city affords more opportunities for the exhibition of virtues as well as of vices, and " if our annals of virtue were kept as carefully as our annals of vice, we might find that town life stood higher in the one than in the other." Every day the city witnesses the performance not merely of acts of generosity and self-denial, but of heroic self-sacrifice. Over against the

---

[1] In using statistics of offenses to compare the moral conditions of different places, care must be taken to exclude such offenses as consist merely in a violation of a local ordinance, *e. g.*, neglect to clean a sidewalk of snow.

professional criminal is to be put the policeman; against the *roué*, the fireman who uncomplainingly faces danger and death day after day. The records of city charitable societies would reveal innumerable deeds of kindness, but would still leave unrevealed the thousand and one generous acts of service performed by the poor themselves for the relief of the unfortunate in their midst.

CHAPTER VIII

GENERAL EFFECTS OF THE CONCENTRATION OF POPULATION

I. ECONOMIC EFFECTS

BEFORE the effects of the concentration of population in cities can be treated in their broad and general aspect, with reference to the nation or social body as a whole, it will be necessary to compare the economic condition of city-dwellers with that of rural workers. This can be done but imperfectly by means of statistics of wages, cost of living, etc., because averages, in the case of extremes, have little significance. An average height of 5 feet 6 inches would be the numerical mean between 7 feet and 4 feet, but would not be a true average since it approaches neither of the two men compared. So with regard to wealth, it is well known that the wealthy men of this country dwell in the great cities, and that the most degrading poverty is found in the cities. It is almost incredible that men in the country should suffer such deprivation and come so near starvation through lack of employment, as do masses of the urban population,—at least not in this country, where famines are unknown. In Russia or India, when the crops fail, a farm laborer may be reduced to the direst straits; but wherever the modern railway has penetrated, agriculturists as well as other classes are relieved from fear of starvation. Aside from famines, moreover, it is doubtless true that the economic condition of the Polish Jews, Bohemians, etc., now living in New York tenements was considerably worse when they were living on their farms in

Europe and had the scantiest clothing, the most wretched shelter and most miserable surroundings. Bad as are the homes in crowded city tenements, they are an improvement. Still, one would say, comparing city and country as we know them in the United States, that the most hopeless poverty, as well as the most splendid wealth, are found in the cities. The Prussian income-tax returns show that the income tax, which is levied on all single males or heads of families enjoying an annual income of 900 marks ($225) or more, is paid by a larger percentage of people in the city than in the country,—38.4 per cent. as against 24.4 per cent.[1] Among the taxpayers, the cities have a larger percentage among the higher incomes:[2]

TABLE CLXII.

Annual income in marks.	Distribution of each 1,000 taxpayers in	
	Cities.	Rural districts.
900–3,000	429.9	679.5
3,000–6,000	156.4	124.4
6,000–9.500	85.5	44.7
9,500–30,500	154.4	65.0
30,500–100,000	95.1	46.2
100,000+	78.7	40.2
Total	1,000	1,000

Another method of measurement is to compare the wages of unskilled labor in the city and country. Such camparisons have frequently been made, and show that the wages of this unspecialized labor are invariably higher in the cities.[3]

---

[1] Bleicher, 146.

[2] See "incomes for city and country" in *Mittheilungen aus der Verwaltung der directen Steuern im preus. Staat,* "Statistik der Einkommensteuerveranlagung," 1892–3, Berlin, 1892, pages 308, 311.

[3] The compulsory sick-insurance system of the German empire grants an allowance corresponding to the local daily wage of unskilled laborers ("ortsüblicher Tagelohn gewöhnlicher Tagesarbeiter"). The local rate was duly ascertained in every town in the empire, allowance being made in money for wages paid in "truck." From the first official revision (1884) the following comparative sta-

Similarly, comparisons have been made of wages in the various skilled trades, one with another. Here, especially, do city wage-earners maintain a superior rate, partly in consequence of the strength of city trade unions.

What is the comparative cost of living in city and country? Does it tend to counterbalance the advantage of the city in higher wages? First, as to rent and personal services of all kinds, no doubt exists as to the disadvantages of cities. Villagers also secure lower prices in buying vegetables and such provisions as are brought to the market from the surrounding agricultural districts. But here their advantage over the city dwellers ends. The townsman buys his bread and meat and various other staple food-products fully as cheaply as does the villager, and far more cheaply than does the suburbanite. And in all other purchases, the townsman has an immeasurable advantage. Clothing, furniture, books and comforts and luxuries of every kind are offered in a variety and at prices in the cities that are not approached in the village store. In general, it may be said that the consumers' rent is much larger in the cities than in smaller dwelling-centers. By "consumers' rent" economists mean the surplus of enjoyment that a man derives from purchasing an article at a price lower than the price he would be willing to pay in barter. The man with an income of $50,000 would no doubt

tistics were compiled (Hirschberg, "Ergebnisse der für die Arbeiter-Kranken-versicherung vorgenommene Lohnstatistik in Preussen und den freien Städten," *Jahrbücher für National-oekonomie und Statistik* (1885), xliv, 265 :

	Daily wages (in marks) of adults.	
	Males.	Females.
In cities of 100,000+	2.16	1.44
" " " 50,000–100,000	2.06	1.27
" " " 20,000-50,000	1.77	1.14
" " " less than 20,000	1.44	.94
Average	1.46	.95

Additional statistics are given in the article " Arbeitslohn, Statistik " in Conrad's *Hdwbh*.

be willing to give 50 cents or more for a loaf of bread; but in the market, the price has been fixed by the marginal buyer and seller at eight cents, and the rich man, as well as the poor man, can buy bread at that price. The consumers' rent of the rich man would in this case be designated by forty-two cents. It is the fierce competition of the great stores in the cities that lowers prices and secures to the city-dweller a large consumers' rent.

The existence of high rents in the city may more than counterbalance the advantages of lower prices in staple articles, thus making the laborer's cost of living higher, and his actual wages lower than in the country. In the average case, a workingman expends from 12 to 15 per cent. of his income for lodgings.[1] Hence when rents run at a figure that averages between 25 and 33 per cent. of the normal wages of an unskilled laborer, as they did at one time in Munich, Dresden, etc., or even at more than 33 per cent., as they are said to have done in Frankfort, Breslau and Danzig, Stettin and other German cities,[2] there is bound to be much misery and suffering. Either the expenditure for rent will encroach upon the other necessary expenses, or else several families must lives together in narrow quarters.[3] There is reason to

[1] Engel's Law, formulated in 1857. Engel classified the expenditure of three groups of workmen in Saxony: (1) those with an income of $200-300; (2) intermediate class, income of $450-600; (3) well-to-do class, $750-1,000. He found that each class expended 12 per cent. of its income for lodging. (*Cf.* Marshall's *Principles of Economics*, p. 191. *The United States Bureau of Labor's Report on Cost of Production*, 1891, classified the expenditures in normal families, and found that the proportion of income expended in rent closely approached 15 per cent. in ten out of the twelve classes.

[2] *Cf.* Schönberg's *Handbuch der Politischen Oekonomie*, 3d ed., ii, 736.

[3] The direct relation of income to overcrowding is shown by an investigation of 600 families in the New York tenement-house district:

	No. of persons. to a family.	Weekly. wage.	No. of persons. to a room.
Families living in one room	3.3	$8.50	3.3
" " " 2 rooms	4.6	10.90	2.3
" " " 3 "	5.4	12.00	1.8
" " " 4 "	5.4	16.50	1.35

—*Report of N. Y. Tenement House Com. of 1894*, pp. 433-4.

fear that too often both alternatives have had to be accepted. Add to this overcrowding, the negligence of the public authorities in regard to the construction of buildings and their sanitary condition, and you have the city slums, with their sickening odor of disease, vice and crime.

Whose is the fault of the slums? and what are the remedies? are questions that do not demand extended discussion here. Society and the state are to blame for the worst features of the slums and in most civilized countries are now applying the remedies. Minute building regulations and careful supervision will prevent the erection of future death-traps; strict inspection will prevent the use of a building, or part of a building, for a purpose other than the one for which it was built; the requirement of a definite amount of air space to each occupant of a room will prevent some of the worst evils of overcrowding; plenty of water, good paving, drainage etc., will render the sanitary condition good. The existing "death-traps" must be condemned and torn down. These measures, or most of them, have been taken in New York city, whose tenement-house laws are probably as good as any. Additional legislation has been proposed, such as limitation on the right to migrate to a city whose housing accommodations are already insufficient, the prohibition of rent taking above a legal maximum (like usury), and restrictions upon the right of contract and the right to seize household goods in default of rent. These proposals are of German origin and have found little support in other countries.

To effect a reduction in house rents, however, is a less simple matter. In some places, notably in Germany, the overcrowding may have been due to a dislike on the part of the landlords to building and managing laborers' dwellings, which are subject to the annoyance of petty accounts, frequent changes of habitation and numerous losses. But

where the workingmen are able to pay a reasonable rent, as
they usually are in this country, the supply of laborers'
dwellings will usually meet the demand unless there be monopoly sites.[1] Where the building space in the vicinity of a
group of factories and other industries is limited, the law
may not be able to prevent overcrowding without inflicting
hardship upon the workingmen. Thus, in Glasgow after an
era of reform in which strictly sanitary buildings had been
constructed by the city on the site of old tenements, there
were too few dwellings for the accommodation of those who
wished to remain in the center of the city, and overcrowding
was almost an immediate result. In such a case, the only
successful way out is an improved transit service which will
permit more of the workingmen to reside in the suburbs.
The London County Council has come to recognize this as
the only really effectual remedy against overcrowding, and
while it has secured Parliamentary Acts which will forbid the
future erection of insanitary tenements, and has also devoted
some attention to the condemnation and destruction of existing " death traps," the Council's principal aim is the development of a rapid-transit system between London and the
suburbs. " Cheap trains for workingmen " is a rallying cry
which has caused Parliament to abate the passenger-taxes in
favor of railways that afford facilities for suburban travel.
In New York city, whose island situation prevents the population settling round the business center in circular fashion,
rapid transit is the only hope of keeping rents down.

It is hardly worth while to set forth the statistics regarding
overcrowding. The elaborate statistics of the Eleventh
Census showing the average number of persons[2] to a dwell-

[1] There was no known scarcity of laborers' dwellings in Chicago, and no overcrowding, until the arrival of poverty-stricken immigrants from Southern Europe.

[2] The average number of persons to a dwelling in the five principal American

ing possess little value, as everything depends on the manner of construction of dwellings and on the relative number of lodgers (young unmarried men) in the town. Nor can the European comparison of overcrowding in various cities be regarded as entirely trustworthy. An instance in point is a recent essay on overcrowding by one of the most eminent statisticians in Europe.[1]

The English census of 1891, however, affords a valuable comparison between urban and rural overcrowding. Regarding as overcrowded all the "ordinary tenements that had more than two occupants to a room, bedrooms and sitting rooms included," the census statisticians found the

cities in 1890, compared with the commonwealths in which they are situated, was:

	City.	State.
New York	18.52	6.70
Chicago	8.60	5.71
Philadelphia	5.60	5.26
Brooklyn	9.80	6.70
St. Louis	7.41	5.52

The statistics of European cities may be found in the manuals of population statistics.

[1] J. Bertillon, *Essai de statistique comparée du surpeuplement des habitations à Paris et dans les grandes villes Européennes.* Paris, 1895. The table referred to in the text gives the percentage of inhabitants living in overcrowded dwellings (*i. e.,* those *logements* in which the number of persons exceeds double the number of rooms—*pièces*) :

Paris	14
London	20
Berlin	28
Vienna	28
Moscow	31
St. Petersburg	46
Budapest	74

The Budapest statisticians said that Bertillon counted only the chambers among the *pièces* in Budapest, whereas he ought to have included kitchens and other rooms as he had done in the other cities.—*Cf. Eighth Inter. Cong. of Hygiene and Demography at Budapest, 1894,* vii, 425, where a résumé of Bertillon's *Essai* is given.

following percentages of the population to be living in over-crowded tenements:

Size of tenements.	Urban sanitary districts.	Rural sanitary districts.
1 room	1.61	0.25
2 rooms	4.42	2.48
3 "	3.46	2.83
4 "	2.82	2.90
Total	12.31	8.46

But with the recent improvements in city tenements, it is reasonably open to doubt if they are not cleaner and healthier habitations than thousands of dwellings in the country. We hear the most about city-tenements; on them is focused all the light of public attention. But no committees have investigated rural dwellings, nor does the metropolitan press spy them out. From personal observation, however, the writer believes that for every ill-kept city tenement, there is at least one rural shanty in as bad or worse condition. The factory having been purified by the pressure of public opinion and legislation, the city-tenement house is now yielding to similar pressure.

That the purely economic effects of the concentration of population are beneficial to society as a whole clearly follows from the fact that the movement itself is mainly in obedience to economic causes. Did it not result in the production of greater wealth, it would soon cease. Production increases with increasing density, and more particularly with increasing concentration, because there is opportunity for greater specialization; every man is placed where his strength and skill are exerted to the best advantage. Ambition has a wider field, and preëminent talent is more frequently brought to light. The statesman, from his acquaintance with the tax revenue returns, knows that cities, especially commercial

cities, are the seats of wealth.[1] And the economists have
shown that the urban wealth redounds to the advantage of
the rural districts as well, for, as Adam Smith long ago
pointed out, the cities afford a convenient and profitable
market for the rude products of the country. The volumi-
nous reports of the recent British Parliamentary commissions
merely serve to emphasize the statement, for they show that
the only agricultural districts in England that have been able
to endure the long agricultural depression without showing
signs of distress, are those around London and the industrial
towns. City markets stimulate intensive cultivation and improvements in agricultural methods; while commerce and
manufactures introduce order and good government, and
guarantee the liberty and security of individuals in both city
and country.[2]

Larger production, other things being equal, is identical
with greater individual wealth, for distribution is merely the
process of assigning to each worker the value of his product. If the average individual's share is expressed by
the quotient of total production divided by total population,
it must naturally increase when the dividend increases faster
than the divisor, as it does in the case of agglomerations.

[1] James Lowe, author of the famous *Present State of England* (1821), constantly refers to the poverty of rural places and their small share of the taxes. The
rich and powerful countries are those in which the concentration of population
has gone farthest, *e. g.*, the Dutch provinces. England is in proportion to population a richer and happier country than France; "in the size of her towns, this
great kingdom, so long the dread of our forefathers and of Europe, has in the last
present age been altogether surpassed by England and Scotland; for although
our island boast only half her population, the distribution of it is made in a
manner far more conducive to efficiency in a commercial and financial sense"
(p. 217).

[2] *Wealth of Nations*, Bk. iii, ch. 4. Smith also notes that the wealth acquired
in cities is often employed in purchasing lands, and thus devoted to agriculture.
But this ambition to enter the landed aristocracy was peculiar to England and
some other European countries, and is now fading away.

Bút normal distribution presupposes perfect competition, which in turn depends a great deal on the legal norms. When, for instance, laborers are forbidden by law to unite in associations for their own protection, the competition among employers for their services is imperfect. Given a tacit agreement among them not to pay more than a certain wage, and the weakening of a single workingman will establish an abnormally low wage for the entire body of laborers. Statesmen have learned that *laissez-faire* is the last thing to secure the competition on which all economic laws are based. On the other hand, there are many laws which interfere with this perfect competition. Among these are restraints upon freedom of movement,[1] which is one of the greatest factors in bringing about competition and justice in distribution. One of the conditions of the high wages prevailing in the United States is, without doubt, the unhampered ability of a laborer to migrate wherever his best interests lead him.[2]

Now with just public laws supplementing economic law in the regulation of the process of distribution, the concentration of population is particularly favorable to the workingmen. It gives every man the chance to show " what is in him." Moreover, and here is the strongest point, a dense population is the most favorable to strong organization. The trade-union movement, which has been a conspicuous force in improving the condition of English workingmen in the 19th century, (not so much, perhaps, from the economic or materialistic standpoint, as from the moral, intellectual and educative standpoint), would have been impossible without the association of large numbers in the cities. The trade union is in fact the only hope of those who have seen materialism prevail over spiritualism ever since the disrup-

[1] But there is considerable justification for such an exception to this rule as the United States contract labor immigration law.

[2] Cf. Walker, *Wages Question*, pp. 178–88.

tion of the familiar and friendly relations of master and employee by corporations and the system of centralized industry. And the trade union is peculiarly a city institution.

The movement towards the cities is therefore justified from the economic point of view, provided it does not go too far. But what is the limit? In the first place, it must be recognized that such a movement may continue after the forces that generated it have ceased to act. The reputation that cities enjoy for the payment of high wages may attract laborers after the adjustment between urban and rural rates of wages has been affected. The information on which men act may be misleading. Or men may over-estimate their prospects of success, just as they do when they flock to the gold fields. As a matter of fact, the average income in a mining camp is almost always small: it is even affirmed that less wealth has been taken out of the Klondike than men took into it. But men went there on the *expectation* of acquiring wealth. Moreover, it is possible that a goodly portion of the migrants to cities may not act on economic motives at all, but rush to the cities out of general discontent and a desire for change, rather than from any real inferiority in their economic rewards. The result would be superfluity of labor in the city and scarcity in the country.

It is hard to say whether this condition actually exists. We hear a great deal at times about the masses of the unemployed in our cities; but this is occasional and comes with commercial crises, which seem, unfortunately, to be a necessary part of the modern industrial system with its separation of producer and consumer, its rapid dynamic movement and its substructure of credit. In a time of ordinary business prosperity there are not many capable men permanently out of work in the cities. The complaints of pauperism result from the influx of tramps and country good-for-nothings, who are attracted by reports of extensive city charities. As a matter of fact, the number of really efficient workers who cannot find remunerative employment in our great cities is small; the testimony of those who have been connected with charity organization societies or with private employment bureaus will, it is believed, entirely substantiate this opinion.[1]

Nevertheless there is a widespread opinion in many countries that the movement has proceeded too far; that so long as the city received only the best blood of the rural districts, the cream of rural youth, it was a healthful tendency. Now, however, it is thought that the migratory current sweeps along vast numbers who are not adapted to town life.[2] This lower grade of labor (represented in American cities by the foreign-born) is said to imperil the standard of life of city laborers, undermining their forces in the battle with capital.

But there is another side to the picture, and before government or society attempts to put up the bars to the migration

---

[1] Messrs. R. Fulton Cutting and Walter L. Suydam, in reporting to the New York Association for Improving the Condition of the Poor on the subject of "Agricultural Depression in New York State" (*Leaflet No. 1*), came to the conclusion that "some attempt should at least be made to check that tide of migration to the city that threatens to make the condition of multitudes there quite intolerable. . . . . It is quite true that as far as regards the difficulty of obtaining employment in New York City for able-bodied men, we are far better situated than is London or many continental cities; yet we have a vast number of the very poor against whom the door of material improvement is well-nigh closed. Unskilled labor is always traveling too near the dead-line of dependence. The intermission of employment and occasional enforced idleness from sickness, coupled with the terrible rent-charge in New York city, makes it well-nigh impossible for the common laborer to save anything from his earnings" (p. 17). But this was written at a time of business depression (1896).

[2] *Vide* Graham's *Rural Exodus*, p. 2, and *passim*. Kingsbury ("The Tendency of Men to Live in Cities," an address at the 1895 meeting of the American Social Science Association, published in the *Journal* of the Association) observes that the newspaper advertisements for boys as clerks no longer read "one from the country preferred" as they did fifty or sixty years ago; which may signify either deterioration on the part of the rural migrants or improvement in city youths.

from country to city, it should consider the advantages which cities possess for assimilating elements that could not be utilized elsewhere, and of educating or taking care of the more helpless persons. On this point the conclusion reached by Dr. Devine in his discussion of the " Shiftless and Floating City Population " must be accepted by every one who really stops to consider the matter: [1] " Taking into account the national interest as a whole, the city is a better and less dangerous and less expensive place for the vagrant than the country. His migration to the city should be welcomed rather than discouraged. If he is in the city we shall be more conscious of his existence, but for that very reason we shall be better able to deal with him. There is greater taxable wealth and therefore greater resources for charitable relief and for correctional discipline. The whole of the repressive and remedial work can be done more efficiently and with better opportunities to watch the results than in the country."

On the other side, it is possible that a scarcity of labor may exist on the farm. Professor Sering affirms that in the agricultural fields of East Prussia, which are being depopulated by emigration, harvests have rotted for lack of labor.[2] And the extensive investigations of the German Socio-political Association show that the wages of farm hands have risen to a height that makes it impossible for many farmers to employ the labor they need.[3] It is complained that there is also a scarcity of farm servants in England,[4] but such is not the finding of the Royal Commission on Agriculture. In an

---

[1] *Annals of the Am. Acad.* (Sept., 1897), x, 159.

[2] *Die innere Colonisation im östlichen Deutschland* (vol. lvi of the publications of the Verein für Socialpolitik).

[3] *Die Verhältnisse der Landarbeiter in Deutschland, Schriften des Vereins für Socialpolitik*, vols. liii-lviii.

[4] Graham, *Rural Exodus*, p. 20.

investigation into the causes of agricultural depression in New York State it was found that the scarcity of good farm labor played a part; ten per cent. of the replies to the question, "What is the cause of the tendency among farmers and their families to leave their farms and live in towns and cities," assigned as a cause "the difficulty of obtaining good help in the house and on the farm." [1]

Now it may well be that urban expansion has at times outrun the growth of the contributory territory, so that the cities have become swollen with a surplus population without employment. This condition has been sorely felt in Australia, where vast government works have been completed and the laborers, temporarily thrown out of employment, have remained in the cities. But as to the alleged scarcity of labor in the agricultural districts being due to an excessive rush to the cities, it is sufficient to observe that the very provinces in Germany that make the loudest complaints have sent the largest number of emigrants across the ocean. Clearly, the migratory movement is not called into being by the cities alone; there must be dissatisfaction at home to cause such an outpouring across the sea as well as toward the city. The spirit of adventure, or the pressure of subsistence, or some other impelling motive, induced this great movement; not the mere attraction of the city on well-paid, comfortably-housed agricultural laborers.

In the United States there has always been a relative scarcity of good farm labor, from the fact that most men desired to own their farms and were usually able to do so on account of our vast domain. To-day, the depopulation of the rural districts in the East is caused not less by the migration westward than by the movement toward the cities.

As to England, evidence was presented in the second

[1] *A. I. C. P. Leaflet*, cited above, p. 8.

chapter of this essay [1] to the effect that no real depopulation of the rural districts had taken place. The conclusions of Drs. Ogle and Longstaff are confirmed in the Report of the Royal Commission on Labor, which states positively that rural emigration proceeds without reference to the local rate of wages, whether labor is relatively scarce and wages high or the opposite.[2]

It is worse than useless to attempt to stem the current of emigration from distressed farming districts, since migration is the one efficient remedy for such distress. And it should be thoroughly understood that a large migration from the country to the city is a perfectly natural phenomenon. Sir James Steuart has analyzed the movement in his excellent treatment of the distribution of population. "What occasion," he inquires, "has the country for supernumerary hands? If it has enough for the supply of its own wants and of the demands of the cities, has it not enough? Had it more, the supernumeraries would either consume without working, or if added to the class of laborers instead of being added to the number of free hands, would overturn the balance between the two classes; grain would become too plentiful and that would cost a general discouragement of agriculture, whereas by going to the cities they acquire money and therewith purchase the grain they would have consumed had they remained in the country; and this money which their additional labor in cities will force into circulation would otherwise have remained locked up, or at least would not have gone into the country but in consequence of the desertion of the supernumeraries. The proper and only right encouragement for agriculture is a moderate and gradual increase of demand for the productions of the earth, . . . and this demand must come from

[1] *Supra*, p. 45.

[2] *Fifth Report* (W. C. Little) in *Parl. Documents*, 1894, xxxv, 110.

cities, for the husbandmen never have occasion to demand;
it is they who offer for sale." [1]

II. POLITICAL EFFECTS.

The changes in the distribution of population which have
been considered in the present paper have necessarily
effected changes in State and national politics and national
power.

In the first place, it will be observed that the causes of
concentration are forces which augment national wealth.
Compare the distribution of wealth in the United States at
the present time and in 1787. In the Constitutional Con-
vention it was held [2] that the distribution of wealth was so
even throughout the country, that any system of taxation
might safely be based on numbers. How different in 1898!
The rural population is not less wealthy now than it was a
century since, but the urban population has amassed incal-
culably greater wealth.

Had England remained an agricultural country without
commerce and cities, she would not now be the powerful and
wealthy state that she is; and in saying this, it is not forgotten that national power depends not so much upon wealth
as upon manhood. But the controversy as to the relative
fighting capacity of the townsman and the countryman is
after all an idle one. Man for man, it is possible that the
agriculturists might be able to overpower the industrials,
though even this is very doubtful, as we saw in the last chapter. But on a given area industry will support so many
more men than agriculture will, that the former would
easily triumph in an armed conflict. A German student has
recently shown that the agricultural countries of England

[1] Sir James D. Steuart: *An Inquiry into the Principles of Political Economy
being an Essay on the Science of Domestic Policy in Free Nations;* in *Works,* i,
70. London, 1805.

[2] *Eliot's Debates,* v. 297 ff.

merely doubled their population in the period 1801–91, and even this increase depended in part on the presence of wealthy consumers in the cities.[1] Hence had England remained an agricultural country she would now have a population of about 16 million, instead of 28 million. The territory of England could not afford support to 28 million people producing their own food supply. The policy of German statesmen who would keep Germany an agricultural country for the sake of her army is therefore seen to be mistaken.

Of even more fundamental importance than national power is national stability. Anything affecting the constitution of the electorate must be of great interest; anything that diminishes the elector's love of country or interest in its preservation must excite distrust. Now land ownership has in the past been recognized as the most important conservative force in politics, and the statesman's ideal—even in England, the land of great landlords—has been a country of small landowners like France. But with increasing concentration of population goes an increase of tenancy, both as regards land and dwelling houses. The American statistics concerning the private ownership of dwelling houses show the following proportions of tenants in 1890:[2]

	Per cent.
Farms	34.08
Rural population	56.22
Cities of 8,000–100,000	64.04
" " 100,000+	77.17
United States	52.20

[1] J. Goldstein, *Berufsgliederung und Reichtum* (Stuttgart, 1897), p. 16, is an interesting monograph on the subject. It contains a full bibliography. On the opposite side of the question, see von Bindewald, " Eine Untersuchung über den Unterschied der Militärtauglichkeit ländlicher und städischer Bevölkerung," in *Jahrb. für N.-O. und Statistik*, lxx, 649 *seq.*

[2] *Abstract of the 11th Cens.*, 223. Holmes, "Tenancy in the United States," *Quar. Jour. of Econ.*, x, 37.

Several cities exceed the average of 77.17 per cent. for the great cities; thus New York's percentage was 93.67 (Greater New York about 85), Brooklyn, 81.44; Jersey City, 81.20; Boston, 81.57, etc. Rochester (56.02) and Milwaukee (57.87) make the most favorable showing. It may be worth while to note that the percentage of tenancy in Berlin (96.65) exceeds that of any American city.

Thus statistics show that the ownership of the home becomes less common in the degree that we leave the farm and village and proceed up (or down) the scale to the great cities. We do not wish to minimize the importance of this fact from the political point of view, and yet we must remember that there are other forms of property than real estate. If a man who rents his home has a good bank-account, he is not likely to vote for the overthrow of government.[1]

The extensive distribution of government bonds among French citizens is felt to be an influence favorable to conservatism scarcely inferior to the ownership of the soil of France by millions of peasant proprietors. And the American election of 1896 proved that the land-owner is not necessarily a conservative, nor the city man necessarily a radical. For whatever our opinion as to the merits of the controversy, it must be conceded that the cause supported by the farmers involved radical changes, while the city populations voted to conserve the *status quo*.

Nevertheless, the danger of class antagonism is particularly grave in the cities. Dives and Lazarus become figures too familiar to let us rest in peace. The chasm created by the industrial system yawns widest in the cities; and the means of bridging it will require careful consideration.

In internal politics the changes causing or accompanying

---

[1] And it may be observed that England's government has been more stable than any continental government, notwithstanding the concentration of its landed property in a few hands.

the concentration of population have brought many new problems to the front, of which the question of taxation is a good specimen. As previously noted, wealth followed population so evenly in the United States of 1790 that even a per capita tax would have been equitable, while the general property tax generally adopted gave perfect satisfaction. But the general property tax has utterly broken down in the last few years on account of the growth of other forms of wealth than immovable property.[1] And so it is generally; the complexity of modern city civilization demands new laws and new policies. And the most conspicuous problem is the difficulty of governing the cities themselves.

Aristotle saw the difficulty of governing a vast agglomeration of people, and limited the population of his ideal city-state to 10,000.[2] There is, indeed, a vast difference between the government of a city and that of a village. A dense population engenders problems that are never thought of in a village. Run the eye over a directory of the public officials of a great city and observe how few of them are known to village governments. Building departments, paving, fire, health, park, public improvement, library, public building boards; city auditor, corporation counsel, city architect, surveyor, superintendent of markets, sewers, bridges, printing; inspectors of milk, provisions, lime, petroleum; a sealer of weights and measures, etc., etc. It would take pages merely to enumerate the officials of New York city, the majority of whom perform functions to which no parallel is found in the village.

The complexity of a city government, the multifariousness of its duties, make it the most difficult kind of government to watch. Even the national government does not undertake to regulate so many details, and the general supervision

[1] Seligman, *Essays in Taxation*, chs. i and ii.
[2] De Republica, l. 7.

to which it is mainly limited can be more easily watched. The city is in many respects a great business corporation; it calls for a careful, systematic, business-like administration. Now, administration is a branch of politics in which Americans have hitherto shown more awkwardness than is pleasant to think of. Corruption if not inefficiency has been the characteristic mark of public administration, especially in the cities. And the reason why Americans have submitted to such service, has been its small sphere, as compared with the sphere of local (*i. e.* rural) government, which has been the strength of our democratic institutions. As Mr. Bryce has said: "Americans constantly reply to the criticisms which Europeans pass on the faults of their State legislatures and the shortcomings of Congress by pointing to the healthful efficiency of their rural administration, which enables them to bear with composure the defects of the higher organs of government."[1] Now it is obvious that with the rapid movement of population from the rural districts to the cities, the sphere of local rural government (typified in the town-meeting, the glory of New England and New England's sons in every part of the Union) has been continually narrowed. With only 25 or 35 per cent. of our people residing in the rural districts (Massachusetts), the "healthy efficiency of rural administration" signifies but little.

The difficulties of city government ("the one conspicuous failure in American politics") are enhanced by the large floating population which is a necessary accompaniment of a great migratory movement toward the cities. The thousands of new residents are strangers to the city's history and traditions, have no local attachments, and do not readily acquire any civic pride. The vast majority are non-taxpayers, and feel little concern in the city's government.

[1] *American Commonwealth*, 2d ed., i, 591.

The ignorance of local history and geography is in fact almost appalling, and our municipalities have but just begun to provide instruction on these subjects, which may in time awaken civic pride.[1]

On top of these obstacles to good government comes the problem of assimilating the foreign nationalities. When the foreign immigrants settle in isolated "quarters," which is the natural tendency, much effort is required to raise them to the city's standard. This is perhaps the one danger of the "movement toward the cities" so far as the United States is concerned: the influx of a shiftless and degraded population from foreign lands, which cannot be readily distributed throughout the country.

Inasmuch as this is not a treatise on municipal government, no discussion of proposed reforms is in place. But one thing is to be strenuously insisted upon, and that is the right of the cities to self-government. The strength of our political institutions has always been in local government, and the only hope for our cities is freedom to work out for themselves a plan of government which shall take the place of the rural local administration that has been our boast in times past. "The problem of modern times is how to make life possible in large cities devoted to industrial activities, and this is a problem which cannot be dealt with except by the cities themselves." The only hope for the cities is to educate the mass of the propertyless, and this will never be accomplished until the liberal and generous minds of the city have the assurance that their work is not liable to be undone at any moment by the State legislature.

[1] New York and other large cities have popular lecture courses in which these themes are sometimes handled. Many of the cities also have societies of large membership devoted to the investigation of local history and propagation of results. The city of Brookline, Mass., has recently prepared a text-book for its school children, which is a local geography, a botany, a geology, a history, and a treatise on civil government as related to that town.

Amidst the discouragements incited by a contemplation of the failure of our city governments to achieve anything like the success of American rural local government, we may derive some small consolation from the fact that things are not now so bad as they used to be. Let us read De Tocqueville's description of our cities in the thirties, and take fresh courage to renew the struggle for municipal reform. Says the illustrious author of *Democracy of America* (Reeve's trans. 2d Am. ed., p. 270):

" The United States have no metropolis; but they already contain several very large cities. Philadelphia reckoned 161,000 inhabitants, and New York 202,000 in 1830. The lower orders which inhabit these cities constitute a rabble even more formidable than the populace of European towns. They consist of freed Blacks in the first place, who are condemned by the laws and by public opinion to an hereditary state of misery and degradation. They also contain a multitude of Europeans who have been driven to the shores of the New World by their misfortunes or their misconduct, and these men inoculate the United States with all their vices, without bringing with them any of those interests which counteract their baneful influence. As inhabitants of a country where they have no civil rights, they are ready to turn all the passions which agitate the community to their own advantage; thus, within the last few months serious riots have broken out in Philadelphia and New York. Disturbances of this kind are unknown in the rest of the country, which is nowise alarmed by them because the population of the cities has hitherto exercised neither power nor influence over the rural districts.

" Nevertheless, I look upon the size of certain American cities, and especially on the nature of their population, as a real danger which threatens the future security of the democratic republic of the New World; and I venture to predict that they will perish from this circumstance, unless the Government succeeds in creating an armed force, which, whilst it remains under the control of the majority of the nation, will be independent of the town population and able to repress its excesses."

III. SOCIAL EFFECTS

Having considered the economic and political effects of the concentration of population, we may now conclude with an estimation of the social effects upon urban and rural communities, and a general summary from the point of view of society as a whole.

As to the cities themselves, we have just noted how good government and even social solidarity are threatened by class antagonisms. The actual cause of such social antipathies will be found in an exaggerated individualism, which has been developed by an era of industrialism, out of mediæval militarism. The new industrial forces which transformed the solidified Age of Authority into a liquefied Age of Freedom, have naturally been more predominant in the cities than elsewhere, for the close contact of man with man in a dense population removes prejudices and engenders liberalism. The cities have always been the cradles of liberty, just as they are to-day the centers of radicalism. Every man of the world knows that isolation and solitude are found in a much higher degree in the crowded city than in a country village, where one individual's concerns are the concern of all. The cities, then, are favorable to free thought and the sense of individual responsibility.[1]

But it is a question whether the loosening of the ties of individual responsibility has not gone too far. " The great danger to morality and good government," says Roscher, " is that the individual is lost in the multitude of atoms,—a condition that may abolish the sense of duty and make the great city as insecure as the opposite extreme, the wilderness."[2] Now this extreme individualism of the cities is merely one manifestation of the—shall we say excessive—fluidity of modern society, and its cause is chiefly industrial. Cities vary in their lack of social feeling (*i. e.*, individualism), and those cities have the least portion of it which are most given

---

[1] An exception is here made in favor of the strength of social opinion in the matter of Fashion. Manufacturers testify that their only market for goods that have gone out of fashion is in the agricultural districts. This exception will be discussed as a part of the subject of Materialism.

[2] Roscher's *System*, vol. iii, *Nationalœkonomik des Handels und Gewerbefleisses* § 6, 5th ed., p. 37.

to industrial enterprises in which the competitive system has obtained full sway.

It may be said, indeed, that it is our industrial system, and not city life, which engenders the essentially egoistic, self-seeking and materialistic attitude; but so long as the cities remain the results of the competitive industrial régime, they must share the blame. No one can view with equanimity the continual drift of population to the cities where it will be subject to such demoralizing influences.

"The modern town is a result of the desire to produce and distribute most economically the largest aggregate of material goods; economy of work, not convenience of life, is the object. Now, the economy of factory co-operation is only social to a very limited extent; anti-social feelings are touched and stimulated at every point by the competition of workers with one another, the antagonism between employers and employed, between sellers and buyers, factory and factory, shop and shop.[1] Where the density of population is determined by industrial competition rather than by human-social causes, it would seem that the force of sound public opinion is in inverse proportion to the density of population, being weakest in the most crowded cities. In spite of the machinery of political, religious, social and trade organizations in large towns, it is probable that the true spiritual cohesiveness between individual members is feebler than in any other form of society. If it is true that as the larger village grows into the town, and the town into the ever larger city, there is a progressive weakening of the bonds of moral cohesion between individuals, that the larger the town the feebler the spiritual unity, we are face to face with the heaviest indictment that can be brought against modern industrial progress, and the forces driving an increased proportion of our population into towns are bringing about a

[1] Hobson, *Evolution of Capitalism*, 340.

decadence of *morale*, which is the necessary counterpart of the deterioration of national physique." [1]

This separation of classes which has so nearly destroyed social solidarity in all large cities, is especially dangerous in the United States (where, under democratic forms, solidarity is especially indispensable) on account of differences in race and religion, as well as social rank and condition. In American cities the "upper" social ranks—the commercial and professional classes—are predominantly American and Protestant; the "lower" ranks—the hewers of wood and drawers of water—are on the contrary chiefly of foreign origin and of the Roman Catholic faith. The danger of class antagonism is therefore peculiarly great in our cities.

What can be done to wipe out class feelings and unify the community? A brief survey of what has already been done will encourage those who have most clearly perceived the dangers of the competitive system and the concentration of population in modern cities, which have been called the "most impersonal combinations of individuals that have ever been formed in the world's history."

Social observers have for some time been aware that society is emerging from the period of Industrialism into a period of Humanitarianism.[2] Criticism of Industrialism began as soon as it was discovered that its fundamental idea (Individualism) was not identical with personal welfare. Scepticism, *laissez-faire*, the insistence upon rights as opposed to mediæval restrictions and obligations, succeeded in freeing the individual from the authority of superiors, but turned him over to the tender mercy of things that society had created and not learned to control. Matter was exalted over mind, and the twin-companion of Individualism was

---

[1] Hobson, *Evolution of Capitalism*, 342.

[2] Cf. the exceedingly interesting and instructive work of J. S. Mackenzie, *Introduction to Social Philosophy*, ch. ii, and *passim*.

Materialism. The guild-laws had scarcely been abolished in England before factory legislation began—the opening of a new period of Reconstruction. Carlyle and Ruskin were the prophets of the new order; Owen, Kingsley, Maurice, its active servants. In recent years every enlightened country has enacted laws along the line of *personal welfare.* Some call such legislation Socialism; it is in the spirit of coöperation—Humanitarianism.

Now, it is perfectly natural that the most noticeable traces of the humanitarian movement should be found in the cities, where the greatest abuses of industrialism and materialism existed. Men cannot live long in close contact without acquiring a painful sense of the separateness of individual interests, of the absurdity of identifying the individual's interest with the interest of society and the consequent policy of *laissez-faire.* I may enjoy playing a cornet during the cool summer evenings; but that is not to the interest of my neighbor who has to go to work early in the morning and so needs early sleep. It may be greatly to my interest to build a tannery on a vacant city lot that comes to me cheap; but it is not the interest of people who have fine residences on adjoining property. It may be to my interest to employ poverty-stricken families, living amidst filth and contagious diseases, to make cheap shirts and clothing; but it is not to the interest of my fellow-citizens. In short, there arise a thousand and one conflicts between individual interests and social interests, and in their adjustment selfishness is curbed and a social feeling excited. This explains why Socialism has so far been largely Municipal Socialism. It is easier, and at the same time more necessary, for the people in a city to coöperate.[1]

Political coöperation, however, will not operate to remedy

[1] This idea is further developed by Dr. Maltbie in *Municipal Socialism* (*Municipal Affairs*, Dec., 1898).

all the evils of an extreme individualism.[1]   Accordingly, we see a multitude of philanthropic associations and enterprises in every great city.   The guide-book to reform clubs in New York city is a volume of no mean dimensions.   All these associations unite to foster civic pride and a spirit of mutual helpfulness.   And still something is lacking to overcome the indifference of the "West Side" to the "East Side" and the lack of neighborly feelings expressed in the North Country proverb: "Friends are far when neighbors are near."   The poor become hopeless, "the submerged tenth," from want of stimulus and help, and the rich become "charityless" from want of the insight that personal contact gives.[2]   To bring together rich and poor is the office of university and other social settlements—Toynbee Hall in London, Hull House in Chicago, and many others.   This is perhaps the most promising of all social movements.[3]   It

[1] Prof. Patten, however, believes the contrary.   As an instance, he says that just as national feelings grow when the wealthy classes can no longer hire substitutes for the army, so civic pride will grow when they cannot have private filters for city water, etc.—*Theory of Social Forces, Annals of Am. Acad. of Pol. & Soc. Sc.*, Sup., Jan., 1896, p. 149.

[2] "The isolation of classes is an evil for all; and as those of us who have means and leisure go to the mountains or to the seaside for the health of our bodies and the relaxation of our minds, so may we ultimately find it necessary to betake ourselves to the centres of our overcrowded populations for the health of our souls. Many at least begin to feel this as a duty."—Mackenzie, *Introd. to Soc. Phil.*, p. 320.

[3] Prof. Patten apparently sympathizes little with such reformatory efforts.   Take the case of a drunkard.   "Mortality tries to reform and only checks social differentiation; the aesthetic feeling pushes him and the saloon out into the back alleys, and thus promotes differentiation by freeing home life and public places from the worst evils, and allowing the growth of refined social feelings.   The integrating tendencies can then produce higher types of men and give them vantage ground for the displacement of the lower types." (*Theory of Social Forces*, p. 151.) As regards *institutions*, we all agree with Prof. Patten, but we can hope for nothing from such treatment of *men*.   If the drunkards and criminals could actually be displaced in this manner, it might be otherwise (but the inhumanity of it!).   But, as it is, these classes are the very ones who will propagate their kind and contaminate the whole neighborhood if left to themselves.

signifies charity in the highest sense—not the selfish opening of the pocket to free oneself from the annoyance of a
beggar or to buy entrance into Paradise.

We may conclude, then, that the cities have a great many
difficult problems to solve; that they have begun to face
these problems and have already applied certain remedies;
that much effort is still needed to make city life what it
should be, and that the principal basis of hope lies in the
decentralizing forces that have recently appeared.[1]

Concerning the effects of the movement toward the cities
upon the rural population, we have already said something
from the economic point of view. Socially regarded, it is a
misfortune *for the villages* that their most enterprising and
choice youth should be drawn away. This must certainly
lower the tone of town and village life and even produce a
local stagnation. The recruits that the villages receive from
the farms partially replace their losses to the city, but on the
whole the villages give more than they receive. Hence they
do not so readily keep up with the march of progress, being
less quick to adopt improvements from the city. The process of equalization proceeds less rapidly. The evil effects
upon the villages of the emigration of their fresh blood is
noticeable in their schools. The superintendent of public
instruction of New York affirms that the cities have sucked
the life out of the country schools,[2] and the governor of
Pennsylvania in his annual message (1897) recommends the
provision of better schools (high schools) in the districts in
order to keep the youth from going to the towns and cities
for their education.

The fact is that a radical change in educational methods

---

[1] *Infra*, ch. ix. That the conditions of life in our great cities can be improved
and must be improved is strongly urged by Dr. Shaw, *Municipal Government in
Great Britain*, 9. *Cf.* also Gladden, *Social Facts and Forces*, 161.

[2] *Report*, 1896.

has been silently effected by the industrial forces of which this essay treats. Under the regime of domestic industry, children were educated by co-operating with their parents on the farm, where the pursuit of both agriculture and the useful arts furnished industrial training, and constant association with adults (especially with the children's parents) provided mental and moral training. In the handicraft regime, boys learned trades as apprentices. Under the modern regime (factory system), country boys have no opportunity to learn trades on the farm or in a village shop. Mental and manual training have been differentiated; the latter cannot be acquired outside the cities, and the former until lately has suffered in village communities from lack of facilities. But the fact has already been noted that a comprehensive report on the subject of rural schools was presented in 1897 to the National Educational Association, and now that the faults have been pointed out, intelligent efforts for reform may be made. Unification of school districts, better teachers, more instruction in nature study and practical agriculture, are needed. About 11,000,000 out of a total 14,000,000 school children are in the schools of towns of less than 8,000 inhabitants, and the nation or State cannot afford to overlook their interests.

The "religious destitution of villages" is a recognized problem, strange as it may seem to those who have observed the evils of city life alone. To many people the Fast Day proclamation of the governor of New Hampshire issued April 6, 1899, came as a revelation by reason of its explicit reference to the decline of the Christian religion in rural communities, which he affirmed is a marked feature of the times. The governor's official recognition of the decay of religion in villages may invite attention to the considerable body of literature on the subject.[1]

[1] *Vide* the pertinent chapter in Crooker's *Problems in American Society*, together with the references therein.

Henry George puts the case against city growth in its worst light when he says [1] that " just as the wen or tumor, drawing the wholesome juice of the body into its vortex, impoverishes all other parts of the frame, so does the crowding of human beings in the city impoverish human life in the country. The unnatural life of the great cities means an equally unnatural life in the country." [1]

What, if any, are the benefits secured to the entire social body in compensation for these evil effects of concentration of population upon the life of the non-urban population? And is there no advantage to the villages themselves?

Economically, as we have learned, the concentration of large masses of people upon small areas at once multiplies human wants and furnishes the means of their satisfaction ; and the benefits are communicated to the surrounding country, which finds in the cities a market for its production and a stimulus to the diversification of the same.

Socially, the influence of the cities is similarly exerted in favor of liberal and progressive thought. The variety of occupation, interests and opinions in the city produces an intellectual friction, which leads to a broader and freer judgment and a great inclination to and appreciation of new thoughts, manners, and ideals. City life may not have produced genius, but it has brought thinkers into touch with one another, and has stimulated the divine impulse to originate by sympathy or antagonism. [2] As the seat of political power, as the nursery of the arts and sciences, as the center of industry and commerce, the city represents the highest achievements of political, intellectual and industrial life. [3] The rural population is not merely conservative ; it is

[1] *Social Problems*, 317.

[2] Pearson, *National Life and Character*, p. 150.

[3] Rümelin, *Reden und Aufsätze*, i, 352.

full of error and prejudice; it receives what enlightenment
it possesses from the city. Nor is the small city free from
the same reproach; while it performs the useful function of
an intermediary between the progressiveness, liberalism,
radicalism of the great city, and the conservatism, bigotry,
of the country, it is the chief seat of the pseudo-bourgeois
Philistine. *Kleinstädtisch* is in German almost as much a reproach as the *paganus* or *rusticus* of the Latin. The contrast
between city and rural populations and civilizations is as
clearly marked in the United States as in any other modern
country; the North represents one, the South the other.
While not denying the many admirable traits of Southern
character, we cannot overlook the prevalence of prejudice
and provincialism which has cut off the South from participation in the lofty patriotism and national feeling existent in
other parts of the United States. Americans of the present
generation are destined to see this provincialism vanish before the powerful influences of large cities, which the introduction of manufactures and commerce on a large scale will
in a short time produce. The South will be brought into
contact with the current of world-thought. To the negro
race justice will at length be accorded, and a stronger feeling of fraternity toward the North will grow up, strengthen-
ing the bonds of patriotism.

It is emphatically true that the growth of cities not only
increases a nation's economic power and energy, but quick-
ens the national pulse. In the present age, the influence of
the cities is not perhaps so strong in the direction of the
noblest thought and culture, because the present age is
essentially materialistic. But there is some reason for believ-
ing that Materialism is gradually giving way before Humanitarianism, and we may hope in time to see the great cities
exercise as noble a domination in the world of thought as
was maintained by the Athens of Pericles and Aeschylus, by

the Rome of Lucretius and Juvenal, by the Florence of Michel Angelo, by the London of Elizabeth, and by the Paris of the second half of the seventeenth century. [1]

It is at least ground for encouragement that the leading nations of the modern world are those which have the largest city populations. That cities are both cause and consequence of a high *Cultur* can hardly be doubted.

But the highest social service performed by the cities will not be realized until we have made clear to ourselves their function in the process of natural selection. Otto Ammon's comparison of this process of natural selection in human society with that of horse-breeding is not flattering to a human being's sense of dignity; but he expresses the facts when he likens cities to folds (*Pferche*) into which the most desirable bloods are brought and nourished on a superior diet. Inside the fold are divisions to secure the concentration of the breeder's attention upon the very few superior animals. These divisions in the cities are the social classes (*Stände*): the laborers, small undertakers, etc., in the lower classes; business men, large undertakers and subordinate public officials in the middle class; the professional men and higher officials in the upper class. [2] Ammon, and others of his school, have gone so far as to claim that the process of natural selection involved in migration cityward produces a distinct race—the dolicocephalic or long heads, as distinguished from the brachycephalic or round heads, who remain in the rural districts. [3] But such facts, when once es-

---

[1] Pearson, *op. cit.*, 152.

[2] *Die Natürliche Auslese*, sec. 404.

[3] Ammon and Lapouge are the leading representatives of this theory, which may be found in the former's *Die Natürliche Auslese beim Menschen* (p. 183 ff), *Gesellschaftsordnung*, etc., and in English in the latter's article entitled "The Fundamental Laws of Anthropo-Sociology," in the *Jour. of Pol. Econ.*, vi. 54-92. The theory is also set forth by Glosson in the articles " Dissociation by Displace-

tablished, will have an interest only for the anthropologist, since any real connection between cranial development and mental capacity still remains to be recognized. While the Anglo-Saxons and North Germans are dolicocephalic, so are the negroes, Hottentots, native Australians and other inferior races.[1]

The city is the spectroscope of society; it analyzes and sifts the population, separating and classifying the diverse elements. The entire progress of civilization is a process of differentiation, and the city is the greatest differentiator. The mediocrity of the country is transformed by the city into the highest talent or the lowest criminal. Genius is often born in the country, but it is brought to light and developed by the city. On the other hand, the opportunities of the city work just as powerfully in the opposite direction upon the countrymen of an ignoble cast; the boy thief of the village becomes the daring bank robber of the metropolis.

Taking this view of the cities as the central instruments of the process of differentiation, we shall be able to reconcile the differences of those who regard the cities as "ulcers on the body politic" (Jefferson) and those who place them at

ment," *Quar. Jour. of Econ.*, x, 156, and "The Hierarchy of Races," *Amer. Jour. of Sociology*, iii. Lapouge attempts to show that the *Homo Europeus* or dolicocephalic type, as contrasted with the *Homo Alpinus* (brachycephalic) is the more active and dominant race. This view is critically examined by Ripley, "Racial Geography of Europe," *Pop. Science Monthly*, 52: 479. Dr. Ripley promises a complete bibliography on Anthropology (to be issued by the Boston Public Library). Short bibliographies may be found in Lapouge's article above cited, in *Pol. Sc. Quar.*, x, 647, and in *Bulletin of the Inter. Institute of Statistics.* viii, 266.

[1] The cephalic index here referred to is the ratio of the breadth of head to its length. When the index is less than 80, the skull is said to be dolicocephalic (long-head); when more than 80, brachycephalic. The cephalic index of the three inferior races mentioned is between 71 and 75, of Celts and Anglo-Saxons, 76–78, of the South Germans, 83–84.

the apex of civilization.[1]   The fact that the cities make the
opinions, fashions and ideals of mankind, rests upon the vast-
ness of opportunity that they afford.   But it is clear that
opportunity to do good and become great involves opportunity to accomplish evil, that is, temptation.   Compare the
devices against burglary in an advanced country with those
in a more backward country; the Yale lock of America with
the ponderous keys and old-fashioned locks, that almost any
one can pick with a button-hook, in Germany.   Compare
the wonderfully complicated equipment against burglars in
a metropolitan bank with the ordinary safes and vaults of a
country bank.   A progressive or dynamic civilization implies
the good and bad alike.   The cities, as the foci of progress,
inevitably contain both good and bad.

Insanity and suicide, both essentially characteristic of industrialism, are naturally more prevalent in the centers of
industry and business, where the real stress and competition
in life are found.   The downward stream of failures explains
the excess of insanity, suicide and crime in the city, the result of a process thrust upon the cities by society and performed for the benefit of society.   It is the penalty paid for
progress.[2]

[1] " The life that men live in the cities, gives the type and measure of their
civilization.   The word 'civilization' means the manner of life of the civilized
part of the community; that is, of the city men, not of the countrymen, who are
called rustics, and were once called pagans (*pagani*), or the heathen of the
villages."—*Frederic Harrison.*

[2] Prof. Ripley has brought out the contrasts between urban and rural communities in somewhat exaggerated form: "In every population we may distinguish
two modes of increase or evolution, which vary according to economic opportunity for advancement.   One community grows from its own loins; children
born in it remain there, grow up to maturity, and transmit their mental and
physical peculiarities unaltered to the next generation.   Such a group of population develops from within, mentally as well as physically, by inheritance.   Such
is the type of the average rural community.   It is conservative in all respects,
holding to the past with unalterable tenacity.   Compare with that a community
which grows almost entirely by immigration.   Stress of competition is severe.

It is the fallacy of averages that obscures much of the best in city life. Thus, in the matter of death rates, the cities appear to poor advantage when compared with rural communities. But in almost every large city one or more wards may be found in which not only the crude death-rate, but also the refined rate and the still more expressive rate of infant mortality, are lower than in the rural districts.[1]

The only doubt of the efficiency of the city's process of natural selection is thus removed, because these healthful wards, it is hardly necessary to say, are the better residential quarters. It is not, therefore, the unfit that survive, which is the complaint of Dr. Ogle, who declares that "the combined effect of the constantly higher mortality in the town and of the constant immigration into it of the pick of the rural population must clearly be a gradual deterioration of the whole, inasmuch as the more energetic and vigorous members of the community are consumed more rapidly than the rest of the population. The system is one which leads to the survival of the unfittest."[2]   Even if the "fittest" mem-

There is no time for rearing children; nor is it deemed desirable, for every child is a handicap for further social advancement. Marriage, even, unless it be deferred until late in life, is an expensive luxury. . . . . Such is the type known as the modern great city," which is the type of progress. (*Pop. Sc. Monthly*, 52 : 480).

[1] This is true of at least half of the 28 large cities of the United States (Cf. *Vital Statistics of Cities of 100,000+ at the 11th Census*). A few examples follow:

		Deaths per 1,000.	
		All ages.	Under 5 years.
Rural part of registration States		15.66	40.65
Cities in registration States		23.48	93.43
Allegheny, Pa. (Ward 5)		14.72	44.82
Cincinnati " 26		10.27	40.34
Cleveland " 6		9.44	31.25
Detroit " 4		15.01	37.87
Pittsburg " 31		15.55	34.58
St. Louis " 27		13.88	39.42

[2] *Jour. of St. Soc.*, 52 : 208. This was virtually the complaint of Süssmilch over a hundred years ago. Cf. *Die göttliche Ordnung*, vol. i, ch. iii, sec. 52 (p. 162 of 2d ed., 1761).

bers of society did perish earlier in the struggle for existence in the city than in the country, it would be open to doubt if society would not gain more by their residence in the city where they can find scope for their abilities than in the country without opportunities for performing the highest social service of which they are capable. But with the modern combination of city business life and rural residence, or at least open-air holidays and recreation periods, and the opportunities that cities alone offer for the carrying on of athletic sports and games, the best blood of the race is not liable to extinction. Even Professor Marshall, who is inclined to over-rate the dangers of city life, reaches an optimistic conclusion in his final review of modern tendencies: [4]

"The progress of knowledge and in particular of medical science, the ever-growing activity and wisdom of Government in all matters relating to health, and the increase of material wealth, all tend to lessen mortality and to increase health and strength and to lengthen life. On the other hand, vitality is lowered and the death-rate raised by the rapid increase of town-life, and by the tendency of the higher strain of population to marry later and to have fewer children than the lower. If the former set of causes were alone in action, but so regulated as to avoid the danger of over-population, it is probable that man would quickly rise to a physical and mental excellence superior to any that the world has yet known; while if the latter set acted unchecked he would speedily degenerate.

"As it is, the two sets hold one another very nearly in balance, the former slightly preponderating. While the population of England is growing nearly as fast as ever, those who are out of health in body and mind are certainly not an increasing part of the whole; and the rest are much better fed and clothed, and, with a few exceptions, are stronger than they were."

[1] *Principles of Economics*, p. 285.

CHAPTER IX

TENDENCIES AND REMEDIES

ONE of the conclusions derived from the statistics of urban growth presented in the second chapter of this essay is that the process of concentration of population is centralizing in its tendencies; that is, the large cities are growing more rapidly than the small cities and absorbing the great bulk of the urban increase. Levasseur's hypothesis that " the power of attraction of human groups is, in general, proportionate to their mass "[1] was nearly everywhere sustained. The only important exceptions were the United States, England and Austria; but it was shown that the large cities in Austria were leading all the others so soon as their boundaries were extended to take in the city populations in the suburbs. In England, where it is also true that the middle-sized cities have been growing more rapidly than London and other large cities, a similar explanation can be made. The middle-sized cities which are leaving the other cities behind are suburbs of the metropolis and other large cities. In the decade 1881–91 there were six cities in England which showed an increase of more than 50 per cent., and the first four of these were suburbs of London.[2] At the present time the great cities spread out over such an enormous territory that their growth can best be viewed in the light of county

[1] *La Pop. fran.*, ii, 355.

[2] Leyton, 133.3 per cent. increase; Willesden, 121.9; Tottenham, 95.1; West Ham, 58.9; Ystradyfodwg, 58.8; Cardiff, 55.8. (*Census of England and Wales*, iv, 12, 13.) The latter two are Welsh mining towns.

446

statistics. Now, in the last decade, 20 of the 55 English (registration) counties increased in population by more than ten per cent.[1] The leading four counties with their percentages of increase were:

Middlesex 50.93
Essex 37.82
Glamorganshire 33.70
Surrey 24.09

Now Middlesex, Essex and Surrey are adjacent to London and contain the London suburbs; all three had a larger increase than the middle-sized cities (22.9 per cent.), which led London and the great towns proper. Kent (13.7) and Sussex (12.2), are also close to London and are within the first fourteen counties of most rapid growth in 1881–91. Inasmuch as the counties preserved approximately the same rank in 1881–91 as in 1871–81, it may be regarded as established that London (including its tributary population) is the most rapidly-growing group in England.

As regards the United States, the figures are not quite so convincing. In Chapter II it was indeed shown that among Massachusetts cities the most rapid growth is in the suburbs of Boston; but even there it remains a fact that " Greater Boston " (either the 8 or 12 mile radius) had a smaller increase than the aggregate population of the 32 towns under municipal government.[2] In New York State, although some individual cities, notably Buffalo, have outstripped New York—and even the New York suburbs,—as a class the inland towns rank below the metropolis, especially when the legal boundries of the latter are extended so as to embrace the towns and cities constituting the metropolitian groups.[3]

[1] *Ibid.*, p. 7. Glamorganshire is a mining county, as are five or six other counties of rapid growth.

[2] *Ante*, p. 38. Cf. *Mass. Census of 1895*, Pt. i, 45–49.

[3] *Supra*, Table CXLIX, footnote. *Cf.* the writer's article in *North Amer. Rev.*, 166: 615.

While, on the whole, there is a strong tendency in the United States for manufacturing industry to locate in small cities like Fall River, Lawrence, New Bedford, etc., even such cities sooner or later enter the class of large cities; and commerce is wholly centralizing. Hence even in the United States, the general proposition remains true that the great cities (the class of 100,000+ population) are bound to absorb an ever-increasing proportion of the country's population; for the class of great cities increases not only by the growth of the cities themselves, but also by the constant accession of smaller cities, without any corresponding loss.

The fact, then, that urban growth is essentially a great-city growth, prompts us to examine with more care than we have yet done the position of the great city, the direction of its development, and if possible the limits of its growth. Then we may be able to suggest remedies for certain of the ills inherent in the situation.

The ancient world was acquainted with great cites whose magnificence and wickedness do not yield to modern capitals. There are no accurate figures concerning the population of Thebes, Memphis, Babylon, Nineveh, Susa and Egbatana; but the fact that the Greeks spoke of them with wonder argues their magnitude. For the Greeks themselves had several cities exceeding 100,000 in population. In the fifth century both Athens and Syracuse certainly surpassed this figure, and Syracuse had not then touched the zenith of her power. Carthage probably reached the figure of 700,-000. At the beginning of the Christian era, Alexandria contained 500,000, possibly 700,000 inhabitants, and a considerable number of Roman cities reached the 100,000 class; but all of them, with the exception of Rome herself, were outside of Italy. Rome's population was 600,000–800,000; certainly not over 1,000,000; and during the first three centuries of the present era, it fluctuated about the number

500,000. After Rome's decay, Constantinople was the only European city whose population exceeded 100,000; but Constantinople in the early middle ages was overshadowed by Bagdad and rivalled by Damascus and Cairo. The modern period was well begun (1600) before Paris wrested the first place from Constantinople, only to be overtaken and passed by London before the end of the seventeenth century.

At the beginning of the sixteenth century Europe had six or seven cities of the 100,000+ class; at its end some 13–14. This century was the period of commercial expansion and New World conquests.

The seventeenth century was the period of the civil and religious wars. The great cities did not increase in number, Vienna and Madrid merely taking the place of Antwerp and Messina, which dropped out of the class. But their population increased about forty per cent. during the century, while Europe's population was nearly stationary.

During the eighteenth century the population both of Europe and of the great cities increased about 50 per cent, and the number of great cities rose to 22. Their aggregate population in 1800 constituted about three per cent of Europe's population (say 4,100,000 in 120,000,000).

During the nineteenth century the number of great cities has increased tremendously. In Europe alone the increase is calculated by Meuriot[1] as follows:

CITIES OF 100,000 +.

Year.	No.	Aggregate pop.	Ratio to total pop.
1850	42	9,000,000	3.80
1870	70	20,000,000	6.66
1895	120	37,000,000	10.00

[1] In his recent work (pp. 30–31) devoted especially to the great cities: *Des Agglomérations urbaines dans l'Europe contemporaine; Essai sur les causes, les conditions, les conséquences de leur developpement.* Paris, 1897.

Table CLXIII.

	Rank of European cities in the years: 1500. 1600. 1800.			Population in 1800. 1850. 1890. (oo omitted.)			Annual increase per cent. 1800–90. 1850–90.	
Group A.								
1.	2.	3.	4.	5.	6.	7.	8.	9.
1. London		9	1	958,8	2,362,1	4,211,7	3.77	1.96
2. New York.....	..	..	..	62,9	660,8	2,740,6	47.3	7.89
3. Paris................	2	1	2	546,9	1,053,3	2,448,0	3.81	3.31
4. Berlin...............	..	..	10	173,4	378,2	1,578,8	9.08	7.94
5. Vienna..............	..	..	8	232,0	431,1	1,341,9	5.31	5.28
6. Chicago.............	..	..	..	0,0	30,0	1,099,9	....	89 21
7. Philadelphia.......	..	..	..	81,0	408,8	1,047,0	19.25	3 90
8. St. Petersburg.....	..	..	7	270,0	490,0	1,003,3	3.01	2.61
Group B.								
9. Constantinople	1	2	5	300,0–1,000,0	ca 400,0+	873,6	?	ca 2.96
10. Moscow	..	14	6	ca 300,0	ca 360,0	822,4	?	ca 3.21
11. Bombay	..	..	..	ca 150,0	ca 560,0	821,8	4.97	ca 1.17
12. Rio de Janeiro.....	..	..	..	ca 125,0	ca 170,0	ca 800,0	ca 6.0	ca 9.30
13. Calcutta	..	..	..	ca 800,0	ca 400,0	741,1	0.	ca 2.10
14. Hamburg Altona ..	..	..	16	ca 120,0	205,0	711,9	5.48	6.18
15. Manchester-Salford.	..	..	..	90,4	388,5	703,5	7.63	2.03
16. Buenos Ayres	..	..	..	ca 70,0	ca 120,0 (1895)	677,8	ca 9.6	ca 11.5
17. Glasgow	..	..	..	77,1	329,1	658,2	8.37	2.5
18. Liverpool	..	..	..	82,3	376,0	518,0	6.21	.95
Group C.								
19. Budapest...........	..	..	..	ca 61,0	156,5	491,9	ca 8.0	5.36
20. Melbourne	..	..	..	0,0	23,1	490,9	....	50.6
21. Warsaw	..	..	..	ca 65,0	ca 160,0	485,3	ca 7.2	ca 5.1
22. Birmingham.......	..	..	..	70,7	232,8	478,1	6.4	2.63
23. Madrid	..	..	12	156,7	281,2	470,3	2.2	1.68
24. Brussels	..	..	..	66,3	188,5	465,5	6.7	3.67
25. Naples	3	3	3	ca 400,0	ca 415,0	463,2	ca .19	ca .29
26. Madras	..	..	..	ca 800,0	ca 700,0	452,5	decr.	decr.
27. Boston	..	..	..	24,9	136,9	448,5	19.0	5.69
28. Baltimore........	..	..	..	26,5	169,1	434,4	18.2	3.92
29. Lyons	..	..	19	109,5	177,2	429,3	3.2	3.56
30. Hyderabad	..	..	..	ca 200,0	ca 200,0	415,0	ca 1.4	ca 2.6
31. Amsterdam	12	9 (1795)	217,0	224,0	408,1	.92	2.16
32. Marseilles	..	..	18	111,1	195,3	403,7	2.94	2.67
Group D.								
33. Sydney............	..	..	..	2,5	53,9	383,3	169.2	15.28
34. Copenhagen	..	..	21	101,0	ca 143,0	375,7	3.1	4.07
35. Cairo..............	..	..	..	250–700,0	ca 250,0	374,8	?	ca 1.3
36. Leeds	..	..	..	53,2	172,3	367,5	6.57	2.84
37. Leipzig.......	..	..	..	32,1	62,4	357,1	11.2	11.8
38. Munich	..	..	..	40,6	109,5	350,6	8.5	5.5
39. Pittsburg-Allegheny ..	..	..	..	1,6	67,9	343,9	251.6	10.16
40. Breslau...........	..	..	..	62,9	110,7	335,2	4.81	5.07
41. Edinburgh-Leith ..	..	..	..	81,4	191,2	329,9	3.4	1.81
42. Mexico	..	..	..	ca 137,0	ca 150,0	('89) 329,5	ca 1.6	ca 3.0
43. Sheffield	..	..	..	45,8	135,3	324,2	6.76	3.49
44. Milan	5	5	15	ca 134,5	ca 190,0	32 ,8	ca 1.4	ca 1.7
45. Odessa	..	..	..	?	('56) 101,3	313,7	?	ca 5.0
46. Dublin	..	..	11	ca 160,0	261,7	311,2	ca 1.05	.47
47. Lisbon	6	10	4	350,0	275,0	307,7	decr.	ca 3.0
48. Minneapolis-St.Paul..	..	..	..	0,0	1,1	302,3	....	680.
49. Rome	..	8	13	ca 153,0	175,9	300,5	ca 1.1	1.8
Group E.								
202. Venice	4	4	14	ca 150,0	? 128,0	132,8		(The numbers preceding the names of these cities indicate their rank in Supan's list of the great cities of the world.)
113. Palermo	..	6	22	ca 100,0	175,8	245,0		
—. Messina	..	7	..	?	ca 75,0	78,4		
81. Antwerp...........	..	11	..	56,3	97,9	268,4		
183. Seville........ ...	..	13	..	80,3	112,5	143,2		
79. Barcelona	..	..	17	111,4	183,8	272,5		
155. Valencia...........	..	..	20	105,0	106,4	170,8		

It is estimated that to-day more than ten per cent. of Europeans dwell in great cities. In individual countries, the proportion is much larger, as will be seen by reference to Table CXII. Thus, in England, one-third of the entire population are inhabitants of great cities, while in the Australian colonies of New South Wales and Victoria, 40 per cent. of the people are resident in such cities (suburbs included).

In Table CLXIII, some of the facts already given are summarized; columns 2, 3, 4 giving the rank of the great cities in Europe since the beginning of the modern period; while the succeeding columns give the population of the world's great cities of 300,000 and upward. The table does not include the Chinese and Japanese cities, because statistical information is lacking (save in the latest period for Japan). The estimates of population in Chinese cities vary nearly as much as did the estimate given of Constantinople's population at the beginning of the present century—between 300,-000 and 1,500,000. The annual rate of growth in 1800–1890 and in 1850–90 has been calculated for each city; but only the latter period affords really trustworthy statistics on which to base comparisons. The American cities, together with the Australian cities, naturally lead the older countries, where population has not increased so rapidly either in cities or in rural districts. But in the period 1850–90 there is, on the average, no perceptible difference between the growth of cities in the Eastern commonwealths of the United States and that of European cities. The larger New York[1] is more than rivaled by Berlin; Philadelphia is outstripped by Vienna; while on the other hand, Boston and Baltimore compare favorably with European cities of corresponding magnitude.

One is tempted here to ask if any limit to the growth of a great city exists,—a question that has always interested

---

[1] Including Brooklyn, Newark, Jersey City, Hoboken, and Long Island City, with Manhattan Island and the Bronx.

speculative statisticians. Aristotle's ideal city is limited to 10,000 inhabitants for political reasons. Hume, in his essay " On the Populousness of Ancient Nations," set the maximum population of Carthage, Pekin, Constantinople, London and Paris at about 700,000 each, and conjectured " from the experience of past and present ages that there is a kind of impossibility that any city can ever rise much beyond this proportion." [1]

This is entertaining; but so is the course of reasoning by which the eminent statistician Sir William Petty, writing a hundred years earlier than Hume, came to the conclusion that 5,000,000 was the upper limit of London's population. If the population of London went on doubling every 40 years as it was then doing, wrote Petty in 1686,[2] by 1842 it would have 10,718,889; but in 1842 England, whose population doubled once in 360 years, would have only 10,917,389. Obviously, the 200,000 people in England outside of London could not supply the city with provisions. For one man in the city, another would have to be an agriculturist. Hence Petty concluded that London would stop growing in the next preceding period (1800) when it would have a population of about 5,000,000, leaving nearly 5,000,000 " to perform the tillage, pasturage, and other rural work necessary to be done without the said city." But Petty did not foresee the revolution in transportation systems that enables London to draw its wheat from Dakota, Manitoba, Argentina and India. In fact, he demonstrated to his own satisfaction that a city's food supply could not be brought from a greater distance than 35 miles. Cattle, he said, can bring themselves from a distance of about 35 miles; the ground enclosed in a circle whose radius is 35 miles will provide bread and drink, corn,

---

[1] *Essays* (Edinburgh, 1817), i, 430.

[2] *Essays on the Growth of the City of London, in Essays on Political Arithmetic,* 1755, p. 16.

hay and fodder, and timber for 600,000 houses,[1]—equal to a population of 5,000,000.

Petty has had any number of followers, and they are not all dead yet. A very recent newspaper article, philosophizing on London's diminishing rate of growth, concludes thus: "Yet Petty was not far from guessing rightly. He estimated 5,000,000 as the largest number of souls that nature would tolerate in one civic bond. The 5,000,000 limit is nearly reached in London, and the resilient wave is perceptible." How far London's growth is from stopping we have already seen in taking account of the "overflow" population; how far short it comes from being limited at 5,000,000 we may see below:

Date.	District.	Area.	Population.
1891	Registration county	118 sq. mi.	4,211,056
1891	London and West Ham	....	4,415,958
1891	Metropolitan police district	690 sq. mi.	5,633,332
1895	" " "	" " "	est. 6,048,555

A fair estimate of the present population of the metropolitan police district, which includes every parish within 12 miles of Charing Cross, would be six and one-half million souls.

And the New World agglomerations are following close after London. A careful estimate by Dr. Roger Tracy, registrar of vital statistics in New York city, gave the present New York on January 1, 1898, a population of 3,388,771; to which should be added Hudson county, Newark and Elizabeth, New Jersey, making a grand total of 4,029,517. "Greater Paris" had over 2,700,000 already in 1891 and now has at least 3,000,000; while "Greater Berlin" on January 1, 1896, was credited with a population of 2,666,000. Even Boston, which ranked sixth among Americans cities in 1890, with a population of 448,477, was credited with 1,004,424

[1] *Ibid.*, p. 23.

at the State census of 1895 in the territory within a radius of 12 miles of the State House.[1]

The advantages and disadvantages of such concentration of population have been discussed at length in a previous chapter. The discussion of remedies began at least twenty centuries ago, and will perhaps continue twenty centuries hence. Plutarch's warning against the overgrowth of the great cities[2] and Cicero's constant effort[3] to turn back the current of emigration from the country alike came to naught. Justinian tried to stop the current by legal measures,[4] and mediæval statesmen and monarchs followed a similar course. The extension of Paris beyond certain limits was prohibited by law in 1549, 1554, 1560, 1563, 1564 and 1672.[5] In the time of the later Tudors and Stuarts, proclamation after proclamation was issued forbidding the erection of new houses in London and enjoining the country people to return to their homes.[6] There were many good reasons for such action—the difficulties of municipal government, the fear of local pressure on Parliament, the difficulty of providing an adequate food-supply,[7] and water-supply, the danger of fires (the Great Fire of 1665!), and especially the danger of plagues and epidemics arising from unsanitary conditions. The evils enumerated in the Act of 1593[8] are almost identical with those depicted in the recent report of the New York tenement-house commission. "For the reforming of the

---

[1] *Op. cit.*, pt. i, p. 47.

[2] *Præcepta Politica.*

[3] *Add. Att.*, i, 19.

[4] Pöhlmann, *Uebervölkerung der antiken Grossstädte,* 169.

[5] Roscher, *System der Volkswirthschaft,* iii, 39.

[6] Cunningham, *Growth of English Industry and Commerce,* ii, 172.

[7] One of James I's proclamations was issued " on account of the present scarcity and dearth and of the high prices of corn and grain."

[8] 35 Eliz., c. 6.

great mischiefs and inconveniences that daily grow and increase by reason of the pestering of houses with diverse families, harboring of inmates and converting of great houses into several tenements or dwellings, and erecting of new buildings within the cities of London and Westminster and other places near thereunto, whereby great infection of sickness and dearths of victuals and fuel hath grown and increased," it ordained that no new buildings should be erected (except for inhabitants of the "better sort,") and that houses should not be broken up into tenements, etc.

While legislative prohibitions of city growth are now a thing of the past, it has been seriously proposed in Germany [1] to check the overflow of rural laborers into the great cities by means of settlement fees. Any such proposal to limit individual freedom of movement would not be entertained in Anglo-Saxon communities.

Not less hopeless are the schemes promoted by agriculturists to make farming more attractive and more remunerative with the help of scientific cultivation, allotments for laborers, and various legislative measures of relief.[2] In themselves such measures are often praiseworthy, as is every plan of improving the moral and material condition of farmers.[3] But it is idle to hope that the adoption of any of these plans will stop the drift of farmers' sons cityward. The production of the world's food-supply calls for a definite amount of labor; any project for increasing the per-capita product of agricultural labor simply releases a certain amount of such labor for other occupations. From the same point of view are to be judged schemes of colonization of the city poor on farm-

[1] By Roscher and others. *Cf.* Art " Wohnungsfrage " in Conrad's *Hdwbh.* 6: 751, and 7: 21.

[2] Cf. *Leaflet No. 1* of the New York Association for the Improvement of the Condition of the Poor, on " Agricultural Depression."

[3] Cf. Emerick, " An Analysis of Agricultural Discontent," in *Pol. Sci. Quarterly,* vol. xi.

ing lands. Aside from the difficulty of getting the tenement classes permanently away from the city,[1] and the questionability of trying to make farmers out of men who fail in other trades, the world already has all the farmers it needs. Colonization of the city poor may, indeed, be the salvation of individuals; but it simply necessitates the transfer of other people in corresponding numbers from the country to the city.[2]

Another scheme of stopping migration cityward is to make village life more attractive. There is certainly opportunity for work in this direction. But so long as the present industrial organization endures, no amount of village improvement will keep ambitious youths at home, for the reason that all the opportunities for rising in the world are in the cities. If domestic industries could be re-established, villages would soon pick up. Efforts are making on the part of philanthropists to put out portions of their work in the country, but the success attained has been exceedingly limited, for employers have to contend not only with the irregularity of country labor, but with the hostility of city trade-unionists, who resent the policy. In analyzing the conditions of production, we found little encouragement for the hope that improvements in electric motors would bring about decentralization of industry. It is a mistake to regard this as "at present the most hopeful method of withdrawing the pressure from our large industrial centers."[3]

Still another remedy proposed is administrative decentralization,[4] the building-up of rural self-government and the

---

[1] *Supra*, p. 221.

[2] Altogether different is the plan of sending city children into the country for part of the year. Such schemes as the George Junior Republic have as their object the training of *citizens*, not simply the making of farmers.

[3] McKenzie, *Introduction to Social Philosophy*, 108.

[4] A popular cry in England. *Cf.* Stephens, *Rural Administration*, 1896.

removal of garrisons and government offices to villages or small towns. But strategic reasons compel the concentration of military forces in cities, and the tendency toward consolidation is antagonistic to the dispersion of government offices. On the other hand, it cannot be doubted that the conferring of more responsibility upon village officials than they enjoy at present on the continent of Europe, would afford a field for the ambition of men who now have to remove from the village if they desire to enter politics.

Perhaps some of the many gratuities (such as hospitals and medical service) in cities might be restricted with advantage. There are those who advocate an abrupt discontinuance of all public improvements in the city, lest they attract more migrants from the country; such persons would prefer to have the city remain a mud-hole. They are to be found in the class that can own country homes and thus escape city dangers.

Is there, then, "no remedy until the accumulated miseries of overgrown cities drive the people back to the country?" One remedy is to admit the harmful tendencies of city life, to fight city degeneration on its own ground, and free city life from as many ills as possible. This work is now proceeding on a vast scale, and in a vast number of ways. Private philanthropy and public supervision go hand in hand. Not only complete drainage, paving, water-supply, inspection of food, etc., are required from the municipality, but also small parks, playgrounds, public baths and laundries, and a variety of other institutions. A vast deal has been accomplished in this line, and the work is only begun. Much may be expected from the progress of invention and discovery and the growth of capital. Prof. Marshall indicates how certain improvements (some of which have already been made in American cities) would "enable a large part of the population to live in towns and yet be free from many of the present evils of town life. The first step is to make under all the streets large tunnels, in which many pipes and wires can be laid side by side, and repaired when they get out of order, without any interruption of the general traffic and without great expense. Motive power, and possibly even heat, might then be generated at great distances from the towns (in some cases in coal mines) and laid on whenever wanted. Soft water and spring water, and perhaps even sea water and ozonized air, might be laid on in separate pipes to nearly every house; while steam-pipes might be used for giving warmth in winter, and compressed air for lowering the heat of summer; or the heat might be supplied by gas of great heating power laid on in special pipes, while light was derived from gas especially suited for the purpose, or from electricity; and every house might be in electric communication with the rest of the town. All unwholesome vapors, including those given off by any domestic fires which were still used, might be carried away by strong draughts through long conduits, to be purified by passing through large furnaces and thence away through huge chimneys into the higher air." [1]

But while much is to be expected in this direction in the near future, the most encouraging feature of the whole situation is the tendency, heretofore alluded to in the present essay, toward the development of suburban towns. [2] The

---

[1] *Principles of Economics*, 3d ed., p. 305, note.

[2] In Vienna the suburbs in close connection with the city itself have long had a rapid growth. After 1870, with a population equal to about one-third of the city, they had larger increments of increase than the city itself. In 1891 they were incorporated into the city having a population of 464,110 as compared with 798,719 for the old city (figures for 1890; cf. Rauchberg, in *St. Mon.*, xix, 140 ff). Similar statistics might be given for the Saxon cities: Dresden, for instance, in-

significance of this tendency is that it denotes, not a cessation in the movement toward concentration, but a diminution in the *intensity* of concentration. Such a new distribution of population combines at once the open air and spaciousness of the country with the sanitary improvements, comforts and associated life of the city. The question is, however, whether the marked growth of the suburbs is because the cities are already too full to hold more, or because the populations of the congested districts are overflowing into the suburbs and thereby leaving a more tolerable condition for those behind. Hon. C. D. Wright, Superintendent of the eleventh census, takes the latter view and presents the following statistics in substantiation thereof:[1]

INCREASE OR DECREASE PER CENT. OF POPULATION, 1870–90.

	New York.[2]	Philadelphia.[3]	Boston.[4]
Congested wards	9.38	—6.56	16.
Remaining "	131.56	168.91	156.
Entire city	60.81	55.33	76.

The only one of the three cities in which the crowded districts actually lost population in 1870–90 was Philadelphia.

creased by 56 per cent. 1871–90, while 28 of her suburbs increased by 233 per cent.:[5]

	Increase, or decrease, per cent., 1870–90.	Population, 1890.
28 towns under	—.3	39,091
93 towns 2,000–10,000	+ 26.4	454,910
22 towns over 10,000	+ 57.1	987,460
150 suburbs of the 22 cities	+146.3	462,575

[1] "Urban Population," in *Popular Science Monthly*, xl (Feb., 1892), p. 463.

[2] The congested wards are 1–17, with the exception of 12, which is in the upper part of the city; this includes that part of the city below Fourteenth street and one ward (16) above.

[3] Congested wards, 2–20, except 15.

[4] Here the "congested wards" designate Boston proper, and the "remaining wards" the annexations.

[5] Cf. Lommatzch, *Die Bewegung der Bevölkerung Sachsens*, pp. 24–8. For growth of the cities and suburbs, 1834–75, *vide Zeitschrift des Kngl. Sächs. Stat. Bureaus*, 1876, p. 302.

TABLE CLXIV.

POPULATION PER ACRE IN NEW YORK CITY WARDS.[1]

Ward.	1860.	1880.	1890.
1	+117.8	116.5	72.2
2	+ 30.9	19.8	11.4
3	39.5	37.7	+ 39.6
4[2]	264.9	252.9	214.5
5	+132.9	94.3	73.7
6	+310.4	233.9	268.8
7	201.9	252.9	+239.7
8	+215.3	196.0	170.6
9	137.8	+169.5	169.0
10	272.7	432.3	+523.6
11	303.9	350.9	+384.3
12	5.5	14.8	+ 44.5
13	307.6	353.2	+428.8
14	292.5	+314.3	292.6
15	139.3	+161.0	128.3
16	129.4	+149.5	140.8
17	220.4	+316.7	311.6
18	127.7	+148.0	140.6
19	22.1	106.8	+158.5
20	152.0	+193.7	189.9
21	119.5	+161.8	153.3
22	40.3	72.9	+100.6
23	....	6.6	+ 12.6
24	....	1.6	+ 2.5

Table CLXIV affords means of analyzing New York's growth more carefully; it shows the average number of inhabitants per acre in each ward at the censuses of 1860, 1880 and 1890, the years in which the greatest density (*i. e.*, largest population) was attained being marked with a + sign. It is at once seen that there is a group of wards which attained their maximum population in 1860 and have since declined. Another group attained their maximum density in 1880, and a third group was still growing in 1890. The

[1] *Report N. Y. Tenement House Com.*, 1894, p. 273. Ward maps will be found in this report and also in the *11th Census, Vital Statistics of New York and Brooklyn.*

[2] Maximum population in 1870, 286.1.

figures for 1870 are omitted since only one ward (No.4 in the first group) showed a maximum (286.1) in that year.

In the table the various groups do not seem to consist of contiguous wards, but this merely follows from the method of numbering. As a matter of fact the four groups do consist of contiguous and homogeneous districts.

Group I (wards 1–6, 8, 14) comprises that part of the city south of Houston street and west of the Bowery and Catherine street. Ward 14 (between Houston and Canal, Broadway and the Bowery) might perhaps be put with equal reason in Group II, but as it lost population in 1860–70, its gain in 1880 may be called temporary. Group I, then, is the "down-town" district, the financial and commercial centre of the city,—the seat of the banks, and the great importing houses. Here there has been a crowding out of dwellings by the building of business blocks and offices; its density is lowest of any of the groups.

Group II (wards 9, 15, 16, 18, 20, 21) consists of all the territory between 14th and 42d streets and also of that between 14th and Houston streets, west of the Bowery. This is the district of retail trade, of hotels and theatres. It is now losing its residential character, having attained its largest growth in 1880.

Group III consists of two districts: (a) Wards 7, 10, 13, 11, 17, which lie east of the Bowery and Catherine street and south of 14th street; (b) Wards 19, 22, 12, 23, 24, which lie north of 42d street. The latter sub-group, comprising the upper part of the city's territory, is the least densely populated of any and is the most rapidly growing of any. It is coming to be distinctly the residential section. But sub-group (a) consists of the most densely populated wards in the city; with a population of 523.6 persons to the acre, the Tenth Ward is probably the densest district in the Western world, Josefstadt in Prague having 485.4, the *quartier* Bonne-

Nouvelle in *arrondissement* Bourse in Paris 434.19, and Bethnal Green North in London 365.3. The Eleventh and Thirteenth Wards are also very densely populated. They are the really congested districts of New York, and yet their population has continued to increase since 1860.

An explanation of this may be found by turning to the map of nationalities in the *Report of the 1894 Tenement House Committee*, which shows wards 10, 13 and 7, and in a less degree ward 11, to be the seat of the Russian and Polish Jews, the Bohemians, and other nationalities of similar standard of life. These nationalities, as we have seen, have come to us chiefly within the decade 1880–90; they naturally settled among their own countrymen and have not yet had time to scatter. At the same time their low standard of life made it easy for them to submit to live in the crowded and squalid quarters there provided. Ward 17, containing mainly Germans, is in this district but it really belongs to group II, as it lost population in 1880–90. It is to be remarked that the Italians, who in New York are concentrated in the Sixth, Fourteenth and Eighth wards, showed a disposition to disperse throughout the country between 1880–90 (*ante* ch. v.) Hence these wards are not so crowded as they formerly were.

On the whole it may fearlessly be said that the congested districts of New York are losing population, with the exception of those inhabited by the most recent immigrants. The latter make a new problem, which can be solved only by adequate building and sanitary laws and rigid inspection by prevent overcrowding and living amidst unhealthy surroundings.

The growth of London's population points even more conclusively to the diminution of congestion in the business districts and the outflow toward the suburbs. In the decade of 1881–91, there was a decrease of population in 11 of the 30 historic districts of registration London. The 11 districts constitute the oldest and central portion of the metropolis, a portion that has been losing its population since 1861, and in a few districts even longer. Comparing the growth of the central area with the remaining districts of registration London and with the outer ring in " Greater London," we have the following results: [1]

TABLE CLXV.

	Increase or decrease per cent.			
	1861-71.	1871-81.	1881-91.	Pop., 1891.
Central area (11)........	—2.7	—4.6	—7.2	1,022,951
Other districts (19)	29.8	29.3	17.5	3,188,792
London (Registr. Co.).	16.0	17.3	10.4	4,211,743
Outer ring............	50.8	50.5	49.5	1,422,063
Greater London [2]........	20.6	22.7	18.2	5,633,806

The decrease in the central area as a whole has taken place only since 1861, as the following table shows:

TABLE CLXVI.

	Population of central area (11 districts).			Pop. of other (19) districts per acre.
	Aggregate.	Percentage of London.	Per acre.	
1801.................	588,264	61.3	60.9	5.7
1851.................	1,129,599	48.0	116.9	19.0
1861.................	1,187,687	42.3	122.9	25.0
1871.................	1,155,462	35.5	119.6	32.4
1881.................	1,101,994	28 8	114.1	41.9
1891.................	1,022,951	24.3	105.9	49.2

But while the central area grew in absolute numbers and in density up to 1861, it did not keep pace with the outer districts, because its proportion to the population of entire London steadily fell throughout the century. The increase

[1] *Census of England*, 1891, iv, 16.

[2] Includes every parish of which any part is within 12 miles of Charing Cross. (Metropolitan police district.)

in the density of the outer districts has been rapid since 1801, rising from 5.7 to 49.2.

In four or five of the districts of the central area, the process of depopulation began earlier than 1861. For our purpose it will be sufficient to trace the process in the two oldest districts, London City and Strand:[1]

TABLE CLXVII.

	London City.		The Strand.	
	Population.	Increase or decrease %.	Population.	Increase or decrease %.
1801	128,833	......	50,854	
1811	121,124	—15.98	51,334	+.94
1821	125,065	+3.26	55,152	+7.44
1831	123,608	—1.17	50,385	—8.64
1841	124,717	+.90	52,209	+3.62
1851	129,128	+3.54	51,765	—.85
1861	113,387	—12.19	48,242	—6.81
1871	75,983	—32.99	41,339	—14.31
1881	51,439	—32.30	33,582	—18.76
1891	38,320	—25.50	27,516	—18.1

The Strand attained its maximum population as far back as 1821, and since then it has regularly lost, except in the decade 1831–41. London City reached its maximum population in 1851, but this scarcely exceeded its population of 1801, so that we can say that its population was stationary during the first half of the century and has since declined, the rate of decrease like that of the Strand becoming very considerable after 1861.

Now in 1801 London City with a population of 192.86 to the acre was the densest district in the metropolis, with the exception of Westminster (213.42) whose population began to decrease after 1841; in 1881, its density was 77. Taken

[1] The following data are from Price Williams's article, "The Population of London, 1801–1881," in *Jour. of St. Soc.*, xlviii (1885), pp. 398–9, and *Census of 1891*, ii, 8.

in connection with the comparative density of the central
area and the other districts (Table CLXVI), it may be regarded as proved that in London the congested districts
have been relieved by the efflux of a part of their population
to the outer districts or to the suburbs.[1]

The German census of 1895 gave Berlin an increase over
1890 of only 6.2 per cent., whereas its growth in the previous
five-year periods had been from 16 to 20 per cent. It was
soon discovered that the towns surrounding Berlin had increased tremendously, thus showing that Berlin had reached
the point of "saturation" and was overflowing. While Berlin added 98,342 persons to her population, the suburbs
within a radius of 10 kilometers (6.2 English miles) added
167.135, although in 1890 they had scarcely one-sixth as
large a population as Berlin itself. (Cf. Table CLXVIII.)
All the districts in the business center (Berlin, Alt-Cöln,
Friedrichswerder, Dorotheenstadt, Friedrichstadt) have been
losing population since about 1861—a few earlier and some
later.

While the old city within the walls has nearly ceased growing, its decrease, as a whole, has not yet begun. Individual
districts, however, have lost population so that the number
of inhabitants to the square kilometer in the innermost ring

---

[1] The tables by Mr. Price Williams, *loc. cit.*, p. 430, indicate a similar conclusion :

	Pop., 1881.	Average per acre.
10 districts—pop. diminishing	878,556	128
sub-districts "	335,140	146
Total......................... ...	1,213,696	133
11 districts—pop. above the average per acre and increasing (excl. of above sub-districts)	1,573,602	87
8 districts—pop. below the average per acre and increasing rapidly	1,029,185	22
29 Grand total	3,816,483	51

TABLE CLXVIII.—GROWTH OF BERLIN AND SUBURBS.

	1801.	1822.	1840.	1858.	1871.	1875.	1880.	1885.	1890.	1895.
Old territory—inside the walls	......	181,838	279,782	367,532	} 721,270 {	576,894	590,646	634,714	662,673	
Old territory—outside the walls	......		7,708	70,635		233,302	302,441	362,763	461,646	
Annexation of 1861	......		......	(29,951)	101,665	152,774	223,730	310,347	442,371	
Annexations of '78, '81	......		......	......	......	......	2,970	4,891	8,323	
Military, ship pop.	......	a 16,763	a 18,739	b 20,470	c 3,002	c 3,888	c 2,543	c 2,572	c 3,781	
Present city limits	173,440	206,309	322,626	458,637	825,937	966,858	1,122,330	1,315,287	1,578,794	1,677,136
Suburbs within 10 km	8,735	16,398	27,420	39,558	57,802	103,949	123,333	163,546	268,507	435,642
Metropolitan police dist.	182,175	222,707	350,046	489,195	883,739	1,070,807	1,245,663	1,478,833	1,847,301	2,112,778
Greater Berlin (radius of 15 km.)	196,266	......	......	521,118	929,041	1,131,249	1,314,442	1,537,924	1,956,581	2,266,000 (est.)

a Military population.　　b Military,19, 676; ship population, 794.　　c Ship population.

(within a radius of one kilometer of the city hall) was 32,589, while in the second ring (radius, 1–2 kilometers) it was 54,-024.[1] Similarly in Vienna, the respective figures of density in two concentric districts were 25,154 and 38,894.[2] A striking example of the tendency is revealed in the statistics of Hamburg:[3]

| | Population, in thousands. | | |
	1867.	1880.	1890.
Inner city	157	171	161
Remainder	64	116	158
15 suburbs	45	120	245

The process thus sketched for New York, London, etc., is known as " city-building." The original settlement becomes the business center and for some time continues to grow rapidly. But if the city prospers, the time will come when this old center is more and more needed for strictly business purposes; houses disappear before the march of office-buildings, government buildings, banks, etc., until the only residents left are the janitors and *portiers*, the keepers of the great buildings.[4] With continued growth, the business center extends itself and steadily pushes the dwellings toward the circumference, until at length the municipal limits are reached and passed.

American cities are not so compactly built as European cities. On the continent especially, where it is still the practice to live in rooms connected with one's store or workshop,

---

[1] *Die Bevölkerungs- und Wohnungsaufnahme vom 1 Dez. 1890 in der Stadt Berlin*, i Heft., Berlin, 1893, p. xiv, ff.

[2] See the article of E. Hasse, entitled "Die Intensität grossstädtischer Menschenanhäufungen, *Allg. Stat. Archiv*, ii, 615 ff. It is only the very largest cities, as Hasse's investigation shows, which have reached this condition. In Paris several of the central *arrondissements* have been losing population. (Cf. Meuriot, *op. cit.*, ch. xii, where the subject is more extensively treated.)

[3] *Statistik des Hamburgischen Staates*, Heft xvi, Census of 1890.

[4] In 1851 there were 14,580 inhabited dwellings in London City; in 1881, 6,493.

the density of population is remarkable in comparison with American cities, thus:[1]

	No. of cities considered.	Area in acres.	Population Total.	Per acre.
United States	28	638,235	9,670,000	15.2
England	22	231,150	8,840,000	38.3
Germany	15	193,290	5,000,000	25.9

Almost as many English urbanites dwell on 230,000 acres as Americans on 638,000 acres. The German percentage is somewhat more favorable, until we restrict the comparison to the building area. Then the population per acre in fifteen American cities is 22 as compared with 157.6 in thirteen German cities.[2]

Paris is one of the most densely populated cities in the world. Upon an area slightly smaller than Kansas City's (20,774 acres), Paris concentrates about two and one-half million persons as contrasted with the latter's 133,000. The following comparative table of individual cities will further illustrate the point here insisted upon:[3]

TABLE CLXIX.

	Acreage.	Pop.	Per acre.
London	74,692	56.4	
Present New York	230,000	....	13.0
Paris	19,295	126.9	
Berlin	14,661	100.8	
Chicago	102,765	....	10.7
Philadelphia	82,807	....	12.6
Brooklyn	18,084	....	44.6
Liverpool	5,210	99.4	
Manchester	12,788	39.5	
Hamburg	18,544	30.7	
St. Louis	39,276	....	11.5
Boston	24,231	....	18.5
Baltimore	18,867	....	23.0
Birmingham	8,400	51.1	

[1] *11th Cen., Social Statistics of Cities*, p. 14. Population is given in round numbers.

[2] *Ibid.*

[3] *Ibid.*, 13. Names of American cities are indented, and their density put in a separate column.

These figures are to be used cautiously, as they depend somewhat upon the amount of suburban territory recently annexed : [1] but on the whole, they demonstrate that population is spread out over a larger territory in American than in European cities.   It has sometimes been urged that this is largely a result of the development of the electric street railway in America, but the causal connection is not apparent.   The first street railway using electric propulsion was opened in 1886, and the number of miles in operation at the time of the latest census was not only small in the aggregate, but was restricted for the most part to smaller cities than those at present under consideration.   It should rather be said that the American *penchant* for dwelling in cottage homes instead of business blocks after the fashion of Europe is the cause, and the trolley car the effect.   Philadelphia was the "city of homes" long before *rapid* transit.   Philadelphia in 1880 led all other American cities in length of horse-car lines, but the horse-car is too slow to carry the majority of workingmen to and from their work each day.   Hence the comparative figures of mileage and number of rides per inhabitant of American and European cities are indications of low or high density of population, which may be regarded as the cause of street railway building.[2]

[1] Thus, in the old New York there were 58.7 inhabitants to the acre in 1890-1, while Paris had 126.9 and Berlin 100.8; and yet it is altogether probable that New York suffers more from dense crowding than do the two European capitals, for the vast majority of New Yorkers live below the Harlem, where the density in 1894 was 143.2 (*N. Y. Tenement House Committee Report*, p. 256).

[2] *The 11th Cen. Rep. on Transportation by Land* (p. 685) contains comparative figures of the average number of rides annually per inhabitant:

New York	297	Buffalo	65
Kansas City	286	London	74
San Francisco	270	Liverpool	51
Boston, Lynn and Cambridge	225	Glasgow	61
Brooklyn	183	Berlin	87
Chicago	164	Hamburg	78
Philadelphia	158	Vienna	43
St. Louis	150	Budapest	37

Berlin, with the best street railway system in Europe, would rank twenty-second among the 28 American cities of 100,000+.

A better index of suburban travel is the number of commuters carried by the steam railways and their percentage in
the total number of passengers. Such statistics are furnished
by the Eleventh Census (*Social Statistics of Cities*, pp. 49–
50) and it appears that, on the whole, suburban traffic increases in the same ratio with the magnitude of cities:

TABLE CLXX.

Cities.	No. of cities.	Commuters.	Ratio of commuters to all passengers.
10,000–25,000	75	4,764,884	28.6
25,000–50,000	29	6,667,220	29.3
50,000–100,000	23	3,956,938	31.1
100,000+	24	79,945,182	52.1
Total	151	95,335,224	46.4

In the matter of street railway travel, Chicago and Philadelphia ranked far below New York. Evidently this is connected with the fact that they have a larger traffic on the
regular railway lines. But the palm for suburban travel belongs to Boston, which had almost as many commuters as
New York and Chicago put together: [1]

	Commuters.	Ratio to all passengers.
Boston	24,587,000	62.9
Chicago	16,903,000	85.9
Philadelphia	10,714,000	70.7
New York	8,643,000	26.9
Cincinnati	3,697,000	86.9
Pittsburg	2,698,000	48.8
San Francisco	2,367,000	37.3
St. Louis	2,164,000	75.8

It is clear that we are now in sight of a solution of the
problem of concentration of population. The trolley car and
the bicycle may serve the purpose in middle-sized cities or
even in the less populous cities of the first class. But when
the city attains a population of a quarter of a million, more

[1] *Ibid.*, 50.

rapid transit than the electric surface railway can furnish is imperatively demanded. A surface railway cannot well run cars at a speed of more than nine miles an hour, and the legal limit in New York State is ten miles an hour. But, as few workingmen can afford to spend more than half an hour in going to their work, they would then be compelled to dwell within three or four miles of the factory and could not have homes in the open country or suburbs, which are at least seven miles beyond the center of the large city. Even the elevated system would not serve the purpose with its regular trains, which cannot be run at a speed in excess of 12 miles an hour. On the other hand, the regular railway lines with fast suburban trains are too few in number to serve a large territory. The sole remedy is the multiplication of steam railroads or the building of elevated and underground four-track systems, thus providing for express trains with a speed of at least 25 miles an hour. Then the workingman could establish his dwelling in the suburbs anywhere within a radius of ten miles of the center of the city. Moreover, by virtue of the geometrical proposition that the areas of two circles are to each other as the squares of their radii, you will quadruple the area for residences every time you double the distance traveled. If in the first case (3 miles radius), the land within the circle affords room for 20,000 dwellings, when you double the speed (ordinary elevated system) you will have an area large enough for 80,000 dwellings. Double it again (the underground railway supposition) and you will have ground for 320,000 houses.

The transcendent importance of rapid transit as a remedy for overcrowding has been recognized most adequately in Belgium, where the railways are principally state-owned. The government there has not only provided an adequate train service for workingmen residing in suburban towns, but has established the rates of fare on a cheap basis that permits the train service to be used daily by workingmen. The service to and from work costs 21 cents a week to those traveling three miles or less, and gradually increases up to 57 cents for 42 miles.

By the Cheap Train Acts of 1883, the English Parliament subsidized the railways entering London with about $2,000,-000 a year, in the shape of remission of taxes, for the provision of workmen's trains. A season ticket for one year (600 journeys for a distance of 22 miles) can be obtained for about four cents per journey. New York still lags behind, but Chicago and more especially Boston (where the legislature has aided the public) are developing a first-rate system of suburban communication. It cannot be doubted that the extremely satisfactory housing of Bostonians as compared with European urbanites,[1] is due not less to the fostering of suburban travel by the steam railways than to the development of the trolley system. Another striking example is that of Sydney, New South Wales : [2]

	Population of	
	The city.	The suburbs.
1841	29,973	
1851	44,240	9,684
1861	56,840	38,949
1871	74,566	63,210
1881	100,152	124,787
1891	107,652	275,631

In the city itself growth has almost ceased, while the suburbs more than doubled their population in the last decade. But the city cannot be called overcrowded, for in

---

[1] Robert P. Porter in the *Report of the Mass. Special Commission on the Relations Between Cities and Street Railway Companies* (1898, p. 218) calls attention to the fact that Boston has only 1,053 families dwelling in a single room as compared with 120,000 in Glasgow. The percentage of all families are respectively 1⅙ and 33.

[2] *Census of N. S. W., 1891, Statistician's Report,* p. 120.

1891 it had only 37.4 inhabitants to the acre. This is a very low density; in New York city there are only three wards in which the population is less dense—the Second, which is almost wholly given over to business, and the Twenty-third and Twenty-fourth, north of the Harlem river. (Table CLXIV).

Attention has often been called to another encouraging tendency favoring suburban growth, namely, the transference of manufacturing industries to the suburbs. The local advantages of a suburban town have been pointed out; they include not only a great saving in rent and insurance, but economy in the handling and storing of goods. All carting is avoided by having a switch run directly into the factory; saving to machinery is effected by placing it all on solid foundations on the first floor; and plenty of space is at hand for the storing of fuel and materials, so that these may be bought when the market offers the most favorable terms. Finally, the suburban employer is likely to secure a high grade of employees. On the one hand, he is not antagonized by the trade unions, who can treat with him as effectively as if he were in the city itself; on the other hand, his large workshops, and the prospect of a cottage and garden, and open-air life, attract operatives of the best class. Statistical data regarding the location of factories in suburbs are not available, but the strong tendency in that direction is familiar to all Americans. A similar tendency is noticeable in Europe, and it has been remarked that although Manchester, Leeds and Lyons are still the chief centers of the trade in cotton, woollen and silk goods, they no longer produce any great part of these stuffs. Manchester is surrounded with scores of industrial cities and villages.

Suburban growth as a result of this tendency cannot be forced; it must wait upon economic forces. But the growth of purely residential suburbs can be influenced a great deal by public policy. In the past it was chiefly the middle classes who could afford to dwell in the suburbs. But if society wishes to minimize the evils of concentration of population, it must abandon the hope of accomplishing great things by such palliatives as model tenements, (which, if located in the city, often serve merely to prevent factories from moving to the suburbs), building laws, inspection of buildings, and the various other ameliorations already discussed. Four goals are of fundamental importance: (1) a shorter working day, which will permit the workingman to live at a distance from the factory; (2) associations for promoting the ownership of suburban homes by workingmen; (3) cheap transit; (4) rapid transit. The importance of the two latter policies has been urged in so eloquent words by Dr. Cooley that they deserve quotation:

" Humanity demands that men should have sunlight, fresh air, the sight of grass and trees. It demands these things for the man himself, and it demands them still more urgently for his wife and children. No child has a fair chance in the world who is condemned to grow up in the dirt and confinement, the dreariness, ugliness and vice of the poorer quarters of a great city. It is impossible to think with patience of any future condition of things in which such a childhood shall fall to the lot of any large part of the human race. Whatever struggles manhood must endure, childhood should have room and opportunity for healthy moral and physical growth. Fair play and the welfare of the human race alike demand it. There is, then, a permanent conflict between the needs of industry and the needs of humanity. Industry says men must aggregate. Humanity says they must not, or if they must, let it be only during working hours and let the necessity not extend to their wives and children. *It is the office of the city railways to reconcile these conflicting requirements.*"

The extent to which this function may be fulfilled is indicated by the progress already made in Boston, Sydney, etc. Even in the European city of Frankfort it was found in 1893 that about 60 per cent. of the population doing business there lived outside.[1] The electric trolley car is helping in the transformation, and its influence will undoubtedly be apparent in the Twelfth Census.

[1] Bleicher, in *Proceedings of Budapest Congreg.*, vii, 466.

The " rise of the suburbs " it is, which furnishes the solid basis of a hope that the evils of city life, so far as they result from overcrowding, may be in large part removed. If concentration of population seems destined to continue, it will be a modified concentration which offers the advantages of both city and country life. It will realize the wish and the prediction of Kingsley, (*Miscellanies :* " Great Cities "),—" a complete interpretation of city and country, a complete fusion of their different modes of life and a combination of the advantages of both, such as no country in the world has ever seen."

BIBLIOGRAPHICAL NOTE.

The first scientific monograph devoted to the subject of urban and rural populations and the migration from the latter to the former was written by M. A. Legoyt, the distinguished chief of the French bureau of statistics: Du Progrès des Agglomérations Urbaines et de l'Émigration Rurale,[1] Paris, 1870, pp. 280. It was an admirable piece of work for the period in which it was written, but is now rendered obsolete by the publication of new material. The second monograph worthy of mention was by the Swede, J. Gamborg: Om Byerne og Landt, i deres indbyrdes forhold med hensyn til Befolkring og Produktion, Christiana, 1877. Nothing more in the shape of scientific treatises appeared, to the author's knowledge, until very recently, when several writers on the continent of Europe have put out monographs in rapid succession: (1) M. Heins, La Belgique et ses grandes Villes au XIXe Siècle, La Population, Ghent, 1897; (2) R. Kuczynski, Der Zug nach der Stadt; Statistische Studien über Vorgänge der Bevölkerungsbewegung im Deutschen Reiche,[2] München, 1897; (3) Paul Meuriot, Des Agglomérations urbaines dans l'Europe contemporaine; Essai sur les Causes, les Conditiones, les Conséquences de leur Developpement, Paris, 1897. The last is a Doctor's thesis and is the most thorough study made since Legoyt, but is greatly inferior to the latter in originality and freshness, as well as arrangement. Nothing at once systematic and scientific has been published in English, altho the city problem has been attacked by Robt. Vaughan, The Age of Great Cities, 2d edition, London, 1843; Fothergill, The Town Dweller; and Strong, The Twentieth Century City, New York, 1898.

In periodical literature and encyclopedias there is a valuable body of writings on this subject. Dr. G. B. Longstaff has a short but well-written chapter in his Studies in Statistics, and has contributed noteworthy articles on Rural Depopulation to Palgrave's Dictionary of Political Economy, and the Journal of the London Statistical Society, 56: 380 (Sept., 1893). The chapter on Les Populations Urbaines in Levasseur's La Population Française (vol. ii, Paris, 1891) can not be neglected, nor can the pertinent chapters in Rauchberg's Die Bevölkerung Oesterreichs. One of the most important résumés of the recent results is given by A. Wirminghaus, Stadt und Land, unter dem Einfluss der Binnenwanderungen, in Jahrbücher für Nationalœkonomie und Statistik, lxiv, pp. 1, 161. Writers who have touched the subject incidentally but luminously are Bücher, essay on Die inneren Wanderungen in his Entstehung der Volkswirthschaft; Hobson, Evolution of Modern Capitalism; Pearson, National Life and Character. Finally, it remains

---

[1] Cited in text as Legoyt.

[2] Cited in text as Kuczynski.

476

to mention some of the fuller text-books, such as Roscher's System der National-ökonomie, vol. III; Wagner's System, etc., vol. I (Grundlagen der Volkswirth-schaft), etc. Reference should also be made to Schönberg's Handbuch der Politischen Oekonomie, Art. Bevölkerungslehre, and Conrad's Handwörterbuch der Staatswissenschaften, Art. Bevölkerungswesen, etc. An extended discussion of numerous phases of the subject was held at the Eighth International Congress of Hygiene and Demography at Budapest, 1894, a full report of which is published in the Proceedings (Vol. VII).

Most of the works above mentioned contain numerous references to authorities or sources of information, but the best bibliographies are to be found in the following:

For Chapter II.

A recent account of the organization of government statistical offices and their publications on population statistics will be found in Meuriot, *op. cit.* Additional references to the German statistics are to be found in the article of Wirminghaus, above cited, and, especially for the municipal statistics, in the article of Brückner, Allgemeines Statistis hes Archiv, i, 135. For the United States, see E. C. Lunt, Key to the Publications of the United States Census, in publications of the American Statistical Association, i, 105.

The most important compendium of recent statistics of the population of towns and cities is the Ortsstatistik of Alexander Supan, constituting the ninth number of Wagner-Supan's Bevölkerung der Erde [1] and Ergänzungsheft No. 107 of Petermann's Mitteilungen, Gotha, 1893. Nearly every country in the world is embraced in this compendium, and their statistical publications containing data respecting the population of towns are, of course, cited in full.

Statistical data for the first half of the century have frequently to be sought in the handbook of *Staatenkunde*, of which the more important are:

Hassel, Statistische Uebersichtstabellen der sämmtlichen Europaischen Staaten, Göttingen. 1809. (Cited as Hassel, 1809, in text.)

Hassel, Statischer Umriss der sämmtlichen Europaischen und der vornehmsten aussereuropaischen Staaten in ihrer Entwicklung, Grösse, Volksmenge, Finanz- und Militärverfassung tabellarisch dargestellt. 3 Hefte. Weimar, 1823–4. (Cited in text as Hassel, 1822.)

J. E. Worcester, Geographical Dictionary or Universal Gazetteer, 2 vols., Andover, 1817. (Cited as Worcester in text.)

Malchus, Statistik und Staatenkunde von Europa. Stuttgart and Tübingen, 1826. (Contains ample bibliography, pp. 20–39.)

Bernoulli, Handbuch der Populationsstatistik. Ulm, 1841.

Harper's Statistical Gazetteer of the world. New York, 1855. (Cited as Harper.)

Wappäus, Allgemeine Bevölkerungsstatistik. Leipzig, 1861. (Especially important for the statistics of 1845–55.)

---

[1] Cited in text as Supan.

Kolb, Handbuch der vergleichenden Statistik. 2d edition, 1860; 8th edition, 1879. (Cited as Kolb, 1860, and Kolb, 1879, respectively.)

Almanach de Gotha.

Statesman's Year Book, since 1864.

Brachelli, Die Staaten Europas. 4th ed., 1884.

The books above mentioned, together with the citation of authorities in the statistical tables of Chapter II, comprise the principal sources of information.

Chapters IV to IX.

The authorities used in Chapter III are enumerated under the several sections of that chapter, and through the remaining chapters of the essay in foot-note references. It is not, therefore, necessary to repeat titles here, especially as classified bibliographies are accessible in the encyclopedias or handbooks of economics and social sciences, notably those of Conrad and Schönberg and Wagner. Particularly valuable are the bibliographies appended to the separate sections of Mayr's Bevölkerungsstatistik, 1897 (especially Secs. 26, 27, 37, 39, 81), and the classified bibliography of 100 pages in Bevölkerungslehre und Bevölkerungspolitik by A. von Fircks (Leipzig, 1898).

As to the municipal conditions and the problems of city life, see Robt. C. Brooks's Bibliography of Municipal Administration and City Conditions (Municipal Affairs, March, 1897).

INDEX OF AUTHORS

INDEX OF SUBJECTS

the food supply 164; agricultural improvements 164–7; agricultural population 166; end of feudalism 178; national unity 178; Black Plague 178–179; natural increase in cities 243–4; internal migration 249–53; mortality in town and country 345, 347, 355; deaths by sex and age, 358–9; crime 404; increase in wealth and power 425–6; rapid growth of the suburbs 446–7; density and acreage of cities 468. *See* also London.

Englishmen, mobility of 250

Entrepreneur, appearance of the 178; city vs. country born 375–80, 391. *See* also Employer.

Environment, physical and population 2, 5; in Uruguay 148; Argentina 149; India 149–150; Australia 149

Erie canal and New York city 25

Essex contains London suburbs 447

Evolution of industrial society 158–160; bibliography of 169; periods of 170; stages in 185

Excitement in cities 368

Factories, advantageous location of 197–209; movement of toward suburbs 8, 202, 203, 224, 228, 473

Factory system, in England 53; France 78; Germany 88; Russia 105; beginnings of 188, 192–3; ancient Egypt 193; advantages of 193–6; and distribution of population 196; education under 438

Factory towns and the marriage rate 321; birth rate 337–8; 341–2

Fairs develop out of weekly town market 179

Families, city, extinction of 370, 386–9; 445

Family life in city and country 322–30; size of families 336–7; life in Paris 405

Famine in Austria 96; Hungary 102; and distribution of population 169

Farm labor, scarcity of 422–4; wages of 422

Farmers, isolation of 221; the radical party in 1896, 427

Farms, increase of in the United States 26; plans to make more attractive 455

Fashion dominates city dwellers 432

Fecundity of women 330–43

Fees for settlement 455

Fertilizer and the law of diminishing returns 225

Flanders, seat of the woollen trade 179

Florence, influence of 6

Food in cities 368

Fords, sites of cities 172

Forecast concerning city growth 225–9

Foreigners, female, in American cities 279–80; concentration of in cities 304–9; percentage of in cities 306: conjugal condition 326; birth-rates among 334; size of family 337; tendency of to herd together 430

Forts as nuclei of towns 174

France, agglomerated population 9; definition of cities 14; urban growth 67–80; rural depopulation 68, 69; natural increase 1881–91, 69; internal migration 1881–91, 69; industrial development 76–80; agricultural progress 167; national unity 180; railway policy 200; natural increase vs. immigration in cities 245; internal migration 249–252; sex at birth, 294; marriage-rate 319; conjugal condition 324; divorces 330; size of families 336; death-rates, 345; crime 404; illegitimacy 405. *See* also Paris.

Frankfort, excess of births over deaths 237; military rolls 269; birth-place of immigrants 271; return of migrants to native places 272; urban and rural origin of immigrants 273; sex of immigrants 278; age of immigrants 280; sex and age of immigrants 293; sex at birth 294; deaths in the sexes 298; mortality among natives and immigrants 366; residence of natives and immigrants 372–3; occupation of natives and immigrants 381; pauperism of natives and immigrants 383

Functions, municipal 353–5

Garrisons in cities 457

Gemeënte, average area of, in Holland 142

Gemeinde, average area of, in Hungary, Austria, Germany, Prussia 142

Genius, in city and country 439, 442

Genoa, influence of 6

Germany, classification of dwelling-centers 15; city growth 80–94; industrial development 87–9; immigrants to the United States 152; railways and cities 200; freedom of move-